Explore the

# LONDON
## ENGLAND AND WALES

*Authors:*
*David Arscott, Heather Barraclough, Michael Z. Brooke,*
*Joe de Casa, Gill Davies, Martin Marix Evans,*
*Angus McGeoch, Andrea Russ, Alexander Sabo,*
*Philipp Zitzlsperger*

*An Up-to-date travel guide with 152 color photos*
*and 18 maps*

**First Edition**
**1996**

*IMPRINT / LEGEND*

**Dear Reader**,

Being up-to-date is the main goal of the Nelles series. To achieve it, we have a network of far-flung correspondents who keep us abreast of the latest developments in the travel scene, and our cartographers always make sure that maps and texts are adjusted to each other.

Each travel chapter ends with its own list of useful tips, accommodations, restaurants, tourist offices, sights. At the end of the book you will find practical information from A to Z. But the travel world is fast moving, and we cannot guarantee that all the contents are always valid. Should you come across a discrepancy, please write us at: Nelles Verlag GmbH, Schleissheimer Str. 371 b, D-80935 München, Germany, Tel: (089) 3515084, Fax: (089) 3542544.

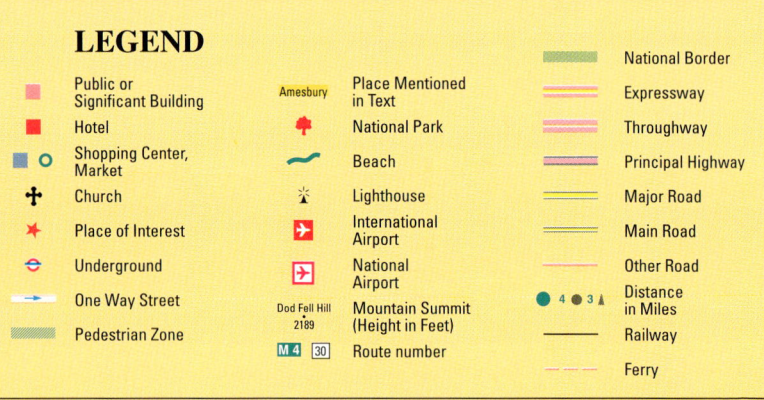

**LONDON, ENGLAND AND WALES**
© Nelles Verlag GmbH, 80935 München
All rights reserved

First Edition 1996
Printed in Slovenia
ISBN 3-88618-413-7

| | | | |
|---|---|---|---|
| **Publisher:** | Günter Nelles | **Cartography:** | Nelles Verlag GmbH |
| **Editor-In-Chief:** | Berthold Schwarz | | RV-Verlag |
| **English Editor:** | Anne Midgette | **Color** | |
| **Translation:** | Ross Greville | **Separation:** | Priegnitz, München |
| **Picture Editor:** | K. Bärmann-Thümmel | **Printed by:** | Gorenjski Tisk |

No part of this book, not even excerpts, may be reproduced without prior permission of Nelles Verlag
- X02 -

## *TABLE OF CONTENTS*

**Imprint / Legend** . . . . . . . . . . . . . . . . . . . . . . . 2
**List of Maps** . . . . . . . . . . . . . . . . . . . . . . . . . 6

**HISTORY AND CULTURE** . . . . . . . . . . . . . . . . 13

### *TRAVELLING IN ENGLAND AND WALES*

**LONDON** . . . . . . . . . . . . . . . . . . . . . . . . . . . 37
**The City** . . . . . . . . . . . . . . . . . . . . . . . . . . . 40
**Central London** . . . . . . . . . . . . . . . . . . . . . . 54
**South of the Thames** . . . . . . . . . . . . . . . . . . . 56
**Outer London** . . . . . . . . . . . . . . . . . . . . . . . 75
**London by Night** . . . . . . . . . . . . . . . . . . . . . 81
*GUIDEPOST: Hotels, Restaurants, Sights* . . . . . . . . 83

**SOUTHERN ENGLAND**
**Kent** . . . . . . . . . . . . . . . . . . . . . . . . . . . . . 87
**Sussex** . . . . . . . . . . . . . . . . . . . . . . . . . . . 92
**Surrey** . . . . . . . . . . . . . . . . . . . . . . . . . . . 97
**Hampshire and the Isle of Wight** . . . . . . . . . . . . 97
**Dorset** . . . . . . . . . . . . . . . . . . . . . . . . . . . 103
*GUIDEPOST: Hotels, Restaurants, Sights* . . . . . . . . 106

**THE HOME COUNTIES**
**Hertfordshire** . . . . . . . . . . . . . . . . . . . . . . . 109
**Bedfordshire** . . . . . . . . . . . . . . . . . . . . . . . 110
**North Buckinghamshire** . . . . . . . . . . . . . . . . . 112
**The Thames Valley** . . . . . . . . . . . . . . . . . . . . 115
**Oxford** . . . . . . . . . . . . . . . . . . . . . . . . . . . 116
**Berkshire** . . . . . . . . . . . . . . . . . . . . . . . . . 118
*GUIDEPOST: Hotels, Restaurants, Sights* . . . . . . . . 119

**EAST ANGLIA**
**Cambridgeshire** . . . . . . . . . . . . . . . . . . . . . . 123
**The Fens** . . . . . . . . . . . . . . . . . . . . . . . . . 125
**Norfolk** . . . . . . . . . . . . . . . . . . . . . . . . . . 128
**Norwich and the Brecklands** . . . . . . . . . . . . . . 129
**Suffolk** . . . . . . . . . . . . . . . . . . . . . . . . . . 131
**Essex** . . . . . . . . . . . . . . . . . . . . . . . . . . . 131
*GUIDEPOST: Hotels, Restaurants, Sights* . . . . . . . . 133

**THE WEST COUNTRY**
**Around Stonehenge** . . . . . . . . . . . . . . . . . . . 137
**Salisbury** . . . . . . . . . . . . . . . . . . . . . . . . . 138

# TABLE OF CONTENTS

**Somerset** . . . . . . . . . . . . . . . . . . . . . . . . 139
**Bristol** . . . . . . . . . . . . . . . . . . . . . . . . . . 142
**Bath and Environs** . . . . . . . . . . . . . . . . . . 143
**Prehistoric Monuments** . . . . . . . . . . . . . . . 127
**Devon** . . . . . . . . . . . . . . . . . . . . . . . . . . 144
**Cornwall** . . . . . . . . . . . . . . . . . . . . . . . . 148
**North Devon Coast** . . . . . . . . . . . . . . . . . 152
*GUIDEPOST: Hotels, Restaurants, Sights* . . . . . . . . 153

## WALES
**South Wales** . . . . . . . . . . . . . . . . . . . . . . 157
**Mid Wales** . . . . . . . . . . . . . . . . . . . . . . . 162
**North Wales** . . . . . . . . . . . . . . . . . . . . . 163
**Isle of Anglesey** . . . . . . . . . . . . . . . . . . . 167
**North Wales Coast** . . . . . . . . . . . . . . . . . 168
*GUIDEPOST: Hotels, Restaurants, Sights* . . . . . . . . 169

## THE HEART OF ENGLAND
**The Cotswolds** . . . . . . . . . . . . . . . . . . . . 173
**Birmingham** . . . . . . . . . . . . . . . . . . . . . 178
**Warwickshire** . . . . . . . . . . . . . . . . . . . . . 181
**Northamptonshire** . . . . . . . . . . . . . . . . . . 184
**Leicestershire** . . . . . . . . . . . . . . . . . . . . . 186
**Lincolnshire** . . . . . . . . . . . . . . . . . . . . . . 187
**Nottinghamshire** . . . . . . . . . . . . . . . . . . . 189
**The Peak District** . . . . . . . . . . . . . . . . . . 191
*GUIDEPOST: Hotels, Restaurants, Sights* . . . . . . . . 195

## NORTHERN ENGLAND
**Cheshire** . . . . . . . . . . . . . . . . . . . . . . . . 199
**Manchester** . . . . . . . . . . . . . . . . . . . . . . 200
**Liverpool** . . . . . . . . . . . . . . . . . . . . . . . 205
**Humberside** . . . . . . . . . . . . . . . . . . . . . . 207
**Yorkshire** . . . . . . . . . . . . . . . . . . . . . . . 208
**North Yorkshire** . . . . . . . . . . . . . . . . . . . 215
*GUIDEPOST: Hotels, Restaurants, Sights* . . . . . . . . 221

## THE LAKES AND BORDERS
**Cumbria / Lake District** . . . . . . . . . . . . . . . 225
**Carlisle and the Borders** . . . . . . . . . . . . . . 230
**County Durham** . . . . . . . . . . . . . . . . . . . 232
**Northumberland** . . . . . . . . . . . . . . . . . . . 233
*GUIDEPOST: Hotels, Restaurants, Sights* . . . . . . . . 237

## GUIDELINES

**Preparations**
Climate . . . . . . . . . . . . . . . . . . . . . . . . . 238
Arival . . . . . . . . . . . . . . . . . . . . . . . . . . 238
Arrival Formalities . . . . . . . . . . . . . . . . . . . 239
Import and Export Restrictions . . . . . . . . . . . . . 239

**Getting Around**
By Car . . . . . . . . . . . . . . . . . . . . . . . . . 239
By Bus . . . . . . . . . . . . . . . . . . . . . . . . . 240
By Train . . . . . . . . . . . . . . . . . . . . . . . . 240
Combining Means of Transport . . . . . . . . . . . 241
Fare Reductions . . . . . . . . . . . . . . . . . . . . 241

**Practical Tips**
Accommodations . . . . . . . . . . . . . . . . . . . 241
Banks . . . . . . . . . . . . . . . . . . . . . . . . . 242
Electricity . . . . . . . . . . . . . . . . . . . . . . . 242
Emergency Calls . . . . . . . . . . . . . . . . . . . 242
Food and Drink . . . . . . . . . . . . . . . . . . . . 242
Health Insurance . . . . . . . . . . . . . . . . . . . 246
Hours of Business . . . . . . . . . . . . . . . . . . . 246
Language . . . . . . . . . . . . . . . . . . . . . . . 246
Money . . . . . . . . . . . . . . . . . . . . . . . . . 247
Post Offices . . . . . . . . . . . . . . . . . . . . . . 247
Public Holidays . . . . . . . . . . . . . . . . . . . . 247
Telephone . . . . . . . . . . . . . . . . . . . . . . . 247
Time . . . . . . . . . . . . . . . . . . . . . . . . . . 247
Tipping . . . . . . . . . . . . . . . . . . . . . . . . 247
Weights and Measures . . . . . . . . . . . . . . . . 248

**Addresses**
Airlines . . . . . . . . . . . . . . . . . . . . . . . . 248
Automobile Associations . . . . . . . . . . . . . . . 248
British Embassies and Consulates Abroad . . . . . . . 248
British Tourist Authority Abroad . . . . . . . . . . . 248
Embassies and Consulates in the UK . . . . . . . . . 248
Tourist Information . . . . . . . . . . . . . . . . . . 248

**Authors** . . . . . . . . . . . . . . . . . . . . . . . . . 249

**Photographers** . . . . . . . . . . . . . . . . . . . . . 249

**Index** . . . . . . . . . . . . . . . . . . . . . . . . . . 250

## *MAP LIST*

England / Wales ................................... 7

City ............................................. 44

Central London................................... 58

Kensington / Chelsea ............................. 70

Greater London................................... 77

Southeast England ............................ 90 / 91

Hampshire / Dorset............................ 98 / 99

Home Counties ............................. 110 / 111

East Anglia ................................ 126 / 127

Wiltshire / Somerset ........................ 140 / 141

Devon / Cornwall ........................... 146 / 147

North Devon Coast............................... 151

South Wales ............................... 158 / 159

North Wales ............................... 164 / 165

West Midlands .................................. 179

East Midlands................................... 183

Peak District ................................... 192

Lancashire / Cheshire ............................ 201

Yorkshire................................. 210 / 211

Cumbria / Durham .......................... 226 / 227

Northumberland ................................. 233

# ENGLAND AND WALES

## HISTORY AND CULTURE

# HISTORY AND CULTURE

## Prehistoric Origins

The glaciers of the Ice Age covered England as far south as the present site of London. In the Stone Age, as recent findings show, people could still walk dryshod across what is now the English Channel. But the first real settlements date from the Neolithic period: the bare hills of the Lake District and north Yorkshire, for example, show where forests were cleared to make way for agriculture; and the flint mines at Grimes Graves in Norfolk are evidence of the dawn of toolmaking.

More striking relics survive from the Bronze Age: funerary relics from the period between 2500-700 BC prove there were trading links with Greece and Germany, while bronze shields, swords, spearheads and pots attest to Continental influence. On the other hand, mighty monuments such as the megalithic circles of Avebury and Stonehenge in Wiltshire remain enigmas to us. Wiltshire also boasts the largest prehistoric mound in Europe, Silbury Hill.

During the next six hundred years – the Iron Age – Celts, of whom traces are found at Hallstatt in Austria and La Tène in Switzerland, first arrived in southern England. More Celts crossed over to England from the north coast of France around 500 BC, and 200 years after this the Celtic Brythons (Britons). New types of weapons, such as the longsword and iron-tipped lance, as well as bronze and iron clasps decorated with swirling circles, are the legacy of the La Tène culture. Around 75 BC a further wave of Celts, this time from the Rhine-Meuse area, crossed the Channel.

## The Roman Occupation

After two unsuccessful attempts under Caesar in 55 and 54 BC, the Romans finally managed to conquer England in 43 AD, in the reign of the Roman emperor Claudius. Roman rule was to last 400 years. One legacy of this period still in evidence are the roads: as they needed to be able to move troops swiftly, the Romans built a great network of highways. Superbly engineered, they ran as straight as the terrain would permit. One extant specimen is south of Towcester in Northamptonshire, which, now the A5, runs arrow-like towards London. The name Towcester (though distorted in the English vernacular to sound like "toaster") also shows Roman origin; place names ending in *-chester* or *-cester* derive from the Latin *castra,* or "camp."

Towns were developed both as military and commercial centers. Public baths and amphitheaters introduced a higher standard of living, and luxury goods from distant climes were to be found in the markets. The capitals of the Roman provinces in Britannia were London, Colchester, York, Chester, Bath and St. Albans. This period reached its zenith under Constantine, who was proclaimed Emperor in York in 306. Under his rule, Christianity became one of the official religions of the Roman Empire, thus also of England.

The limits of Roman rule were marked by Hadrian's Wall, which ran from sea to sea along the Scottish border. Even today, sections of this wall still stand; the Romans built it as a defense against the northern tribes of Brigands and Picts.

## The Dark Ages

After 410, the province of Britannia was beset by Saxon raiders; and the

*Preceding pages: Victorian terraces in Brighton. The Lake District. Left: Execution of Thomas More (by A. Caron, 1591).*

## HISTORY AND CULTURE

weakened government in Rome was unable to respond to its colonies' plea for assistance. Historical records for the next 150 years, the Dark Ages, are fragmentary. The theologian the Venerable Bede wrote the first English history in the monastery at Jarrow, near Newcastle-upon-Tyne. His *Historia Ecclesiastica Gentis Anglorum,* or *History of the English Church and People*, was completed in 731.

What is clear is that Germanic tribes from the European mainland repeatedly attacked England. Angles from the region of Schleswig-Holstein established themselves in what is now known as East Anglia (Norfolk and Suffolk), while Saxons came to Essex and moved westwards toward Wessex. Jutes from Jutland made Kent their home. The Celts retreated westwards into Wales or crossed into Armorica in northwest France,

*Above: Swords from the late Bronze Age. Right: A Saxon font (8th century) from Curdworth.*

which was renamed Brittany after them. (This, by the way, is why we still refer to *Great* Britain – not out of national pride, but originally to distinguish it from Little Britain across the Channel). Resistance to the invaders may well have led to the legend of King Arthur, whose story Geoffrey of Monmouth recorded in the *Historia Regium Britannia* about 1150.

Modern place-names give clues to the ancient division of the land. Anglo-Saxon towns bear the ending *-ton* (Southampton); woodland clearings, *-leah*, are the source for places now ending in *-ley* or *-leigh* (Bletchley, Cranleigh). The term for a market, *wic*, has yielded names like Norwich.

### The Saxon Kingdoms

By the 8th century, there were three principal kingdoms on the island – Northumbria, Mercia and Wessex – as well as some 200 smaller territories. Roman laws and customs were mingled with the cultures of the invaders; Christianity survived only in the Celtic churches. With the emergence of some stability, Pope Gregory I sent a missionary expedition from Rome in 595 under the monk Augustine. After converting King Ethelbert of Kent, Augustine established Canterbury and York as the seats of bishoprics. Meanwhile, Celtic missionaries were at work. There were significant differences between the two creeds; but these were peacefully resolved in 664 at the Synod of Whitby when the Roman church organization was adopted.

Around 757, the island's political center shifted to Mercia, which stretched from the Welsh borders to the western edge of East Anglia. Offa claimed to be "King of the whole of the land of the English," and his power must indeed have been great, since he was able to erect a massive defensive earthwork against the Celts of Wales. The remains of Offa's Dyke are still to be seen.

## HISTORY AND CULTURE

### The Viking Raiders

Fresh incursions from the north troubled the land. Vikings from Norway and Denmark had already settled the northern islands of Orkney and Shetland, occupied the Isle of Man and sacked Dublin. In 793, they destroyed the monastery at Lindisfarne in Northumbria; over the next 60 years they established themselves in East Anglia and York. Wessex was the first kingdom able to control the menace. In 871, a Viking army attacked Wessex, and the Saxons, under Ethelred and Alfred, fought and conquered them in nine battles. Ethelred died in battle, and Alfred succeeded him as king.

### Saxon, Danish and English Rulers

In 878, Alfred and a small force defeated the Vikings near Chippenham, Wiltshire. Crucial to Alfred's victory was his creation of defensive fortresses or burghs, in which the people could take refuge from the Viking marauders.

The Danish leader Guthrum was baptized, and with the Treaty of Wedmore in 879, the Danes agreed to leave Wessex in peace. In return, Alfred ceded all of England north and east of a line from the mouth of the Thames to Chester. This territory, known as the Danelaw, was thereafter settled by Norsemen, something reflected today in place-names ending in *-by* (Derby, Whitby), *-thorpe* (Grimethorpe) and *-toft* (Lowestoft). In Cumbria, the locals still use the Norse words *fell* for moor, *beck* for stream, and *yat* for gate.

The developments of the next 150 years were a gradual progress towards a unified kingdom of England. The only question was whether it would have an Anglo-Saxon, Danish or Norman king. The first hundred years favored Alfred's heirs. By 973, the situation was sufficiently stable to allow Dunstan, Archbishop of Canterbury, to crown Edgar King at Bath Abbey. But after Edgar's death in 975, Anglo-Saxon dominance began to decline.

*HISTORY AND CULTURE*

The brief reign of Edward was followed by that of Ethelred II. Unable to resist Danish attacks, and attempting to gain peace on at least one flank, Ethelred made the mistake of trying to buy a truce with the Norwegian king, at that time allied to the Danes. This forced him to institute the *Danegeld*, the first general tax levied in a medieval state, which became a huge annual indemnity.

Ethelred died in 1016; the reign of his successor, the Danish King Cnut, or Canute, saw the final unification of the kingdom of England. Although already married to Ethelred's widow, Emma, he also married a Mercian lady, Aelfgifu, whom he later sent to govern Norway. This unusual arrangement allowed him to control an expanding empire stretching from Denmark to Greenland. There followed nearly twenty years of peace and prosperity.

After Canute's death in 1035, his sons Harald and Hardicanute reigned; when they died, the throne was due to pass to King Magnus of Norway. However, the English nobles preferred Ethelred's son Edward, who had remained in exile in Normandy after the family took refuge there in 1013, though his father returned to resume his throne in England; thus Edward had also had a Norman education. As king, his passion was the rebuilding of Westminster Abbey. His deep piety and charitable works earned him the epithet "the Confessor."

The first ten years of Edward's reign were marked by power struggles with Godwin, Earl of Wessex. Edward tended to promote Normans to positions of influence, but after Godwin's death in 1053 his son, Harold, who had a good relationship with the King, took over more and more of the administration of the realm. Upon Edward's death in 1066, Harold became king.

*Right: The Bayeux Tapestry documents the Norman invasion of 1066.*

### The Battle of Hastings

Some two years previously, Harold had had the misfortune to be shipwrecked on the French coast, and was taken into the custody of William of Normandy, to whom he is said to have sworn an oath of allegiance. William, in any case, had a plausible claim to the English throne through his father; and Harold's oath was held to invalidate his election as King by the English nobles. At the same time the Norwegian King, Harald Hardrada, revived the Norwegian interest which dated back to King Magnus.

King Harold kept a close watch on the Channel coast throughout the summer, but with the approach of autumn and the stormy weather, the militia were disbanded. Then, in September, Harald Hardrada landed in Northumbria and gained immediate success. Rushing north, Harold took the Norwegians by surprise and won a decisive victory at Stamford Bridge near York, on September 25, killing one of his rivals for the throne. Two days later William sailed for England and landed unopposed.

Harold hastened south once more, covering the distance from York to London in seven days. Gathering as many men as he could, he moved on to bar the invaders' route to London and the morning of October 14, 1066, found him established on a small hill outside Hastings, a place now called Battle. The English foot-soldiers and militia managed to hold the Norman force of cavalry and archers at bay until Harold himself was slain.

### The Norman Conquest

William the Conqueror, King of England and Normandy, was now the ruler; but he still had to acquire practical control. Military developments included the motte and bailey castle: a motte, or earth mound, surrounded by a bailey area of a moat, wall, or palisade. ditch and wall.

## HISTORY AND CULTURE

Unlike Alfred's burghs, these, and conventional castles such as the White Tower in London and Colchester Castle, were built not to defend against outsiders, but to subdue the land and people.

Landholding was the cornerstone of feudalism. To determine who held what, a massive survey was instituted to compile the *Domesday Book*. This catalogue which covered the entire country, with some exceptions (such as London and parts of northern England), listed every estate, manor and fief, detailing the land tax, field sizes, population and overall value. At the time the Normans began to enforce an oppressive overlordship. The changes wrought by the Normans were extreme; William replaced some 4,000 English landholders with 200 Norman barons loyal to him.

The successors to William I were his sons William Rufus and Henry I. Henry made his daughter Mathilda his heir and married her to Geoffrey of Anjou, Duke of Normandy, known as Geoffrey Plantagenet.

In spite of great problems, including civil war, arising from disputed successions to the throne, the next century saw a general consolidation of centralized government and the legal system. Monastic orders, especially the Cistercians, were on the rise, and built monasteries throughout the country – some of them, because of the austerity espoused by the latter order, in remote and challenging places, bequeathing to us such beautiful ruins as Rievaulx in Yorkshire and Tintern in Gwent.

### The Plantagenet Dynasty

Henry II, the son of Geoffrey of Anjou-Plantagenet and great-grandson of William the Conqueror, had married Eleanor of Aquitaine before succeeding to the English throne in 1154. Through his marriage he gained further lands, so that his sphere of control extended from the Pyrenees up the west coast of France and through all of England up to the borders of Scotland. That he and his family

## HISTORY AND CULTURE

were more French than English is shown by the tombs at Fontevrault near Chinon in France: Henry II, his wife, and his son Richard Lionheart all lie there.

Henry II initiated a major reform of the legal system. The baronial courts were repressed in favor of the king's courts, which developed the Common Law ("common" meaning that it applied to all of the king's subjects alike). Trial by jury was also introduced. When Henry tried to define the position of the clergy with regard to the secular courts, it led to a break with his friend and former chancellor Thomas à Becket, Archbishop of Canterbury. Becket went into exile. After his return, he was murdered by four of Henry's knights in Canterbury Cathedral. Thomas was canonized by Pope Alexander in 1173.

Richard I spent most of his reign, 1189-1199, outside of England, whether on crusades, in prison, or in foreign wars. The abuses that flourished while he was away were the basis for the legend of Robin Hood, a noble bandit who robbed from the rich to give to the poor. The brother of Richard Lionheart, King John Lackland (1199-1216), managed to lose not only most of the country's French lands, but also the struggle for power with his barons. They forced him to sign the Magna Carta on the meadows of Runnymede, near Windsor, in 1215. While many of the provisions were matters of purely contemporary interest, two of them have endured down the ages: no imprisonment without trial and no offering of bribes to the courts.

Henry III (1216-1272) was pious, peaceful and politically somewhat naïve. Under him, the power of the church and the bishops increased, and the first Gothic cathedrals were built in the Early English style at Lincoln and Salisbury. The power of the barons also increased; they effectively ruled for seven years before Edward, the king's son, overthrew

*Above: King John signs the Magna Carta (1215). Right: At the archery butts with the English longbow.*

them. On his death, Henry was buried in Westminster Abbey, which he had labored to restore.

Westminster Abbey is one of the first examples of the typically English "Decorated Style," which is characterized by rich tracery and ornamentation. The Perpendicular Style arose around 1350; it is typified by large window areas divided vertically by heavy mullions.

## From Edward I to Edward III

When Henry III died, his son, Edward, was returning from a crusade to the Holy Land, in Sicily; he did not reach England for another two years. Horrified by the corruption he found, he instituted a massive investigation into official malpractice and undertook the codification and reform of English law. His political control was challenged by the Welsh. Henry had recognized the Lord of Snowdonia, Llewelyn ap Gruffydd, as Prince of Wales in 1267, but this noble refused to pay homage to Edward. Edward conquered Wales in two campaigns in 1277; in 1301, he made his son Edward, born in Caernarfon, Prince of Wales, a title that is still given the heir to the throne to this day. Edward sealed his control and subjugation of the Welsh with the last great program of castle-building of the Middle Ages, bequeathing to us such magnificent structures as Harlech, Caernarfon and Beaumaris.

In 1290, Edward's beloved wife Eleanor of Castille died at Lincoln; the King's anguished grief is marked today by the crosses he erected at each night's resting place along the way to her burial place at Westminster. Perhaps his agony inspired the most ignoble action of his reign, the expulsion of the Jews, who had come to England with the Normans and were tolerated on account of their financial support of the crown. His plans to marry his son to Margaret, the infant successor to the throne of Scotland, miscarried; and

the uneasy relationship with this kingdom to the north finally deteriorated into war in 1297. The next ten years saw continued fighting, with varied results. These wars were marked by a new weapon, the English longbow, capable of firing 12 arrows a minute a distance of 660 feet (200 m). The effect was to revolutionize warfare, as events in France in the next century would show.

Edward died just south of the Scottish border on his last advance against Robert Bruce in 1307. His son, Edward II, was a far inferior statesman. Although he married Isabella of France and sired a son, he appeared chiefly interested in giving in to his homosexual proclivities. The disastrous defeat at the hands of Robert Bruce at Bannockburn in 1314 left the borders open to repeated raids, and rebellion in England scarred the land. Isabella went to France and conspired against Edward; she finally returned to England with her lover and an army, and forced her husband to abdicate. Although confined under hellish conditions in Berkeley

## HISTORY AND CULTURE

Castle, Edward persisted in living, and so was tortured to death with red-hot irons.

Edward III's coronation in 1327 ushered in an age of chivalry and military glory. Needing money for his wars against France, Edward convened Parliament often; it was under him that Parliament was separated into the Houses of Lords and Commons. The English language became the country's official tongue, even in courts of law.

Edward's Arthurian leanings were shown in the creation of the Order of the Garter, still England's highest order of chivalry. While dancing, so the story goes, Edward's mistress, Alice, lost her garter. Edward outfaced giggling courtiers by fixing it to his own leg and remarking *Honi soit qui mal y pense* (Shame on him who thinks ill of it), which remains the motto of the order to this day.

*Above: A battle in the Hundred Years' War.*
*Right: Henry VIII as depicted by Hans Holbein the Younger (1536).*

### The Hundred Years' War, Plague, and Peasants' Revolt

After the death of Charles IV of France in 1328, Edward claimed the French throne, and what is known as the Hundred Years' War commenced in 1339. After a number of minor skirmishes, 1346 saw the great victory at Crécy, in which the English archers proved the worth of their weapons. The King's son, also Edward, known as the Black Prince on account of the color of his armor, was denied assistance by his father in order to earn his spurs. Calais fell in 1347 after a siege of several months. The Black Prince, who was the darling of his people, chalked up a further victory at Poitiers in 1356, but was to die in 1376, predeceasing his father.

On the home front, the country was rocked by natural disaster. In June, 1348, a ship unknowingly carried plague-infected rats to England, and for two years the Black Death, bubonic plague, ravaged the land. The population was reduced by as much as one-third; it took 200 years for it to regain its pre-plague numbers.

Edward died in 1377, after years of decline and increasing senility. Heir to the throne was his 10-year-old grandson, Richard II, son of the Black Prince; as he was a minor, the regency was taken over by John of Gaunt (Ghent). He was one of the younger sons of Edward III, and by marriage had become the wealthy Duke of Lancaster. The war against France was financed by the imposition of a poll tax, a tax payable by each adult regardless of means. Attempts to levy a third poll tax in 1381 resulted in the Peasants' Revolt under Wat Tyler, which spread even to the urban lower classes of London itself. The young king Richard saved the day by dealing personally with the leaders of the rebellion. The government abandoned the hated tax; and it was not to be revived until the days of Margaret Thatcher, six

## HISTORY AND CULTURE

hundred years later, when it proved to be just as much of a mistake.

In 1389, Richard took power himself. At first, he ruled very moderately, even negotiating an agreement with France to suspend hostilities. However, in 1397 he changed his style of government and became an absolute monarch. When John of Gaunt died in 1399, Richard seized his lands. Henry Bolinbroke, the new Duke of Lancaster, was banished, but came back to England while Richard was in Ireland. The king was outwitted, captured and deposed by Parliament for misrule. He was murdered in Pontefract Castle in 1400, probably by Bolinbroke.

Henry IV, as Bolinbroke now became, was in a precarious position – constantly short of money and with a tenuous claim to the throne. Young Edmund Mortimer had a better claim; Henry IV accordingly incarcerated him. Rebellions of the Welsh and the Northern English aristocracy were put down; but not until Henry V succeeded in 1413 did the situation truly stabilize.

"Good Prince Hal" had led a dissolute life, but as Henry V he assumed the mantle of a virtuous king and successful general. Attacking France in 1415, he was victorious at Agincourt but suffered heavy losses. He made for Calais, only to encounter a French army nearly ten times as great as his own. Yet Henry came out the victor, and in 1417, in Troyes, he married Catherine of Valois, the daughter of the French king Charles V. Henry should thus have succeeded to the French throne, but he died in 1422, leaving a one-year-old son, and his widow married one Owen Tudor, through which union another Tudor was later to lay claim to the English throne.

Where his father left trails of glory, Henry VI left only chaos. His marriage to Margaret of Anjou made him unpopular in England. By the end of the Hundred Years' War in 1453, England had lost all of her possessions in France except for

Calais. A year later, the King went mad, and Richard of York became regent, a post he was extremely unwilling to relinquish when the king regained his sanity two years later.

### The Wars of the Roses

A red rose was the symbol of the House of Lancaster (Henry); a white rose, of the House of York. Hence the name "Wars of the Roses," a long and confused series of struggles lasting from 1455 until 1485. Henry VI was deposed; was later, after a defeat of his army, found wandering in Lancashire; was imprisoned in the Tower of London in 1465; was freed and restored to the throne; lost once again; and was finally beheaded in the Tower in 1471.

Bloody battles were fought at St. Albans (1455), Northampton (1460), Wakefield (1460) and again at St. Albans in 1461. At this stage two kings ruled in England, as Richard of York's son was crowned Edward IV in 1461. Edward was victorious in several battles; upon his death in 1483, the throne passed to his son, Edward V. However, Edward's uncle, Richard of Gloucester, had the marriage of Edward IV declared void and his children illegitimate, and ascended the throne himself as Richard III. Richard had Edward and his young brother murdered in the Tower. Word gradually leaked out about this terrible double infanticide and destroyed the popularity Richard had enjoyed with the people.

Richard III died in 1485 in battle against the next claimant, Henry Tudor, the sole surviving member of the House of Lancaster. Henry was crowned king on the battlefield.

## The Power of the Tudors

With the marriage of Henry VII and Elizabeth of York, the houses of York and Lancaster were united, eliminating the rivalry that had torn the land apart. Centralization of the government and legal reform, coupled with zealous tax collection, were Henry's weapons to secure his power. At his death in 1509, a powerful monarchy was passed on to his second son, who became Henry VIII.

The elder son, Arthur, had died suddenly in 1502, five months after his marriage to Catherine of Aragon. For financial and political reasons, Henry VII persuaded the Pope to permit her remarriage to the younger son. Henry VIII was eighteen years old when he came to the throne. Remarkably good-looking, well-educated, fond of music, dance and good living, he was considered a jewel of a prince. Although successful in war, defeating both a French and a Scottish army in 1513, he cared little for the details of governmental administration so beloved of his father. This opened the way for the rise of powerful advisers such as Thomas

*Right: Elizabeth's reign ushered in a Golden Age of art and culture in England.*

Wolsey, who became exceedingly rich and built himself several palaces, including the one at Hampton Court.

## Henry VIII

Henry's desire for a male heir was to alter the course of British history. Catherine's children all died in infancy, except a girl, Mary. Meanwhile, Henry wanted an heir by his current love, the marriage-seeking Anne Boleyn, and demanded that Wolsey, now a Cardinal and Lord Chancellor, fix him a divorce. The Pope refused. Back in 1521, Henry had published a denunciation of Martin Luther, for which the Pope had given him the title of *Fidei Defensor* (Defender of the Faith), a title still to be seen (F.D.) on British coins today in spite of subsequent events! The arguments over the King's divorce continued for five years until, in 1532, a crisis brought matters to a head. Anne was pregnant, and an heir had to be born in wedlock. Henry split with Rome. The new Archbishop of Canterbury, Thomas Cranmer, declared Henry's first marriage annulled in 1533, and Henry married Anne on June 1; the Pope promptly excommunicated him. Within a year, Parliament had passed the Act of Supremacy declaring Henry head of the Church of England. Members of the church and civil service alike had to swear an oath to the crown, thereby recognizing the king's full supremacy over the church. Anyone refusing to take the oath was executed, among them Thomas More, the author of *Utopia.* However, the problem of the succession to the throne remained unsolved, for Anne's child was a girl, baptized Elizabeth.

Wolsey had been disgraced after his failure to engineer Henry's divorce and his place was taken by Thomas Cromwell, also a man of humble origins. He sought to provide for the income necessary for the King's lifestyle and wars by plundering the riches of the medieval re-

*HISTORY AND CULTURE*

ligious houses of England. By 1539 all of the monasteries had been dissolved.

Henry's desire for a son was still unsatisfied. Anne Boleyn was beheaded on a doubtful charge of adultery, and Jane Seymour became Queen. She gave the King a son, Edward, but died twelve days later. Further marriages followed: to Anne of Cleves, a plain woman who was pensioned off; to Catherine Howard, who lost her head like Anne Boleyn; and, finally, to Catherine Parr, who survived to become a widow. Illness wore Henry down, and the beautiful prince became a foul-tempered, overweight monster. He died in 1547, at the age of 55.

Edward VI was nine years old when he ascended the throne; he died six years later. The regency that exercised power on his behalf saw the growth of the Protestant regime. The Archbishop of Canterbury assembled the *Book of Common Prayer*, and this became the cornerstone of the Anglican Church, Protestant in its teachings, Catholic in its bishops and its masses.

After Edward's death, Lady Jane Grey became the unhappy figurehead for a nine-day continuation of a Protestant monarchy; but she had to yield to the legitimate heir, Mary Tudor, daughter of Henry by his first marriage. Mary was extremely pious, and reinstated the Roman Catholic Church, earning the nickname "Bloody Mary" for her repression of Protestant rebellion. In spite of encouragement from her advisers, however, Mary refused to have her half-sister Elizabeth executed to remove the temptation of a living Protestant heir; Elizabeth wisely withdrew to Woodstock in Oxfordshire and avoided all contact with Mary's enemies.

Mary's desire for a child and heir led her to marry the King of Spain's son, the future Philip II. He, however, found her extremely unattractive and soon returned to Spain, leaving the lonely Mary to concentrate on imposing Catholicism; she had some 300 heretics burnt, including Thomas Cranmer. She died, sick and miserable, in 1588.

23

## The Golden Age of Elizabeth I

The Elizabethan Age (1558-1603) is remembered as a golden age, in part because of the effective propaganda of "Good Queen Bess" herself. She was a remarkable woman. She spoke six languages fluently, displayed outstanding administrative skills, had great powers of concentration and was precise and careful with money. Elizabeth I never married, while her Catholic cousin, Mary Queen of Scots, married three times. As a granddaughter of Henry VI, Mary also had a claim to the English throne, and was thus a focus for the plots of fellow Catholics. After being deposed in 1567 she fled to England, where Elizabeth took her prisoner and finally, in 1587, had her executed.

Trade rivalry, rather than religious differences, drew England and Spain into conflict in 1585. Spain was seeking economic supremacy in Europe; while England's vigorous commercial expansion found partial expression in what her enemies saw as piracy: Francis Drake and John Hawkins plundered Spanish treasure ships and raided her colonies in central and south America. Religion was summoned to the aid of trade, and Philip II of Spain, wanting to bring the Counter-Reformation to England, planned an invasion with the blessing of the Pope. The Spanish Armada sailed in 1588. It was a formidable force, but failed, in part because of the skill of the English seamen in smaller, more maneuverable boats, who harried the fleet all the way up the Channel and set fire to part of it. Storms, moreover, scattered the Armada's vessels, and the fleet had to straggle home as best it could on long and tortuous routes via Scotland and Ireland.

The rare peace and stability of Elizabeth's reign allowed a great artistic flowering: painting, poetry, music and drama thrived in the so-called "English Renaissance." First among the many great artists of the period was William Shakespeare (1564-1616).

## Rule of the Stuarts

On Elizabeth's death in 1603 the crown passed peaceably to the King of Scotland, the son of Mary Queen of Scots, James VI, now also James I of England. A new factor in religious dispute now arose: the growing strength of the Puritans, extreme Protestants. James conceded a new English Bible, a magnificent work of literature which still makes its successors seem dull and flat, quite lacking the poetry of the 1611 "Authorized Version." However, the Puritans could not accept compromise and chose emigration. In 1620, the first 120 Pilgrim Fathers set sail from Plymouth on the *Mayflower,* and became the first colonists of New England.

The poet of the Puritans was John Milton (1608-1674). In his epic *Paradise Lost*, he depicted the struggle between the powers of Heaven and Hell. A different kind of writer was Thomas Hobbes (1588-1679), who developed a theory of the bourgeois state in *Leviathan.*

The Catholics hatched a plot to blow up the King and Parliament. News of this Gunpowder Plot leaked, and Guy Fawkes and his fellow-conspirators were caught and hanged, drawn and quartered. Fawkes is still burnt in effigy each November 5th.

After a few years of successful cooperation between King and Parliament, tension began to develop. Money provided the focus for what became an argument of principle. James, with a wife and family, and with a lavish lifestyle, soon ran short of cash. Parliament was reluctant to approve new taxes, and James therefore ruled largely without parliaments until his death in 1625.

*Right: Oliver Cromwell holds prayers (painting by J.F. Cretius).*

## HISTORY AND CULTURE

His successor, Charles I, also raised taxes without the consent of Parliament. In 1628 he was compelled to sign the *Petition of Rights* which prevented him from levying taxes unless Parliament agreed; furthermore, nobody could be arrested without a clearly stated reason (*Act of Habeas Corpus*). But from 1629 to 1640, Charles again ruled without Parliament. He was forced to recall it in 1640, as he needed money.

In 1642, King Charles attempted to put a stop to attacks on his authority by entering the House of Commons with troops to arrest five radical MPs. This act of despotism failed, and Charles fled London.

Two-thirds of the House of Lords and one-third of the House of Commons, the old land-owning aristocracy ("Cavaliers"), were of the King's party. He was opposed by the "Roundheads," whose interests lay in the development of overseas trade and a modern economy. In the first Civil War, 1642-1646, Cromwell built up an army, the famed and feared *Ironsides,* which annihilated the royal army.

Charles was captured and condemned to death for tyranny and for causing civil war.

In 1649, the army proclaimed the English republic and declared England a free Commonwealth, to be ruled solely by Parliament without a King or the House of Lords. For the first time, Parliament included members from all over Britain. Insurrections in Scotland and Ireland were put down, the latter with a savagery remembered bitterly even to this day.

In 1653, Oliver Cromwell became Lord Protector and sole ruler, and he ruled as a military dictator from 1655 until his death in 1658. Cromwell had made his son his heir, but the inept Richard Cromwell could not even hold onto his office for a year. In 1659 Charles II returned to London as King.

### The Restoration of the Monarchy

It was the two Houses of Parliament which restored the monarchy – which meant that Parliament itself also gained

## HISTORY AND CULTURE

in power and influence. Pleasures forbidden under the Commonwealth – theatergoing, dancing and other jollification – were permitted once more, and Charles's own self-indulgence, including fathering 14 illegitimate children, set the tone.

But the new reign was also beset by public disasters. In 1665 bubonic plague swept through the land, principally in London; the year after, a great fire devastated the capital, reducing the close-packed wooden houses to ashes in a matter of three days. The Great Fire of London made way for new buildings in brick and stone and gave scope to the genius of Sir Christopher Wren, creator of St. Paul's Cathedral.

Between 1679 and 1681 Parliament split into two camps, the aristocratic landowners, or Tories, and the liberal commercial class, or Whigs. The Tories insisted on the principle of legitimacy and defended the divine right of kings. The Whigs represented Protestant freedoms and a social contract.

In this period, England stood at the forefront of contemporary developments in mathematics, physics, and astronomy, thanks to the work of the speculative genius Isaac Newton (1643-1727). He published the results of his research in 1687 in *Philosophia naturalis principia mathematica*, his greatest work, which also includes the law of gravity.

### 1688: The Glorious Revolution

On his succession in 1685, Charles's Catholic brother, James II, recognized the Church of England as the established church; yet he was unable to curb his desire to promote Catholics in public office. In 1688, therefore, the Bishop of London and his supporters in the House of Lords summoned the Protestant William of Orange and his wife Mary,

*Right: In 1666, four-fifths of the City of London was destroyed in the Great Fire.*

James's daughter, to England. William landed in Devon and James II fled to France and exile. Parliament deposed James and declared William III and his wife Mary II heirs to the throne. A constitutional restriction of the monarchy was laid down in the *Declaration of Rights*.

Philosopher of the revolution was John Locke. In his *Epistola de tolerantia* (On Tolerance), he stated that religion was a private matter, while his *Second Treatise on Civil Government* demanded that power be divided between the king and people. This found expression in the Bill of Rights, passed by William III in 1689.

The royal couple had no children, and Mary's sister, Anne, was their successor. She was married to Prince George of Denmark, an amiable fellow and attentive to his duty; Anne had many offspring. Most, however, died in infancy; Parliament therefore had to decide the succession, and it fell to James I's Protestant granddaughter, Sophia, Electress of Hanover, and thus to the House of Hanover. Anne came to the throne in 1702, just as the War of the Spanish Succession was looming. The Duke of Marlborough was rewarded for his victories in this war with the gift of a new, magnificent palace, Blenheim, named after the site of a great battle on the Danube. Blenheim Palace was the most important work of John Vanbrugh (1664-1726) who built many other great English houses as well.

### The Hanoverian Succession

In 1714, George, Elector of Hanover, assumed the throne. He had no love for his new kingdom, spoke little English, and took small part in the governance of the country, leaving administration in the hands of the Prime Minister and his cabinet ministers. The Prime Minister's office therefore gained in importance. The Whigs ruled for decades, initially under Prime Minister Robert Walpole.

## HISTORY AND CULTURE

George I died suddenly in 1727, and his son, George II, came to the throne at the age of 44. A war with Spain over conflicts of commercial interests in the Caribbean led to Walpole's resignation. In the Seven Years' War (1756-1763), France's defeats in America and India cleared the way for Britain's rise to become the leading sea and colonial power in the world. British politics were now directed by William Pitt the Elder.

The rule of George II saw an event with long-range consequences for British history: Robert Clive and Warren Hastings established English government in the East Indies. Money flowed back to the home country seemingly without cease; while the island people suddenly became a race of overseas traders.

Charles Edward Stuart, known as "Bonnie Prince Charlie," the young claimant to the throne and son of James II, believed his chance had come to drive out the Hanoverians, and landed in Scotland in 1745. He took Edinburgh, but could only advance southwards very slowly; all the same, London was seized with panic, as defense troops had to be brought in from Hanover. But the rebels turned away northwards. The Duke of Cumberland pursued them with his army and defeated the Scots at Culloden.

An important literary event for the growing middle classes was the development of the English newspaper. In 1709, *Tatler* commenced publication; the *Spectator* followed in 1711, and the *Guardian* in 1713. Another literary event was the publication, in 1754, of the much-touted *Dictionary of the English Language* by critic and author Samuel Johnson. In the visual arts, the painter William Hogarth was recounting the story of *A Rake's Progress* in pictures; while Gainsborough and Sir Joshua Reynolds documented the gentry in magnificent portraits.

The pivotal figure in British philosophy, meanwhile, was Scotsman David Hume (1711-1776). He represented a school of extreme empiricism which maintained that all knowledge was based

27

## HISTORY AND CULTURE

upon experience and was subject to its control. It was also the foundation of philosophic positivism, according to which human cognition was restricted to empirical reality (the "positive").

Between 1750 and 1785 landscape gardening blossomed for the first time under Lancelot "Capability" Brown (1716-1783). He received his nickname because he was in the habit of assuring his patrons that their lands had "great capabilities" for landscaping.

The 40-year reign of George III, who had been brought up in England and was thus the first monarch since Anne able to participate fully in affairs of state, was marked by the loss of the North American colonies. The cause of the War of Independence was an attempt to enforce taxation on citizens not represented in Parliament. This difficult period saw the rise of William Pitt the Younger, who be-

*Above: Wellington and Napoleon I (caricature of 1814). Right: First use of a steam engine in coal mining, 1792.*

came Prime Minister at the age of 24. He reacted to the loss of America with extensive additions to British territory in other parts of the globe. In 1770 James Cook discovered Australia, which subsequently became a useful place to which to deport convicted criminals; and India remained a source of wealth for Britain.

The Duke of Wellington was convinced that the continual repression of the Catholics in Ireland was a threat to the country, and forced the king to allow them access to Parliament in England. In 1801 the Act of Union came into force, uniting England and Ireland. The Irish sent 32 members to the House of Lords, and 100 to the Commons. Following the Act of Emancipation in 1829, Catholics, too, were permitted to be members of Parliament and hold public office.

England was one of the main foes of revolutionary France. Nelson's victories at sea over the French fleet – in 1798 at Abukir and in 1805 at Trafalgar – gave England maritime superiority. Napoleon's Continental blockade of England's industrial products put the brakes on the Industrial Revolution. But at the battle of Waterloo in 1815 a British-Dutch-Prussian army, under the joint command of the Duke of Wellington and Count Blücher, achieved the final defeat of Napoleon.

### The Regency

For the last 25 years of his life George suffered from mental instability, and his son became Prince Regent in 1812. "Prinny," as he was known, had extravagant tastes (an example of which is the Royal Pavilion at Brighton) and led a self-indulgent life, both as Regent and, later, as George IV.

Political power lay with the Tories, who brought about two significant reforms for law and order: Prime Minister Robert Peel abolished the death penalty for more than 100 crimes and founded

# HISTORY AND CULTURE

the first regular police force – nicknamed "Bobbies" after him.

Under King William IV (1830-1837), the Reform Laws of 1832 achieved a long-overdue reform of the electoral laws. The old allocation of Parliamentary seats had become ridiculous. The borough of Old Sarum, near Salisbury, had the right to send two members to Parliament, although it had been years since anyone had lived there. Liverpool and Manchester, on the other hand, were not even represented. Fifty-six "rotten boroughs" were swept away by the Reform Bill, and the franchise was extended.

In literature, the Romantics held sway through the works of poets Wordsworth, Keats and Shelley. Hero of the century, however, was Lord Byron, inventor of the concept of "world-weariness." Mary Shelley, meanwhile, wrote the classic novel *Frankenstein*, giving rise to the development of the genre of the Gothic novel. And Constable and Turner were busy revolutionizing painting with their powerful landscapes.

**Agriculture and Industry**

More peaceful revolutions were also taking place: between 1760 and 1815 there were major changes in agriculture. Common land was enclosed and redistributed, with the result that non-propertied farm laborers began migrating to the cities. At the same time, improved agricultural techniques increased productivity and thus profits.

At the same time, innovations in industrial technology – spinning machines, mechanical looms, the steam engine – had placed England far ahead of the Continent in terms of industrial development. New methods of factory production were introduced; and these new developments led to the improvement of transportation routes: streets, bridges and canals were built, and the first railway line was constructed in 1825. None of this, however, did anything to improve life for the workers, accustomed to miserable living conditions and child labor. Richard Cobden recognized that one cause of urban

## HISTORY AND CULTURE

poverty was high bread prices, which in turn was due to the corn tax.

The House of Lords, comprised almost exclusively of major landowners, had pushed this duty through in 1815. Cobden founded the *Anti-Corn Law League*; only after a protracted struggle was the duty on corn abolished in 1846. In 1833 a factory act was passed which limited the hours which children could work. In 1836 the Working Men's Association was founded in London, leading to a reorganization and new beginning of the workers' movement. Parliament, meanwhile, was seeing the crystallization of a two-party system. The Conservative Party was founded in 1832, the Liberals in 1836.

With no children of his own, William IV clung on to life until a month after the eighteenth birthday of his niece Victoria. And so Victoria became Queen in 1837.

*Above: Child labor in 19th-century mining. Right: Queen Victoria and Prince Albert's family life shaped the values of an epoch.*

### The Victorian Age

The young Queen's marriage to her cousin, Prince Albert of Saxe-Coburg-Gotha, in 1840 was a love match. It was also profoundly influential. Albert was intelligent, interested in science and technology, and a strong believer in the sanctity of family life. Indeed, the expectation that the Royal Family should serve as an example to the country at large derives from this marriage, unusual though it was. The Prince Consort's death from typhoid in 1861 shattered Victoria; she mourned her husband for the rest of her days.

The Great Exhibition of 1851 celebrated Britain's technological and industrial supremacy. One concrete example of this was the Crystal Palace of glass and cast-iron, a marvelous feat of engineering by Joseph Paxton. The event was a success both in terms of national morale and of profit. The revenues were used to buy land for a new complex of museums, including the Science Museum and the Victoria and Albert Museum, and Imperial College in South Kensington.

The Great Exhibition had demonstrated that artisanship, too, had to take strides in order to keep pace with the times. In 1861, William Morris founded a workshop specializing in the production of objects that were at once attractive and useful – stained-glass windows, textiles, and furniture – which he began producing in series after the mid-1870s. Morris's workshop served as a model for a host of artists' guilds that sprang up, ultimately giving rise to the Arts and Crafts Movement which spread to the Continent and led to the development of Art Nouveau and Bauhaus.

Great Britain was now a world power and empire, and keeping the "Pax Britannica," actually the maintenance of conditions favorable to British trade and influence, led to a series of wars and the concept of "gunboat diplomacy." The

## HISTORY AND CULTURE

colonies served at once as certain markets for British products and sources of raw materials. On the home front, the "public" schools (public in the sense that entry was not restricted to any particular social, religious, ethnic or vocational group as long as they could afford to pay) fostered an ethos of fair play and unprejudiced public service. The concept of "the White Man's Burden," a duty to care for the people of the Empire, was not entirely ignoble or cynical, though the system rested, in essence, on the exploitation of the weak.

After two reforms of the electoral laws, workers in the city and on the land were finally able to vote and to be elected to Parliament.

The second wave of the Industrial Revolution changed the face of the landscape. Noxious fumes and poisonous waste water earned the Midlands around Birmingham the sobriquet of the "Black Country," but conditions were equally bad in many other cities. Within Britain, critical voices began to be raised against the exploitation of the working classes. The novels of Charles Dickens exposed the misery and injustice of the age. In *Vanity Fair*, William Makepeace Thackeray penned a savage and satirical picture of society. Before the turn of the century Robert Louis Stevenson was writing his adventure stories, which included the famous *Treasure Island*. Rudyard Kipling, the first Englishman to win the Nobel Prize for literature, published *Kim* and *The Jungle Book*.

The year 1859 saw the publication of the book *On the Origin of Species by Means of Natural Selection* by Charles Darwin. The first edition of 1,250 copies was sold out on the day of publication. Darwin's experiences in South America and the Galapagos Islands had shown him that today's life forms must be the result of a long process of evolution. In this foundation work of evolution theory, man was only mentioned in the last sentence: "Light will fall on the origins of man and his history." He did not actually publish this theory until 1871, as he knew

## HISTORY AND CULTURE

that due to the social mores of the times his *Descent of Man* would unleash a storm of indignation.

**The 20th Century**

The nation was emotionally shattered by Victoria's death in 1901. Her reign had seen the transformation of a largely agrarian country into an industrial nation; and, although production was levelling off, England was still the heart of an empire on which the sun never set. The new King, Edward VII, was a jovial fellow, but not at all the steady symbol of Imperial greatness which his mother had been.

Domestically, resistance in the House of Lords to tax and other reforms proposed by the House of Commons led to the reduction of the powers of the Lords; while the suffragette movement was

*Above: Suffragettes fight for women's emancipation, 1905. Right: Britain is fast turning into a multicultural society.*

using tactics of civil disobedience and even violence to promote the right of women to vote.

Abroad, Britain's world dominance was challenged in the new century by industrial development and imperial ambition in other quarters, particularly in Germany, Japan and the United States of America. Edward contributed to the resistance to German expansion by improving relations with other European states, and laid the foundations for the Entente Cordiale (1904) with the country's old enemy, France. By the time of his death in 1910, the seeds were sown for conflict between the power blocs of Germany and the Austro-Hungarian Empire on the one hand and Britain, France and Italy on the other.

**World Wars**

In 1910, the popular George V succeeded his father Edward to the throne. During World War I, the royal house dropped its German name to become the House of Windsor. The effects of the Great War were as profound in Britain as elsewhere. In 1918, the right to vote was extended to all men over 21 and women over 30. Until 1926, the country experienced frequent strikes and economic recession. Unemployment brought Fascism to power in Germany but not in England, where Mosley's Blackshirts remained relatively insignificant while the intelligentsia tended more to the left, favoring Communism.

Britain's first Labour government came to power in 1924. After the death of George V in 1936, a fresh crisis arose when Edward VIII abdicated, finding himself unable to resist marrying an American divorcée, Wallis Simpson. The throne passed to his brother Albert, Duke of York, who used another of his given names, George, to help restore confidence and stability. Having himself fought in the First World War, he shared

# HISTORY AND CULTURE

the desire not to see another, and supported the policy of appeasement of the rising power of Germany. But in 1939 war came nonetheless, and Winston Churchill, aged 65, emerged from years in the political wilderness to lead his country.

**The post-war Years**

World War II further loosened the structure of the British Empire, and its former colonies gradually attained independence, not always altogether without trouble, over the next 20 years. Most of them chose to remain within the Commonwealth, which is still under the aegis of the British monarch. The social complexion of Britain altered significantly in these years with the arrival of immigrants from the West Indies, India, Pakistan and Africa. However, due to their "insular outlook", the British were reluctant to accept the immigrants, in spite of the enrichment the latter brought to the culture and lifestyle of the country.

George VI died in 1952, and Elizabeth II came to the throne at the age of 25. She married Lt. Philip Mountbatten, who was also descended from Queen Victoria.

The second half of the 20th century has been a confusing time for the British. Membership in the EEC, now the EU, promised material prosperity; dissolution of the Empire eroded the old concept of national identity; and a natural linguistic and cultural bond with America has pulled the country in yet another direction.

There is, in fact, no such entity as "Britishness." Aside from a general sense of loyalty to a common fatherland, the people of these islands see themselves variously as English, Welsh, Scots, Indian, West Indian and so on. Indeed, the English may well respond to enquiry by identifying themselves as Yorkshiremen, Cornish, Londoners or Lancastrians. It is precisely this variety and multiplicity of historical heritage and culture that make England and Wales such treasure troves for the visitor to explore.

*LONDON*

# LONDON

**THE CITY**
**CENTRAL LONDON**
**SOUTH OF THE THAMES**
**OUTER LONDON**
**LONDON BY NIGHT**

## LONDON – WORLD CAPITAL, CULTURAL CAPITAL

One hundred years ago London was the largest city in the world, the capital of the foremost industrial nation on earth and center of the largest empire the world had ever seen. Today, London is still a city of superlatives, although its pre-eminence is more cultural than economic. The heart of the metropolis, the City, may have to share with Tokyo and New York the honors of being one of the largest financial and business centers in the world, but culturally London is still at the forefront of theater, classical music, popular music and television production.

Every year, more than 100 theaters mount more than 600 productions, including musicals by Sir Andrew Lloyd Webber, serious plays and comedies by everyone from Shakespeare to new and unknown authors. The Royal Shakespeare Company has its London base at the Barbican Centre; six world-famous orchestras (including the Royal Symphony Orchestra and the Royal Philharmonic Orchestra) play at two famous concert halls: the Royal Albert Hall and the Royal Festival Hall. Almost every day, famous bands give pop and rock concerts, a tradition which goes back to the era of the "Swinging Sixties" when the Beatles and the Rolling Stones were causing a sensation and London became the center of the pop world.

As the capital of the United Kingdom of Great Britain and Northern Ireland, London is the seat of the royal family, Parliament, and the government. Covering an area of 624 square miles (1,600 sq. km), London is the only metropolis in the world which does not have a single unified city government. Since Margaret Thatcher dissolved the Greater London Council in 1986, the individual boroughs have been administratively independent.

This administrative heterogeneity is reflected in the wide variety of races and languages found in London. One-quarter of the population of more than 7 million hails from other parts of the world, which means that more than 150 languages are spoken here. The large numbers of immigrants from the former Empire and their children who were born in Britain create a variegated tapestry of skin colors and peoples. Eating is fun in London – in hardly any other city can you find such a wide and excellent selection of Indian, Chinese, French, Italian, Pakistani and Greek restaurants.

*Preceding pages: Tower Bridge by night.*
*Left: It isn't only lovers who meet under the statue of Eros at Piccadilly Circus.*

If London defined itself in the 60s through its cultural life, the 80s, on the other hand, were a time of economic boom. The world recession at the beginning of that decade destroyed old industrial centers in Britain and wiped out one-third of all jobs. With the recovery in the middle of the 80s, the service sector moved to center stage. As a consequence of this, more than 500 banks and insurance companies from more than 70 countries are concentrated in the City of London, attracted by the commercial legislation of Thatcher's Conservative government, making London the financial capital of the European Community. Others who profited were advertising companies, the administrative infrastructure, retailers and the catering trade. New television and video companies sprang up like mushrooms in Soho; publishing houses and design studios in Covent Garden. The people who fell by the wayside were the newly-unemployed from the old companies, especially in the East End, Tottenham and Brixton. Street riots in these poorer districts were an attempt to attract the attention of a wider population, but didn't achieve much in the way of improvement. In the 70s, the Labour goverment planned to convert the old docks area into public housing, but under the Conservatives ten years later this became the Docklands project, a complex of offices – many of which remain empty – and luxury apartments too expensive for the area's original population.

Most of London's sights are north of the Thames. You can easily explore entire districts on foot, and you will again and again come across small green squares or parks where you can rest your feet. Buckingham Palace alone is flanked by two of the largest parks, Green Park and St. James's park, and within a radius of one mile (1.5 km) are the Tate Gallery on the Thames to the south; to the west

*Above: The Monument and the City. Right: Bus 38 (Victoria Station to Clapton) has become a new tourist attraction due to Duke Bassey, its reggae-singing conductor.*

the world-famous department store, Harrods; to the east the lively Covent Garden district; and to the north the luxury shopping mile of Bond Street and its exclusive stores.

Modern London embraces numerous small villages and hamlets that once surrounded the city. In the course of time they grew and fused with one another, and were ultimately incorporated into the metropolis. The former villages of Chelsea, Hampstead, Kensington and Mayfair have remained, until the present day, residential areas particularly favored by the wealthy. Each part of London has its own history and its own atmosphere: Bloomsbury or South Kensington, for example, are meccas for the art-lover and dedicated museum-goer. Other areas, Soho and Covent Garden in particular, attract the young and the young-at-heart with their lively, happening ambience and the variety of theaters, opera houses and cinemas.

Conserve your energy by travelling longer distances by underground (as the British call the subway), bus, taxi or Thames riverboat. Taxis are not expensive in London and are worth taking when public transportation connections are fiddly, or you are simply weary and would appreciate a little pampering. You can also see a lot of the city from the top deck of the red double-decker buses. For example, the number 11 bus between Liverpool Street Station and Hammersmith passes a dozen major sights, including St. Paul's Cathedral, the Bank of England, Trafalgar Square, Whitehall, the Houses of Parliament and Westminster Abbey. A little more expensive, but with a cleverly thought-out route through the city, are the sightseeing tours offered by London Transport – in summer, open-topped double-deckers are used. It's when the roads are clogged up and traffic is crawling forward at 10 mph that the underground becomes an ideal method of transportation. The *tube*, as locals call it, has a network of some 250 miles (400 km) and 273 stations, which makes it the largest subway system in the world. You

## THE CITY

really can reach every sight in London by underground.

### The Origins of London

The origins of London can be traced back to three separate parts of the capital: the City, Westminster and Southwark. The oldest nucleus is the City, whose present area goes back to the 10th century. Westminster was already in existence at that time, and began a centuries-long rivalry with the City for political, economic and cultural predominance. As early as Roman times, another part of the city had access to the area north of the Thames: Southwark. The Romans built the first bridge over the Thames here, the wooden *London Bridge*, which remained until 1749 (often renovated, of course, and replaced by a stone bridge in the 12th century) the sole connection between the

*Above: When in doubt, ask a friendly policeman or policewoman. Right: The Embankment is the main mooring for Thames craft.*

sections of London north and south of the river. Since the Middle Ages this geographic separation has also marked a social division: the citizens living within the city walls (north of the river) had civil rights, while those living outside the city gates (south of the river) enjoyed no rights or protection. This social differentiation survives even today: the people with money live "above," the poorer classes "below," on the south bank.

Most of the other outlying villages were not incorporated until around 150 years ago. Today, Greater London consists of 33 boroughs: 12 inner-city or metropolitan boroughs and 20 outer boroughs. Central London resembles an oval dish: it lies in the center of a basin crossed by the Thames and bordered by a low chain of hills to the north and south (the highest point is all of 474 ft/145 m).

### THE CITY

Traces of a Celtic settlement have been found near the City. In 43 AD the Romans founded the city of *Londinium*. They established a harbor, built London Bridge, fortified the area of today's City with a wall (whose remains can still be seen, for example, near Tower Hill underground station), and flung a well-planned network of Roman roads over the whole country. In the year 410 the Romans abandoned Londinium, leaving behind them a flourishing, cosmopolitan city of around 10,000 inhabitants. Over the ensuing centuries, this population had to endure attacks of the Picts and Scots from the north, and raids by the Angles, Saxons, Jutes and Vikings. King Alfred the Great was able to beat the latter group back time and time again; in 883, he rebuilt the ravaged city, making it his second capital (in addition to Winchester). Trade flourished anew; German and French merchants and traders settled here and extended the boundaries of the city northwards and westwards. To improve

*THE CITY*

its defense against the Danes, King Alfred divided the city into wards, which have remained the basis of the city administration up to the present day. However, Canute the Dane was still able to take London and had himself crowned king here in 1016.

Christianity had already found a foothold here due to the missionary activities of St. Augustine, who had been sent out by Pope Gregory at the end of the 6th century. The new faith spread rapidly with the first (wooden) St. Paul's, the cathedral of the See of London, built in the 7th century. At the beginning of the 11th century, Edward the Confessor started work on Westminster Abbey. After his coronation in the abbey, William the Conqueror had the first part of the Tower of London built, the stronghold known now as the White Tower (it once really was painted white). Up until the time of Cromwell, the fortress also served as the royal palace, but since King Canute the English monarchs have preferred to reside 2 miles (3 km) outside the walled city in the "village" of Westminster. In this period Westminster consisted of little more than the royal palace, some roads with houses, and the abbey. The monarchs moved back and forth by royal barge between the Tower and the royal residence, usually along the main route via "Le Straund" (today's Strand). Not until around 100 years ago were the bankside areas, which were for the most part mud flats and marshes, reinforced with the strong walls of the *Embankment*. At the end of the 12th century, the City of London was officially declared an autonomous city republic by Richard I. As he was constantly in need of money due to his involvement in the Crusades, he sold usufruct of the Thames to the City. This special status exists even today: the City of London is the only borough which has its own administration with its own mayor, the Lord Mayor.

At the beginning of the 14th century, various trading and crafts guilds came into existence, which passed on their particular expertise and knowledge within

## THE CITY

the guild, developed contacts and offered each other mutual protection. They wore their own special liveries, and street names such as Tailor's Road or Wine Street attest to the fact that the guilds were located in particular streets. The 15th and 16th centuries were a particularly prosperous period for England. Under the rule of the Tudors, who had put an end to the Wars of the Roses, both the arts and the sciences experienced an upswing. During this period, the City finally managed to gain the upper hand over Westminster, economically and culturally. Nine-tenths of overseas trade were controlled from London, the first Stock Exchange was set up in the City, and the economic boom led to incredible population growth. If 75,000 people were living in London at the beginning of the 16th century, 150 years later this number had swelled to 450,000 or so. The 17th century did bring two black years with it: in 1665, thousands of the people living in the City died of the bubonic plague; the poor suffered most, as the wealthier were able to flee to healthier areas such as Knightsbridge and Highgate. Just one year later, the Great Fire of London broke out, destroying more than 13,000 houses and 85 churches. The greatest architect of the period following the conflagration was Sir Christopher Wren, who built not only the new St. Paul's Cathedral but also another 52 churches in the City, of which 23 have survived to the present day.

Today, the City extends over around 500 acres (200 ha). As a center of finance and trade, it is no longer a city where people live but rather one where they work. Every day more than 350,000 people stream in to their jobs, but only around 5,000 actually live and sleep here.

### The Railway Stations

*Above: As the terminus of the Eurostar, Waterloo Station has a new flair. Right: The inner courtyard of the Barbican Centre.*

The great London railway termini, from which trains depart for every corner of the island, are arranged in a great circle around the City. These stations are linked to one another by "interstation buses." Some of the great station concourses of ironwork and glass date back to the 19th century; they have been restored and extended to meet modern requirements (such as Victoria Station). A special case is **Waterloo Station**: this is where the trains arrive from the English south coast and the boat trains which connect with the cross-Channel ferries; it's also the terminal for the *Eurostar* express which travels at 185 mph (300 km/h) through the Channel tunnel which was finally opened in 1994. The train is not quite so fast on the English side of the Channel; the present 3-hour trip to Paris will take only 2 hours and 30 minutes once the new Folkestone-to-London section is completed.

The glass tubes of the new station, almost elliptical in cross-section, are 1,300 feet long (400 m) and between 115 and 165 feet wide (35-50 m); at the Thames end they abut smoothly onto the platforms and hall of the old Waterloo Station. The station was completed in 1993 to the designs of English architect Nicholas Grimshaw, and continues the tradtion of London train stations as a modern steel-and-glass structure for our time.

### The Barbican Centre

The Barbican Centre, built after World War II, is a gigantic complex which blends function and form. Two-thirds of the City's population live in the not exactly cheap high-rises (up to 400 feet/125 m high) named Shakespeare, Cromwell and Lauderdale Towers and located between Aldersgate Street and Moorgate (underground station: Barbican). It is not an easy matter to find the hidden entrance on the corner of Whitecross Street and Silk Street, but once inside you will be richly rewarded. On the ten different levels (four of them underground) of this cultural center, opened in 1981, your only problem will be choosing what to do: listen to a concert in the **Barbican Hall**, home of the London Symphony Orchestra; watch a performance by the Royal Shakespeare Company; or see an experimental production in the associated studio theater "The Pit." There are also three cinemas and a two-storey art gallery with rotating exhibitions. If you have had enough culture, you can recover in the open air by an artificial lake, or in one of the restaurants or coffee shops. At lunchtimes and on weekends, jazz or classical concerts are often given free of charge.

At the edge of the Barbican complex, you can still see remnants of the medieval city walls. Here, too, is the **Museum of London**, where you can travel through time from prehistoric times via Roman London and the Middle Ages before you arrive back in the 20th century. As the exhibits are set up according to the very latest trends in museum pedagogy – with an eye, that is, to entertainment – they're thoroughly enjoyable for kids as well as

## THE CITY

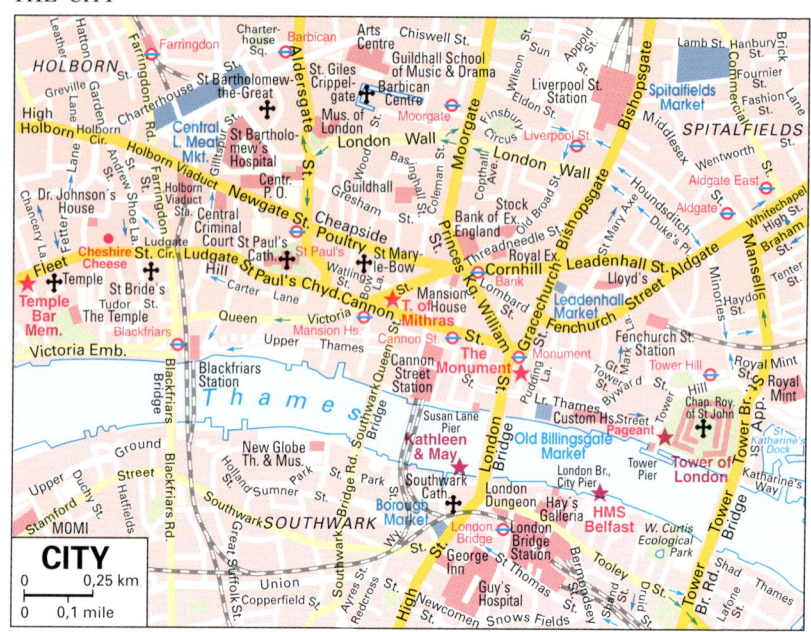

adults. A multimedia show brings the 1666 Great Fire of London so near that you can almost feel the heat of the flames on your skin; and just before the exit is a splendid piece of pomp and circumstance: the gilded coach of the Lord Mayor, used once a year when the new Lord Mayor celebrates taking up office by processing through the City (the Lord Mayor's Show takes place each year on the second Saturday in November).

### The Old City Walls

To the east, beyond the Barbican Centre and the Museum of London, you will come across the medieval church of the Barbican district: **St. Giles Cripplegate**. As it was outside the city walls, this 16th-century parish church survived the Great Fire of London, but was gutted by German bombs during the blitz; it's since been rebuilt. The name of the church alludes to the city gate which formerly stood here at the intersection of Wood Street and the London Wall. It was its location outside the walls which protected the church from the Great Fire. A previous church on the same site dated back to the 11th century and was dedicated to St. Giles, the patron saint of cripples. Some famous Englishmen are buried here, including the writers John Milton and Daniel Defoe, author of *Robinson Crusoe*. In 1620 Oliver Cromwell married Elizabeth Boucher in this church. To the left of St. Giles are remnants of the **Roman City Walls**. Nearby, a blue plaque indicates the beginning of the **London Wall Walk**, which follows the route of the old walls for nearly two miles (2.8 km).

### The Financial District

Going east from the Barbican Centre or St. Giles Cripplegate, you'll pass the renowned **Guildhall School of Music and Drama**. From here it is not far to the

*Right: Smarter than their patrons: the shoeshine men at Leadenhall Market.*

44

## FINANCIAL DISTRICT

wide thoroughfare of Moorgate, which leads south to Princess Street and the **Bank of England** (underground station: Bank). For the English, the "Old Lady of Threadneedle Street" is as much a part of the national culture as fish and chips or football. The Bank was founded as a private company in 1694; until it relocated to Threadneedle Street in 1734, its offices were quartered in the guild halls of two of the great Companies, the Grocers and Drapers. A **museum** was opened in the bank in 1988, covering the founding of the bank, the history of the building, and the early years of banking in England.

Directly opposite the Bank of England is another building steeped in history: the **Royal Exchange**, founded in 1566 by Sir Thomas Gresham (his crest, the grasshopper, adorns the flag flying above the roof). Gresham's building fell victim to the Great Fire; its replacement also burned down in 1838; and the third and present building, a classical design by Sir William Tite with a portico supported on eight Corinthian columns, was erected in 1844. Traditionally the accession of a new monarch to the throne is announced from the front steps. The tympanum over the columns depicts an allegorical figure of world trade, presenting the charter of the exchange to the Lord Mayor and merchants from various countries.

If you keep the Royal Exchange on your right and proceed along Leadenhall Street, which is the continuation of Cornhill, you will find a small side street on the left which leads to **Leadenhall Market**. This market was originally set up as a poultry market in the 14th century and was reopened in the 19th century. That it is located on the site of the **forum** and **basilica** of Roman Londinium is demonstrated by remnants dating from the late 1st and early 2nd centuries. Unlike Covent Garden, with its slightly touristy artificiality, Leadenhall Market still has a genuine market atmosphere; and you can pick up some fresh fruit to restore your flagging energies.

A few yards further along Leadenhall Street is the new **Lloyd's** building, a

## FINANCIAL DISTRICT

high-tech palace of glass and steel which was opened in 1986. Architect Richard Rogers placed pipes, ducts and conduits, elevators, stairs, and the like in plain sight in six towers on the exterior of the building, in much the same manner as he did in his Centre Georges Pompidou in Paris.

From the Royal Exchange, it's only a few minutes to the **Stock Exchange**, which was founded in 1773. Since the reform of the Stock Exchange in 1986 (the so-called "Big Bang"), stockbroking has been largely conducted by computer and telephone, and this 1970s-vintage building sees less and less use by the brokers. The visitor's gallery still allows a view down over the trading floor.

On the south side of the Bank of England is **Mansion House**; here, on the first floor, the Lord Mayor resides for the single year of his office. During this period he is the second most important person in the City, after the monarch, and has his own police force and jurisdiction. He is even informed daily of the day's password for the Tower. Behind Mansion House is **St. Stephen Walbrook**, which many consider to be the most beautiful of Wren's creations. Outside, it's almost drab, but the interior, divided by Corinthian columns, is illuminated with clear light that draws your attention forwards and up to the coffered dome. It was built between 1672 and 1679, as a kind of practice run for Wren's life's work, St. Paul's Cathedral. In one corner of the churchyard garden (open only at lunchtime) is a sundial by Henry Moore.

A few blocks to the north, off Gresham Street, is the Lord Mayor's place of work, the **Guildhall**. Of the original building from 1411, all that remains are the porch, parts of the *Great Hall* (used for meetings and celebrations), the crypt and the outer wall. The 18th-century facade with Gothic and classical elements was restored after the war. The stone wall of the Great Hall is worth seeing, decorated as it is with the arms of the twelve great guilds, or Companies: Grocers, Clothworkers, Fishmongers, Haberdashers, Vintners, Salters, Ironmongers, Mercers, Drapers, Merchant Taylors, Skinners and Goldsmiths.

### St. Paul's Cathedral

Emblem of the City and one of the highlights of London is Sir Christopher Wren's masterpiece, **St. Paul's Cathedral** (underground: St. Paul's). In 604 the Saxon king Ethelbert erected the first Christian church in England on this site. Like its four destroyed predecessors, the present cathedral is dedicated to St. Paul, the patron saint of London. It is the only domed church in England and serves not only as the seat of the Bishop of London but also as the parish church for Christians from the entire Commonwealth.

*Above: An interesting specimen of modern architecture: the Lloyds building in the City.*
*Right: A nation of dog lovers.*

## ST. PAUL'S CATHEDRAL

In only 36 years of construction (1675-1711), Wren managed to create one of the most original and distinguished churches in England, inspired in part by the dome of St. Peter's in Rome. Although the English dome, 363 feet (111 m) tall, is not as high as its model, St. Paul's is still the third-highest domed building in the world today (after Yamasouhro in the Ivory Coast).

The entrance on the West Side leads up a stairway to a columned portico, above which is a second smaller storey with a pediment containing a relief by Francis Bird which depicts the conversion of Saul into the apostle Paul. Bird also sculpted the statues above it: the apostle Peter on the left, James on the right, and St. Paul himself at the center. Above this rises the mighty bulk of the **dome**, supported on Corinthian pillars. For structural reasons the dome actually consists of three shells, one enclosing the other: this is because, on the one hand, the dome should impress with its size and height when seen from without, while on the other hand, it needs to be low enough in the interior not to skew the proportions of the space and to enable the congregation to see the paintings of the eight scenes from the life of Paul on the dome's inner surface. Wren solved this problem by inserting a conical brickwork structure, reinforced with iron, between the outer and inner shells.

The Cathedral's interior has a marvelous airy elegance; despite Baroque details, the traditional Gothic three-level wall structure is dominant. On the way to the crypt, you pass the marble statue of Wellington (north aisle) and the memorials for the heroes of the Napoleonic Wars (north transept), as well as the choir with its ceiling paintings and the high altar (these last not constructed until this century, to the original designs of Wren). In the north deambulatory, or the aisle which goes round behind the choir, is the **Chapel of the Modern Martyrs**, where the South African freedom fighter Steve Biko, who was tortured to death in 1977, is also commemorated.

## OLD BAILEY

At the south end of the crossing you descend to the **crypt**, which is the largest of its type in the world. Of the famous people commemorated by 350 memorials and 100 sarcophagi here, there is space to name only a few: the architect Sir Christopher Wren himself, the painters Turner, Constable and Reynolds, the writer and adventurer T. E. Lawrence (the original Lawrence of Arabia), the Pre-Raphaelites Hunt and Millais, and Lords Wellington and Nelson.

Finally, there's the ascent to the dome; a climb of 627 steps, which is done in three stages. The first section takes you to the **Whispering Gallery**, named for its unusual acoustic properties: you can clearly hear someone whispering 100 feet (30 m) away on the other side of the gallery. After the next section, the **Stone Gallery** commands a first view of London; and the last 166 steps lead up to the **Golden Gallery**, with its stunning panorama of the London skyline.

North of the cathedral is the pedestrian zone of **Paternoster Row**, which was where the paternoster or rosary makers sold their wares in the Middle Ages. In the 16th century, however, the taverns in this area were meeting-places of the actors and the like from the Elizabethan theatre district nearby. After the Great Fire of 1666, many of the booksellers driven away from St. Paul's Churchyard, once the most famous publishing address in England, settled here in Paternoster Row: Daniel Defoe's *Robinson Crusoe*, for example, was published here in 1719. West of this you will come to **Amen Court**, a picturesque collection of red brick houses from the 17th century which once housed the canons of St. Paul's; you can reach these houses along Ave Maria Lane. From here, Warwick Street leads into Newgate Street, where a left turn takes you to the **Central Criminal Court**, more familiarly known as the **Old Bailey**. These courts were built on the site of **Newgate Prison,** which was demolished in 1903. This is where Oscar Wilde stood trial, and more recently (1981) Peter Sutcliffe, known as the Yorkshire Ripper. Newgate Prison stood for nearly seven centuries; notable sometime denizens included Daniel Defoe and the Quaker William Penn, who later founded Pennsylvania. Public executions took place here until as recently as 1868, and since these occasions were almost festive, the prison was a favorite destination for Sunday excursions of the Londoners. An old tradition of Newgate judges has survived to the present day: twice a month in spring and summer, the judges enter the court carrying a fragrant bouquet of flowers. This goes back to earlier times when hygienic conditions in the prison were so bad that the stink carried into the court; the scent of the flowers was intended to ward off the

*Above: St. Paul's Cathedral. Right: The Master and Court of the Vintners' Company process to church – similar to the judges who bring their flower bouquets into the courts.*

## ST. BARTHOLOMEW / FLEET STREET

smell and also diseases carried in the air. On the Old Bailey's 210-foot (65 m) copper dome, completed in 1907, soars the bronze statue of Justice by William Pomeroy. The stone sculptures above the entrance represent Truth and Patience.

Newgate Street will take you past the **General Post Office**, which has a small museum with an extensive collection of postage stamps. Take Giltspur Street to **St. Bartholomew's Hospital**, more commonly known as "Bart's," founded in 1123 by the Augustinian monk Rahère, and which is both the oldest hospital and the oldest teaching hospital in London.

At the northern end of the hospital you can see one of the oldest churches in London: **St. Bartholomew the Great**. The original Norman church was once part of Rahère's monastery, but only parts of the choir survive from this period. The font is also original, dating from the 15th century; here, the future painter and engraver William Hogarth was baptized in 1697. Opposite the hospital and the church was the site of London's largest market for cloth and meat, **Smithfield** (from "smooth field"), which moved to the borough of Islington in 1855. Since 1868, this has been the home of the **Central London Meat Market**, which employs more than 3,000 people; here, you will find the only pub in England permitted to serve beer at six-thirty in the morning.

### Fleet Street

In 1702, England's first daily newspaper, the *Daily Courant*, appeared on Fleet Street. This was quickly followed by more and more publications, until the street's name had become a synonym for the English press. The name of the street is derived from the river Fleet, a major traffic route in the Middle Ages, which flowed along here until it was built over in 1765 (it now runs invisibly beneath the surface). Until the mid-1980s, the buildings along Fleet Street echoed with the thunder of the printing presses; today, however, nearly all publications have moved out of the city center, notably to

## FLEET STREET / TEMPLE

the Isle of Dogs, where there's room to implement new printing technologies. Still, a number of newspapers, publishing houses and press agencies have retained their city offices here. The *Daily Telegraph* headquarters, for example, are opposite **St. Bride's Church**, which due to its location is the press's place of worship. It houses a small museum dedicated to the history of Fleet Street.

That this area has traditionally been a forum not only for the labors of journalists, but also for the work and discussions of sundry literati who convened in its pubs and coffeehouses, is reflected in the sobriquet the *Street of Ink*. The **Cheshire Cheese**, a cozy, authentically restored pub from the 17th century, is supposed to have been frequented not only by Dr. Johnson and his friend and biographer James Boswell, but also by Mark Twain and Charles Dickens.

*Above: The Tower of London. Right: Security checks are strict at the entrance to the Tower to protect the Crown Jewels.*

A little way down Fleet Street towards the Strand, on the right, are Gough Square and **Dr. Johnson's House**. No. 17, a wooden gate with later masonry above it, is the entrance into the legal district of **The Temple**. On the first floor of this house, which dates back to before the Great Fire of London, you can visit the **Pepys Exhibition**, dedicated to the outstanding 17th-century diarist Samuel Pepys. In his diaries Pepys gives a detailed description of the course and consequences of the Great Fire; they also constitute a fascinating insight into the society of the time, and into Pepys' own love life.

Go through the gate and you will come to two of London's four venerable Inns of Court, the **Inner** and the **Middle Temple**. The two others, Gray's Inn and Lincoln's Inn, are on the other side of Fleet Street. Formerly the principal schools for the study of the law, the Inns still determine who is admitted to the bar and are the examining bodies for law, although most law students now study elsewhere.

*THE TOWER OF LONDON*

Each Inn has its own chambers, gardens, refectories and classrooms. The Inner and Middle Temples share a church, the **Temple Church**, which was built by the Knights Templar in 1185 and restored by Wren in 1682. Famous former students include Charles Dickens, Sir Walter Raleigh, and William Thackeray.

Returning to Fleet Street, you'll see the **Temple Bar Memorial** on your left: this dragon-topped stone monument marks the boundary between the City and Westminster. This is the point where the Queen must halt when making official visits; the Lord Mayor awaits her there and gives her official permission to proceed. An arched gateway once stood here, with spikes on which the heads of executed criminals were impaled until as recently as 1745.

### The Tower of London

When you emerge from the Tower Hill underground station, follow the signs to the entrance to the Tower, located in the westernmost tower on the Thames, the **Middle Tower**. Until the London Zoo opened in 1834, the tower to the left of this one, the so-called Lion Tower (now gone) was the home of the royal zoo.

At the southeastern corner of the Roman city walls, William the Conqueror had the first building of today's sprawling castle, the **White Tower**, erected in the 11th century. Two hundred years later, under Henry III, the tower was first whitewashed, whence its name. At the end of the 12th century, Richard I added a moat, and a hundred years after that Henry III added a wall with 13 towers around the inner courtyard to increase its security. By the 14th century, the outer fortifications were virtually completed with the addition of a new outer ward by Edward I. Only a few utilitarian buildings were to be added to the inner courtyard.

Right from the start the Tower had a number of different jobs to perform: to protect the capital, to control the city population, to secure the safety of navi-

51

## THE TOWER OF LONDON

gation on the river and of the palace. It also functioned as an armory, treasury and prison. Among its many famous prisoners we may list the Bishop of Durham, builder of the White Tower; the queen of nine days, 17-year-old Lady Jane Grey; Sir Walter Raleigh; Elizabeth I before her accession; and two wives of Henry VIII, Anne Boleyn and Catherine Howard. A small **memorial tablet** to the left of the White Tower marks the site where the scaffold once stood and heads of enemies of state rolled in the dust. Commoners were hanged at Tyburn, near today's Marble Arch. The old observatory in the Tower was relocated to Greenwich in 1675, while the Royal Mint moved out to a nearby building in 1810.

Today the Tower attracts more than two million visitors a year. One special attraction are the **Crown Jewels** in the **Jewels House** behind the White Tower.

*Above: A Beefeater in his Tudor uniform. Right: St. Katharine's Docks are among London's most exclusive residential areas.*

Since renovations in 1994, 20,000 visitors a day can view the glittering regalia from an automatic walkway. At the entrance to the treasure chamber there's an informative exhibition on the history and significance of the Crown Jewels, most of which date from the period after 1660, as during the Revolution Oliver Cromwell had nearly all pieces of jewelry melted down or sold to raise funds.

Worth a look is the **crypt** of the oldest surviving Norman church in London on the second floor of the White Tower. The two-story barrel vaulting of the fortress's church, built in 1080, rests on plain columns decorated only on the capitals and bases. The only new features here are the windows, which date from the Victorian period. As you leave the White Tower you pass Henry VIII's extensive **collection of weapons and armor**, which today includes exhibits from up to the period of World War I. The most impressive pieces are certainly the four bombastic suits of armor of the monarch which clearly show the stature of the man – in every respect.

Anne Boleyn, Henry's second wife and mother of Elizabeth, was imprisoned for the 18 days preceding her execution in the picturesque, half-timbered **Queen's House**, built in Henry's reign and adjoining the Bell Tower. The house is now the Governor's residence, but has also seen Guy Fawkes and Rudolf Hess as unwilling guests. The countless ravens strutting on **Tower Green**, the expanse of grass on the west side of the White Tower and site of the scaffold, are not there simply to provide the "local color" in tourists' snapshots, but are official members of the Tower, by royal statute, and serve an important function. According to an old Celtic myth about a god of war being metamorphosed into a raven, the crown will fall should the ravens ever quit the Tower. Their wings, therefore, are regularly clipped and the birds fed on meat paid for from the royal purse.

*TOWER BRIDGE*

If you wish to leave the Tower by a different route, you will come to the **Bloody Tower**, built under Richard II, where Sir Walter Raleigh, during some 13 years of imprisonment (1603-1616) following conviction for treason, wrote his *History of the World*. Upon his release he undertook an unsuccessful expedition to South America, after which he was again arrested, incarcerated anew in the Tower, and this time executed.

After crossing the outer ward you will see St. Thomas's Tower, below which is the exit **Traitor's Gate**, guarded by the *Yeoman Warders* or *Beefeaters* in their red Tudor uniforms. Contrary to popular opinion, their name does not derive from their predilection for beef but from the French word *buffetier*, meaning a cupbearer. Every night the Beefeaters perform the *Ceremony of the Keys* or the locking up of the Tower; by 9:53 p.m. at the latest they must have reached and locked the main gate. From the path in front of the walls you can enjoy a fine view of Tower Pier and **Tower Bridge**, which was renovated in 1994 for its 100-year jubilee; it commands a fantastic panorama over the City and the docklands. Along with the Tower, Big Ben and St. Paul's, Tower Bridge is one of the trademarks of London. It is a drawbridge which can open fully within 90 seconds to allow the passage of large ships, although this happens only a few times a week. Built by the engineer John Barry, this bridge over the Thames is a technical masterpiece whose old hydraulic lifting gear was later replaced by an electrical system. Since 1982, the towers of the bridge have housed a museum of the history and technology of the bridge; here, you can find out when the bridge will open next.

Proceed along Tower Pier underneath the bridge and past the Tower Hotel, and you will come to **St. Katharine's Docks**. This harbor was shut down in 1968, to be successfully transformed five years later into a yacht harbor and recreation center with exclusive apartment blocks, galleries, stores and restaurants. On your

## LONDON BRIDGE / ST. MARY-LE-BOW

way back toward Tower Pier, turn left into Lower Thames Street, and at the corner of Byward Street you will pass **Billingsgate Market**, the old central fish market. Today's main fish market has been relocated to the Isle of Dogs, and this hundred-year-old structure now houses offices of City finance companies. The adjoining **Customs House** still functions as offices of the Customs and Excise service; there has been a customs house on this site since the 14th century. Not far after this, **London Bridge** connects the City to Southwark. The first bridge we know of, the wooden one built by the Romans, was torn down almost 1,000 years ago and replaced by a bridge made of stone. Today's bridge is only 20 years old, its predecessor not having been able to cope with the increasing volume of traffic (it was dismantled and shipped to the U.S.A.). The

*Above: A London hallmark: Big Ben at dusk.
Right: Westminster Hall with its famous oak ceiling.*

extension of the bridge leads northwards directly to the **Monument**, a column of white Portland stone erected by Wren in 1671-77 to commemorate the Great Fire of London. It is exactly 202 feet high (61.5 m) and this reputedly is the distance to the baker's shop in nearby Pudding Lane where the fire broke out on September 2, 1666. A spiral staircase on the inside takes you up 311 steps to a viewing platform.

Continue northwards to Cannon Street and there turn left: on your right is 11 Victoria Street where the ruins of a Roman **Mithraic temple** were discovered in 1954; it is thought the temple was used between 90 and 350 AD. The remains have been reconstructed in the temple courtyard, while the head of Mithras found here is exhibited in the Museum of London.

Left of Cannon Street your route leads via Watling Street to Bow Street and another Wren church, **St. Mary-le-Bow**. A church stood on this site back in Anglo-Saxon times, and even Wren's church needed to be renovated due to the bomb damage it suffered during the war. This church is famous for its bells; no one can call himself a true Cockney unless he was born within earshot of Bow Bells.

## CENTRAL LONDON

Central London includes Kensington, Knightsbridge, Chelsea, Marylebone, Islington, the City of London and Westminster. The Thames forms its southern boundary.

### Westminster

From the Westminster underground station at the north end of **Westminster Bridge** it is only a few steps to the Houses of Parliament. This cast-iron bridge is 130 years old; its predecessor, built in the mid-18th century, was only the second bridge crossing the Thames

## BIG BEN / HOUSES OF PARLIAMENT / WESTMINSTER ABBEY

for London's 675,000 inhabitants. With the bridge behind you, you will see on your left what is perhaps London's most famous landmark: **Big Ben**. This name not only refers to the clock tower itself, but also to the 16-ton bell whose voice is known all over the world thanks to the BBC. It is disputed however whether the bell was named for Sir Benjamin Hall, under whose supervision the bell was hung in 1858, or after the boxer Benjamin Caunt.

Stretching along the Thames behind Big Ben are the neo-Gothic **Parliament Buildings**, built in the middle of the 19th century in golden-brown York stone to the plans of Charles Barry and August Pugin. In the 11th century the original building, raised as a royal palace for Edward the Confessor, burned down. After the signing of the *Magna Carta* in 1215 it also functioned as both Parliament and law court. Today it is home only to Parliament, which works on a two-chamber system (**House of Lords** and **House of Commons**). Sittings of both houses are open to the public; you can obtain tickets at St. Stephen's Entrance. Worth seeing inside is **Westminster Hall**, built in 1097 under William Rufus, son of William the Conqueror. Despite some structural changes, you can still see the original hammer-beam ceiling of oak, weighing 660 tons, which was completed in 1402. This hall once housed the supreme courts of England, and saw the trials of Charles I and Guy Fawkes, who tried to blow up Parliament in 1605. He failed, however, and the Queen is still able to open the new session of Parliament every year.

On **Parliament Square**, laid out by Barry, there are a number of monuments to eminent former M.P.s such as Benjamin Disraeli or Sir Robert Peel. Not far off is the little parish church of **St. Margaret's**, which is where many of the Lower House marry.

Alongside St. Margaret's and dwarfing it is the shining coronation church, **Westminster Abbey**, now cleaned of years of soot and grime. The abbey is dedicated to St. Peter, and is not subject to a bishop,

## WESTMINSTER ABBEY

but rather directly to the royal house. Henry III wished to provide his predecessor, Edward the Confessor, who had built a monastery church here in the 11th century, with a worthy monument. Henry's builder demolished parts of the Norman church and then rebuilt the nave, aisles, chapterhouse and the shrine along the lines of the Gothic cathedrals of Reims and Amiens. 300 years later, the vaulting of the nave roof was finished and the building of King Henry VII's Chapel started. The towers of the west facade were completed in 1740. This 500 years of building history resulted in an outstanding church which has the highest nave in England (111 feet/34 m).

Despite the impressive height and width, what tends to strike you as you enter through the West Entrance is the sheer quantity of tombs (400), memorial tablets (3,000), and statues. Immediately after the portal there is a marble tablet to the memory of Sir Winston Churchill; on the left, the *Socialists' Corner* dedicated to British left-wingers; in the nave itself, a memorial to the architect Barry; in the north nave, a tablet commemorating Charles Darwin and famous musicians and composers; in the north transept, statues of eminent 19th century politicians such as Disraeli, Gladstone, Peel, Canning. The *Poet's Corner* is in the south transept and honors, among others, Shakespeare, the Romantics Keats and Shelley, the Brontë sisters, and many, many more.

For centuries, the coronation ceremony has been held in the **Sanctuary** to the east of the crossing. The monarch sits on a wooden throne, the *Coronation Chair*, supported by four lions; at other times, this 13th-century throne is kept in **St. Edward's Chapel** next to the shrine of the royal saint. Beneath the throne is the rectangular Stone of Scone, the coronation stone of all Scottish kings until 1296, when Edward conquered Scotland and brought the stone back to London. It's said that as long as England possesses the stone, Scotland will never gain independence, and not so long ago Scottish Nationalists actually kidnaped it. The eastern end of the Abbey terminates in the wonderful **Henry VII's Chapel**, with a marvellously intricate fan-vaulted ceiling. This chapel is not only the final resting place of Henry VII, but also of his wife, Elizabeth of York; Queen Elizabeth I; her sister, Mary Tudor; and her rival Mary Stuart, Queen of Scots.

If you want a breath of fresh air, leave the Abbey by way of the **cloister** (the door is in the south transept), where you can see an oval memorial tablet with a world map dedicated to the circumnavigators Sir Francis Drake, Captain James Cook and the lone sailor of this century, Sir Francis Chichester.

Behind the Abbey, on your way to the Tate Gallery, you will pass **Westminster School** in Great College Street, founded in 1560 by Elizabeth I. It is still one of the great "public" schools of England (alongside Eton and Winchester); and its alumni have included notables from Ben Jonson, Dryden, and Wren to the actor Peter Ustinov.

Millbank runs parallel to the Thames and brings you to the neo-classical entrance of the **Tate Gallery** (underground station: Pimlico). The gallery stands on the site of what was once the largest prison of London and was opened in 1897 by the sugar millionaire Sir Henry Tate. It exhibits works by British artists from the 16th to 19th centuries, international modern art after 1880. In 1987 the post-modern extension, the **Clore Gallery** (architect: James Stirling) was opened. Paintings by Turner are displayed here on two floors.

A fifteen-minute walk northwards brings you to **Westminster Cathedral**, England's most important Catholic

*Right: Waiting for the changing of the guard at Buckingham Palace – even in the rain.*

# BUCKINGHAM PALACE

church (underground station: Victoria). This Romanesque-Byzantine basilica of red brick striped with white Portland stone is externally very different indeed from the Anglican Westminster Abbey. The tower, almost 330 feet high (100 m), has an elevator and provides a wonderful view of the government district.

## St. James's

A few streets further beckons the residence of the royal family, **Buckingham Palace**. Lord Buckingham had his town house built here in 1705. Later, George IV commissioned his favorite architect, John Nash, to make extensive additions to the complex (1825-30). The classical east facade, which is 390 feet long (120 m) and points towards Trafalgar Square, was designed by Aston Webb in 1913.

Queen Victoria was the first English monarch to reside in the palace, moving into some of its 600 rooms in 1837. Today Queen Elizabeth and her husband actually live in just twelve rooms on the north side; the other rooms are used as offices or reception rooms. On official occasions members of the royal family wave to the crowds from the middle balcony on the east facade. If you are one of the select few invited to one of the Queen's garden parties, you may walk through the gates of the palace, but they are generally closed to the casual visitor. Since the summer of 1993, however, the Palace has had a second attraction to add to the **Changing of the Guard**, which takes place in front of the Palace every day at 11:30 (between August and April, only every other day). While the royal family is taking its annual summer vacation at Balmoral Castle in Scotland in August and September, 18 rooms of the palace are opened to visitors. The background to this gesture, which is not exactly cheap for the tourist, was the fire at Windsor Castle in 1992: renovations will cost some 100 million pounds, two-thirds of which is to be financed by receipts from this new attraction.

# CENTRAL LONDON

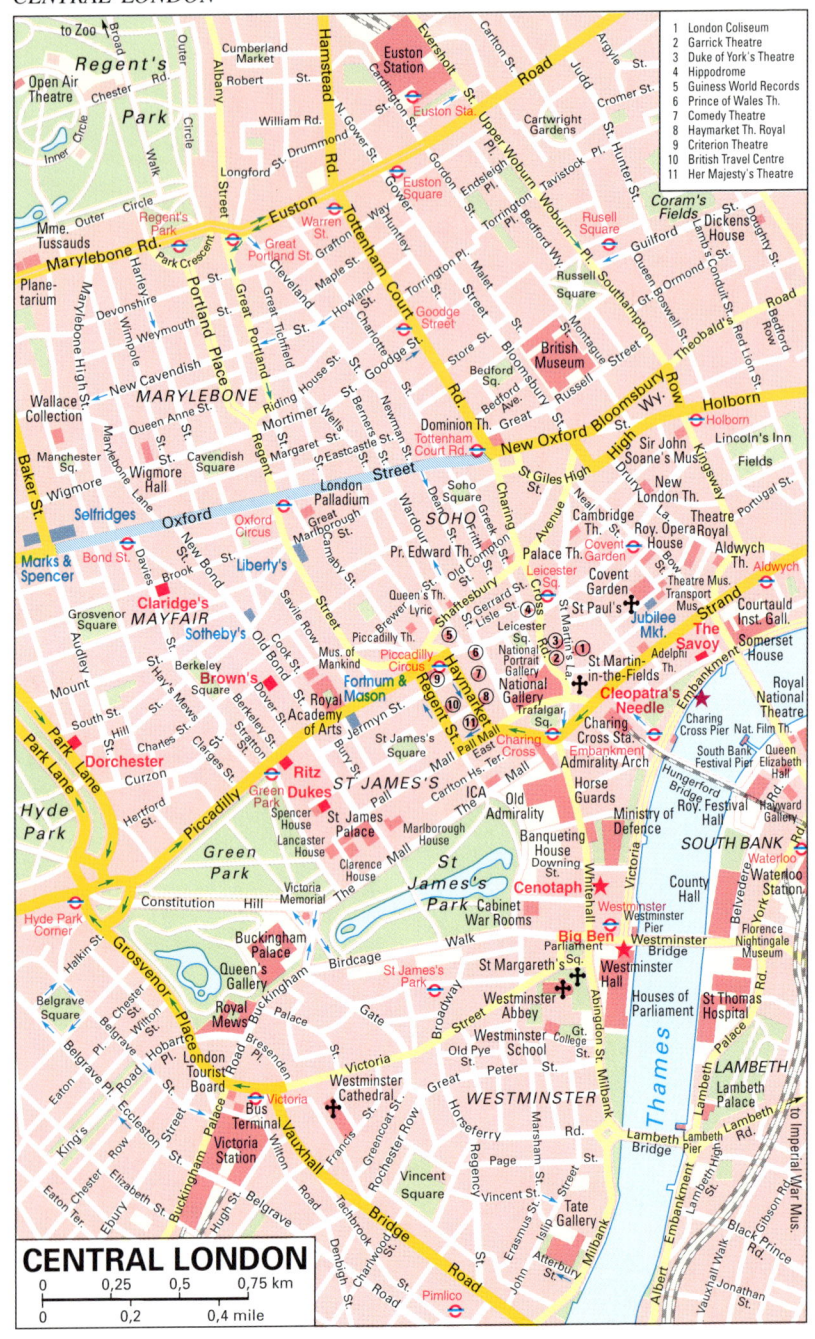

1. London Coliseum
2. Garrick Theatre
3. Duke of York's Theatre
4. Hippodrome
5. Guiness World Records
6. Prince of Wales Th.
7. Comedy Theatre
8. Haymarket Th. Royal
9. Criterion Theatre
10. British Travel Centre
11. Her Majesty's Theatre

**CENTRAL LONDON**

| 0 | 0,25 | 0,5 | 0,75 km |
| 0 | 0,2 | 0,4 mile |

## THE MALL / TRAFALGAR SQUARE

In any case, you can visit the **Queen's Gallery** in the south wing of the Palace, with its rotating exhibitions of works of art from the royal collections, all year round. Also open all year to visitors are the **Royal Mews** to the southwest of the Palace, housing 30 royal horses, 70 or so state coaches and 20 luxury cars of the Queen.

After sightseeing, you can unwind in the two parks adjoining Buckingham Palace. The first, **Green Park**, created in the 17th century, is a green triangle between the north wall of Buckingham Palace Gardens and Piccadilly; in the spring, it turns into a sea of yellow daffodils. The oldest royal park, and one of the loveliest in London, is **St. James's Park**, located to the east of the Palace and the broad avenue leading up to it, **the Mall** (underground station: St. James's Park). The Mall dates to 1660 and, like the parallel avenue of Pall Mall, takes its name from *paille maille*, a game resembling croquet, which Charles II is supposed to have played here. At the southwest end of the Mall is the **Victoria Memorial**: after a design by Webb, the sculptor Thomas Brook surrounded Queen Victoria with a plethora of allegorical figures representing such Victorian values as justice, truth, motherhood, peace and progress. The general feeling was that the edifice rather resembled an enormous wedding cake, but both Brook and Webb were knighted for their work.

If you turn round and walk back along the Mall towards its northwest end, **Admiralty Arch**, you will pass three palaces on the left: **Lancaster House**, today used only for banquets and receptions; **Clarence House**, residence of the Queen Mother; and **St. James's Palace**. This last was planned as a hunting lodge by Henry VIII and converted into a royal palace 150 years later after its predecessor

*Above: St. James's Park is a favorite place for unwinding.*

in Whitehall burned down in 1698. Prince Charles has lived here since his separation from his wife in 1992.

In the red brick building next door, **Marlborough House**, another Wren creation, the Commonwealth Centre has been housed since 1962. Just before you reach the triumphal arch giving onto Trafalgar Square, you will see a light, elegant row of classical houses fronted by Doric pillars, **Carlton House Terrace**. In the 1930s this was the German Embassy; during the war it became the headquarters of the Free French; and today it is the home of the **ICA** (the Institute of Contemporary Arts), Britain's leading museum of avant-garde art.

### Trafalgar Square

In the center of the West End is London's only really generously proportioned square, **Trafalgar Square** (underground station: Charing Cross), favorite hangout of innumerable London pigeons. The square is dominated by the granite

## TRAFALGAR SQUARE / NATIONAL GALLERY

**Nelson's Column**, 184 feet (56 m) high. The column was completed by 1842 to the designs of Regency architect John Nash. One-armed and one-eyed, Nelson, Britain's greatest naval hero, who died in 1805 at the battle of Trafalgar which secured the Royal Navy's dominance of the seas for another hundred years, stands high above the bronze reliefs around its base which depict his greatest victories: Abukir on the Nile, Copenhagen, Trafalgar and St. Vincent. Four huge bronze lions gaze out from their plinths over the pigeons and tourists, while Nelson's eye high above looks south down Whitehall, toward the equestran **Statue of Charles I** (1633) at the traffic hub of Charing Cross. Here, in 1291, Edward I set up the last of 13 crosses marking the route of the funeral cortège for his beloved Queen, Eleanor of Castille. On New Year's Eve, Trafalgar Square is the arena for a huge open-air event. It's jam-packed with people, and its two fountains, which each day spew 400,000 liters of water into the air, are switched off to ensure that none of the 50,000 revellers drowns unnoticed in their icy waters.

This famous and extremely busy square is surrounded by important buildings. To the north is the classical architecture of the **National Gallery**, built in 1838 to plans by Wilkins and Barry: it contains more than 2,200 paintings representing every major European school and era, from the 13th to the 20th centuries. Masterpieces ranging from the Middle Ages to Impressionism are distributed over four wings and 66 rooms (including Leonardo da Vinci's *Virgin of the Rocks*, Albrecht Dürer's *Father of the Artist*, Titian's *Bacchus and Ariadne*). Aids to orientation are the general plan of the museum (free of charge) or the booklet *20 Great Paintings*, which provides a quick introduction to the most important works and where you can find them.

1991 saw the opening of the post-modern **Sainsbury Wing** (named after the donors, who also own the well-known supermarket chain), housing more than 250 works of the early Renaissance, as well as various rotating exhibitions. Behind the National Gallery, at the south end of Charing Cross Road, you will find the **National Portrait Gallery** with five floors of portraits of British notables from Tudor times (Henry VIII) to today (Princess Di, Paul McCartney) – not only paintings, but also sculptures and photographs.

Opposite this gallery stands the oldest building on the square, the church of **St.-Martin-in-the-Fields**, with a steeple 183 feet (56 m) high. Wren's pupil James Gibbs built it in 1721-26 in Baroque-Classical style on the site of the old oratory of the monks of Westminster who 500 years ago used to work here "in the fields." St.-Martin-in-the-Fields has long been the church of the Admiralty, and

*Above: Trafalgar Square, with Nelson's Column and the National Gallery. Right: The Horse Guards are a favorite with tourists.*

# WHITEHALL

since 1954 a shelter for the homeless. Music too plays an important role here: lunchtime concerts are held here at 1:05 pm on weekdays (except Thursdays), and there are often candlelight concerts in the evenings. Classical music is even played in the crypt, where there is a small café. The Academy of St.-Martin-in-the-Fields, an ensemble specializing in early music which attained prominence under the direction of Sir Neville Marriner, is famous around the world. The church also has a *Brass Rubbing Centre*, where children can rub their own pictures of medieval knights.

Passing the South Africa House, you come to **Whitehall**, which leads to the Houses of Parliament.

## Whitehall

Whitehall is a street of government; the first large building on the right is the 17th-century **Old Admiralty**, where Nelson picked up his orders. Linking it with the Treasury building further down Whitehall is the Palladian-style headquarters of the **Horse Guards**, immediately recognizable by the mounted troopers standing like statues outside the sentry boxes flanking the entrance. These impassive cavalrymen are members of one of the seven regiments of Household Cavalry: red tunics indicate the Life Guards, blue the Royal Horse Guards. Every hour between 11 a.m. and 4 p.m. the sentries and horses (gray or black only) change, and every two hours the entire guard. On the second Saturday in June, the guards take part in the colorful celebration of the Queen's official birthday, the *Trooping of the Color*; they march past the Queen, Colonel of the seven regiments, bearing bright banners, to the music of the military bands.

On the opposite side of the street is the only building to survive of the old Whitehall Palace, which burned down in 1698. This is the **Banqueting House**, which Inigo Jones built for James I between 1619-22, thus founding Palladianism in England. Above the main entrance is a bust of Charles I, who is supposed to have walked down from the upper floor on his last journey to the scaffold in 1649. Twenty years earlier, the king had commissioned Rubens to paint the impressive ceiling mural glorifying the Stuarts. Back on the other side of the street, before you reach the guarded (and inaccessible) side street of **Downing Street** (where the Prime Minister lives and works at No. 10, and the Chancellor of the Exchequer at No. 11), you will pass statues of Sir Walter Raleigh and Field Marshal Lord Montgomery. Further down Whitehall, in the center of traffic, is the sparse elegance of the **Cenotaph**, a memorial to the fallen in the two World Wars. Every year on Remembrance Day, the second Sunday in November, the Queen, officers from the armed forces and leading politicians lay wreaths here. Just before Westminster underground station are the **Cabinet**

## COVENT GARDEN

War Rooms, an underground nerve center and Churchill's headquarters during the war, and now a museum.

### Covent Garden

The light and airy atmosphere of Covent Garden has made this market and theater district into a favorite area for young artists and visitors (underground station: Covent Garden). As its name suggests, this was once the site of a convent garden; today, it's a center for professionals and artisans. Furniture designers, architects, or hair stylists live and work in these buildings which Inigo Jones originally designed for the upper classes.

Center of Covent Garden is the market hall, built in 1828 by Charles Fowler, and notable for its Georgian elegance. For a good three hundred years, this was London's largest fruit and vegetable market, until activities were relocated in 1974 to Nine Elms south of the river. Today, it's been restored into a mall with an assortment of small boutiques, arts and crafts shops, bookstores, cafés, art galleries and restaurants. In addition, every Saturday, the stalls of the **Jubilee Market** on the piazza before the market hall offer more arts and crafts products for sale.

Inigo Jones laid out this Italianate **piazza** in the 17th century; today, street performers earn their pennies here between the market hall and the diminutive **St. Paul's Church**. The Earl of Bedford, so the story goes, commissioned Jones to build a chapel no more ornate than a barn; Jones, accordingly, built him "the most elegant barn in England." Although it burned down in 1796, it was rebuilt to the original design; today, it's known as the actors' church. Particularly noteworthy is the pretty churchyard at the back, which is open at lunchtime.

The southeast edge of the piazza was once home to the **Floral Market**, which inspired George Bernard Shaw's 1912 play *Pygmalion*. This is the story of the Cockney flower-girl Eliza Doolittle of Covent Garden, whom Henry Higgins, a professor of phonetics, bets he can transform into a well-spoken and elegant member of society. Shaw's comedy of nature and nurture was successfully turned into the musical *My Fair Lady*. If you would like to experience the color and bustle of an original flower market today, go one Saturday morning to the **Columbia Road Market** (underground station: Shoreditch), as Shaw's market is now occupied by the **London Transport Museum**. The museum is well-designed, particularly for children, and presents many aspects of the history of the tube and the buses. Also worth seeing is a collection of old Art Deco posters. Next door you can view photographs, programs, sets and costumes of the London stage in the **Theatre Museum**.

*Above: There's nearly always something going on at Covent Garden. Right: An evening stroll through the streets of Soho.*

In the next street parallel, on the corner of Bow and Floral Streets, is the **Royal Opera House**. Built by Barry 150 years ago – two previous opera houses had burned down – this theater stages productions with prominent guest artists together with the royal opera and ballet ensembles. Tickets are hard to come by, but you can always try to get hold of one of the 100 or so standing-room tickets by standing in line at the box office a couple of hours before the evening performance. Two streets further on, between Drury Lane and Catherine Street, are the classical columns of the **Theatre Royal**, built by Nash in 1820, which has seen many plays by Oscar Wilde, as well as more than 2,000 performances of *My Fair Lady*. One street further on is **Neal Street**; you can sample the pleasant and busy atmosphere of the West End in its boutiques, cafés, pubs and courtyards.

Going south, you'll come to the **Courtauld Institute Galleries** (entrance on the Strand, underground station: Aldwych or Temple) where **Somerset House** has since 1990 maintained a small but excellent collection of French Impressionists (the most important collection of its kind outside France), as well as 19th- and 20th-century British artists. The exit at the rear leads you down steps to the Thames Embankment, where to your right looms **Cleopatra's Needle**, nearly 70 feet high (20 m), weighing 20 tons and around 3,500 years old; Egypt presented this obelisk to London in 1819, but it was not set up until 1878. Before its erection, various contemporary objects were interred beneath it for the edification of posterity: a photograph of Queen Victoria, a hairpin, a copy of the *Times*, and a train timetable.

## Soho

North of Trafalgar Square and west of Covent Garden is the district of Soho (underground stations: Leicester Square or Piccadilly Circus). It was once one of the hunting grounds of Henry VIII, and one explanation for the name of this

## LEICESTER SQUARE / PICCADILLY CIRCUS

lively district in the West End is the hunting call "so ho!" For 250 years, Soho has been the most ethnically diverse part of London; here came Huguenots from France, Italians, Jews, Indians and Chinese. The latter are a particularly strong force; the shops and restaurants of **Chinatown** are concentrated in Lisle and Gerrard Streets, marked by a recently-erected Chinese gate. Even the telephone boxes have been given a Chinese touch.

A few steps further on is the principal open space of Soho, **Leicester Square**, which housed theaters as long as 150 years ago. Today, numerous cinemas draw the crowds. At the center of this green square are statues of Shakespeare and Charlie Chaplin, and at the south end there is a ticket office offering half-price tickets for performances that same day. Alone on the main thoroughfare of London's stage world, **Shaftesbury Avenue**,

*Above: A Chinese gateway marks the entrance to Chinatown. Right: Leicester Square, the lively center of Soho.*

you can count six theaters and two cinemas. At the corner of Shaftesbury Avenue and **Charing Cross Road** (which is a Mecca for book lovers, with Foyles and a host of second-hand bookstores) is the **Limelight**, a popular nightclub in a converted church. To the north, two streets past Shaftesbury Avenue, is pulsing **Old Compton Street**. This former Bohemian quarter is worth visiting for its innumerable pubs and restaurants. Nearby **Carnaby Street** came to fame in the 60s as *the* place to buy hip clothes, but today the only people gravitating here are tourists. Real, if fairly seedy, life is found in **Berwick Street**.

To the west, around Brewer Street, is the nearest London comes to a real redlight district, with strip clubs and dirty bookshops. It peters out just before **Piccadilly Circus**. "Circus" here has nothing to do with the big top, but rather refers to the *circulation* of traffic and people around the central fountain with its statue of **Eros**, erected in 1893. This monument doesn't have much to do with physical love, but rather, incongruously, with Christian charity; it is dedicated to the Earl of Shaftesbury (who also gave his name to the avenue) who fought for better social and hygienic conditions in the 19th century. To the north is **Regent Street** with the large stores which symbolize England to many visitors: Austin Reed, Aquascutum, the Art Nouveau edifice of Liberty's, and so on.

### Mayfair

West of Piccadilly Circus is the elegant district of **Mayfair**. Piccadilly (underground station: Piccadilly Circus) is a shopping street with exclusive clothing stores, the top bookstore **Hatchard's**, and delightfully but extremely old-fashioned shops where you can buy hunting pink or split-cane fishing rods, as well as the famous delicatessen and tea store **Fortnum & Mason**, suppliers to

## MAYFAIR / MADAME TUSSAUD'S

the court since 1707. Every hour the store's founders, Fortnum and Mason, strike the hour on a clock above the entrance. Opposite this, the **Burlington Arcade** (particularly good for expensive silk ties and cravats) is also the home of **Royal Academy of Arts**, which includes an art school and gallery with changing exhibitions. When you come out at the other end of the arcade you're just a few steps from a branch of the British Museum, the **Museum of Mankind**, with exhibits from past and present cultures from the entire world.

Luxurious clothing and antique shops are the attractions of Mayfair's principal thoroughfare, **Bond Street** (underground station: Piccadilly Circus or Bond Street). Here and in **Cork Street**, you'll find one private art gallery after another, while Bond Street is home to the established auction house **Sotheby's**. The area around **Berkeley Square** and **Grosvenor Square** has been a preferred residential area of the upper classes for 300 years, although today more and more houses are being converted into offices and embassies. You can still sense the original atmosphere in the small side streets southwest of Berkeley Square, particularly in the small shops, cafés, pubs and restaurants of **Shepherd's Market**. It was here that the original *May fairs* were held – on the site of the earlier cattle and feed market – until the aristocracy started settling here around 1700. In Mayfair you will find such famous hotels as **Claridge's** in Brook Street or the **Ritz** on Piccadilly opposite Berkeley Street.

**Marylebone and Bloomsbury**

To reach **Madame Tussaud's** in Marylebone, travel a few stops on the underground north of Green Park station (underground station: Baker Street). Madame Tussaud's real name was Marie Grossholtz; she was a wax modeller at the court of Louis XVI. After the French Revolution she lost her position and finally, in 1802, came to England where after an unsettled life, at the age of 74, she established herself in London, founding her museum in 1835. Today, the wax figures displayed here range from the worlds of politics, film and television (Joan Collins), sport (Boris Becker), pop music (the Beatles), and the royal family to the most infamous of criminals and rogues. Since the separation of the Prince and Princess of Wales, Princess Di has been shifted a noticeable distance from the rest of the royal family. Long queues form almost daily in front of the entrance, but you can avoid these if you buy a combination ticket in the **Planetarium** next door. Around the corner, in Baker Street, detective-story fans can immerse themselves in the four-storey **Sherlock Holmes Museum** – although Holmes's fictional address, 221B Baker Street, does not actually exist.

Elegant streets frame one of the most attractive of London's parks, **Regent's**

*Above: Breathtakingly lifelike: Alfred Hitchcock and Humphrey Bogart at Madame Tussaud's. Right: Speaker's Corner.*

**Park** (underground station: Regent's Park). In 1812, the architect Nash designed a stylish garden city on the site of the old royal hunting grounds; note the breathtaking semicircle of façades along **Park Crescent**; with the park next door. Here there is an **open-air theater**, where Shakespeare is staged on summer evenings; and on the north edge of the park, the **London Zoo**.

Particularly recommended is a romantic boat trip on **Regent's Canal**, which leads to the zoo in one direction and to **Little Venice** in the other. Flower-bedecked houseboats are moored here, some of which serve as floating restaurants (underground station: Warwick Avenue). You can continue your boat trip north of the zoo to **Camden Lock** (underground station: Camden Town or Chalk Farm). This lively quarter is home to many artists, and you can often watch them at work. Every weekend a flea market is held at Camden Lock.

South of the park, **Marylebone High Street** makes for a pleasant stroll and

## OXFORD STREET / BRITISH MUSEUM

leads you to the **Wallace Collection**, an important art collection located in an 18th-century town house (underground station: Bond Street). Next to the Bond Street underground station in Oxford Street are the inexpensive department stores **Selfridge's** and **Marks & Spencer**. Not far away **Hyde Park** begins, with **Speaker's Corner** at its northeast corner (underground station: Marble Arch). Here anyone can simply turn up, with or without a soapbox to stand on, give vent to his opinions, and gather an audience of listeners and hecklers without fear of being asked to move on by the police. Freedom of speech is not restricted to Speaker's Corner, but here the laws regarding obstruction are not enforced, unless the speaker is obscene, racist or threatening public order. Across the road is **Marble Arch,** which was designed by Nash in 1828 as a worthy entrance for Buckingham Palace but which proved to be too narrow for the royal coaches and was therefore erected here in 1851 on the site of the old Tyburn gallows (which were used until 1783).

**Oxford Street**, the giant but now somewhat seedy shopping street, leads due east to the district of **Bloomsbury** and the **British Museum**, *the* leading temple of the past in London (underground station: Tottenham Court Road, Russell Square or Holborn). The ponderous entrance 400 feet wide (125 m) with 44 Ionic columns supporting a tympanum with a frieze showing the progress of civilization really is reminiscent of a temple. Behind the main entrance stands a statue dedicated to the founder of the museum, the physician and world traveler Sir Hans Sloane, who died in 1753 and bequeathed his collection, numbering some 80,000 pieces, to the state. Since then, treasures have been coming in from all over the world – so many, by now, that you almost suffocate not from the masses of people but from the sheer quantity of objects in the museum's 94 rooms. For this reason, the best times to visit are just after the museum opens or two hours before it closes.

There is only space here to mention a few highlights: the **Rosetta Stone** (Room 25), the piece of black basalt discovered in Egypt in 1799 which helped the Frenchman Champollion decipher the hieroglyphs; the **Elgin Marbles** from the frieze of the Parthenon in Athens (Room 8); the **Lion Hunt** relief in the Assyrian department (Room 17); the **Egyptian mummies** (Rooms 60 and 61); the **Manuscripts Collection** in Room 30, where two of the four existing originals of the *Magna Carta* are displayed next to such contemporary items as the manuscript of the Beatles' *Yesterday*. Look in, too, at the pale-blue, Victorian-era **Reading Room**, where once worked such diverse notables as Karl Marx, Mahatma Gandhi and George Bernard Shaw.

A few streets further on is **Sir John Soane's Museum** (underground station: Holborn), a lively if chaotic collection of art and curios. The architect spent the last

67

*KENSINGTON GARDENS*

24 years of his life here; the house contains, among other things, an important alabaster sarcophagus of Seti I.

A must for Dickens fans is the **Dickens House** in Doughty Street (underground station; Russell Square); here, the writer penned *Oliver Twist* and enjoyed his rise in society in 1837-39. In addition to the writer's furniture, objects of general use, letters, and photographs, the house also holds every single first edition of his work and an extensive library.

**South Kensington and Knightsbridge**

Until the Great Exhibition in Hyde Park in 1851, these districts were rural in character; it was only after the exhibition that rapid building began, and **South Kensington** became the apple of Prince Albert's eye. Under his supervision there arose a museum and educational district,

*Above: Attractive and expensive living in Kensington. Right: Whale and dinosaur skeletons in the Natural History Museum.*

which Queen Victoria extended after her consort's death. South Kensington and, even more so, Knightsbridge developed into upscale residential and shopping districts for the prosperous classes who settled in luxurious villas alongside small crafts workshops.

To the north, South Kensington is bounded by the oaks and chestnuts of **Kensington Gardens**, separated from **Hyde Park** by the **Serpentine**, a lake shaped like an elongated whale and fed by another of London's hidden streams. Since the 17th century, members of the royal family have lived in the simple brickwork of **Kensington Palace** (underground station: Kensington High Street); this is where Queen Victoria was born, and today it's home to Princess Margaret and Princess Di. The Palace itself is located at the southwestern edge of the Gardens. To the east of it sits an extraordinary edifice: the neo-Gothic **Albert Memorial**, 180 feet (55 m) high, which Victoria had erected to the memory of her "dear Albert." Under the ornate canopy the Prince Consort sits enthroned, holding in his hands the catalogue of the Great Exhibition, which drew six million visitors to Hyde Park in 1851 and raised a quarter of a million pounds, money Albert used to buy the land for his building plans. The Prince is surrounded by four figures symbolizing his fields of interest: agriculture, manufacture, commerce and engineering. The marble frieze around the base of the plinth depicts 178 famous – male – persons of the period.

On the other side of the street is the oval structure of the **Royal Albert Hall**, red brickwork with light terra-cotta bands; it was built in 1867-71 to the designs of engineers Fowke and Scott. Despite its poor acoustics, this concert hall with its impressive glass and cast-iron dome 295 feet high (90 m) is beloved of the Londoners. Its neighbors to the south are the Imperial College of Science and Technology, the Royal College of Music, the Royal School of Mines, and of course the **Science Museum**, which covers science and technology. Particularly worth a visit is the **Natural History Museum** (underground station: South Kensington), remarkable for its striped terra-cotta façade of beige, white and pale blue. The entrance hall accommodates an enormous dinosaur skeleton. A visit to the world of the dinosaurs or the "creepy-crawlies" department, with various household critters, has plenty to hold the interest of adults as well as children. The **Geological Museum** next door is famous not only for its rock collection, but also for its gems and precious stones.

Cross Exhibition Road to the **Victoria & Albert Museum**, which began as Prince Albert's collection of beautiful, unusual or notable objects. It has 150 galleries, and you really will need the plan of the museum which can be obtained free of charge at the entrance. Highlights include the Green Dining Room, furnished and decorated by William Morris, and the Rodin sculptures in the Henry Cole Wing. Behind the museum and shaded by the trees stands the Roman-Catholic **Brompton Oratory**, which frequently

*KENSINGTON / CHELSEA*

hosts concerts. From here you can see the red terra-cotta facade of **Harrods**, one of the most famous department stores in the world (underground station: Knightsbridge). Founded by the tea dealer Harrod in 1840, it now belongs to an Egyptian businessman. 4,000 employees cater to the whims of visitors from all over the world. The opulent Art Nouveau Food Hall on the ground floor is an El Dorado for eye and nose.

**Kensington and Notting Hill**

For the last 300 years or so, **Kensington** and the area around **Holland Park** have been, like Chelsea, accounted desirable addresses by those in the know. Blue plaques mounted on house façades throughout the area indicate the one-time residences of various luminaries; walking along **Kensington High Street**, Kensington's main drag, you pass a number of such plaques, as well as a range of nice little shops. On the parallel Stafford Terrace is the **Linley Sambourne House**, once home to the Punch caricaturist of that name; inside, you can get a taste of the somewhat lugubrious atmosphere of a respectable Victorian-era home, with its dark velvet curtains and William Morris wallpaper.

A couple of streets further on is the beflagged **Commonwealth Institute**, a 1962 tent-roof construction which acts as a cultural and educational center providing information about the history, economy, politics and lifestyles of the 50 Commonwealth states. A few blocks past this, at number 12 Holland Park Road, is the exquisite **Leighton House**, home of Pre-Raphaelite artist Lord Leighton; its oriental *Arab Hall* with its domed roof is particularly striking. No artifice here: the tiles on the walls are the genuine article, which the lord himself brought back from Damascus and Cairo.

Small but striking, **Holland Park** lies to the northeast, surrounded by a number

*Right: Good vibes every year at the Notting Hill Carnival.*

## PORTOBELLO ROAD / NOTTING HILL

of embassies. One attraction here is the wildlife park with its peacocks and emus; another is the wealth of trees and flowers. Here, too, is **Holland House**, in the 19th century a center of political and social intrigue, and today, more prosaically, a youth hostel.

By contrast, **Bayswater** (underground station: Queensway) and **Notting Hill** (underground station: Notting Hill Gate), north of the park, are a whole different world, reflecting the influence of the spectrum of colorful cultures of immigrants from throughout the Commonwealth. Bayswater's main street, **Queensway**, tempts the palate with a panoply of inexpensive restaurants offering a wealth of regional cuisines; but a better-known attraction is the annual **Notting Hill Carnival** at the end of August, celebrated since 1966 by immigrants from the West Indies. For three days the festival rocks to the sound of reggae, ska, calypso, and other regional musical specialties; while the streets are filled with bright costumes and the aromas of exotic food. But even during the rest of the year, Notting Hill remains a favorite haunt of flea-market fans and lovers of antiques. Along **Portobello Road**, the longest street market in England, there is a junk, antiques and knickknacks market starting at 10 a.m., Monday to Saturday. In addition to the dealers who set up their stalls here every day, there are others with permanent shops; some of these have added audaciously overpriced souvenirs to their range of wares, and it's always worth your while to try to haggle a bit. Less crowded than Portobello Road is the parallel **Ladbroke Grove**, which offers more second-hand goods. Many shops post maps to show what is on offer where. This street market started off around 1870 as a gypsies' market where horses and herbs were traded; later came fruit and vegetable sellers, and since 1948 more and more antiques dealers. Yet 250 years ago, this street was no more than a narrow sandy path leading through open fields to Porto Bello Farm.

71

## Chelsea

Like Kensington, Chelsea has been regarded as an elegant residential area for the last 300 years. During the "Swinging Sixties," it was in Chelsea's main drag, **King's Road** (underground station: Sloane Square) that the miniskirt began its conquest of the world; even today, many people account this thoroughfare one of the city's leading shopping streets, lined as it is with innumerable trendy boutiques. Today's well-to-do professionals (doctors, lawyers, successful artists, the sons and daughters of wealthy families) live in the chic houses around **Sloane Square**, with its classy cafés and restaurants. The square was still a meadow in 1771; but today, it's hard to believe that Chelsea was once a small fishing village.

This part of London has a particular flair, partly by virtue of its residents. In the eighties, it was the haunt of the so-called "Sloane Rangers," a group of youngish, upper-middle-class scions of families with old money (not, God forbid, "nouveaus"), who dressed unremarkably and expensively and took off on Fridays in their Jeeps to their weekend cottages. Best-known example of this set was the then-Lady Di; they had, and still have, many imitators.

But Chelsea has always been home to notable people, and **Cheyne Walk**, which runs parallel to the Thames Embankment, is still a much-sought after address. No. 3 Cheyne Walk was once the abode of Keith Richard, No. 4 of George Eliot, No. 16 of William Morris, Nos. 19-26 Sir Hans Sloane, No. 48 Mick Jagger, No. 119 J.M.W. Turner. At the eastern end of Cheyne Walk, at 66 Royal Hospital Road, is the lovely **Chelsea Physic Garden**, which was founded by apothecaries in 1673 as a teaching and herb garden, and is still filled with exotic plants and trees. A few streets farther on is the **Royal Hospital**, which has been accommodating army veterans (at least 22 years of service to qualify) for 300 years. There are around 400 of them; their old-fashioned red tunics and black tricorn hats are a familiar sight in Chelsea. The Hospital also houses the smallish **National Army Museum**, with exhibits documenting the history of the British army since the 15th century.

## SOUTH OF THE THAMES

### Lambeth, the South Bank and Southwark

South of the Thames, you can get a fantastic view of Westminster and the Houses of Parliament from **Lambeth Palace** (underground station: Lambeth North), a brick building with white facings dating from the Middle Ages and since 1207 the London residence of the Archbishop of Canterbury. A stroll along the river will take you past **St. Thomas's Hospital**, where Florence Nightingale founded the first college of nursing in Europe (next door is the small **Florence Nightingale Museum**). A few streets further on, set in a park, the **Imperial War Museum** is dedicated to the history of war in the 20th century. Further down the Thames and after Westminster Bridge comes the sprawling and now empty edifice of **London County Hall**, which was the home of the Greater London Council (GLC) until its dissolution in 1986. Now, between Westminster Bridge and Waterloo Bridge (the view from the top is well worth the effort) comes the district known as the South Bank. Site of the 1951 Festival of Britain, it is now occupied by the monolithic blocks of concrete which make up the **South Bank Arts Centre**, a cultural complex which has developed into a major center for concerts, exhibitions, plays and films. Among its

*Right: To the American his hamburger, to the Briton his fish and chips.*

*SOUTH BANK / SOUTHWARK CATHEDRAL*

concrete blocks is the **Royal Festival Hall**, opened in 1951 and extended until the 1960s; it boasts a seating capacity of 3,400 and famously good acoustics. The smaller halls, the Queen Elizabeth Hall and the Purcell Room, are venues for recitals and chamber concerts. By day as well as in the evening, the Festival Hall restaurant offers a grandiose view of the skyline of the opposite bank of the river. Another concrete building is home to one of the most important museums of modern art and international travelling exhibitions: the **Hayward Gallery**. It is adjacent to the **Museum of the Moving Image (MOMI)**; opened in 1988, and financed principally by John Paul Getty, this is the largest film museum in the world. Its imaginative displays present both the history of the cinema and the fictional worlds it has created. Next door, directly beneath Waterloo Bridge, the two cinemas of the **National Film Theatre** each show a different film every day – series arranged around specific themes, cult films, or outsider productions. Finally, the three stages of the **Royal National Theatre** are venues for a variety of plays.

Your stroll along the river now leads you into **Southwark** (pronounced Suth'k), the impoverished and oldest district of South London, famous for centuries for its theaters, inns, brothels and prison. In the Middle Ages it was a pleasure district outside both the city gates and the city's jurisdiction. It was here that Shakespeare's company performed in the Globe Theater in 1599; the building burned down in 1613, but was reconstructed a few years ago. Also vanished are Southwark's seven prisons, one of which held Charles Dickens's father in 1824; Dickens depicted the bleakness of life in this neighborhood in *Oliver Twist* and other novels.

One surviving relic of the past is **Southwark Cathedral** (underground station: London Bridge), a Gothic church 700 years old which was not made a cathedral until 1905. It was partly in ruins when it was restored at the end of the last

*NEW GLOBE THEATER*

century. Above the crossing a square tower rises on four enormous piers; inside, take a look at Harvard Chapel, dedicated to the founder of Harvard University in Cambridge, Massachusetts. John Harvard was baptized here in 1608. In addition to the remains of the first Norman church (archways on the left and opposite the entrance, as well as in front of the Harvard Chapel), the choir is a particularly interesting example of the Early English style (end of the 13th century). The altar and chancel weren't built until the Late Gothic period at the beginning of the 16th century. In 1912, a memorial was erected in the south transept to Southwark's most famous parishioner, William Shakespeare. Every Monday and Tuesday at 1 p.m., one-hour concerts are held in the church.

After Southwark Bridge and west of the Cathedral, the **New Globe Theatre** was opened on April 23, 1993, Shake-

*Above: A trip to the Docklands will interest fans of modern architecture.*

speare's birthday. The American director Sam Wanamaker built a copy of the original theater with 1,500 seats, and it includes a small **museum**. Opposite the cathedral, moored at the quay of St. Mary Overie, lies the wooden three-master *Kathleen & May*, which has been restored to its original condition. South of the cathedral are the old market halls of (today's) wholesale fruit and vegetable market, the **Borough Market**. On the other side of the High Street is the **George Inn**. Built in 1554 and restored after the Great Fire in 1666, it is the only galleried coaching inn left in London. Here, Shakespeare is supposed to have appeared. Every summer the George mounts some of his plays in his honor. Behind the inn is the rectangular red brick tower of **Guy's Hospital**, where you can get an idea of what an operating theater looked like a hundred years ago. Under the operating table a box filled with sawdust still waits to catch the blood. Further gruesomeness is provided a few blocks away in Tooley Street at the

**London Dungeon Museum**. Opposite this is the entrance into the two former warehouses which have been converted into **Hay's Galleria**, today connected by a glass roof and containing shops and restaurants intended to revive this old harbor area. Moored off the gallery is one of the largest warships in Europe, *HMS Belfast*, which saw active service in World War II, housing a company of 800 men on seven decks, and with guns with a range of 14 miles (22 km). Today a **museum**, the vessel is nonetheless still part of the Royal Navy, as is indicated by the White Ensign flying at the stern. From here you can look across to the Tower of London on the other side of the Thames.

## OUTER LONDON

### East and South London: Docklands, Greenwich and Dulwich

Since between 1967 and 1981 all of the warehouses and docks for around 20 miles (30 km) east of Tower Bridge closed, the number of unemployed dockworkers has risen. For nearly two centuries the **Docks** on the Thames were the most important loading and unloading point for all goods and commodities from the British Empire. Containerized shipping, introduced in the 1950s, shifted the center of gravity for ocean transportation downstream to Tilbury on the Thames estuary, thereby dealing the death blow to the old wet docks. The original plan was to erect council housing in their place, but the Thatcher government's nearly autonomous building agency set up in 1981, the *London Docklands Development Corporation*, created a construction boom due to the lack of building restrictions and attracted all kinds of speculators. Rents shot up and old warehouses, where the rats had in some cases already made their homes, were converted into luxury apartments for yuppies. Their horrendous rents seemed almost realistic in light of the materialistic spirit and economic excess of the age.

Today, however, the boom is past, and many of the buildings are still empty, as virtually no one, private individual or small company, can afford monthly rents of up to two thousand pounds. This futuristic satellite city is, like the City, almost exclusively the provenance of those who work there by day, and virtually uninhabited at night. You can see this, for example, from the fact that the *Docklands Light Railway* or DLR, which was specially built for the new Docklands, only runs until 9:30 p.m., and in the evenings there is hardly a soul to be found in the pubs and restaurants.

All the same this major project, where architecturally successful individual buildings stand cheek by jowl with shapeless lumps of concrete, is worth a look. Since 1987, the DLR has linked the underground station Tower Hill with Greenwich. Center of this four-part construction area (the Isle of Dogs, Wapping, the Royal Docks, Surrey Docks) is the **Isle of Dogs** (DLR station: Canary Wharf; river bus: Docklands Pier). Many of the newspaper houses from Fleet Street have settled here: *The Daily Telegraph, The Guardian, The Sunday Telegraph*. Immediately striking is the **Canary Wharf Tower**, almost 800 feet (250 m) high, with 50 floors where some 50,000 people will work once all the space has been rented out. The **Docklands Visitor's Centre** (DLR station: Crossharbour) provides free maps and information on its newest developments; you can even book guided tours here. Apart from the Isle of Dogs, the only walk worth doing so far is around **Wapping** (DLR station: Limehouse).

A pleasant and interesting 90-minute boat trip from Westminster down the Thames will bring you to **Greenwich** (by boat from Westminster Pier or Charing Cross to Greenwich Pier); you can also take the DLR to the terminus at Island

## GREENWICH / THAMES BARRIER

Gardens and then go through the pedestrian tunnel. Greenwich, whose name derives from the Old English for "green village," is famous worldwide for the meridian which passes through the Observatory here. Historically, Greenwich has also been an important place: this is where England began her rise as a seafaring nation. Here, too, Henry VIII was born and had one of his favorite palaces.

Past the tea clipper the *Cutty Sark*, which sped from China to England in 1871 in only 107 days; past *Gypsy Moth IV*, the little yacht in which Sir Frances Chichester sailed alone around the world in 1966/67, you come to King William's Walk, where there are plenty of small shops, pubs and restaurants. In the side street College Approach, the **Greenwich Market** is held every weekend, offering crafts, books and antiques.

Now comes **Greenwich Park**. Up in the grounds of the **Old Royal Observatory** runs the dividing line between the Eastern and Western Hemispheres (the entrance price is only worth it if you want to see the collection of old astronomical instruments as well). A little way below it, a footpath crosses the meridian, a favorite place for photographs. Due to London's once-chronic thick smogs, the observatory was moved to Sussex in the 1950s. From the hill next to the old observatory, you can look down on **Queen's House**, designed in 1616 by Inigo Jones for the wife of James I and today, together with its Palladian-style extensions, housing the **National Maritime Museum**, which documents the history of British seafaring and its importance for the British Empire. Its western wing accommodates old ships and ship models, while on the upper floors the James Cook exhibition explains the political importance of his world voyages and the flora and fauna of the South Seas. The Navigation Room displays four chronometers which were of decisive importance for exact navigation. Behind the museum is the **Royal Naval College** with its two onion domes, originally designed as a naval hospital for veterans; Wren was one of its architects. Naval officers have been trained here since 1873, although today it looks as if the college might have to close.

To the east, separated from Greenwich by a great bend in the river, is London's bulwark against the flooding that could happen with a high tide and a wind from the east, the **Thames Barrier** (railway station: Charlton; or by boat from Greenwich Pier). London has experienced four great floods in its history – in 1236, 1663, 1928 and 1953 – and in 1965 the Greater London Council decided to build a barrier. In 1984 the barrier, 1,700 feet (520 m) wide with 10 gates, was finally opened; since then, it's been used once or twice a year.

At the southwest end of Greenwich Park is the small mansion of **Ranger's**

*Above: Astronomy of days gone by at the Old Royal Observatory in Greenwich.*

# GREATER LONDON AREA

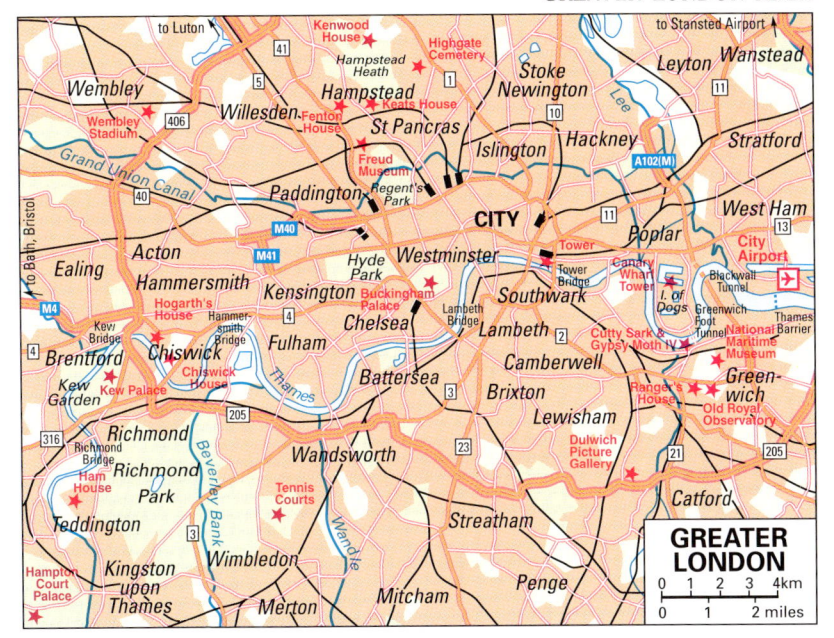

Heath (railway station: Blackheath) which holds the *Suffolk Collection*, a collection of paintings from the Stuart period.

Five miles (8 km) south of London is the oldest public art gallery in England, the **Dulwich Picture Gallery** (railway station: West or North Dulwich). It was opened in 1817 by Sir John Soane and contains outstanding works by Rembrandt (his *Jakob II de Gheyn* has already been stolen four times from here), Raphael, Canaletto, Murillo, Poussin and Watteau.

## North London: Hampstead and Hampstead Heath

The well-kept and idyllic suburb of **Hampstead** with its neighboring parklands of **Hampstead Heath** (underground station: Hampstead Heath) has for 200 years been considered one of the most attractive and desirable places to live in London. Only 4 miles (7 km) from the city center, this village on the hill has over the years attracted such residents as John Keats, Charles de Gaulle, John Constable, and Sigmund Freud. Some of their houses have been converted into interesting small museums.

Also noteworthy are the attractive Georgian houses along **Heath Street** and **Church Row**. In Hampstead Grove, parallel to Heath Street, stands the red brick building of **Fenton House**, a mansion built in the 17th century which houses 18th-century furniture and porcelain from China, England and Germany as well as a comprehensive collection of musical instruments (with an emphasis on keyboards) which are actually played during house concerts.

Not far away to the south you may gaze in wonder at the famous couch of the first psychoanalyst Sigmund Freud in the **Freud Museum** (underground station: Finchley Road) at 20 Maresfield Gardens. In 1938, the 82-year-old Freud fled from the Nazis with his family and important papers, and passed his last years here. His daughter Anna Freud has

77

left six of the rooms as they were; in 1986, four years after her death, the house was opened as a museum with a library.

A few streets further east, in Keats Grove, is the Regency-style **Keats Memorial House** (railway station: Hampstead Heath) in one half of which the poet lived from 1818-20, next door to the woman who later became his fiancée, Fanny Brawne. On show are his books, manuscripts, letters and her engagement ring. They never married, however: in 1821, the poet died in Italy of tuberculosis at the age of 25.

At the north end of the expansive park (measuring 810 acres/325 ha in area), which is dotted with small lakes and woods, stands the imposing mansion of **Kenwood House** (underground station: Golders Green). It was was built at the beginning of the 17th century, and then remodelled in 1767-69 by Robert Adam, England's leading interior decorator. Its last owner, the Earl of Iveagh, built up a valuable art collection of works from the 18th and early 19th centuries (including paintings by Rembrandt, Gainsborough, Vermeer, and Turner). After the Earl's death in 1928, the state set up the **Iveagh Bequest Museum** in Kenwood House, his former home, which also accommodates an attractively-designed library.

East of the park is one of the most famous cemeteries in London, the Victorian **Highgate Cemetery**, last resting place of many notables (underground station: Archway or Highgate). This hilltop cemetery, laid out with the help of the landscape gardener David Ramsay, was opened in 1839; attractive as it was and is, it soon developed into a favorite destination for day trips. Today the cemetery is divided into two parts: you can only visit the western part with an official guided tour, but the eastern part (where Karl Marx lies, among others) is open without restrictions.

*Above: Historic coaches take visitors through Kew Gardens. Right: The façade of Hampton Court.*

## West London: Mansions, Kew Gardens and Hampton Court

To the west and southwest of London, and usually less than an hour by underground or train, are a number of noteworthy mansions, parks and museums. Virtually every one of the old country seats of the aristocracy lies on the Thames and can be reached by boat (frequent sailings daily from Westminster Pier). A boat trip to the famed botanical gardens of Kew Gardens (2 hours) or to Henry VIII's historic palace of Hampton Court (4 hours) will revive a sense of the days when nobles and members of the royal family travelled by sumptuous barges between their summer residences and the capital. There are so many sights to see here that we can only present the highlights, taken in geographical order as you leave London.

The third Earl of Burlington was a great enthusiast of all things Italian, and he had his country seat of **Chiswick House** modelled on Palladio's Villa Capra at Vicenza in 1725-29 (underground station: Chiswick). Two impressive symmetrical flights of steps lead through the portico of Corinthian columns and into the two-story house, whose center is an octagonal dome. Opening off from here are elegant rooms where the Earl held evening receptions. The upper rooms and the attractive, hilly park were designed by English landscape architect William Kent. Nearby is the small **Hogarth's House** (underground station: Turnham Green), in which painter and engraver William Hogarth lived between 1749 and 1764, and which today contains a small exhibition of his personal mementos and some of his work. The house became famous in 1917 when Virginia Woolf and her husband Leonard founded a publishing house here which they named *Hogarth Press*.

One stop further on the underground (underground station: Gunnersbury) brings you to magnificent **Syon House** in Syon Park. For centuries, this has been the family seat of the Dukes of Northum-

## KEW GARDENS / RICHMOND

berland. Open to the public are the reception rooms, which were fully remodelled by Robert Adam in the 1760s; the *Great Hall* is the most attractive. A work of art in itself is the surrounding park, laid out by landscape gardener "Capability" Brown from 1767 to 1773. In addition to a rose garden and a butterfly house, the park contains the impressive Victorian greenhouse of the **Great Conservatory**.

Get off at the next station for one of the most beautiful botanical gardens in the world, **Kew Gardens** (underground station: Kew Gardens; train: Kew Gardens Station; boat: Kew Gardens Pier). Botany fans can spend an entire day here with ease; equally impressive is the architecture of the 18 great glass-houses and buildings in Chinese, Japanese and Victorian styles. The gardens extend over 280 acres (120 ha), encompassing 2 artificial lakes, and contain 50,000 different species of plants from every corner of the globe, collected in part on trips by the former director of the gardens, Sir Joseph Banks, who sailed around the world with Captain Cook. The gardens were founded in 1759 by Princess Augusta, the mother of George III. Right from the start they were intended not solely for scientific research but also leisure and relaxation. The **Orangery** on the northern edge (today a tea room and shop) and the **Chinese Pagoda** on the southern edge were designed by the architect Sir William Chambers. George III had the gardens extended by "Capability" Brown and appointed botanist Sir Joseph Banks as honorary director. In the 19th century, the Royal Botanical Gardens were turned over to the state; a library was founded (which today holds over 100,000 volumes); and what were then the largest conservatories in the world were built: the **Palm House** and the **Temperate House**. These two Victorian conservatories – an early glass and ironwork design by Burton, containing exotic palms and plants – are the main attraction of the gardens today. Other highlights include the biotopes in the **Princess of Wales Conservatory**, with flora from a variety of regions, from the Arizona desert to the jungles of Borneo, and a lotus the size of a table. Nearby is the Georgian-style **Kew Palace**, with personal items which belonged to George III and his wife Charlotte.

One underground station and a loop of the Thames further south brings you to **Richmond**, idyllically situated in a landscape of gently rolling hills (underground station: Richmond; boat: Richmond Bridge). During the period between Henry I and Charles I, Richmond was the royal residence; it later attracted the upper classes from London as well. It remains elegant and well-groomed: note the impressive villas along **Richmond Terrace**, lying directly on the river, or **Richmond Hill**. From here, in fine weather, there is a breathtaking view which has inspired many poets and landscape painters (including Turner).

If you fancy a long, peaceful stroll, try **Richmond Park**, south of the town center. Nearly 150 acres (600 ha) in area, it is the largest park in London, with more than 200,000 old trees. On the fringe of the park is **Ham House**, open to the public. It is one of the best-preserved stately homes of the 17th century and contains valuable furniture, tapestries and paintings (by Van Dyck, among others). (Underground station: Richmond, then the 71 bus as far as the Fox and Duck.)

About 16 miles (25 km) southwest of London is one of the most attractive and historic castles in England: **Hampton Court Palace** (train: Hampton Court Station; boat: Hampton Court Pier). Erected by Cardinal Wolsey at the beginning of the 16th century, this late Gothic red brick building was confiscated by Henry VIII when his cardinal refused to

*Right: Loud, colorful, and varied: night life in London.*

allow him to divorce his first wife, Catherine of Aragon. Wolsey was thrown into prison as a traitor, and the king lived in the cardinal's palace with each one of his next five wives. It has often been extended, and remained the royal residence until Queen Victoria opened up the State Apartments to the public for the first time in 1839. Today pensioned employees of Queen Elizabeth live here. Among its most important sights are the **astronomical clock** from the Tudor period on Anne Boleyn's Gate (the clock even shows the level of high tide at London Bridge), the **State Apartments** with their tapestries, and the ceiling paintings in the *Cartoon Gallery*. Don't miss the *Great Hall* from the time of Henry VII with its hammer-beam ceiling, or the royal painting collection, with works by Mantegna, Titian, Tintoretto, Holbein and Brueghel the Elder. Also impressive is the vast **kitchen**, which had to feed 800 people a day in winter and up to 1,200 in summer.

The **castle gardens** also contain the 200-year old *Great Vine*, which "Capability" Brown is supposed to have planted and which in good years even today can provide up to 700 pounds of grapes. The other major sight in the gardens is the *Maze*, a labyrinth of hedges almost 7 feet (2 m) high and more than 800 yards (750 m) long. Dating from the time of William III, it was immortalized in Jerome K. Jerome's classic comic novel *Three Men in a Boat*. If you do get lost in the maze, don't worry, as the keepers will come and rescue you when the park closes for the night...

## LONDON BY NIGHT

By night as by day, London offers a plethora of activities, be it a simple stroll along the Thames, with an especially beautiful view from Westminster Bridge of the illuminated Houses of Parliament, and through the pulsating streets of **Soho** and **Covent Garden**, or a meal in one of the city's fine restaurants. Theatre, of course, springs to mind; with good reason London is renowned as one of the

## LONDON BY NIGHT

leading theatrical cities of the world, and a metropolis of musicals. More than 100 theatres put on classical, modern or avant-garde plays. The largest and most well-known theatres are, like the first-release cinemas, mostly located in the West End: the classical **Royal Drury Lane** theatre, the elegant **Royal Haymarket** theatre or the **Palace**. The **Royal National Theatre** is part of the South Bank Arts Centre, while the **Royal Shakespeare Company** plays at the Barbican. In summer there are also open-air performances, including Shakespeare, in **Holland Park** and **Regent's Park**. In other districts, smaller theaters often put on unusual plays (for example, the **Almeida** theatre in Islington, or the **Canal Theatre Café** in Little Venice).

Listings of what's running in London, as well as all of the other things you can do, appear in the weekly magazines *Time Out* and *What's On*, which come out on

*Above: The pubs are at their fullest just before last orders.*

Wednesdays and are sold at newsstands and bookshops. The West End is also home to the famed opera houses, such as the **Coliseum**, where the *Royal Ballet* appears when the *English National Opera* is taking its summer break, and the **Royal Opera House**, which frequently presents famous guest soloists (such as Placido Domingo or Kiri te Kanawa).

In the less expensive **Sadler's Wells**, in addition to opera and ballet, there are also dance performances by international troupes; while the small **Wigmore Hall**, famed for its excellent acoustics, is best known for chamber music in an intimate atmosphere.

If you are hungry after the theatre or cinema you can find somewhere to eat until midnight in Soho, although the English usually dine beforehand. The **pubs** close at the latest by 11 pm, after which open the doors of the exclusive discos and nightclubs: the **Hippodrome,** the **Empire Ballroom** or **Annabel's**, to name a few. The leading jazz club is **Ronnie Scott's**. Larger rock or pop concerts are generally held at **Wembley Stadium** or the **Hammersmith Odeon**. The underground runs until around 11:30 p.m., starting up again at 5:30 a.m. During the night, special night bus services are available; all of them stop at **Trafalgar Square.** It can take a long time to find a taxi; the best thing is to ask the way to the nearest taxi rank.

The question remains: how do I get a ticket for the theater or other events? There are various options: at the theatre box office itself (during the day as well, or by phone using a credit card); via an agency (they charge around 15% commission); at Leicester Square for half-price tickets for performances that evening (but here you may find long lines); or – the easiest way – through your hotel reception. Buying tickets from touts on the street cannot be recommended: the prices are exorbitant, and the tickets often turn out to be forged.

# GUIDEPOST LONDON

## LONDON
### Accommodation

*LUXURY:* **Blakes**, 33 Roland Gdns., SW7 3PF, tel. 0171 3706701. **Brown's**, Albermarle St., W1A 4SW, tel. 0171 4939381. **Claridges**, Brook St., W1A 2JQ, tel. 0171 6298860. **Dorchester**, 53 Park Lane, W1A 2HJ, tel. 0171 629 8888. **Dukes**, 35 St. James's Pl., SW1A 1NY, tel. 0171 491 4840. **Halcyon**, 81 Holland Park, W11 3RZ, tel. 0171 7277288. **Hyde Park Hotel**, 66 Knightsbridge, SW1Y 7LA, tel. 0171 2352000. **Forte Grand Westbury**, Bond Street, Mayfair, W1A 4UH, tel. 0171 6297755. **The Savoy**, The Strand, WC2R 0EU, tel. 0171 8364343.
*MODERATE:* **Academy**, 17-21 Gower St., WC1E 6HG, tel. 0171 6314115. **Aster House**, 3 Sumner Pl., SW7 3EE, tel. 0171 5844925. **Blandford**, 80 Chiltern St., W1M 1PS, tel. 0171 4863103. **Charles Bernard**, 5 Frognal, Hampstead, NW3 6AL, tel. 0171 7940101. **La Place**, 17 Nottingham Pl., W1M 3FB, tel. 0171 4862323. **Mabledon Court**, 10-11 Mabledon Pl., WC1H 9BA, tel. 0171 3883866. **Rembrandt**, 11, Thurlow Place, tel. 0171 5898100. **Windermere**, 142-144 Warwick Way, Victoria, SW1V 4JE, tel. 0171 8345163.
*BUDGET:* **Abbey House**, 11 Vicarage Gate, W8 4AG, tel. 0171 7272594. **Alexander House**, 32 Hugh Street, SW1 1RT, tel. 0171 8345320. **Chumleigh Lodge**, 226-228 Nether Street, Finchley, N3 1HU, tel. 0181 3461614. **Edward Lear**, 30 Seymour Street, W1H 5WD, tel. 0171 4025401. **Fielding**, 4 Broad Court, Bow St., WC2B 5QZ, tel. 0171 8368305. **Kensington Palace Thistle**, Devere Gardens, tel. 0171 937 8121. **Knightsbridge**, 12 Beaufort Gardens, London SW3 1PT, tel. 0171 5899271. **Swiss House**, 171 Old Brompton Rd., SW5 0AN, tel. 0171 3732769. **Windermere**, 142 Warwick Way, SW1V 4JE, tel. 0171 8345163. **WoodvilleHouse**, 107 Ebury St., SW1W 9QU, tel. 0171 7301048.

### Hotel Booking
**London Telephone Accommodation Booking Service**, for Access, Visa, and Mastercard, tel. 0171 8248844, Mon-Fri 9.30-17.00. **Hotel Booking Service Ltd.**, 4 New Burlington Place, tel. 0171 4375052. **British Hotel Reservation Centre**, 10 Buckingham Palace Rd., tel. 0171 828 2425/6 (for groups). Office at Victoria Station, platform 8, tel. 0171-8281027/ 828 6439.

### Restaurants
Prices in London are higher than out-of-town, so what is moderate in this context is fairly expensive in wider terms. Advance booking is necessary in the more popular restaurants.

*LUXURY:* **Blue Elephant**, 4-6 Fulham Broadway, SW6, tel. 0171 3856595, exotic Thai. **Nico at Ninety**, 90 Park Lane, W1, tel. 0171 4091290. **The English Garden**, 10 Lincoln St., SW3, tel. 0171 5847272, light, delicate food. **Langan's Brasserie**, Stratton St., W1, tel. 0171 4936437, In-restaurant, prominent diners. **Memories of China**, 67-69 Ebury Street, SW1, tel. 0171 7307734.
*MODERATELY EXPENSIVE:* **Aubergine**, 11 Park Walk, SW10, tel. 0171 3523449. **Bentley's**, fish and oysters, 11-15 Swallow Street, W1, tel. 0171 7344756. **Bibendum**, bistro-style, Michelin House, 81 Fulham Road, SW3, tel. 0171 5815817. **Bombay Brasserie**, Courtfield Close, Courtfield, SW7, tel. 0171 3704040, Indian. **The Greenhouse**, British, 27a Hay's Mews, W1, tel. 0171 5895171. **The Ivy**, 1 West Street, Covent Garden, WC2, tel. 0171 8364751. **Joe Allen**, 13 Exeter St., WC2, tel. 0171 8360651, relaxed American. **L'Escargot**, 48 Greek Street, Soho, W1, tel. 0171 4372679. **Mirabelle**, 56 Curzon Street, W1, tel. 0171 4994636. **Neal Street**, Italian, 26 Neal Street, WC2, tel. 0171 8368368. **Planet Hollywood**, 13 Coventry St., W1, tel. 0171 2871000, wild and loud, good food. **Quaglino's**, 16 Bury Street, St James's, SW1, tel. 0171 9306767. **Rules**, classic English, game, 35 Maiden Lane, Covent Garden, WC2, tel. 0171 8365314. **Simpson's in the Strand**, British, 110 Strand, WC2, tel. 0171 8369112. **Turner's**, French, 87-89 Walton Street, W3, tel. 0171 5846711.
*LESS EXPENSIVE:* **Ajimura**, Japanese, 51-53 Shelton Street, WC2, tel. 0171 2400178. **Anwar's**, 64 Grafton Way, W1, tel. 0171 3876664, vegetarian. **Bahn Thai**, 21a Frith Street, W1, tel. 0171 4378504. **The Berkshire**, British, Oxford Street, W1, tel. 0171 6297474. **Food for Thought**, 31 Neal Street, Covent Garden WC2, tel. 0171 8360239, vegetarian. **Good Earth**, Chinese, 233 Brompton Road, SW3, tel. 0171 5843658. **Harbour City**, Chinese, 46 Gerrard Street, W1, tel. 0171 4397859. **Le Boundin Blanc**, 5 Trebeck Street, W1, tel. 0171 4993292. **Old Delhi**, Indian, 48 Kendal Street, W2, tel. 0171 724 9580. **Olivio**, Sardinian, 21 Eccleston Street, SW1, tel. 0171 7302502. **Osmani**, North African, 46 Inverness Street, N6, tel. 0171 2674682. **Quality Chop House**, 94 Farringdon Road, EC1, tel. 0171 8375093.

### Cafés / Tearooms
**Benedicte**, 106 Kensington High St, W8, tel. 0171 9377580, coffee, tea, great cakes. **Café Laville**, 453 Edgware Rd., W2, tel. 0171 7062620, cakes, fabulous club sandwiches. **Café Royale**, 68 Regent St., W1, tel. 0171 4379090, European-style coffee house, lunch and dinner. **Fortnum & Mason**, 181 Piccadilly, W1, tel. 0171 7348040. **Lisboa Patisserie**, 57 Goldbourne Rd., tel. 0171 2292907, Portuguese café. **Richoux**, 172 Piccadilly, W1, tel. 0171 4932204.

## GUIDEPOST LONDON

### Museums

**Army Museum**, tel. 0171 7300717, daily 10.00-17.30. **Bank of England Museum**, Bartholomew Lane, tel. 0171 6015545, open all year Mon-Fri 10.00-17.00. **Bethnal Green Museum of Childhood**, Cambridge Street, tel. 0181 9802415, Mon-Thur, Sat 10.00-18.00, Sun 14.30-18.00. **British Museum**, Great Russell Street, tel. 0171 6361555, open all year Mon-Sat 10.00-17.00, Sun 14.30-18.00. **Dickens House Museum**, 48, Doughty Street, tel. 0171 4052127, open 2 Jan-23 Dec Mon-Sat 10.00-17.00. **Florence Nightingale Museum**, 2 Lambeth Palace Road, tel. 0171 6200374, open all year Tue-Sun 10.00-16.00. **Freud Museum**, 20 Maresfield Gardens, tel. 0171 4352002, open all year Mon-Fri 10.00-17.00. **Institute of Contemporary Art**, Nash House tel. 0171 9300493, open all year Mon-Sat 12.00-23.00, Sun 12.00-23.00. **Lawn Tennis Museum**, Church Road, Wimbledon, tel. 0181 9466131, open all year Tue-Sat 10.30-17.00. **Museum of Mankind**, Burlington Gardens, tel. 0171 3238043, Mon-Sat 10.00-17.00, Sun 14.30-18.00. **The Museum of London**, 150 London Wall, tel. 0171 6003699, all open Tue-Sat 10.00-18.00, Sun 12.00-18.00. **Museum of the Moving Image**, National Film Theatre, South Bank, tel. 0171 4012636, daily 10.00-18.00. **Natural History Museum**, tel. 0171 9389123, open all year Mon-Sat 10.00-18.00; Sun 11.00-18.00. **National Maritime Museum**, Greenwich, SE10, tel. 0181 8584422, Mon-Sat 10.00-18.00, Sun 12.00-18.00 (until 17.00 in winter). **National Portrait Gallery**, St. Martin's Place, tel. 0171 306055, open all year Mon-Sat 10.00-18.00, Sun 12.00-18.00. **Royal Academy of Arts**, Green Park, tel. 0171 4397438, open all year Sun-Sat 10.00 -18.00. **Science Museum**, Exhibition Road, South Kensington, tel. 0171 9388000, Mon-Sat 10.00-18.00, Sun 11.00 -18.00. **Shakespeare Globe Museum**, 1, Bear Gardens, tel. 0171 9286342, Mon-Sat 10.00-17.00, Sun 14.00-17.30. **Tate Gallery**, Millbank, SW1, tel. 0171 8878000, weekdays 10.00-17.50, Sun 14.00-17.50. **Theatre Museum**, 1E Tavistock Street, tel. 0171 8367891, Tue-Sun 11.00-19.00. **Victoria and Albert Museum**, Cromwell Road, tel. 0171 9388500, Tue-Sun 10.00-17.50, Mon 12.00-17.50. **The Wallace Collection**, Hertford House, Manchester Square, tel. 0171 9350687, open all year Mon-Sat 10.00-17.00, Sun 14.00-17.00. **Tower Hill Pageant**, Tower Hill, EC3, tel. 0171 7090181.

### Tips and Trips

**Banqueting House**, Horse Guards Avenue, Whitehall, tel. 0171 9304179, Mon-Sat 10.00-17.00. **Buckingham Palace**, The Mall, Victoria, tel. 0171 4933175, Aug-Sept daily 9.30-17.30. **Commonwealth Institute**, Kensington High Street, tel. 0171 6034535, Mon-Sat 10.00-17.00, Sun 14.00-17.00. **Cutty Sark Clipper**, Greenwich, tel. 0181 8583445, April-Sept Mon-Sat 10.00-18.00, Sun 12.00-18.00; Oct-March Mon-Sat 10.00-17.00, Sun 12.00-17.00. **Guiness World Records**, The Trocadero, Coventry Street, tel. 0171 4397331, open daily all year except Dec 25. **Hampton Court**, East Molesey, Surrey, tel. 0181 7819500, March-Oct Mon 10.15-18.00, Tue-Sun 9.30-18.00; mid Oct-mid March Mon 10.15-16.30, Tue-Sun 9.30-16.30. **HMS Belfast**, Morgan's Lane, tel. 0171 4076434, open 20 March-31 Oct 10.00-17.20. 1 November-19 March daily 10.00-16.00. **Hogarth's House**, Hogarth Lane, Great West Road, tel. 0181 9946757, open April-Sept 11.00-18.00, Mon and Sat 14.00-18.00. Oct-March 11.00-16.00 Mon and Sat 14.00-16.00, closed Tuesdays, the first two weeks in September and the last three weeks in December. **Houses of Parliament**, Westminster, tel. 0171 2193000, galleries open Mon-Thur 14.30-22.30, Fri 9.30-15.30, crypt open Fridays only. Book in advance. **Kensington Palace**, Kensington Gardens, tel. 0171 9379561, Mon-Sat 9.00-17.30, Sun 11.00-17.30. **Kenwood House**, Hampstead Lane, tel. 0181 3481286, April-Sept daily 10.00-18.00; Oct-March daily 10.00-16.00. **London Brass Rubbing Centre**, St. Martin-in-the-Fields, tel. 0171 4376023, open all year Mon-Sat 10.00-18.00, Sun 12.00-18.00. **London Docklands Visitor Centre**, 3 Lime Harbour, Isle of Dogs, tel. 0171 512111, Mon-Fri 8.30-18.00, Sat, Sun and Bank Holiday Mon 9.30-17.00. **London Dungeon**, 28-34 Tooley Street, tel. 0171 4030606, April-Sept daily 10.00-18.30; Oct-March daily 10.00-17.30. **London Zoo**, Regents Park, tel. 01891 505767, open all year daily 10.00-17.00 except Dec 25. **Madame Tussauds**, Marylebone Road, tel. 0171 9356861, open Mon-Fri 10.00-17.30, Sun 9.30-17.30. **Pepy's Exhibition**, tel. 0171 13537323, open all year 9.30-17.00. **Royal Mews**, The Mall, tel. 0171 7992331, open 5 Jan-23 March, Wednesday only 12.00-16.00. 29 March-29 Sept Tue, Wed, Thur 12.00-16.00. **St. Paul's Cathedral**, St. Paul's Churchyard, tel. 0171 2482705, Mon-Sat 8.30-16.30, galleries open 9.45-16.45. **Spencer House**, 27 St. James Palace, tel. 0171 4998620, open all year daily 11.30-17.30. **Queen's Gallery**, The Mall, tel. 0171 7992331, open 4 March-23 Dec Tue-Sat 10.00-17.00. **Tower of London**, Tower Bridge, tel. 0171 6003699, open early March-Oct Mon-Sat 9.00-18.00; early Nov-Feb Mon-Sat 9.00-17.00, Sun 10.00-17.00. **Westminster Abbey**, Westminster, tel. 0171 2225152, open all year Mon-Fri 9.20-16.00, Sat 9.20-14.45. **Westminster Hall**, Westminster, tel. 0171 2194272, visits by appointment only.

# GUIDEPOST LONDON

### Theaters
Credit card booking (additional fee payable) is available for most theaters, tel. 0171 3444444. Further theatres and fringe theatres are listed in the weekly magazines *What's On* and *Time Out*.
**Adelphi**, The Strand, WC2, tel. 0171 3440055 (booking fee). Group bookings, tel. 0171 4133302. **Aldwych**, Aldwych, WC2, tel. 0171 836 6404. Group bookings, tel. 0171 9306123. **Almeida**, Almeida St., N1, tel. 0171 3594404. **Cambridge Theatre**, Earlham Street, WC2, tel. 0171 4979977. **Canal Theatre Café**, The Bridge House, Delamere Ter., Little Venice WC, tel. 0171 2896054. **Comedy**, Panton Street, SW1, tel. 0171 3691731. Group bookings, tel. 0171 4133321. **Dominion**, Tottenham Court Road, W1, tel. 0171 4166060. Group bookings, tel. 0171 4166075/4133321/2407941. **Drury Lane Theatre Royal**, Catherine Street, WC2, tel. 0171 4945000. Group booking, tel. 0171 8318625/4945454. **Duke of York's**, St Martin's Lane, WC2, tel. 0171 8365122. **Garrick**, Charing Cross Road, WC2, tel. 0171 4945085. **Haymarket Theatre Royal**, Haymarket, SW1, tel. 0171 9308800. **Her Majesty's**, Haymarket, SW1, tel. 0171 494 5400. Group bookings, tel. 0171 9306123. **London Palladium**, Argyll Street, W1, tel. 0171 4945020/ 4979977. Group bookings, tel. 0171 4945459. **Lyric**, Shaftesbury Avenue, W1, tel. 0171 4945045. Group bookings, tel. 0171 9306123. **National Theatre (Olivier, Lyttleton** and **Cottesloe)**, South Bank, SE1, tel. 0171 9282252. Group bookings, tel. 0171 6200741. **New London**, Drury Lane, WC2, tel. 0171 4050072. Group bookings, tel. 0171 9306123. **Old Vic**, Waterloo Road, SE1, tel. 0171 9287616. **Palace**, Shaftesbury Avenue, W1, tel. 0171 4340909. Group bookings, tel. 0171 9306123. **Piccadilly**, Denman Street, W1, tel. 0171 3691734. **Prince of Wales**, Coventry Street, W1, tel. 0171 8395987. Group bookings, tel. 0171 4133321. **Prince Edward**, Old Compton Street, W1, tel. 0171 7348951. Group bookings, tel. 0171 9306123. **Queens**, Shaftesbury Avenue, W1, tel. 0171 4945040. **Regent's Park Theatre**, Regent's Park, NW1, tel. 0171 4862431. **Royal Shakespeare Company London** (The Barbican, EC2 (and other theaters), tel. 0171 6388891. **Royal Court**, Sloane Square, SW1, tel. 0171 7301745/ 7302554. **Savoy**, The Strand, WC2, tel. 0171 8368888. Group bookings, tel. 0171 4133321. **St Martin's**, Cambridge Circus, West Street, tel. 0171 8361443. Group bookings, tel. 0171 3121994.

### Opera / Concerts / Ballet
**London Coliseum**, St Martin's Lane, WC2, tel. 0171 6328300. **Queen Elizabeth Hall**, South Bank, SE1, tel. 0171 9288800. **Royal Opera House**, Floral Street, WC2, tel. 0171 3044000. **Royal Albert Hall**, Kensington Gore, SW7, tel. 0171 5898212. **Royal Festival Hall**, South Bank, SE1, tel. 0171 9288800. **Sadler's Wells**, Rosebery Avenue, EC1, tel. 0171 2788916. Group bookings tel. 0171 4133321. **Wigmore Hall**, 36 Wigmore St., W1, tel. 0171 9352141.

### Music / Clubs
**Annabel's**, 44 Berkeley Sq., W1, tel. 0171 6291096. **Hippodrome**, Charing Cross Rd., WC2, tel. 0171 4374311. **100 Club**, 100 Oxford St., W1, tel. 0171 6360933, jazz. **Pizza Express**, 10 Dean St., W1, tel. 0171 4379595, pizza and jazz. **Ronnie Scott's**, 47 Frith St., W1, tel. 0171 4390747, jazz. **The Forum**, 9-17 Highgate Rd., NW5, tel. 0171 2842200, small club, rock and pop. **Hammersmith Odeon**, Queen Caroline St., W6, tel. 0181 7484081, rock palace. **Wembley Stadium**, Wembley, tel. 0181 9001234.

### Markets
**Alfie's Antique Market**, 13-15 Church St., NW8, Tue-Sat 10.00-18.00. **Antiquarius**, 135-141 King's Road, SW3, antiques, clothes, lace, Mon-Sat 10.00-18.00. **Bermondsey Antiques Market**, corner Longlane/Bermondsey St., SE1, Fridays from 5.00. **Camden Lock**, NW1, at the canal, Camden town underground, arts and crafts, bric-à-brac, clothes, antiques, Mon-Fri 10.00-18.00. **Camden Passage**, Islington High St., N1, antiques, books, Sat 8.00-17.00, Wed 6.45-16.00, Thur 7.00-16.00. **Gabriel's Wharf**, SE1, at the National Theatre, Waterloo, bric-à-brac, antiques, arts and crafts, Tue-Sun 11.00-18.00. **Jubilee Market**, Covent Garden, WC2, bric-à-brac, antiques, Mon 6.00-17.00, Tue-Sun 9.00-18.00. **Leather Lane**, EC1, underground Chancery Lane, Mon-Fri 10.00-14.30. **Portobello Road**, Notting Hill Gate underground, Mon-Sat from 10.00.

### Sightseeing
**Open Top Guide Buses** run all year daily except Dec 25 and Jan 1, every 15 minutes from 9.30-17.00 (London Transports, tel. 0171 2273456). No advanced booking needed. Pick-up points: Victoria Bus Station, Marble Arch, Baker Street near Madame Tussaud's.

### Tourist Information
**British Travel Centre**, 12 Lower Regent Street, SW1, tel. 0171 7303400, Mon-Fri 9.00-18.30, Sat and Sun 10.00-16.00. **London Tourist Board**, 26 Grosvenor Gardens, SW1W 0DU, tel. 0171 7303450. Information counters: Victoria Station, SW1, Easter-Oct daily 8.00-19.00. Underground-station Heathrow, Terminals 1,2,3, tel. 0171 8248844, daily 8.30-18.00. Office in the department store Selfridges, Oxford St., W1, basement. **Artsline**, information for the handicapped, tel. 0171 3882227, Mon-Fri 10.00-17.00. **London Transport Information** (buses, underground), tel. 0171 2221234. **Airports**: See travel information page 238.

85

*SOUTHERN ENGLAND*

# SOUTHERN ENGLAND

KENT
SUSSEX
SURREY
HAMPSHIRE / ISLE OF WIGHT
DORSET

The famous white cliffs of Dover are part of a chain of chalk hills which run in a great arc through Kent as the North Downs and through Surrey as the South Downs until they meet the coast again at Beachy Head in Sussex. Between them, in East Sussex, rises the Weald, a hilly and partly wooded area which is still one of the most densely-populated parts of Europe and which holds a great many surprises for visitors who have the time and curiosity to take detours off the beaten track.

## KENT

From London, the A2 leads to **Rochester**, an industrial town on the banks of the River Medway. The first **cathedral** here was consecrated in 604 AD, while the Norman building was erected 1077 - 1108. The **castle**, built in 1127 during the reign of Henry I, is one of the finest examples of Norman military architecture and the highest fortress in England. The city museum is housed in **Eastgate House** (16th century), while **Restoration House** (16th century) is probably the most attractive in the city. **The Dickens Centre** celebrates the life and work of the great Victorian novelist, who spent the happiest years of his childhood in nearby of **Chatham**. Rochester was the birthplace of the Royal Navy, and the historic 18th-century **Royal Dockyard**, extending over 80 acres (32 ha) and once the most important naval base in Britain, is now a museum where the submarine *HMS Ocelot* is on display.

Before you visit Canterbury, take a short excursion south on the A229 to the idyllic village of **Aylesford** with its 13th-century Carmelite house, Aylesford Friary. **Maidstone**, the county town of Kent, boasts the largest church in the county, All Saints Church, which was started in 1395. Here a former palace of the Archbishop of Canterbury has been turned into a **heritage center** with displays about local history. East of Maidstone on the A20 is the large and picturesque **Leeds Castle**. Located in a 500-acre park with two islands and a golf course, the castle was a favorite residence of the Queens of England in the Middle Ages. Henry VIII converted the main building with its vast banqueting hall into a luxurious royal palace and had the Gloriette built on the north island. At the exit from the castle there is a **dog-collar museum**. From here, the A20 runs along the foot of the steep scarp of the downs; if you turn northeast onto the A252 at

*Left: Thatched roofs require regular maintenance.*

*CANTERBURY*

**Charing**, you can still make out traces of the old pilgrimage route medieval pilgrims followed to the shrine of Archbishop Thomas à Becket, murdered in the cathedral in 1170 by knights believing they were carrying out the wishes of Henry II.

## Canterbury

The principal attraction of Canterbury, a city which still bears the stamp of the Middle Ages in places, is the **Cathedral,** which was built between the 11th and 16th centuries. As early as 597, the first bishop's church in England stood on this site; Canterbury has been the seat of the head of the primate of the Anglican church ever since.

The present building rests on 11th-century Norman foundations. After a fire in 1174, the church was rebuilt by the architect William of Sens, who brought in the Early Gothic style from France in the tripartite division of the walls, the ogival arches and the doubled transept; such stylistic elements made Canterbury Cathedral a model for other English cathedrals. Between 1391 and 1405, the architect Henry Yevele oversaw the building of the High Gothic nave, which attained a stylistic unity rare in English Gothic. Some fine medieval stained-glass windows survived both the Civil War and World War II. The spot where the Archbishop of Canterbury, Thomas à Becket, was murdered on December 29th, 1170, is called the **Martyrdom**.

Among the many attractions in the historic old town is **The Canterbury Tales Museum** on St. Margret's Street, a recreation, with authentic sounds and smells, of the pilgrimage taken by the colorful characters in Chaucer's *Canterbury Tales*. In busy **Mercery Lane**, the old town's pedestrian zone, and the narrow, quaint alleys leading off it, you can see old half-timbered houses; and enough of the 13th-

*Above: Canterbury is dominated by the Cathedral. Right: Oast-houses are typical of this part of Kent.*

and 14th-century city walls have survived that you can imagine yourself in a medieval town. On High Street, you can find the rebuilt **Chequers of Hope** inn, which Chaucer mentioned; while over the bridge, directly on the river Stour, are two 18th-century weavers' houses. Past these is the impressive **West Gate**, which dates from the 16th century and which today functions as the **Museum of City History**.

### Thanet and Dover

The A28 leads northeast to the **Isle of Thanet** and the seaside resorts of Margate, Broadstairs and Ramsgate. The A256 runs south from here, passing **Richborough Castle**, the ruins of the Roman fort known as *Rutupiae*, which played a major part in the Roman invasion of 43 AD, and was later expanded with a triple defense wall and a triumphal arch.

The Romans were at **Dover** too, and their lighthouse, or **pharos** (1st century), still stands today on Castle Hill. Also worth seeing is the **Roman Painted House** (2nd century) with its wall frescoes. The mighty fortress of **Dover Castle** was started under Henry II towards the end of the 12th century and extended during the 13th - 14th centuries. It was one of the last tower fortresses in western Europe. It was used again during the World War II, and there are guided tours of the secret military tunnels at Hellfire Corner which date back to the 13th century The town's newest attraction, the **White Cliffs Experience**, incorporates the remains of the *Classis Britannica*, the headquarters of the Roman fleet in Britain. Through vivid high-tech displays, it tells the story of Dover from the Roman invasion until 1945. Dover remains one of the most important ferry terminals of Britain, but it is now in fierce competition with the recently-completed Channel Tunnel. At **Cheriton**, a suburb of Folkestone, the **Eurotunnel Exhibition Centre** includes models of the tunnel and terminals and a full-size shuttle.

In the well-loved Victorian resort of **Folkestone**, picturesque High Street entices you into the old town with its church of St. Mary and St. Eanswyth before you continue along the A259 coast road to the harbor town of **Hythe**. A highlight here is the Royal Military Canal, cut in 1804 during the Napoleonic Wars, today a favorite destination for sailors and anglers.

### Romney Marsh

At Hythe, you can board the world's smallest narrow-gauge public railway, the *Romney, Hythe and Dymchurch Line*, which runs across the flat and fertile grazing lands of Romney Marsh as far as the shingle bank of **Dungeness**. The fishermen's cottages here are overshadowed by a gigantic nuclear power station, open for visits.

Running parallel to the railway, the A259 leads across the marshes through

*THE GARDEN OF ENGLAND*

**New Romney**, with its Norman parish church of St. Nicholas (12th century) and to the curiosity of **St. Augustine's Church** (12th-14th centuries) in **Brookland**. This church's three-story wooden bell-tower stands at a little distance from the main building, presumably because of the instability of the ground. Another interesting feature is the Norman baptismal font made of lead.

Shortly after the Sussex border, you can see the splendid town of **Rye** rising above the horizon on its sandstone bluff. With its fortifications, ancient gateway (14th century) and narrow, hilly cobbled streets with antique shops and pubs, the place is indisputably a delight. The half-timbered houses in Mermaid Street and High Street are especially worth seeing, while the parish church of **St. Mary** houses the last church window that Burne-Jones and William Morris designed together. The tower holds one of the oldest clocks in England.

Also on a hilltop, **Winchelsea** is a medieval town preserved in aspic. When Old Winchelsea was drowned by the sea at the end of the 13th century, King Edward I ordered the building of a new port town on higher ground, laying out the streets in a grid or checkerboard pattern to enclose 40 fields. Alas, the harbor soon silted up again and building was stopped. Only three town gates and a few dead-straight streets remain of the original plan, while many of today's authentically restored Georgian houses have the original cellars below ground. The incomplete church of St. Thomas, built in the Decorated Style around 1300, is also worth seeing.

### Gardens and Stately Homes

Take the A268 and A262 to reach the horticultural jewel of **Sissinghurst Garden**. Its 6 acres were laid out in the 1930s by writer Vita Sackville-West (1892-1962) and her diplomat husband Sir Harold Nicholson. At the center of the gardens is a brick tower, the only surviving remnant of the Elizabethan **Sissinghurst Castle**. Vita had her study in the tower, and it still contains her furniture and the printing press used by Virginia and Leonard Woolf for the first publications of their Hogarth Press in the early 1920s.

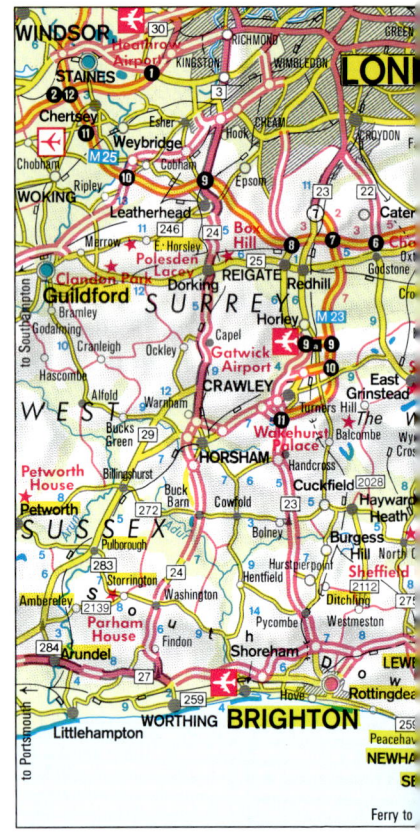

This is a green and beautiful countryside, quite unlike the rest of Kent, and oast-houses, with their distinctive white conical roofs, are a feature of the landscape. They were used for drying hops, reminding us that, because of the fertile soil, fruit-growing Kent was once known as "The Garden of England."

West of Hawkhurst lies **Scotney Castle** where, in the late 1840s, the Hussey family created one of England's most romantic gardens around the ruins of a small 14th-century moated castle. There are more ruins a few miles along the B2169 to the west – the remains of **Bayham Abbey**, which was dissolved by Cardinal Wolsey in the 16th century and, likewise, has become a pretty decoration in a rich man's garden.

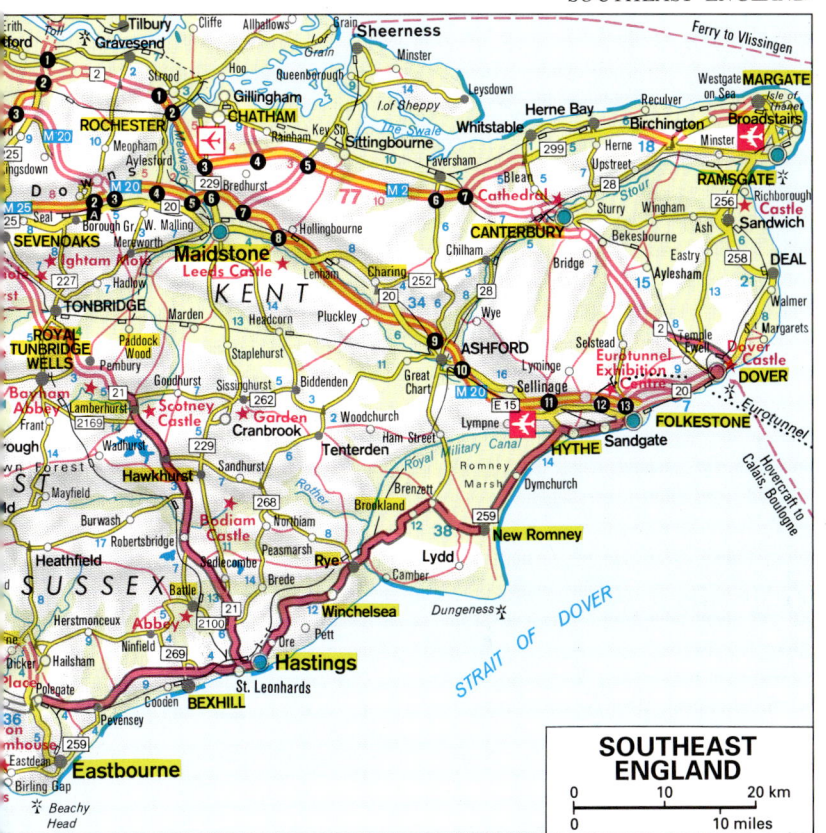

**Tunbridge Wells**, a spacious spa town with numerous parks and commons, became famous in the early 17th century for its curative, iron-rich waters, but its heyday really began with the arrival of the fashionable society figure known as Beau Nash in 1735. Its most famous street is the **Pantiles**, an 18th-century pedestrian precinct which was the first such in England. An excursion northeast of Tunbridge Wells takes you to more oasthouses at the Whitbread Hop Farm in **Paddock Wood**. This is the home of the *shire horses*, the draft horses which still pull the drays of Whitbread's Brewery.

North of Tonbridge, the A227 leads to **Ightham Mote** (14th century), a small moated medieval manor house. **Knole**, to the west on the edge of Sevenoaks in a deer park, is altogether grander. The home of the Sackville family for four hundred years, and birthplace of Vita Sackville-West, this 15th-century manor accommodates a notable art collection with costly Persian carpets, porcelain, tapestries and paintings (including some by Reynolds and Gainsborough). From

Knole you can go on to visit the other interesting great houses of northwest Kent. At **Westerham**, west of Sevenoaks on the A25, is **Quebec House** (17th century), whose stables house an exhibition on the Battle of Quebec. South on the B2026 is **Chartwell**, the home of Sir Winston Churchill from 1922 until the end of his life, and much of it unchanged since then; several museum rooms tell the story of his career.

A turnoff at Crockham Hill leads east to **Hever Castle** (13th century), a romantic moated castle which was the childhood home of Anne Boleyn. From its loggia and colonnaded piazza, you can look down on a large lake set in the middle of its gardens.

The turreted **Penshurst Place** was built in 1341 as a Gothic manor house and rebuilt in the 15th century. There is a lofty Barons' Hall 85 feet high, an art collection (including portraits of the former owners, the Sidney family), and lovely gardens with precisely clipped yew hedges.

## SUSSEX

**Hastings**, in Sussex, was one of the five harbor towns known in the Middle Ages as the Cinque Ports (the other four were in Kent), which received special rights and privileges from the Crown in return for providing the King with fishing boats and crews to create what was, in effect, the country's first navy. There is still a thriving fishing industry today: the boats are hauled up on the shingle at **Rock-a-Nore**. The 19th-century Fishermen's Chapel now houses a small fishing museum. On the beach itself are the **Net Lofts**, curious tall wooden buildings made of tarred wood shingles and once used for drying nets. The seafaring theme is further emphasized at the **Fishermen's Museum**, the **Shipwreck Heritage Centre** and the **Sea Life Centre**.

*Above: View of the Novices' Hall at Battle Abbey. Right: The white cliffs of the Seven Sisters shine out far over the sea.*

Hastings' old town center has to be explored on foot. The ancient High Street and All Saints Street ascend between medieval houses, with steps mounting the steep hillsides to hidden gardens and courtyards. High above everything stand the ruins of the **castle**, which William the Conqueror built in 1096. A cable car can take you up to the castle and St. Clement's Caves, while another (far steeper) leads up the cliffs of East Hill to the splendid scenery of **Hastings Country Park**.

The route now continues westwards along the coast, but not before an essential diversion northwest on the A2100 to **Battle**, the actual site of the 1066 conflict that has misleadingly become known as the Battle of Hastings. After his victory, William the Conqueror had a great **abbey** (consecrated in 1094) built in thanks; the high altar of the church marks the spot where King Harold fell in the battle.

When Henry VIII dissolved the monasteries, he turned the massive building over to a courtier, who tore down the Norman church and converted part of the monastic buildings; still, today you can see the gatehouse, ruins of the dormitory, and the impressive vaulted undercroft.

### The Sussex Coast

Most of the Sussex coastal resorts have grown up within the past 200 years, their development generally financed by wealthy men with an eye to the future. First you reach the genteel seaside town of **Bexhill** with its golf course and pleasant Victorian houses. The little fishing village of **Eastbourne** was turned into a fashionable bathing resort in Victorian style by the seventh Duke of Devonshire in 1835. Elegant pastel-colored houses and luxury hotels line the three-mile promenade. Language schools, three golf courses, 60 tennis courts and a theatre more than 100 years old attract plenty of visitors throughout the year, both from home and abroad.

Between Eastbourne and Seaford, the A259 crosses one of the most celebrated tracts of scenery in southeast England.

## ALFRISTON / LEWES

Anyone who enjoys walking should allow time to ramble across the springy, flowered turf of the South Downs above the gleaming white chalk cliffs of **Beachy Head** and the **Seven Sisters**. There are steps down to the beach at **Birling Gap** and **Hope Gap**, but the rescue services have been summoned to the aid of many an optimist who set out to walk from one to the other and was surprised by high tide. It is essential to check tide times before you start.

The A259 coast road continues to Seaford, the port of **Newhaven** and via Peacehaven and Rottingdean to Brighton. A more attractive route, however, leads north from the eastern outskirts of Seaford towards the attractive little village of **Alfriston** with its Tudor half-timbered houses. The narrow main street easily becomes a bottleneck in the height of the season. **St. Andrew's Church** (14th century Decorated) stands on the village green; next door is **Clergy House**, a thatched and half-timbered vicarage from the 14th century.

After Alfriston, take the A27 west to Lewes. **Firle Place**, a mansion from the time of Henry VIII, was been the home of the Gage family for 500 years. General Thomas Gage commanded the British troops at the Battle of Bunker Hill in the American War of Independence, an event well-documented in this house. A turn-off here leads to **Glyndebourne**, home of the world-famous country opera festival held every year between May and August, which draws music-lovers from the entire world.

### From Lewes to Brighton

The hilltop town of **Lewes** is East Sussex's administrative capital. Note the Norman castle, **Barbican House**, built in 1088 and today an archaeological museum. On the southern edge of the town is the medieval **Anne of Cleves House**,

*Above: On Brighton's Palace Pier. Right: The Royal Pavilion is like something out of the Arabian Nights.*

reputedly once owned by Anne, the fourth wife of Henry VIII. The old town itself preserved its harmony as it grew over the years; its steep alleys are lined with a mix of half-timbered houses and buildings from the Georgian period.

From Lewes, you can take an attractive detour north to explore the high heathland of **Ashdown Forest**. The A275 from Lewes passes the extensive woodland garden at **Sheffield Park**, some of which was laid out by the 18th-century landscaper "Capability" Brown. Another attractive route, the A2028, leads northwest to the 140 acres of **Wakehurst Place**, another of the internationally-known gardens of the High Weald whose acid soils yield wonderful displays of rhododendrons and azaleas in the spring. At **Haywards Heath**, the B2112 branches off to Ditchling. Beyond the village a minor road makes its way steeply upward to **Ditchling Beacon** on the South Downs, from where you have glorious views of the Weald to the north before descending into Brighton.

### Brighton, the Royal Resort

In the early 19th century, George, the Prince Regent (later King George IV) gave the expanding seaside town his patronage, and all of Society followed his lead. Here he realized his oriental fantasy, the **Royal Pavilion**.

Built in 1815-22 by his favorite architect John Nash, it is fitted out with minarets and topped with white domes reminiscent of Indian architecture; even so, all of this pomp only hints at the extravagant *chinoiserie* of the interior, which includes a magnificent banqueting hall. Architectural purists will perhaps prefer the town's Regency terraces, with Lewes Crescent and Sussex Square to the east matched by Brunswick Terrace to the west in neighboring Hove.

A great deal of Brighton's flamboyant seaside architecture is Victorian, including the two **piers** (one sadly in a state of decay) which thrust out far into the sea, and the filigree arches of **Madeira Drive** on the eastern seafront – which is also a favorite venue for various automobile races. The most famous is the London-to-Brighton "old crocks" race held each year in November.

The **Brighton Museum and Art Gallery** in Church Street houses an excellent collection of art deco, Art Nouveau furniture, fashions from the last 100 years, and old musical instruments.

In the district known as **The Lanes**, antique shops, elegant boutiques and small restaurants have settled in the old 17th-century fisherman's cottages. Since 1841, when the railway first connected Brighton to London, this former harbor town has grown into the largest and best-known seaside resort on the Channel coast.

The former Goldstone pumping station in **Hove** is now the home of the **British Engineerium**, which fittingly celebrates the engineering achievements of the

*WEST SUSSEX / CHICHESTER*

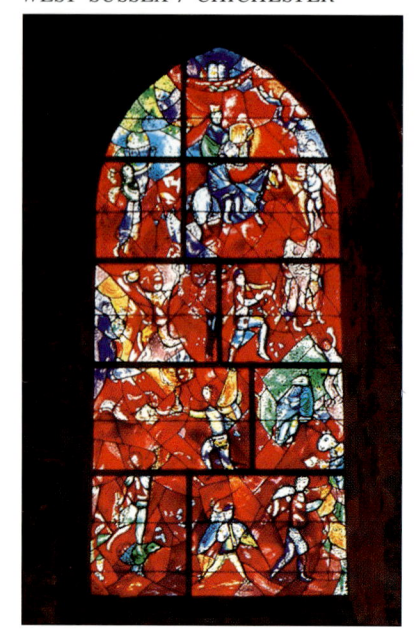

Regency period. **Volk's Railway**, the world's first electric railway when it began in 1883, runs from Palace Pier towards the large yacht marina which has grown up under the cliffs since the 1960s.

## Into West Sussex

**Arundel**, an attractive little town on the River Arun at the edge of the South Downs, is dominated by its great **castle**, which since the 11th century has been in the possession of the leading Roman Catholic family of England, the Dukes of Norfolk. Narrow winding alleys lead past ancient houses to the turreted castle walls, which command a wonderful panoramic view. Lots of paths by the river promise enchanting walks and the **Great Park** with its beautiful lake and **Potter's Curiosity Museum** are also worth a visit.

*Above: Marc Chagall's famous window in Chichester Cathedral. Right: A figurehead in the Royal Navy Museum, Portsmouth.*

If you take the A284 north and turn off east onto the B2139, you'll come first to the **Amberley Museum**, a working museum of industrial history. A little further on is the picture-postcard village of **Amberley** itself. From here, there is a lovely drive below a stretch of folded downland to Storrington.

Follow the A283 west a short distance and you arrive at the Elizabethan **Parham House**, set in a great park with oaks and elms. The *Great Hall* has a splendid stucco ceiling and the *Long Gallery* is almost 170 feet (50 m) long. Beyond Pulborough there is another stately home with an extensive deer park: **Petworth House**. The house took on its present form in 1688-96, while the grounds were designed by "Capability" Brown. For a time Turner had his studio here, and 20 of his paintings are exhibited in the Turner Room. Petworth itself is a lovely little town with narrow cobbled streets. From here the road runs south to Chichester.

## Chichester

Northeast of Chichester is **Goodwood House** (18th century) which houses a collection of furniture, tapestries, porcelain and paintings by Reynolds, Canaletto, van Dyck and Gainsborough. You can only visit the house as part of a guided tour.

It was the Romans who laid out **Chichester**; and remnants of their city wall, as well as the formal geometric pattern of their streets, radiating out from the ornate octagonal Late Gothic market cross, are still in evidence today. However, the city itself has a marked Georgian flair. The **Cathedral**, a blend of Norman and Gothic elements, was completed – all but its towers – by the end of the 12th century. Inside are two impressive stone reliefs dating from between 1120 and 1225: *Christ, Mary and Martha at the Gates of Bethany* and *The Resurrection of Lazarus*. Even modern craftsmen have contributed to the interior: there is a stained-glass window by Marc Chagall. **St. Mary's Hospital Almshouses** were built as a hospital around 1290. In the Georgian quarter of **Pallants**, you can see an impressive collection of modern art in **Pallant House**.

## SURREY

The A286 heads north from Chichester and passes the little village of Singleton, which is a center for riding and hunting and is known for its open-air museum with reconstructions of English farmhouses from the 14th to 19th centuries. The road takes you on to the market town of **Midhurst**, with some fine medieval houses in Knockhundred Row.

At the prosperous county town of **Guildford**, stroll up or down High Street, one of the steepest streets in England, with buildings from the time of the Tudors and James I. East of Guildford, the A246 passes **Clandon Park**, a Palladian-style house (1713-29) with a famous collection of furniture and porcelain. At East Horsley is another fine house, **Polesden Lacey**, a Regency villa with terraced gardens. Continue east and turn south on the A24 to **Box Hill**, a wooded chalk outcrop rising to 400 feet (120 m), giving superb views of the country.

## HAMPSHIRE AND
## THE ISLE OF WIGHT

The rolling, wooded countryside of **Hampshire** is the first taste of the charm of rural England that you get after leaving London through its prosperous southwestern suburbs. But the most attractive feature of the county is the coastline. The sea has penetrated far inland, creating not only the fine harbors of Portsmouth and Southampton, but also dozens of quiet, reed-fringed estuaries which are a paradise for yachtsmen, windsurfers, and anyone else who loves salt water.

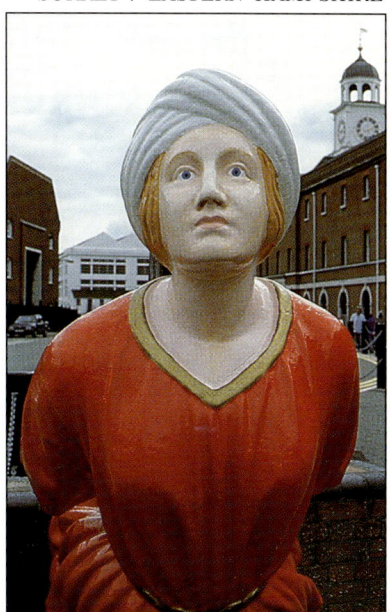

Southwest of Box Hill, the A31 leads to **Chawton** and **Jane Austen's House**. England's great woman novelist lived with her mother and sister in this red brick house, today a museum filled with Austen memorabilia.

Returning to the A31, turn left on to the A32 (for Fareham), a quiet road through the park-like country of the **Meon Valley** with numerous old, picturesque villages. A turn left on to the B2150 leads to **Hambledon**. Cricket-lovers should follow the signpost to **Broadhalfpenny Down**, where the rules of England's oldest national sport were laid down in the 1750s in the **Bat and Ball** inn, which still stands beside the cricket ground. Continue on the B2150 to Denmead; a small road leads right from the middle of this village toward **Southwick**, high on the downs. Southwick became famous in World War II as the headquarters for the D-Day invasion of Normandy. It was in Southwick House, on June 6, 1944, that General Eisenhower gave the immortal order: "OK, let's go!"

## PORTSMOUTH

Behind the village, the road toward Portchester leads up to the crest of the Ports Downs, which commands a magnificent view of Portsmouth Harbor, the Isle of Wight, and the Solent Narrows. At the crossroads turn right and you will see the 150 ft (50 m) **Nelson Monument**, with the 19th-century **Fort Nelson** just beyond it, now containing an **artillery museum**. Opposite the Nelson Monument, a minor road runs down to the spit of Portchester. Towering over the elegant old houses is massive **Portchester Castle**. Built by the Romans in the 4th century to defend the harbor against the Saxons, it was extended by the Normans some 600 years later.

### Portsmouth

Under Henry VIII, **Portsmouth** became the most important harbor of the Royal Navy. The history of the city, known as *Pompey* to generations of sailors, is closely linked with the development of British sea-power. However, it was severely damaged in World War II, and rebuilt fairly haphazardly afterwards. The only places of interest are around the waterfront and dockyard, although you can make a pilgrimage to the **Birthplace of Charles Dickens**, a small early 19th-century house in the north of the city, furnished in the style of the period (signposted from the end of the M275). While the dockyard is still operational, its 18th-century buildings near the main gate have been converted into the **Royal Naval Museum**. The oldest of its three **historic ships** is the *Mary Rose*, the pride of Henry VIII's navy. In 1545, she set sail to meet the French but capsized off the harbor entrance and sank with all 700 hands on board; she was finally raised in 1982 and placed in dry-dock. About half the hull, from deck to keel, has survived; equally fascinating are more than 1,000 artifacts, displayed in a separate museum. The great man-o'-war *HMS Victory*, Lord Nelson's flagship at the Battle of Trafalgar (1805), has been restored in every detail, from its massive masts, rigging and cannons down to Nelson's cabin. The most recent of the restored ships, *HMS Warrior*, was designed as Britain's "secret weapon" in 1860 but never saw action. It was the world's first ironclad, steam-powered warship. Outside the dockyard gates, **The Hard**, or waterfront, leads to the pier, which is both the terminus for trains from London and the departure point for passenger steamers to the Isle of Wight, as well as the waterbus which takes visitors round the harbor.

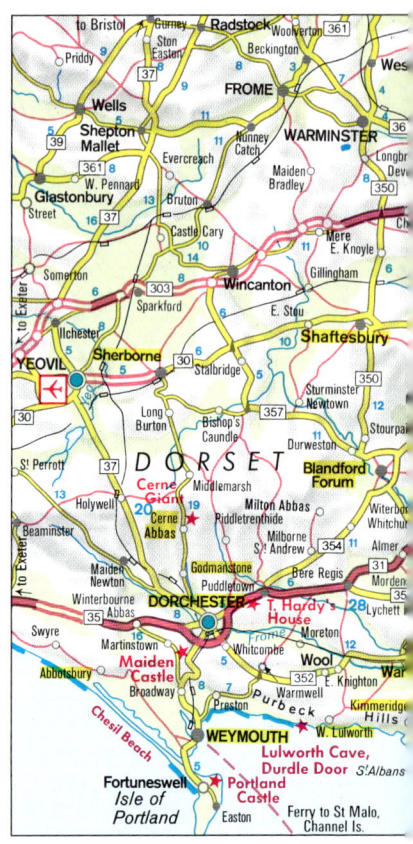

From here, Gunwharf Road leads into **Old Portsmouth**. The oldest house in the

*HAMPSHIRE / DORSET*

city is **Quebec House** (1754). Between the Tudor defensive walls and the little commercial harbor, called **The Camber**, are a few streets of old houses, pubs and shops, where some of the old seafaring atmosphere has survived. Climb the **Round Tower** and watch a continuous procession of ferries, fishing boats and yachts passing through the narrow harbor mouth.

If you follow the fortifications eastward, the scene changes completely as you come to **Southsea**, a Victorian seaside resort. With its **Clarence Pier**, a wide, grassy esplanade, a fun fair and rows of pastel-colored Victorian hotels, it is a cheerful – and crowded – place on a summer weekend.

**The Isle of Wight**

Off the shore of Portsmouth and Southampton, the **Isle of Wight** has a very different flavor. Because of its strategic importance, it was occupied by Romans, Saxons, and Vikings, and was, until the 16th century, frequently raided by the French. Not until the 19th century did the well-to-do discover the island's potential as a holiday resort; and it's been known by such epithets as "Isle of Flowers" or "Diamond in the Sea" ever since. Its climate is mild in comparison with other regions, and it attracts walkers and nature-lovers, particularly in the spring, when everything bursts into blossom, or in the somewhat cooler autumn.

99

## THE ISLE OF WIGHT

The east coast is the more developed, with a line of resorts, while at the western tip of the island there are high chalk cliffs at **Freshwater Bay** and the three famous **Needles** rocks. Also fascinating are the colorful sand cliffs at **Alum Bay**.

**Ventnor** is a peaceful, gray stone Victorian spa clinging to the steep coast, with a picturesque pub, **The Spyglass**, on its tiny beach. Inland is the sleepy capital, **Newport**, the island's second-largest town after Ryde. Just south of the town, on a commanding hilltop, stands **Carisbrooke Castle**, a Norman fortress built on Saxon foundations. The medieval **Great Hall** was the residence of the Governors of the island until 1944; it now houses a museum of the island's history.

Newport stands on a tidal river, the Medina, which flows north to the busy and attractive port of **Cowes**. In August, sailing enthusiasts from all over the world meet here for Cowes Week, a famous regatta. The races start and finish close inshore – spectacular in a stiff breeze. A ferry crosses the Medina to East Cowes, where Prince Albert had the Italianate summer residence **Osborne House** built in 1845-51 for himself and Queen Victoria. After Albert's death in 1861, Victoria spent a lot of time at Osborne and died here in 1901. During the Great War it was an officer's convalescent home for a while, and both Robert Graves and Siegfried Sassoon stayed here. The rooms have been preserved almost unchanged from Victoria's times. Neighboring **Barton Manor** has been producing wine since 1976 (including Müller-Thurgau); most of the vintage is sold locally.

The north coast of the island, west of Cowes, is tranquil and unspoiled. On the marshy estuary of the Newtown river, the silence is only broken by the cries of the seabirds in the **nature reserve**, and the tiny hamlet of **Newtown** is all that is left of a once prosperous borough that was burned by the French in 1377. A few

*Above: Off season, the beaches of the Isle of Wight are pleasantly empty.*

miles further west, the port of **Yarmouth** is dominated by the ruins of a castle, one of many built by Henry VIII. High Street is lined with 17th- and 18th-century houses, shops and pubs. From the old wooden pier, steamers depart on short cruises in the summer, and on the west side of the town is the terminal for the **car ferry** across to Lymington, an attractive New Forest fishing village on the mainland.

### The New Forest

The 150 square miles (400 sq km) of the New Forest, which occupies much of southwest Hampshire, existed long before William the Conqueror decided to make it his private hunting reserve. Ever since then it has been a protected area unique in England: a mixture of broadleaf forest, open heathland and unspoiled villages.

The enclosures that turned the rest of England into a patchwork of hedges and fields are absent here: pigs, horses, donkeys and cattle graze on unfenced pasture and wander across the roads. Signs everywhere warn drivers to be careful of the animals, and picnickers must be prepared to share their food with them.

The small town of **Lyndhurst** lies on the A35 and A337 and is the "capital" of the Forest, with hotels, information center, cycle hire and pony-trekking. In the Victorian parish church of **St. Michael**, the colorful east window and the north transept windows were designed by Burne-Jones.

A few miles northeast is **Beaulieu** (pronounced "Bewly"), a beautiful village at the head of a tidal river. In 1952, the landowner, Lord Montagu, created a discreet but hugely successful tourist complex here with the **Motor Museum,** displaying 200 vintage automobiles, and his own stately home, **Beaulieu Abbey**.

River trips will take you to **Buckler's Hard**, an 18th-century shipyard where Nelson's ships were built from New Forest oak. On the far side of the river, a few miles downstream, lie **Exbury Gardens**. Here you can wander among one of the world's greatest collections of exotic shrubs, whose colors and scents are at their most vibrant in May and June.

### Western Hampshire

Trout fishermen should visit **Stockbridge**, an old coaching town on the river Test in West Hampshire. A footpath, the **Test Way**, leads along the river. 6 miles (10 km) downstream from Stockbridge you reach **Mottisfont Abbey**. This 13th-century Augustinian foundation was converted into a manor house in Elizabethan times, and is set in superb gardens by the river.

A little further downstream is the little market town of **Romsey** with a rare intact medieval hall-house, known as **King John's House**, which was probably part of the infirmary of **Romsey Abbey**. The abbey was built in 1120 and extended in the 12th and 13th centuries. The south aisle is decorated with an Anglo-Saxon relief of the Crucifixion. Just south of the town, in a park laid out by Capability Brown, is **Broadlands**, a Palladian mansion whose two most celebrated owners were Lord Palmerston (1784-1865), the Victorian statesman, and Earl Mountbatten, a member of the royal family who was murdered by Irish terrorists in 1980.

### Southampton and Winchester

**Southampton** was an important port even back in Roman times. In the 19th century new docks were laid out and the railway to London completed, bringing a marked increase in passenger and freight traffic. From Southampton, the *Mayflower* sailed in 1620 and the *Titanic* in 1912. In World War II, the city was heavily bombed and the modern city, though spacious, has few sights to attract the

## SOUTHAMPTON / WINCHESTER

tourist. In the **Old Town**, you can still see the city walls of 1360, while the half-timbered **Tudor House** (16th century) houses a museum with Georgian and Victorian exhibits. The **Wool House**, a 14th-century warehouse, is today a maritime museum, while **God's House Tower** houses a museum of archaeological finds. You can also tipple in two historic pubs: the *Duke of Wellington*, with Tudor half-timbering, and the *Red Lion* on High Street.

The suburbs of Southampton stretch inland almost as far as **Winchester**. When King Alfred the Great united the country, this historic city on the river Itchen became England's first capital; and it remained an important center of power, second only to London, until the 18th century.

A Norman Gothic **cathedral** was built on Saxon foundations between the 11th

*Above: The west front of Wincester cathedral. Right: Clifftop paths are ideal for leisurely walks.*

and 14th centuries; it has the longest medieval nave in Europe (556 ft/169 m). Remnants of the Romanesque walls in the north transept merge into the Late Gothic fan vaulting. The Great Screen (1455-75) behind the altar is a miracle of filigree stone carving. In the choir there are painted mortuary chests containing the bones of early English kings, as well as the tomb of Jane Austen. Also worth noting are the Norman font (north transept) which shows scenes from the life of St. Nichola, and the famous Winchester Bible of the 12th century (south transept). If you leave the cathedral through the west door, turn left and walk through the cloisters to the **Deanery**, the **Pilgrim's Hall** (14th century) with its early hammer-beam roof and the beautiful gabled **Cheyney Court** (15th century), the former bishop's courthouse. South of the church grounds is **Winchester College**, Britain's oldest public school, founded in 1384.

Follow College Street past the **Bishop's Palace** (17th century) and the ruins of **Wolvesey Castle** (1130-70). A path runs alongside the city walls down to the elegant **City Bridge** and an 18th-century water-mill. The **Great Hall**, at the upper end of High Street, was built in 1236 for Henry III and is the finest building of its kind after Westminster Hall in London. In pride of place is the **Round Table**, made of oak and 18 feet (6 m) in diameter, painted with the figure of King Arthur and the names of all his knights.

## DORSET

Despite its relatively small area, Dorset offers a greater variety of scenery than any other region of southern England. Immortalized in the novels of Thomas Hardy, these landscapes still attract many ramblers today.

### The Bournemouth Coast

From Christchurch in the east to Sandbanks in the west, the densely-populated coast around **Bournemouth** is the nearest thing in England to Miami or the Côte d'Azur. It has a mild climate, a wide variety of entertainment and 10 miles (16 km) of sandy beaches backed by low cliffs. Since the 1930s, large hotels, apartment blocks and expensive villas have been built here among the pine trees and rocky "chines" or gorges running down to the sea. The many language schools in Bournemouth attract not only the young but also older people (comfortably-off retirees).

To the west, the suburbs of Bournemouth extend to the shores of **Poole Harbour**, the largest natural harbor in Europe. More like an inland lake, it is over 6 miles (10 km) wide yet its mouth to the sea is barely 650 feet (200 m) across. The **Sandbanks** peninsula closes off most of the harbor mouth. On its seaward side there is a good bathing beach, while the sheltered harbor shore is ideal for windsurfing, waterskiing and swimming.

Though **Poole** and Bournemouth have now grown together, Poole has a much longer history and a very different character. From the south of the town, cargo ships, yachts and ferries head for Cherbourg and the Channel Islands. On the quay there are a number of traditional harbor pubs and workshops, such as the **Poole Pottery**.

Though the town was damaged during the war, some of its old buildings on the **Quay** have survived, including the **Old Town House** (around 1500) which houses a museum of local history; the elegant 18th-century **Fisheries Office**, and the **Customs House**. From the quay you can take the ferry over to the seabird paradise of **Brownsea Island**, 500 acres (200 ha) of heathland and woodland.

West of Poole is **Wareham**, a charming, sleepy town dating from Saxon times and enclosed by ramparts on three sides. Around the tiny quay, a departure point for boat trips, are attractive old pubs and restaurants. The **Priory** next to the parish church today serves as a luxury hotel.

Crossing the Frome, you come to the **Isle of Purbeck**, a peninsula of heath-covered hills with wooded valleys, one of which is guarded by the impressive hilltop ruins of **Corfe Castle**. This Norman fortress was occupied by several medieval kings, and in the Civil War was one of the royalist strongholds which Cromwell destroyed. The pretty village at the foot of the castle is popular not only with walkers. From Corfe, take the B3351 left to **Studland**, an unspoiled village (also reached by car ferry from Sandbanks). Set in National Trust woodland, it has, in addition to one of the finest beaches in England, a large and comfortable hotel.

South of Studland, beyond the chalk stacks of Handfast Point, lies the popular beach resort of **Swanage**. For centuries, chalk and sandstone was shipped out from here but with the advent of the railway in 1880 it grew rapidly as a resort. Some of the medieval alleys survive, but most of the town is Victorian or Edwardian.

From Swanage, a minor road climbs past quarries of the famous Purbeck marble (actually a variety of sandstone) and up to gray stone villages like **Worth Matravers**, high above the sea, and **Kingston**, where a popular old inn, the **Scott Arms**, looks down on Corfe Castle and Poole Harbour. Returning to Corfe, take the minor road west via Kimmeredge to **East Lulworth** with the ruins of Lulworth Castle (17th century). At **West Lulworth** is the nearly circular bay of **Lulworth Cove**, almost shut off from the sea by steep chalk cliffs, and a famous scenic spot. A little way to the west, **Durdle Door** is an impressive rock arch, carved by the action of the waves.

The next town along the coast is **Weymouth**, a pretty seaside resort with Tudor and Georgian houses, a wide, sheltered beach, and an elegant esplanade. From its

*Right: The Giant of Cerne Abbas, etched in the chalk, is visible for miles.*

small but busy commercial harbor, ferries leave for St. Malo and the Channel Islands. Beyond the harbor is a causeway leading to the rocky **Isle of Portland**. For centuries, **Portland Harbour** was an important naval base and is guarded by **Portland Castle**, another of Henry VIII's castles. The lighthouse at the southern tip is open to visitors.

West of Portland is **Chesil Beach**, a remarkable barrier of shingle some 40 feet (12 m) high and 650 feet (200 m) wide. The long lagoon behind it is now a bird sanctuary. Due to the fast, swirling currents, swimming or sailing are very dangerous both here and in Portland. **Abbotsbury**, at the western end of the lagoon, has a ruined abbey (11th century) with attractive gardens and a swannery (800 inhabitants). At the border with Devon, is **Lyme Regis**, an elegant old seaside town well-known to readers of John Fowles' novel *The French Lieutenant's Woman*. West of the town is the beach of **Undercliff**, where you can sometimes find in nature the fossils which you can also admire in the **Philpot Museum**.

### The Country of Thomas Hardy

There is more to Dorset than its dramatic coastline. The hinterland is haunted by the characters of Thomas Hardy's novels of rural passion and tragedy, such as *Far from the Madding Crowd* and *Tess of the D'Urbervilles*. Hardy (1840-1928) was born at Upper Bockhampton, near Dorchester, where he spent most of his life. The thatched cottage where he was born, **Hardy's Cottage**, is open to the public.

**Dorchester** stands on a hill between two rivers and has been settled since the Stone Age. Just to the southwest of the town, **Maiden Castle** is a huge Iron Age fortification, where the Celts made a last stand against the Roman legions in 44 AD. Dorchester was an important center in Roman and Saxon times, and there is a fine Roman town house (4th century) and

## CERNE ABBAS / SHERBORNE

an amphitheater. But most of the other buildings, such as **Judge Jeffrey's Lodgings**, date from the 17th and 18th centuries. Visit the **Dorset County Museum**, which has dedicated a section to Thomas Hardy.

Take the A352 north from Dorchester, and at **Godmanstone** you will find the smallest pub in England, the *Smith's Arms*, formerly a forge. A few miles further north is **Cerne Abbas**, an ancient village at the foot of a hill on which a huge, primitive figure of a man with a club, cut out of the turf, is outlined in white chalk. The **Cerne Giant** is thought to be at least 1,500 years old, and his exaggerated phallus suggests a pre-Christian fertility cult.

The village itself has a tranquil charm. A narrow lane leads off the main street to the **abbey**, founded in 987. The guesthouse and gatehouse are among the best-preserved monastic buildings.

The A352 now climbs a ridge from where you have a fine view across the wide **Blackmore Vale**. On the far side of the valley, **Sherborne** is a handsome old town with a 15th-century abbey, medieval almshouses and Sherborne School, (1350-70) one of England's leading boarding schools for boys. Beside the river Yeo is the ruined **Old Castle** (1109-39) with its massive gatehouse, which Queen Elizabeth I gave to Sir Walter Raleigh. In 1594 Raleigh built a new castle, **Sherborne Castle**, right next to the old one; this now houses a collection of furniture and paintings. From here, the A30 leads east to **Shaftesbury**. This is a Saxon hill-town, unique in England, built on a high bluff above Blackmoor Vale. From the main square a narrow lane called **Gold Hill** opens out into a vista that must be the most-photographed in England: a row of pastel-colored cottages, lining a perilously steep cobbled street against the backdrop of hilly Blackmore Vale.

To complete your tour, head south on the A350 to **Blandford Forum**, a market town offering one of the most perfect Georgian townscapes in England.

*GUIDEPOST KENT / SURREY / EAST SUSSEX*

## KENT / SURREY
### CANTERBURY
#### Accommodation
CANTERBURY: *LUXURY:* **County Hotel**, High Street, tel. 01227 766266. *MODERATE:* **Abba Hotel**, Station Road West, tel. 01227 464771. *BUDGET:* **Ann's Hotel**, 63 London Road, tel. 01227 768767.

#### Restaurants
CANTERBURY: *MODERATE:* **Sully's** at the County Hotel. *INEXPENSIVE:* **Ristorante Tuo e Mio**, 16 The Borough. tel. 01227 761471, Italian.

#### Museums
CANTERBURY: **The Canterbury Tales Museum**, St. Margaret St., tel. 01227 454888, Jan-Feb and Nov-Dec Sun-Fri 10.00-16.30; Sat 9.30-17.30. March-Oct daily 9.30-17.30, closed Dec 25, Jan 1.

#### Tips and Trips
CHERITON: **Eurotunnel Exhibition Centre**, St. Martin's Plain, tel. 01303 270111, daily, winter 10.00-17.00, summer 10.00-18.00. **DOVER: The White Cliffs Experience**, Market Square, tel. 01304 201066, daily 1 Jan-26 March 10.00-16.30, 27 March-31 Oct 10.30-18.30, 1 Nov-31 Dec 10.00-15.00. **BEKESBURY: Howletts Wild Animal Park**, near Canterbury, tel. 01303 264647, daily 10.00-19.00. **FOLKESTONE: Rotunda Amusement Park**, tel. 01303 245245, daily 10.00-18.00. **HYTHE: Lympne Castle**, near Hythe, tel. 01303 267571, 1 April-early Oct daily 10.00-18.00. **Port Lympne Wild Animal Park**, tel. 01303 264647, daily except Dec 25. **GUILDFORD: Clandon Park**, near Guildford, tel. 0483 222482, 1 April-end Oct daily except Thur and Fri (open Good Friday) 13.30-17.30, Bank Holiday Mon 11.00-17.30. **GREAT BROOKHAM: Polesden Lacey**, near Dorking, tel. 01372 458203, house open March Sat and Sun 13.00-16.30, April-Oct Wed-Sun 13.30-17.30, Bank Holiday Mon 11.00-18.00. Gardens daily 11.00-18.00. **HEVER: Hever Castle**, tel. 01732 866368, 2 April-30 Oct, Tue-Thur 12.00-17.30. Sat, Sun and Bank Holiday Monday 11.00-17.30. **MAIDSTONE: Aylesford Friary**, east of Maidstone, tel. 01622 717272, all year daily except Dec 25 and Jan 1, 9.00-dusk. **Leeds Castle**, tel. 01622 765400, daily Nov-March, 10.00-17.00, open 25 June, 2 July, 5 November 10.00-15.00. Closed Dec 25 and 26, Jan 1. **PENSHURST: Penshurst Place**, tel. 01892 870307, 26 March-2 Oct daily. House open 12.00-17.30, grounds 11.00-18.30. **RAMSGATE: Richborough Castle**, tel. 01304 612013, April-31 Oct daily 10.00-18.00. **ROCHESTER: Rochester Castle**, tel. 01634 402276, daily 10.00-17.00. **Dickens Centre**, Chatham near Rochester, tel. 01634 844176, daily 10.00-17.30, closed Dec 25 and Jan 1. **SEVENOAKS:** **Knole**, tel. 01732 450608, April-31 Oct, Wed, Fri, Sat, Sun 11.00-17.00, Thur 14.00-17.00. **Ightham Mote**, east of Sevenoaks, tel. 01732 810378, April-end of Oct daily 12.00-17.30, Sun and Bank Holiday Mon 11.00-17.30, closed Tue and Sat.

#### Tourist Information
CANTERBURY: 34, St. Margaret's Street, tel. 01227 766567.

## EAST SUSSEX / BRIGHTON
#### Accommodation
BRIGHTON: *LUXURY:* **Old Ship Hotel**, Kings Road, tel. 01273 29001.
*MODERATE:* **Kempton House Hotel**, 33-34 Marine Parade, tel. 01273 570248.
*BUDGET:* **York Lodge Hotel**, 22-23, Atlingworth Street, Marine Parade, tel. 01273 605140.

#### Restaurants
BRIGHTON: *LUXURY:* **Le Grandgousier**, 15 Western Street, tel. 01273 772005. **Grand** in the Grand Hotel, Kings Rd., tel. 01273 321188. *MODERATE:* **Black Chapati**, 12 Circus Parade, New England Rd., tel. 01273 699011, Indian. **Langan's Bistro**, 1 Paston Place, tel. 01273 606933. **Whytes**, 33 Western Street, tel. 01273 776618.

#### Museums
HASTINGS: **Fisherman's Museum**, tel. 01424 424787, May-Sept, Mon-Fri 10.30-17.00; Sat and Sun 14.30-17.00. **LEWES: Anne of Cleeve's House Museum**, tel. 01273 47610, open 1 April-30 Oct, Mon-Sat 10.00-17.00, Sun 14.00-17.30.

#### Tips and Trips
ALFRISTON: **Clergy House**, tel. 01323 87001, April-Oct 10.00-17.00. **BATTLE: Battle Abbey** and **Site of the Battle of Hastings**, tel. 01424 773792, 1 April-31 Oct 10.00-18.00, 1 Nov-31 March 10.00-16.00. **BODIAM: Bodiam Castle**, tel. 01580 830436, Jan-March, Tue-Sat 10.00-sunset. April-end of October 10.00-18.00, Nov-Dec 10.00-sunset. **Sissinghurst Garden**, near Bodiam, tel. 01580 712850, April-15 October Tue-Fri 13.00-18.30; Sat, Sun and Good Friday 10.00-17.30. **BRIGHTON: Royal Pavilion**, tel. 01273 603005, Jan-May and Oct-Dec 10.00-17.00. June-Sept 10.00-18.00. **EXCEAT: Living World Exhibition**, tel. 01323 870100, daily mid March-1 November, 10.00-17.30. **FIRLE: Firle Place**, near Lewes, tel. 01237 858335, Easter, May-end of Sept Sun, Wed, Thur 14.00-17.00. **Charleston Farmhouse**, near Lewes, tel. 01323 8111265, 2 April-10 July, 7 Sept-30 Oct Wed-Sun 14.00-18.00; 13 July-4 Sept; additional opening 11.00-14.00 Wed-Sat. **HASTINGS: Shipwreck Heritage Centre**, tel. 01424 437452, all year daily except Dec 25, 11.00-17.00. 19 Sept-30 Oct 14.00-16.00. **LAMBERHURST: Castle Gardens**, tel. 01892 890651,

## GUIDEPOST WEST SUSSEX / HAMPSHIRE / DORSET

open 2 April-end of October Wed-Fri 11.00-18.00; Sat, Sun 14.00-18.00. **RYE: Lamb House**, tel. 01892 890651, April-end of Oct Wed and Sat 14.00-18.00. **WESTERHAM: Quebec House**, tel. 01959 62206, 1 April-30 Oct Sun-Wed and Fri 14.00-18.00.

### Tourist Information
**BRIGHTON**: 10 Bartholomew Square, tel. 01273 323755.

### WEST SUSSEX / CHICHESTER
#### Accommodation
**CHICHESTER**: *LUXURY:* **Ship Hotel**, North Street, tel. 01243 778000.
*MODERATE:* **St. Andrew's Lodge**, Chichester Road, Selsey, tel. 01243 606899. *BUDGET:* **Woodstock House**, Charlton, tel. 01243 63666.

#### Restaurants
**CHICHESTER**: *MODERATE:* **Droveway**, 30a Southgate, tel. 01243 528832. **Comme Ça**, Broyle Road (near Festival Theatre), tel. 01243 788724.

#### Museums
**AMBERLEY: Amberley Museum**, tel. 01798 831370, Wed-Sun 10.00-17.00: 23 March-19 March, 18 April-24 May, 6 June-19 July, 5 Sept-18 Oct. Daily 10.00-17.00: 30 March-17 April, 25 May-5 June, 4 Sept-19 Oct. **SINGLETON: Weald and Downland Open Air Museum**, near Chichester, tel. 01243 871348, open all year daily, 13.00-17.00.

#### Tips and Trips
**ARUNDEL: Arundel Castle**, tel. 01903 883136, 1 April-28 Oct Sun-Fr 11.00-18.00. **Wild Fowl Reserve**, tel. 01903 883355, 1 Jan-31 March, 1 Nov-31 Dec 9.30-16.30. 1 April-31 Oct 9.30-17.30.
**CHICHESTER: Goodwood House**, tel. 01243 774107, May-Sept, Sun and Mon 14.00-17.00. **PETWORTH: Petworth House**, tel. 01798 342207, 1 April-30 Oct, Tue, Thur, Sat, Sun 13.00-17.30, gardens 12.30-18.00. **PULBOROUGH: Parham House**, tel. 01903 744888, open Easter Sun-1 Sun in Oct Wed, Thur, Sun 14.00-18.00.

#### Tourist Information
**CHICHESTER**: 29a, South Street, tel. 01243 775888.

### HAMPSHIRE / PORTSMOUTH
#### Accommodation
**PORTSMOUTH**: *LUXURY:* **The Marriott**, North Harbour, tel. 01705 383151.
*MODERATE:* **Westfield Hall Hotel**, 65, Festing Road, tel. 01705 826971. *BUDGET:* **Post House**, Pembroke Road, tel. 01705 827651.

#### Museums
**BEAULIEU: Beaulieu Motor Museum, Palace House** and **Abbey**, tel. 01590 612345, daily 10.00-18.00, closed Dec 25. **CHAWTON: Jane Austen's House**, Alton, tel. 0420 83262, 11.00-16.30 April-Oct daily; Nov, Dec and March Wed-Sun; Jan and Feb, Sat and Sun only. **PORTSMOUTH:: Royal Naval Museum** and **Naval Heritage**, tel. 01705 733060, daily 10.30-16.30, closed Dec 25 and Jan 1. **ROMSEY: Broadlands**, tel. 0794 516878, Easter to last Sun in Sept 12.00-16.00, closed Fri except Good Friday and during Aug. **STOCKBRIDGE: Mottisfont Abbey Garden**, tel. 0794 340757, House: Tue, Wed, Sun 13.00-17.00, Gardens: April-end Oct, Sat-Wed 12.00-18.00; June Sat-Wed 12.00-20.30. **SOUTHAMPTON: Tudor House Museum**, Bugle St., tel. 01703 332523, Tue-Fri 10.00-12.00 and 13.00-17.00, Sat 10.00-12.00 and 13.00-16.00, Sun 13.30-17.00.

#### Tips and Trips
**PORTCHESTER: Portchester Castle**, tel. 01705 58159, 1 April-31 Oct daily 10.00-18.00; 1 Nov-31 March daily 10.00-16.00.
**PORTSMOUTH: Birthplace Museum of Charles Dickens**, Old Commercial Road, tel. 01705 827261, April-Sept Mon-Fr, 13.00-17.00; Sat and Sun 11.00-17.00. **ISLE OF WIGHT: Carisbrooke Castle**, Newport, tel. 01983 522107, all year 1 April-31 Oct 10.00-16.00. 1 Nov-31 March, 10.00-16.00. **Osborne House**, near Cowes, tel. 01983 420022, open 1 April-31 Oct daily 10.00-18.00. **WINCHESTER: Wolvesey Castle**, tel. 01794 854766, Easter-31 Oct daily 10.00-16.00.

#### Tourist Information
**PORTSMOUTH**: The Hard, tel. 01705 826722.

### DORSET / BOURNEMOUTH
#### Accommodation
**BOURNEMOUTH**: *LUXURY:* **Swallow High Cliff Hotel**, St. Michael's Road, Westcliff, tel. 01202 557702. **Royal Bath Hotel**, Bath Road, tel. 01202 555555. *MODERATE:* **Durley Hall Hotel**, Durley Chine Road, tel. 01202 500100. *BUDGET:* **West Cliff Gardens**, tel. 01202 556218.

#### Tips and Trips
**DORCHESTER**: **Thomas Hardy's Cottage**, southeast of Dorchester, tel. 01305 262366, April-Oct daily 10.00-18.00 except Thur.
**POOLE: Poole Pottery Factory**, tel. 01202 669800, daily 9.00-17.00; Sat and Sun 10.00-17.00, closed Fri afternoon. **SHERBORNE: Sherborne Castle**, tel. 01935 813182, Easter-30 Sept daily 14.00-17.30. **Sherborne Abbey**, tel. 01935 812452, summer 9.00-18.00, winter 09.00-16.00. **SWANAGE: Corfe Castle**, west of Swanage, tel. 01929 481294, open 7 Feb-31 Oct daily 10.00-17.30, Sat and Sun 12.00-15.30.

#### Tourist Information
**BOURNEMOUTH**: Westover Road, tel. 01202 789789.

## THE HOME COUNTIES

# THE HOME COUNTIES

**HERTFORDSHIRE**
**BEDFORDSHIRE**
**BUCKINGHAMSHIRE**
**THE THAMES VALLEY**
**OXFORD**
**BERKSHIRE**

---

The name Home Counties goes back to the days when judges traveled out from London to courts within the so-called "Home Circuit": the territory, that is, within a day's journey of London, allowing for one change of horses along the way.

Virtually all the major roads and the motorways in the Home Counties radiate out from London. Heading directly north from London is the old *Great North Road*, today either signposted as the A1 or as the A1(M). This is an ancient pre-Roman highway, which eventually passes east of the Pennine mountains, and on into Scotland, but initially takes you through Hertfordshire, a county of soft, gently rolling hills.

## HERTFORDSHIRE

### St. Albans

The medieval market town of **St. Albans** is situated on a hill by the river Ver. During the Wars of the Roses two decisive battles were fought here, in 1455 and 1461.

The Romans settled to the southwest of the city. Excavations of their town, *Ve-*

*Left: A guardsman on duty at Windsor Castle, sporting a traditional bearskin hat.*

*rulanium*, one of the leading cities of Roman Britain, have brought to light a Roman amphitheatre, remnants of the fortifications and a mosaic floor. Other finds from the excavations here are displayed in the **Verulanium Museum**.

In the center of the city is the **Abbey Church**, at 550 feet (168 m) the second-longest cathedral in England. An earlier, Saxon building was founded here in 79 AD on the site of the martyrdom of St. Alban (c. 304), a Roman legionary who had become a Christian.

The present cathedral was built between 1077 and 1326. The Norman crossing tower is the oldest part of the Gothic cathedral. Because the cathedral took 250 years to build, it demonstrates a variety of styles and colors, both inside and out. The Norman nave, for instance, has arches in various shades of color; and, while on the north side the pillars are Norman, there are four bays in Early English style behind the west entrance.

In the old city center, the **Museum of St. Albans** specializes in local and natural history as well as a rare collection of traditional artisan tools.

Even more specialized is the **Organ Museum**, which exhibits a collection of old music boxes, working fairground and theatre organs, and other mechanical musical instruments.

## Hatfield and Knebworth

Further east is **Hatfield**, originally a Saxon market town but more recently an important center of the aviation industry. A little outside the town in an enchanting park is **Hatfield House**, an impressive example of Jacobean architecture. Built in 1607 for the Earls of Salisbury, it is still owned by the family, and today contains collections of period furniture and paintings. Within its grounds also stands part of the old **Royal Palace of Hatfield** (1497), where Queen Elizabeth I spent much of her childhood.

A few miles further north is **Knebworth House**, another fine old English stately home, standing in 250 acres (100 ha) of magnificent parkland where herds of deer wander free. Home of the Lytton family since 1493, the house contains many beautiful rooms and a wealth of fine furniture from the 17th and 18th century, objets d'art and a portrait collection. For children the park can offer a large adventure playground and the Fort Knebworth Miniature Railway.

Northwards on the B656 lies **Hitchin**, a medieval market town with many Tudor and Georgian buildings arranged around a spacious market square. Close by stands a large medieval parish church and the 18th-century **Hitchin Priory**, furnished by Robert Adam. The **Hitchin Museum** contains England's largest selection of period costumes as well as an authentic Victorian chemist's shop rebuilt inside. Outside is the **Physic Garden**, devoted to medicinal herbs and shrubs.

Northeast of Hitchin along the A505 lies **Letchworth**, a garden city laid out to the plans of Ebenezer Howard in 1903. From Letchworth the A505 heads east to **Baldock**, a picturesque little town founded by the Knights Templar in the 12th century. Its Church of **St. Mary** boasts an impressive 14th-century steepled tower.

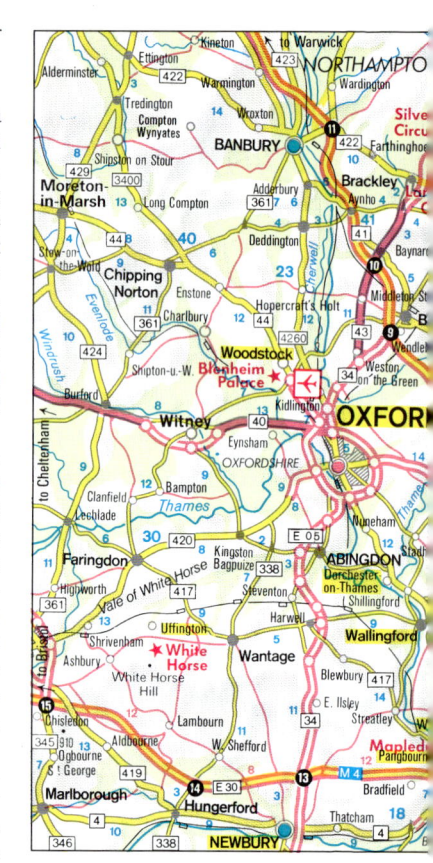

## INTO BEDFORDSHIRE

The county of Bedfordshire begins near the town of Biggleswade. A little way west, on the edge of the village of **Old Warden**, an old aerodrome houses the world-famous **Shuttleworth Collection** of veteran and vintage aircraft (many still regularly flying) and motor vehicles.

Nearby is a remarkable example of Victorian landscape architecture: the **Swiss Garden**, an enchanting blend of ornamental gardening with picturesque architecture.

Further west, take a detour to the bird sanctuary of **Sandy Lodge** before you drive on to **Bedford**, the county town.

*HOME COUNTIES*

Most of Bedford is modern and industrial, but this is ameliorated by a large number of parks. Pride of the town is the **Bunyan Meeting House and Museum,** where John Bunyan gave his nonconformist sermons, which he paid for with 12 years in jail. Here he wrote most of his classic work *The Pilgrim's Progress.*

### Luton and Dunstable

**Luton** is a bustling industrial town, once famous for its straw hat factories, set in a surprisingly rural landscape. Luton has for centuries been a center for the carriage-builder's craft; the town's museums include the **Mossman Collection** of over 70 original and replica horse-drawn vehicles. Today, fittingly, it has the Vauxhall factory. Worth visiting is the Gothic church of **St. Mary** with its stone font and baldachin, and its Wenlock chapel (1461).

Southeast of the town is **Luton Hoo**, a grandiose country home designed by Sir Robert Adam in 1767, but not completed until the late 19th century, when it was owned by the Wernher family. It contains a priceless collection of paintings (including works by Rembrandt, Constable, Memling and Titian), tapestries, jewellery (some by Fabergé), furniture, and porcelain. The marvelous park and gardens, which on their own are worth a visit, are the work of "Capability" Brown.

## DUNSTABLE / WOBURN ABBEY

West of Luton is the town of **Dunstable** with its **Priory Church of St. Peter and Paul**, which has a Norman nave. It was here that the divorce of Henry VIII and Catherine of Aragon was pronounced in 1533.

The B489 climbs out of the town up a high chalk ridge onto **Dunstable Down**s, the northern lip of the chalk hills which edge the London basin. At its highest point (also the highest point in the Home Counties) is **Ivinghoe Beacon** (900 feet/ 276 m). Locals claim you can see seven counties from here on a clear day. The whole of Dunstable Downs is designated as a country park with picnic areas, and many pleasant walks. Not far away, marked by an enormous lion cut into the chalk, are the 500 acres (200 ha) of the **Whipsnade Wild Animal Park**, home to some 2,500 species of rare or endangered animals, birds and reptiles.

*Above: Stowe Landscape Gardens, created by William Kent and "Capability" Brown. Right: Silverstone Circuit.*

### Woburn Abbey

Northwest of Dunstable is **Woburn Abbey** (18th century) with the **Woburn Safari Park**. On the site of the Cistercian abbey the Duke of Bedford built his seat. The interior of the house was furnished by Henry Holland and is packed with a costly collection of French furniture, porcelain and paintings (van Dyck, Holbein, Rembrandt, Gainsborough). Most people, however, come to see the Safari Park, where African big game and smaller animals of all kinds roam freely. The park also has excellent facilities and amusements for children.

## NORTH BUCKINGHAMSHIRE

The road winds northwest via the small Quaker-founded town of Woburn and through pleasant countryside into Buckinghamshire. Here, you'll pass the new city of **Milton Keynes,** which was built on green fields in 1967. The buildings here are low, spread out, and surrounded

## NORTH BUCKINGHAMSHIRE

by plenty of greenery, so that it hardly seems like a city at all. The A422 takes you to **Buckingham**, once the county town. Center point of this attractive little town is the traditional market square (formerly the cattle market), where open-air markets are still held twice a week. At one side of the square is the old **County Gaol**, now a museum. Since 1976, Buckingham has been home to the only independent university in Britain.

A few miles north of the town are the 500 acres (200 ha) of the **Stowe Landscape Gardens**, designed in the 18th century by "Capability" Brown and William Kent for the Duke of Buckingham, and surrounding his stately home (now an independent school). Particularly attractive is the octagonal lake with its Palladian bridge.

On the border with Northamptonshire, is the raceway of the **Silverstone Circuit**, venue for the annual *British Grand Prix*.

From Buckingham, the A413 heads southeast, passing through the small market town of **Winslow** with the attractive **Winslow Hall**. A right turn down a small country lane brings you to **Claydon House**, a fine 18th-century rococo mansion with a Chinese Chippendale room, family portraits, and memorabilia of Florence Nightingale, who was a frequent visitor here. The red brick house was supposedly built by Sir Christopher Wren around 1700.

### The Vale of Aylesbury

The country surrounding Aylesbury is rich, green and fertile, and has for centuries been the home of many famous beef and dairy herds. **Aylesbury** itself is a bustling market town. At its center, a conservation area, is the **Parish Church of St. Mary** (13th century) with an unusual steeple; the spacious market square, and numerous restored half-timbered houses. Near the church is the **Buckinghamshire County Museum**, with a collection of local antiques, the **Aylesbury Gallery**, and the **Special Exhibition Gallery**.

113

## CHILTERN HILLS

Not far away is **The King's Head** pub, whose most famous "regular" was King Henry VIII when he was courting Anne Boleyn. A century later, Aylesbury became an important garrison town for the Parliamentarians during the English Civil War, and the same public house was visited by their leader Oliver Cromwell.

From Aylesbury, you can make several interesting excursions. West along the A41 is the village of **Waddesdon**, and **Waddesdon Manor**, a magnificent French Renaissance-style château built by Baron Ferdinand de Rothschild in the 1870s. It contains 18th-century furniture and tapestries, Sèvres porcelain, manuscripts, and paintings by Rubens and Gainsborough.

Railway enthusiasts will not be disappointed by a detour northwards to **Quainton** and the **Buckinghamshire Railway Centre**, home to a plethora of steam locomotives.

*Above: Windsor Castle is the summer residence of the Royal Family.*

Northeast of Aylesbury, just outside the village of Wing is another Rothschild home, **Ascott House**. Originally a hunting lodge, it was extensively rebuilt at the time of James I. The art collection includes works by Rubens, Hogarth, Gainsborough and Stubbs.

### The Chiltern Hills

Leaving Aylesbury in a southeasterly direction, the A413 enters a delightful river valley at **Wendover**, where among the well-preserved half-timbered houses is Anne Boleyn's cottage.

The road now climbs the gentle, thickly wooded slopes of the Chiltern Hills which rise to around 850 feet (260 m). The beech woods here are among the most beautiful in all England and have long attracted ramblers. These rich stocks of trees have resulted in a flourishing furniture industry in the region's towns such as **High Wycombe**, for centuries a furniture-making center. The **Wycombe Local History and Chair Museum** provides some interesting insights into local history, as well as the process of, and tools required for, making chairs.

North of the town, on the A4128, is **Hughendon Manor**, the Victorian Neo-Gothic home of Benjamin Disraeli, one of the most important Prime Ministers of the last century.

South of Amersham is the village of **Chalfont St. Giles** with the small house of the poet John Milton (1608-1674) and the **Chiltern Open Air Museum** which displays, among other things, a replica Iron Age house and a Victorian farmyard. South of the village, at **Jordans,** is the barn where William Penn and his followers used to convene before the Quaker Meeting House was even built (1688), and before Penn went overseas to the region that was later to become known as Pennsylvania.

## THE THAMES VALLEY

Rising from a source in Gloucestershire, the river Thames winds past Oxford to Windsor, 20 miles (35 km) from the capital. On a hill in the center of this small town is **Windsor Castle,** a commanding structure which for 900 years has served the kings and queens of England as their principal official residence outside the capital.

In 1992, a fire seriously damaged parts of the Royal Apartments and other areas, and repair and restoration will take many years to complete. Nonetheless, the bulk of the castle precincts remain open to visitors – except at times when the Royal Standard is flying over the Round Tower. This indicates that the sovereign is at Windsor, and the castle is then closed to visitors.

The present appearance of this Norman fortress, built by order of William II, owes much to rebuilding under George III and George IV. The burial place of the royal family and the personal chapel of Elizabeth I is **St. George's Chapel** (1475-1528) in Late Perpendicular style with fan vaulting. The entrance, the **King Henry VIII Gate**, was built during the Tudor period in the year 1571.

The **State Apartments** house a superb collection of paintings, with works by such Old Masters as Holbein, Leonardo da Vinci, Raphael, Michelangelo, van Dyck, Rubens, Rembrandt and Canaletto. Other treasures include tapestries, china, porcelain, silver and gold artifacts and, of course, the famous **Queen's Doll's House**, created in 1924 by the architect Sir Edwin Lutyens.

It was at Windsor Castle that Edward III founded the United Kingdom's highest order, the Order of the Garter, in 1348, restricting the number of its members to 26. The story goes that a court lady lost her garter at a banquet, whereupon the king announced, to rescue her from sniggers, that it would be an honor for a knight to wear such a garter. With his order he created a select society of knights who were committed to upholding knightly honor, true to their motto: "*Honi soit qui mal y pense*" (Shame on him who thinks ill of it).

This imposing building is today the largest inhabited castle in the world and Queen Elizabeth's favorite residence. Since Queen Victoria had the castle extended, there are always apartments available for members of the extensive royal family or visiting heads of state.

The castle dominates the landscape for miles around, but Windsor itself, with its half-timbered buildings and winding alleys has much to offer the visitor, from a Town Hall designed by Wren to a range of souvenir and antique shops.

Boat trips can be taken up or down the river Thames as it winds through enchanting parkland. If you prefer to travel on dry land, take a walk to **Windsor Great Park**, which is 2.5 miles (4 km) south of town.

North of town on the A308 is **Runnymede**, where King John signed the

115

## THAMES VALLEY / ETON

Magna Carta in 1215. Today, this is also the site of the John F. Kennedy Memorial.

A short walk across the bridge in Windsor takes you to the little town of **Eton**, famous for its public (i.e. private) school, **Eton College**, founded by King Henry VI in 1440, which claims to have more than twenty Prime Ministers among its past pupils. The boys wear uniform: a black hat and striped trousers. Parts of the college date to the 15th century, such as the late Gothic school chapel (1411) and the oldest schoolroom in England (1443).

Head west on the A308, which roughly follows the Thames, as far as **Maidenhead**, a thriving town with good shopping facilities and many attractive riverside pubs and restaurants.

From Marlow, the road continues to **Henley-on-Thames**, a charming old redbrick town that comes to pulsating life

*Above: Scholars in the traditional academic robes at Founder's Day, All Souls College. Right: Lincoln College Library.*

each year during its international regatta week in July. This great event in the social calendar was started by Prince Albert in 1839.

West of Henley is **Wallingford**, an ancient market town and key river crossing since the days of the Romans, and the lovely little town of **Dorchester-on-Thames**. Occupied since the Bronze Age, the latter is famous for its Norman **abbey** and the half-timbered houses lining High Street.

South of Henley and north of Reading is **Mapledurham**, a red brick manorhouse beside the Thames. Further upstream, at Whitchurch, a toll bridge crosses to the pretty town of **Pangbourne**, with riverside restaurants and boats for hire.

## OXFORD

Oxford is proud of having Britain's oldest university. **Merton College** was founded back in 1266. The oldest colleges are grouped along the south side of High Street (Merton, University College, Corpus Christi) and between "High" and Broad Streets (New College, Jesus, Brasenose, Lincoln, Exeter). But the two largest and most impressive colleges are **Magdalen** (pronounced "Mawdlin") on the right as you cross Magdalen Bridge into the city, built in 1458, and **Christ Church** ("the House") on St. Aldate's Street, on the south side of the city.

The Norman-Early Gothic chapel of Christ Church College, which dates from the first half of the 12th century, was elevated to **cathedral** status in 1546. Its south transept includes a Becket window (c. 1320) as well as five windows by the Pre-Raphaelites Burne-Jones and William Morris. The choir was given fan vaulting around 1500. The whole college concept was based on the architecture of a monastery, linking a cloister, chapel, and community and living spaces. **New College**, built between 1380 and 1386, is a classic example of such a building. The colleges are open to the public most of the time and it is worth taking a guided tour.

It is notable that 24 of Britain's 57 prime ministers were educated at Oxford, and this includes every single prime minister since World War II. Other famous Oxford alumni include Sir Walter Raleigh, Samuel Johnson, Pope Alexander V, Cecil Rhodes, and legion writers and poets, including Shelley, Evelyn Waugh, J.R.R. Tolkien, Dorothy Sayers, and C.S.Lewis.

The name Oxford probably does mean the ford of the oxen. Today, one is saved the difficulty of fording the river by a number of bridges; but certainly the river, here known as the Isis, continues central to the life of the town. A marked contrast to the bustle of the city is a stroll along the idyllic river banks, or even a traditional punting excursion.

In town, the liveliest street is **Cornmarket** with the old defensive tower of St. Michael's. **Carfax** is the name of the crossroads right at the center of Oxford, and it is around Carfax that the townspeople and the university people (the "town and gown") mingle in the stores and covered market. Oxford is a paradise for book lovers, and you'll find some of the largest second-hand bookstores on and around Broad Street.

Broad Street also boasts the greatest concentration of fine buildings of mellow golden stone. At the street's south end are the circular 18th-century **Sheldonian Theatre** (designed by Sir Christopher Wren); the medieval **Divinity School**, with fan vaulting from the 15th century; the first public university library, the **Old Bodleian Library**; and the circular **Radcliffe Camera**, an 18th-century reading room in an English-Italian style.

East from Broad Street runs Holywell Street, lined with historic students' lodgings and the **Holywell Music Room**, Europe's oldest concert hall. On the right is an alley leading to the *Turf*, a popular old pub and beer-garden nestled against the high walls of New College.

## BLENHEIM PALACE / BERKSHIRE

At the other end of Broad Street, running north, is the wide tree-lined St. Giles Street. At the beginning of this street is the **Martyr's Memorial**, which marks the spot where the Protestant bishops Cranmer, Latimer and Ridley were burned in 1556. On the left, facing Beaumont Street, is the oldest museum in England, the **Ashmolean Museum**, with collections of art and antiquities, Greek and Roman pottery, jewelry, and Far Eastern art.

Northwest of Oxford, the A44 towards Stratford-on-Avon brings you to the charming old town of **Woodstock**, which clusters round the gates of magnificent **Blenheim Palace**. Set in extensive parkland, this palace was built in 1701-24 by John Vanburgh for the first Duke of Marlborough. Sir Winston Churchill, a descendant of the Duke, was born at Blenheim and is buried at the nearby village church of Bladon.

*Above: The Bridge of Sighs spans New College Lane.*

The palace stands in the midst of an extensive park which was laid out in French rococo style and is planted with old trees. This green expanse surrounds a building with more than 200 rooms in the palace, ranging from the Churchill memorial rooms to Baroque staterooms with priceless 18th-century tapestries and valuable portraits by such luminaries as van Dyck, Reynolds and Knetter.

### BERKSHIRE

Southwest of Oxford at Uffington a white horse 370 feet (114 m) long carved by the Celts into the chalk downs has given its name to the locality. From White Horse Hill, where there's an Iron Age fort, you have fine views out over the **Vale of the White Horse.**

**Newbury**, once a cloth-trading town, is best known today as one of the leading centers for breeding and training racehorses. There is a large race-course just to the south of the town, and occasionally motorists will have to wait for a string of fine thoroughbreds to cross the road on the way out to their morning or evening exercise.

Besides the attractions associated with horse-racing, Newbury has other historical highlights to interest the visitor. The Battle of Newbury in 1644 was an important turning point in the English Civil War, and both **Newbury Castle** and the **Newbury District Museum** contain interesting exhibits from that and other periods.

Running through the town are the River Kennet and its close partner, the **Kennet and Avon Canal**. Public excursion trips, or private charters, are available in either direction from the town, in a variety of magnificently decorated "narrow boats" (the correct term for canal barges), some of them hauled by massive heavy horses trudging along the tow-paths, just as they were back in the 18th century.

# GUIDEPOST HOME COUNTIES

## HOME COUNTIES
### Accommodation
**HIGH WYCOMBE**: *LUXURY:* **Bell House**, Beaconsfield, tel. 01753 887211. *MODERATE:* **Ethorpe**, Gerrads Cross, tel. 01753 882039. *BUDGET:* **White Hart**, Beaconsfield, tel. 01494 671211. **OXFORD**: *LUXURY:* **Forte Grand Randolph**, Beaumont St., tel. 01865 247481. **The Old Parsonage**, 1 Banbury Rd., tel. 01865 310210. *MODERATE:* **The Old Black Horse**, 102 St. Clements, tel. 01865 244691. **Mount Pleasant**, 76 London Rd., Headington, tel. 01865 62749. *BUDGET:* **Falcon Private Hotel**, 88-90 Abingdon Rd., tel. 01865 722995. **Pickwicks Hotel**, 17 London Rd., Headington, tel. 01865 750587.

### Restaurants
**OXFORD**: *LUXURY:* Out of town to the east at Great Milton, near exit 7 on the M40, **Le Manoir aux Quat' Saisons**, Church Road, tel. 01844 278881. *MODERATE:* **Bath Place**, 4 & 5 Bath Place, Holywell St., tel. 01865 791812. *INEXPENSIVE:* **Munchy Munchy**, 6 Park End Street, tel. 01865 245710.

### Museums
**AYLESBURY**: **Buckinghamshire County Museum**, tel. 01296 88849, all year daily Mon-Sat 10.00-17.30, Sun 11.00-16.00. **BEDFORD**: **Bunyan Meeting House and Museum**, tel. 01234 213722, April-Oct, Tue-Sat 14.00-16.00. July, Aug and Sept 11.00-16.00. **BUCKINGHAM**: **The Old Gaol Museum**, Market Hill, tel. 0128 823020, April-Sept, Nov-Dec Mon-Sat 10.00-16.00, Sun 12.00-16.00, closed Thur. **HERTFORD**: **Hertford Museum**, tel. 01992 582686. Bull Plain, Tue-Sat 10.00-17.00, closed Sun and Mon. **HIGH WYCOMBE**: **Wycombe Local History Museum and Chair Museum**, tel. 01494 421865, Mon-Fri 10.00-17.30. **HITCHIN**: **Hitchin Museum**, tel. 01462 434476, all year daily 10.00-17.00. Sun 14.00-16.30. **LUTON**: **Mossmann Collection, Stockwood Craft Museum**, tel. 01582 38714, April-Oct Wed-Sat 10.00-17.00, Sun 10.00-18.00, Nov-March Fri-Sun 10.00-16.00. **NEWBURY**: **District Museum**, tel. 01635 30511, April-Sept Mon-Sat 10.00-17.00, Sun and Bank Holidays 13.00-17.00, Oct-March Mon-Sat 10.00-16.00, closed Wed. **OXFORD**: **Oxford Museum**, St. Aldate's, tel. 01865 815559, all year Tue-Fri 10.00-16.00, Sat 10.00-17.00. **Ashmolean Museum**, Beaumont St., tel. 01865, open daily all year, except Dec 25 and Easter. **University Museum**, Park Road, tel. 01865 270949, all year Mon-Sat 12.00-17.00. **ST. ALBANS**: **Verulamium Museum**, tel. 01727 819339, Mon-Sat 10.00-17.00, Sun 14.00-17.30. **St. Albans Museum**, tel. 01727 819340, Mon-Sat 10.00-17.00. Sun 14.00-17.00.

### Tips and Trips
**AYLESBURY**: **Waddesdon Manor**, near Aylesbury, tel. 01296 651211, 31 March-16 Oct Thur-Sat 13.00-18.00, Sun and Bank Holiday Mon 11.00-18.00. **BUCKINGHAM**: **Stowe Landscape Gardens**, tel. 01280 822850, 26 March-16 Oct daily. 18 April-1 July Mon, Wed, Fri and Sun. 10.00-17.00. 3 July-4 Sept daily, 5 Sept-21 Oct, Mon, Wed and Fri 22-30 Oct daily, 17-23 Dec daily 10.00-17.00. **CHALFONT ST. GILES**: **Chiltern Open Air Museum**, Newland Park, Gorelands Lane, tel. 01494 872163, April-Oct Wed-Sun 14.00-18.00. **DUNSTABLE DOWNS**: **Whipsnade Animal Park**, tel. 01582 872171, near Ivinghoe, daily except Dec 25, 10.00-18.00; summer Sun and Bank Holiday Mon 10.00-19.00. **HATFIELD**: **Hatfield House**, tel. 01707 262823, 25 March-9 Oct Tue-Sat 12.00-16.00, Sun 13.30-17.00, Bank Holidays 11.00-17.00. **HIGH WYCOMBE**: **Hughendon Manor**, tel. 01494 532580, open 5-27 March Sat and Sun 14.00-18.00. 30 March-31 Oct, Sat 14.00-18.00. Sun and Bank Holiday Mon 12.00-18.00. **JORDANS**: **Mayflower Barn and Quaker Meeting House**, tel. 01494 874146, April-Oct Wed-Sun 10.00-13.00, 14.00-18.00; Nov-March Wed-Sun 10.00-13.00, 14.00-16.00. **KNEBWORTH**: **Knebworth House**, near Stevenage, tel. 01438 812661, 26 March-2 Oct. **LUTON**: **Luton Hoo**, tel. 01582 22955, open 29 March-16 Oct, Tue, Wed, Thur, pre-booked groups only. Otherwise Fri, Sat and Sun 12.00-17.00. Closed Mon except Bank Holiday Mon 10.30-17.00. **OLD WARDEN**: **Shuttleworth Collection**, near Biggleswade, tel. 01767 627745, daily 10.00-16.00. **OXFORD**: **The Oxford Story**, tel. 01892 510001, daily except Dec 25 and Jan 1. April-Oct 9.30-17.00; July and Aug 9.30-19.00; Nov-March 10.00-16.00. **ST. ALBANS**: **Hatfield House**, tel. 01707 262823, 25 March-9 Oct Tue-Sat 12.00-16.00, Sun 13.30-17.00. **WADDESDON**: **Waddesdon Manor**, tel. 0126 651211, 3 March-16 Oct; Thur, Sat, 13.00-18.00. Sun and Bank Holiday Mon 11.00-18.00. **WINDSOR**: **Windsor Castle**, tel. 01753 3831118, daily Nov-March 10.00-18.00. April-Oct 10.00-17.00. **WING**: **Ascott House**, near Aylesbury, tel. 01926 688242, 12 April-30 Sept Tue-Sun 14.00-18.00. **WOBURN**: **Woburn Abbey**, tel. 01525 29666, 27 March-30 Oct daily 10.00-18.00, rest of the year Sat and Sun 11.00-18.00. **Woburn Safari Park**, tel. 01525 290407, March-Oct 10.00-17.00 daily, Nov-Feb Sat and Sun 10.00-15.00. **WOODSTOCK**: **Blenheim Palace**, near Oxford, tel. 01993 811325, mid March-31 Oct daily 10.30-17.30.

### Tourist Information
**HIGH WYCOMBE**: 6, Corn Market, tel. 01494 421892. **OXFORD**: The Old School, Gloucester Green, tel. 01865 726871.

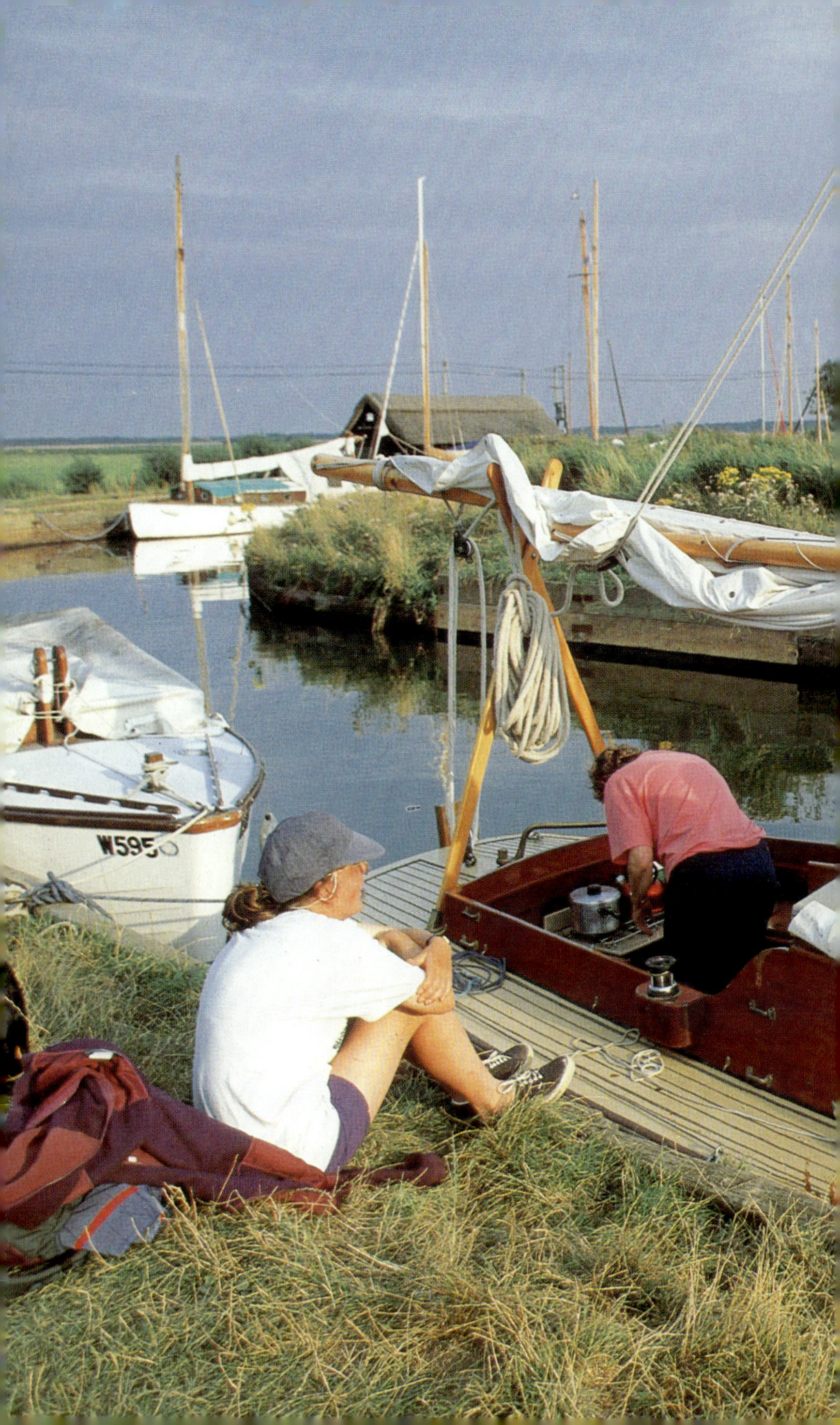
W595

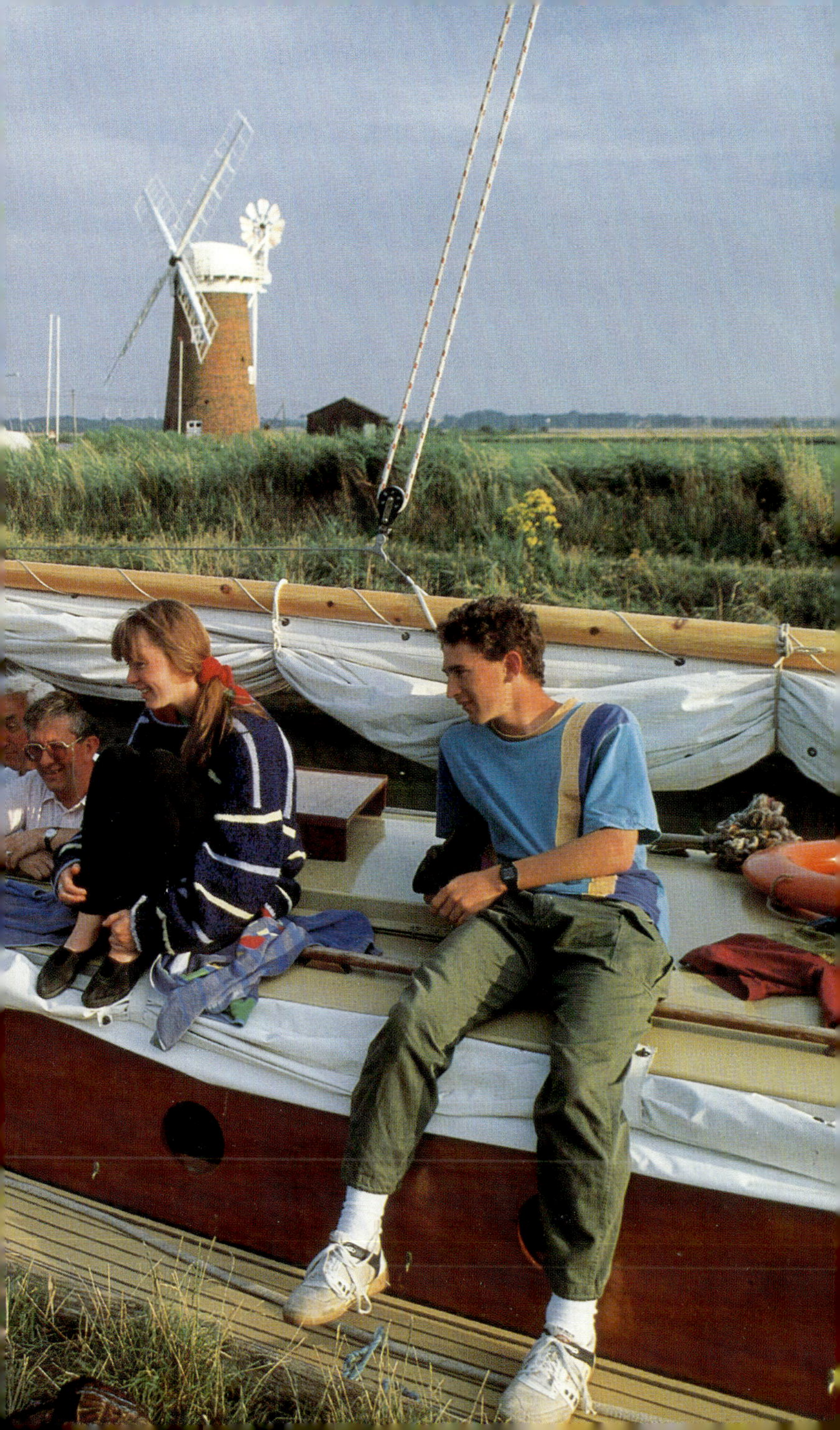

*EAST ANGLIA*

# EAST ANGLIA

**CAMBRIDGESHIRE**
**THE FENS**
**NORFOLK**
**NORWICH**
**SUFFOLK COAST**
**ESSEX**

The region of England known as East Anglia comprises the counties of Cambridgeshire, Norfolk, Suffolk and Essex. Only at a second glance do the attractions is of this unspectacular, mostly flat landscape become evident: the horizon seems infinite, a glorious light falls on the fertile fields and quiet villages with half-timbered buildings and thatched cottages. Great stately homes, castles and cathedrals point to the historic heritage of this part of England. John Constable, England's best-known landscape painter, masterfully succeeding in depicting the interplay of light, clouds and peaceful landscape in his paintings; Gainsborough and Turner were also inspired by East Anglia's magic.

East Anglia has the lowest annual rainfall in Great Britain (21 inches/550 mm), but its good soil has permitted intensive farming which brought great prosperity to the region. Since Antiquity, it's attracted a wide range of peoples: Celts, Romans, Saxons, Normans and Danes settled here and left their mark on local art and culture. In the 17th century, Flemings fled to East Anglia – especially to Norwich and Colchester – bringing with them their weaving skills, which became famous throughout the whole country.

The gentle rolling grassland of the **Brecklands** and the wide plains of the **Norfolk Broads** are ideal for long rambles or cycling tours, while the many lakes, bays and rivers are a paradise for anglers and watersports fans. The largely unspoiled marsh landscapes of the **Fens** and the coastal regions have such an extraordinarily wide selection of flora and fauna that many bird-watchers and botanists spend their vacations here. Traditional seaside resorts stud the coast, offering a wide range of activities and long sand and gravel beaches. Nor should East Anglia's tasty cuisine be ignored: fresh asparagus, Suffolk ham, good solid potato dishes, and freshly-caught fish, lobster, oysters and crab.

## CAMBRIDGESHIRE

**Cambridge**, the most attractive town in the east of England, is world-famous as the seat of a venerable university. The town takes its name from a bridge over the river Cam. In the 13th century, students from Oxford settled here, and soon the first college, **Peterhouse**, was founded. By 1352 there were already seven colleges. What is special about the college system, as distinct from the large,

*Preceding pages: A houseboat idyll near Horsey Mill, Norfolk. Left: Little Hall, a half-timbered house in Lavenham, Suffolk.*

*CAMBRIDGE*

impersonal universities on the Continent, is that students live, study and eat within their colleges, and receive more personal attention in their studies. Each student has an in-house tutor, a professor who guides his or her academic progress; the most important unit of instruction here is not a lecture, but a tutorial. The college system has crossed the Atlantic and is emulated, if not exactly copied, at such elite American universities as Harvard and Yale.

Some of the university's most traditional colleges are **St. John's College**, **Queen's College**, **Trinity College** and **King's College**, where many original buildings survive to remind us that the colleges were originally organized on the model of monasteries. This is why all of the historical colleges have cloisters around which are grouped living quarters, dining halls and lecture halls.

*Above: The Mathematical Bridge at Queen's College, Cambridge. Right: Inside the crossing-tower in Ely Cathedral.*

Henry VI laid the cornerstone of **King's College Chapel** in 1446, starting the construction of one of the loveliest Late Gothic buildings in the land with richly decorated windows in the Perpendicular style and a fan vaulting ceiling 78 feet high (24 m). In 1959, the chapel was presented with a painting by Rubens, *The Adoration of the Magi*, which now adorns the altar. Try to visit in the late afternoon when the college choir is singing evensong.

Musts on a walk around the city include the **Bridge of Sighs** at St. John's College and the **Mathematical Bridge** at Queen's College; the latter is so named because the balance of forces had been calculated so precisely that no nails were needed for its construction.

The **Fitzwilliam Museum**, Cambridge's leading museum, displays, in addition to Egyptian, Greek and Roman collections, a notable collection of paintings that includes works by leading British artists such as Hogarth, Turner and Gainsborough.

The **Holy Sepulchre church** in Bridge Street, one of only four round churches remaining in England today and certainly the oldest (c. 1130), is well worth a visit.

## THE FENS

North of Cambridge stretch the Fens, an area of marshland extending more than 1,350 square miles (3,500 sq. km). The Romans founded many settlements here, growing grain and winning sea salt along the coast. To create more arable land, they started cutting drainage canals in some of the marshes; these also served as transportation routes. But it was not until the 17th century that the Dutchman Sir Cornelius Vermuyden actually succeeded in reclaiming extensive tracts of marshland for farming. Initially there were unforeseen problems: when the water was drained, the peat moors sank to such an extent that windmill-operated pumps had to be used to get water into the main canals. In the 19th century, the windmills were replaced by steam engines. At **Stretham**, near Ely, one of these old engine houses is still standing. But the efforts paid off: today, the fields of the fens are among the most productive in the country.

On the western edge of the fens is the pleasant town of **Huntingdon**, where Oliver Cromwell was born in 1599. In nearby **St. Ives**, a 15th-century stone bridge crosses the Ouse. The small chapel in the middle of the bridge is one of four surviving medieval bridge churches in the country. In **Kimbolton** you can see the castle where Catherine of Aragon, Henry VIII's first wife, spent her last years.

North of Huntingdon is the village of **Stilton**. Actually, this village never actually produced cheese; but in the **Bell Inn**, a major stopping-point on the road to London, the Leicestershire and Fenland farmers came to send off their wares south, including their cheese, which thus became known as "Stilton cheese."

**Peterborough** today is an industrial town with modern shopping arcades in

*PETERBOROUGH / WISBECH / ELY*

the city center. In 654, an abbey was founded on a swampy site, and the impressive 12th-century **cathedral** stands on this spot today. The bones of St. Oswald and particularly of St. Thomas à Becket made the former abbey church (Peterborough was not promoted to a bishopric until 1541) a place of pilgrimage and brought great prosperity to the abbey.

The cathedral is famed for its west façade with three giant portals 78 feet high (24 m). Striking, too, is the spacious majesty of the interior, where heavy arcades and serrated arches show a strong Norman influence. The painted wooden ceiling is one of the most elaborate in the country. The cathedral is also where Catherine of Aragon is buried.

On the river nearby there are a number of historical buildings, including **St. John's Church**, the Guildhall and the Customs House. The **Peterborough Museum and Art Gallery** has some archaeological exhibits of interest.

East of Peterborough is **Wisbech**, the area's most architecturally interesting city after Cambridge. Georgian houses along the canal hearken back to their Dutch models. **Peckover House**, an 18th-century town house on the North Brink bridge, is one of the most attractive examples of the Georgian style. The owner Jonathan Peckover, a Quaker, founded his own bank, which later become Barclays Bank. Wisbech is a seaport, too, and the surrounding tulip fields and orchards turn the area into a sea of flowers in the spring.

Northeast of Cambridge is the enchanting town of **Ely** with its famous **cathedral**. The name Ely means *eel island*, with the *-y* coming from the Old English for *island* (other forms are *-ey* and *-ea*, reflected in many London place-names); and the city really did rise like an island about 65 feet (20 m) above the marshlands before they were drained. You have the best view of the cathedral from the

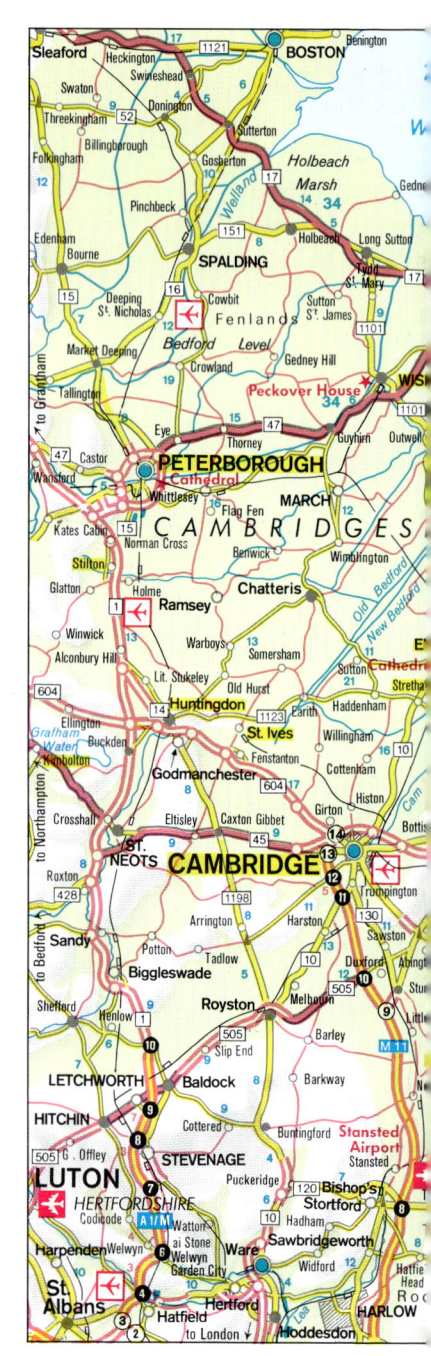

126

EAST ANGLIA
0 10 km
0 10 miles
NORFOLK
SUFFOLK
Brecklands
Blakeney Point Pt.
Wells-next-the-Sea
Burnham Overy Staithe
Brancaster
Burnham Market
Holkham Hall
Burnham Thorpe
Stiffkey
Blakeney
Cley
Weybourne
Sheringham
Cromer
West Runton
Overstrand
Heacham
Docking
Fring
Binham
Holt
Snettisham
Little Walsingham
Dersingham
Sandringham House
Sandringham
Fakenham
Briston
Edgefield Green
Roughton
Thorpe Market
Mundesley
Keswick
Happisburgh
North Walsham
Saxthorpe
Ingworth
Aylsham
Sea Palling
Stalham
Waxham
Hickling
Horsey
Catfield
Norfolk Broads
Hemsby
Horning
Winterton
Scratby
California
Castle
Hillington
Harpley
Great Massingham
Guist
Cawston
Reepham
Marsham
Bure
Wensum
LYNN
Gayton
Brisley
N. Elmham
Bawdeswell
Horstead
Wroxham
Ranworth
E. Wynch
Litcham
Setchey
Narborough
Newton
East Dereham
Attlebridge
Drayton
Filby
Caister-on-Sea
Wendling
Hockering
Honingham
Easton
Blofield
Acle
Runcton
Necton
NORWICH
GREAT YARMOUTH
Swaffham
Trowse Newton
Stradsett
Shipdham
Hethersett
Gorleston
Oxborough Hall
Watton
Kimberley
Hilborough
Swardeston
Yare
Stoke Ferry
Wissey
Caston
Hingham
Wymondham
Swainsthorpe
Reedham
Hopton
Haddiscoe
Loddon
Corton
Methwold
Mundford
G.t Ellingham
Ashwellthorpe
Hempnall
Feltwell
Grimes Graves
Attleborough
LOWESTOFT
Long Stratton
Oulton Broad
Croxton
Larling
New Buckenham
Bungay
Beccles
Little Ouse
Weeting Castle
Thet
E. Harling
Mettingham
Pakefield
N.th Cove
Brandon
Pulham
Lakenheath
THETFORD
Kenninghall
Homersfield
Kessingland
Elveden
Diss
Dickleburgh
Harleston
Brampton
Wrentham
Garboldisham
Scole
Covehithe
Euston
Waveney
Halesworth
Wangford
Southwold
Botesdale
Fressingfield
Walpole
Blythburg
Walberswick
Mildenhall
Barton Mills
Stradbroke
Stanton
Ingham
Lackford
Eye
Laxfield
Bramfield
West Stowe
Ixworth
Yoxford
Dunwich
Kentford
Thwaite
Dennington
Westleton
BURY ST. EDMUNDS
Minsmere Bird Sanctuary
Country Park, Anglo Village
Saxted Green
NEWMARKET
Debenham
Saxmundham
Leiston
Beyton
Framlingham
Woolpit
Farnham
Bradfield Combust
Stowmarket
Deben
Thorpeness
Alde
Wickhambrook
G.t Finborough
Wickham Market
Aldeburgh
Needham Market
Tunstall
Alpheton
Ufford
Orford Ness
Lavenham
Bildeston
Claydon
HAVERHILL
Clare
G.t Blakenham
Woodbridge
Sturmer
Stour
Long Melford
Monks Eleigh
IPSWICH
Brightwell
Sandlings
Baythorn End
Hadleigh
Hintlesham
Alderton
Sudbury
Castle Hedingham
Boxford
Bawdsey
Flatford Mill
Trimley
Bures
Stratford St. Mary
East Bergholt
Swan Street
Halstead
Nayland
Shotley
FELIXSTOWE
Gosfield
Dedham
Manningtree
HARWICH
Wakes Colne
Dovercourt
Earls Colne
Ardleigh
Wix
ESSEX
Paycocke's House
BRAINTREE
Castle
Weeley
Ferry to mainland
Ferry to Zeebrugge
Mark's Tey
Walton-on-the-Naze
Rayne
Coggeshall
COLCHESTER
Thorpe
Kelvedon
Brightlingsea
G.t Clacton
Frinton
Abberton
Tiptree
Witham
Lit. Waltham
Mersea I.
St. Osyth
Hatfield Peverel
Tolleshunt d'Arcy
CLACTON-on-Sea
Maldon
West Mersea
Chelmsford
to London
Tollesbury
Bradwell on Sea

## NORFOLK

**King's Lynn**, on the east bank of the Ouse, is only some 2.5 miles (4 km) from the bay of the Wash, and was once one of the most important seaports in England. *Lynn* is a word of Celtic origin meaning *lake*, and the lake provided both the fish and the salt the inhabitants traded in. For a short time, King's Lynn was a Hanseatic town, which meant inclusion in an extensive network of maritime trading, and thus considerable prosperity. Henry VIII granted further market rights to the city, which is how Lynn became King's Lynn. At the **Saturday Market** by the river stands St. Margaret's church, whose two great towers can be seen from miles away. Opposite is the Guildhall, where since 1978 the sword and cup of King John Lackland, the brother of Richard the Lionheart, have been exhibited.

From the Guildhall, Queen's Street brings you to **Clifton House** (16th/17th centuries) with its single watchtower. Further north, on the quayside, is the Palladian-style **Customs House**; continuing north from here, King's Street is lined with many magnificent Tudor and Georgian houses.

At the end of the street is **St. George's Guildhall**, which served as a theater in the 18th century and today is a museum of art and the theater. The adjacent **Tuesday Market** is another King's Lynn attraction. It's surrounded by a maze of narrow streets with beautiful old houses.

North of King's Lynn is **Heacham**, a little village in the midst of fields of lavender. After the flowers are harvested in July, they are distilled to extract their essence. A lavender-water distillery is open to the public at Fring.

The cliffs at **Hunstanton**, at the tip of the peninsula, are striped with different-colored layers of rock. For thousands of years, the surf has washed against the coast, eroding the shore and bringing these rock strata to light.

northwest, from where you can clearly discern the building's quite considerable bulk (536 ft/164 m long, 216 ft/66 m high). Building started in the 11th century and was completed after 107 years. In the 14th century, the crossing-tower collapsed and was replaced by an octagonal wooden steeple with a lantern.

An excellent example of Norman sculpture is the **Prior's Gate** in the west aisle. The tympanum shows Christ presiding at the Last Judgment. Opposite the west façade is the 17th-century **Bishop's Palace**. An attractive walk leads from the cathedral along the Ouse to **Cherry Hill Park**.

South of Ely at Soham is the **Wicken Fen Nature Reserve**, where you can get a sense of the original flora and fauna of the fen marshlands. As the reserve has not been drained, the ground here is higher than elsewhere.

*Above: Windmills are still typical of the East Anglian landscape. Right: An amusement park on the promenade in Great Yarmouth.*

In **Burnham Thorpe,** Lord Nelson was born in 1758; he is remembered in the local church. Southwest of **Wells-next-the-Sea** (a place famous for its boiled snails) is **Raynham Hall,** where Viscount Townshend lived in the 18th century. He invented crop rotation, thus making a significant contribution to the agricultural revolution in England.

Between Sea Palling and Great Yarmouth on the coast, and extending as far as Norwich, stretch the **Broads,** a lowland plain full of lakes covering over 120 square miles (300 sq. km). The lakes were created by the large-scale removal of peat for fuel. Today, the Broads are especially prized by yachtsmen, motorboat cruisers and anglers; boat tours depart from **Wroxham**. A special feature of the region are the different patterns in the thatch of the cottages.

**Great Yarmouth** is the largest coastal town in Norfolk. Before the city started specializing in supplying the drilling rigs out in the North Sea, herring fishing was the cornerstone of its economy. Yarmouth is also a popular seaside resort with a beach nearly 6 miles (9 km) long. The town center suffered considerable bomb damage in the war, but the **Rows**, a network of narrow streets with old houses, managed to survive.

The **Town Hall** on Hall Quay contains what is probably the most authentic portrait of Lord Nelson, painted by Matthew Keymer in 1801. The **Sailors' Home Museum** on Marine Parade displays a large number of ship models.

## NORWICH AND THE BRECKLANDS

For 900 years, the county town of **Norwich** has been the seat of the bishops of eastern England. The city boasts no fewer than 32 medieval churches; only London can claim more. With a city center which has grown harmoniously over the centuries, Norwich is one of the most pleasant cities in the country to live in. Around **Market Square**, itself one of the largest and most important in East Anglia, are

## NORWICH

ranged the 15th-century **Guildhall**, the **City Hall** (13th century), and the Library (1963). To the south, the church of **St. Peter Mancroft** in Perpendicular style stands on the square in front of the **Royal Theatre** and the **Assembly Rooms** (used for concerts and the like). Passing through the Art Nouveau **Royal Arcade**, you'll come to the base of the castle mound, topped by the 12th-century **Castle**. At the center of this complex is a Norman tower which served as a prison until 1884. Today, the castle houses an archaeological museum, and collections of weapons and paintings.

North of the castle is the **Bridewell Museum** which exhibits local products such as silk shawls, Mackintosh sweets and the first wire netting machine in the world (1844). Right beside the museum is the **Old Curiosity Shop**, which presents another specialty of the town, the famed *Colman's mustard*. John Robinson, pastor of the Pilgrim Fathers, once preached in nearby **St. Andrew's church**. Princess Street leads to **Elm Hill**, a steep cobbled street with a plethora of inviting shops in historic buildings. West of Elm Hill, at the Maddermarket (dyers' market) is **Strangers' Hall**, named for the first Flemish weavers who fled to Norwich as religious refugees. Dating from the late Middle Ages, the building houses a museum of costume and furniture.

The Norman-Gothic **Cathedral** has the second-highest tower in England (314 ft/ 96 m). Building started in 1096 and was completed in 1145. In the early Norman nave with its 14 crossbeams, the windows, in Decorated and Perpendicular styles, have been preserved. Notice the richly-decorated misericords in the choir and the keystones of the arches and capitals. Northeast of the cathedral, **Riverside Walk** leads along the river Wensum past Cow Tower (part of the old city walls) to the 14th-century **Bishop's Bridge**, one of the oldest bridges in England.

*Above: Riverside Walk. Right: Shopping in the Royal Arcade (both in Norwich).*

## THE BRECKLANDS / SUFFOLK

On the western fringes of the city is the campus of the **University of East Anglia**, built in the 1960s in what the students think of as a modern brutalist style, with residences in the form of ziggurats. The creative writing course here, led by Malcolm Bradbury, has produced a slew of successful young writers, including Ian McEwen and Kazuo Ishiguro (*The Remains of the Day*). Also on campus is the **Sainsbury Centre for the Visual Arts**, a collection of modern art with works by Picasso, Giacometti and Moore.

### The Brecklands

Southwest of Norwich is **Thetford**, a bishopric until the 11th century and the birthplace of Thomas Paine, who later crossed the Atlantic and actively worked to bring about American independence. In Thetford, too, you can still see sections and ruins of five of 80 former monasteries and nunneries, as well as a well-preserved medieval motte, castle hill.

North of Thetford, in the wooded **Brecklands**, are **Grimes Graves**, an archaeological site where neolithic flints, spear- and arrow heads have been found. Further north is **Oxborough Hall**, one of the best-preserved medieval castles in Norfolk. At **Mildenhall**, on the river Lark, one of the greatest Roman treasure troves was found in 1946. Called the "Thetford Treasure," it is exhibited today in the British Museum.

**Bury St. Edmunds**, south of Thetford, is named after King Edmund who was buried here after being killed by the Danes in 870. The picturesque ruins of the famous **Benedictine Abbey** (11th century) can be seen in the town's park. The massive Abbey Gate was added later in Perpendicular Style. On November 20, 1214, the mightiest nobles in the land met in the abbey to proclaim the *Magna Carta* and to force King John Lackland to accept it (which he finally did in June, 1215). Worth a visit is one of the oldest houses of East Anglia, **Moyse's House** (12th century), now a museum, and the **Church of St. Mary** (15th century), near the Norman Gate. It contains the grave of Mary Tudor.

**Newmarket**, on the border of Cambridgeshire, is the home of the *Jockey Club*, the horse-racing control board founded in 1840, as well as the **National Horseracing Museum**. You will need a permit to visit stables in Newmarket, but anyone can enjoy watching the thoroughbreds at exercise in the fields, free of charge.

## SUFFOLK

Although rich in rivers, the coastal region of **Suffolk** was not able to develop any major North Sea ports due to coastal erosion. **Dunwich**, for example, an important port in the Middle Ages with a large number of monasteries, is today below sea level.

Further south is **Aldeburgh**, a favorite holiday resort with good hotels. Every

## IPSWICH / COLCHESTER

*Above: Brewing has a long tradition in Suffolk.*

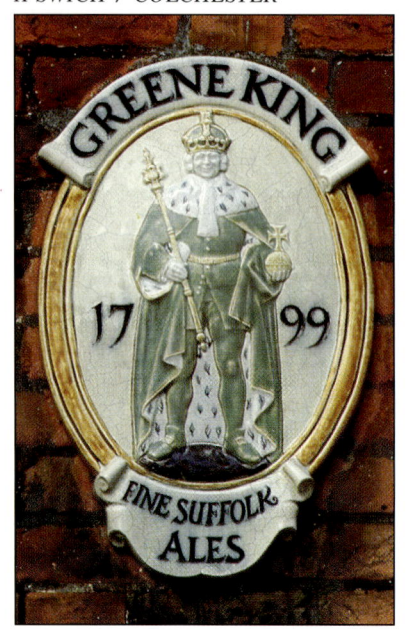

summer, the town hosts the Aldeburgh Music Festival, founded in 1948 by British composer Benjamin Britten, who lived here until his death in 1976.

At the mouth of the river Deben is one of the largest freight ports in Britain, **Felixstowe**. There's regular ferry service to the Continent from here and from neighboring Harwich.

In the past, however, it was the port of **Ipswich** which was the more important transportation hub. Worth seeing here is the **Ancient House** in the Buttermarket, which is decorated with a wealth of ornate Baroque stuccowork. Also well worth a visit is the **Christchurch Mansion** in Christchurch Park in the north part of the city center. It now houses an art gallery with works by Constable and Gainsborough.

The region west of Ipswich is known as "Constable Country," as it was both the home and inspiration of the works of the famous landscape painter John Constable. Constable was born the son of a miller in 1776 in East Bergholt. He studied painting in London, but kept returning, time and again, to his beloved homeland to paint there. Thus were created such works as *The Millstream*, which hangs in the Christchurch Mansion in Ipswich, or *Flatford Mill*, depicting the painter's place of birth (in the Tate Gallery, London).

The other great painter of East Anglia, Thomas Gainsborough, was born in **Sudbury**, also on the Stour, in 1727, the son of a clothmaker. His birthplace at 43 Gainsborough Street become a museum in 1958; here, you can see not only a number of his drawings, engravings and some of his paintings, but also private memorabilia. Unlike Constable, Gainsborough painted portraits, which had the advantage of being a dependable source of income.

### ESSEX

**Colchester** is said to be Britain's oldest recorded town; settled in the 1st century BC by the Trinovantes, it was called *Camulodunum*. Surviving from the Roman period are the ruined walls of a temple, later incorporated into the Norman castle. The castle today houses an **archaeological museum** with very extensive Roman collections. Opposite the castle, a former church now holds a **natural history museum**. Numerous Georgian houses, art galleries, and green parks combine to make Colchester a rewarding destination.

On the border of Cambridgeshire is **Saffron Walden**, an attractive little town known for growing crocuses, from which saffron is harvested for the cloth trade. South of Saffron Walden is the pretty thatched town of **Thaxted**. Dominating the town are its two trademarks, a 14th-century church – one of the largest in Essex – and an old windmill.

## CAMBRIDGESHIRE
### Accommodation
**CAMBRIDGE**: *LUXURY:* **The University Arms Hotel**, 154 Cheston Road, tel. 01223 35388. *MODERATE:* **Gonville Hotel**, Gonville Place, tel. 01223 66611. **Royal Cambridge Lodge**, 139 Huntingdon Road, tel. 01223 352833. **Garden House Hotel**, Granta Place, Mill Lane, tel. 01223 63421. *BUDGET:* **Assis Guesthouse**, 193 Cherry Hinton Rd., tel. 01223 246648.
**STILTON**: **Bell Inn**, tel. 01733 371111.

### Museums
**CAMBRIDGE**: **Fitzwilliam Museum**, Trumpington St., tel. 01233 332900, Tue-Sat 10.00-17.00 (paintings 14.00-17.00), Sun 14.15-17.00. **PETERBOROUGH**: **Museum and Art Gallery**, Priestgate, tel. 01733 343329, Tue-Sat 10.00-17.00.

### Tips and Trips
**ELY**: **Oliver Cromwell's House**, St. Mary's Street, tel. 01353 662062, open daily April-Sept 10.00-17.00. **Ely Cathedral**, tel. 01353 667735, open all year, summer 7.00-19.00, winter 16.30-18.00 Mon-Sat.

### Tourist Information
**CAMBRIDGE**: Wheeler Street, tel. 01223 322640. **ELY**: Cromwell's House, 29 St. Mary's St., tel. 01353 662062. **HUNTINGDON**: The Library, Princes St., tel. 01480 388588. **PETERBOROUGH**: 45 Bridge St., tel. 01733 317336.

## NORFOLK
### Accommodation
**GREAT YARMOUTH**: *LUXURY:* **Imperial**, North Drive, tel. 01493 851113. *BUDGET:* **Spindrift**, 36 Wellesley Rd., tel. 01493 858674.
**KING'S LYNN**: *LUXURY:* **Congham Hall**, Grimston, tel. 01485 600250.
*BUDGET:* **Sixty One Hotel**, 61 King George V Avenue, tel. 01553 774485.
**NORWICH**: *MODERATE:* **Beeches Hotel & Victorian Gardens**, 4-6 Earlham Rd., tel. 01603 621167. *BUDGET:* **The Corner Guesthouse**, 62 Earlham Rd., tel. 01603 627928.

### Museums
**NORWICH**: **Sainsbury Collection**, Sainsbury Centre for the Visual Arts, University of East Anglia, tel. 01603 56060, Tue-Sun 12.00-17.00

### Tips and Trips
**WELLS-NEXT-THE-SEA**: **Holkham Hall**, tel. 01328 710733, open 29 May-30 Sept Sun-Thur 13.30-17.00.

### Tourist Information
**GREAT YARMOUTH**: Marine Parade, tel. 01493 842195. **KING'S LYNN**: The Old Gaol House, Saturday Market Place, tel. 01553 763044. **NORWICH**: The Guildhall, Gaol Hill, tel. 01603 666071.

## SUFFOLK
### Accommodation
**BURY ST. EDMUNDS**: *LUXURY:* **Hamling House Hotel**, Kiln Lane, Elmswell, tel. 01359 230934. *BUDGET:* **Ravenwood Hall Hotel**, Rougham, tel. 01359 270345.
**IPSWICH**: *LUXURY:* **Belstead Brook Hotel**, Belstead Road, tel. 01473 684241.
*MODERATE:* **Queens Cliff House**, Queens Cliff Road, tel. 01473 690293.

### Museums
**BURY ST. EDMUNDS**: **Bury St. Edmunds Art Gallery**, tel. 01284 762081, all year Tue-Sat 10.30-16.30. **NEWMARKET**: **National Horseracing Museum**, 99 High St., tel. 01638 667333, open 29 March-4 Dec Tue-Sat 10.00-17.00, Sun 14.00-17.00, Sun 12.00-17.00.

### Tips and Trips
**FRAMLINGHAM**: **Framlingham Castle**, tel. 012728 724189, open April-Sept 10.00-18.00. Oct-March, Tue-Sun 10.00-16.00.
**SNAPE MALTINGS**: **Concert Hall**, Britten Music Festival; ticket office tel. 01728 453543.
**SUDBURY**: **Gainsborough's House**, 46 Gainsborough St., tel. 01787 372958, Tue-Sat 10.00-17.00, Sun 14.00-17.00.

### Tourist Information
**BURY ST. EDMUNDS**: 6 Angel Hill, tel. 01284 764667. **IPSWICH**: St. Stephen's Church, St. Stephen's Lane, tel. 01473 258070. **NEWMARKET**: 63 The Rookery, tel. 01638 667200. **SUDBURY**: Town Hall, Market Hill, tel. 01787 881320.

## ESSEX
### Accommodation
**COLCHESTER**: *LUXURY:* **Butterfly Hotel**, Old Ipswich Road, tel. 01206 230900. **Mill Hotel Periquito**, East St., tel. 01206 865022.
*MODERATE:* **Peveril Hotel**, 51, North Hill, tel. 01206 574001. **Butlers**, Colne Rd., Bures Hamlet, tel. 01787 227243, very pleasant, recommended. *BUDGET:* **Trust House Forte**, East Horndon, A127 Little Chef, tel. 01277 810819.
**SAFFRON WALDEN**: *LUXURY:* **The Crown House Hotel**, Great Chesterford, tel. 01799 530515.

### Museums
**COLCHESTER**: **Colchester Castle Museum**, tel. 01206 712931, Mon-Sat 10.00-16.30, Sun 14.00-17.00, March-Nov only. **SAFFRON WALDEN**: **Saffron Walden Museum**, tel. 01799 510333, 3-4 April 14.30-17.00, 5 April-31 Oct Mon-Sat 10.00-17.00, Sun 14.30-17.00. 1 Nov-31 March, Tue-Sat 11.00-16.00, Sun 14.00-16.30. Closed Dec 25 and 26.

### Tourist Information
**COLCHESTER**: 1 Queen Street, tel. 01206 282920. **SAFFRON WALDEN**: 1 Market Place, tel. 01799 51044.

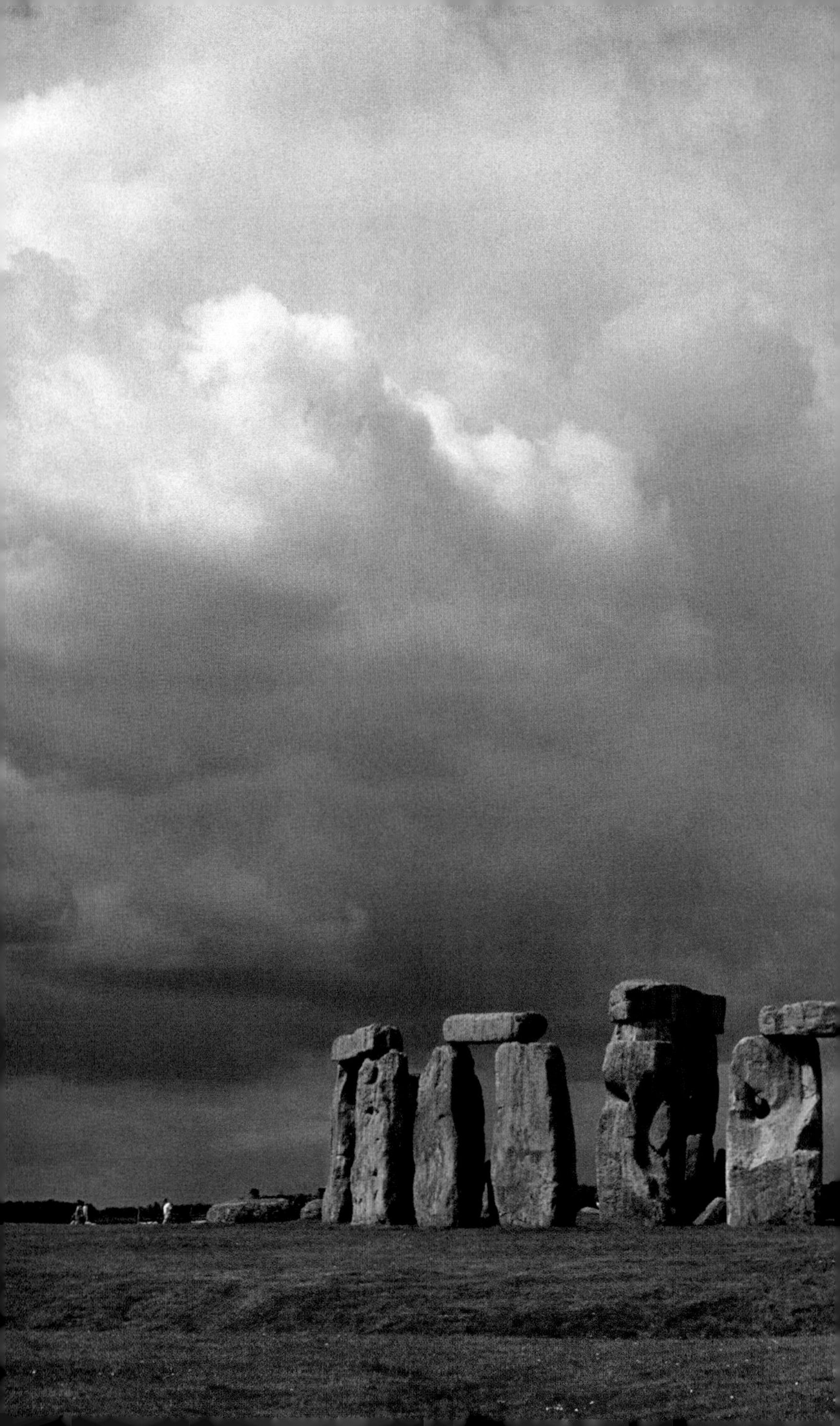

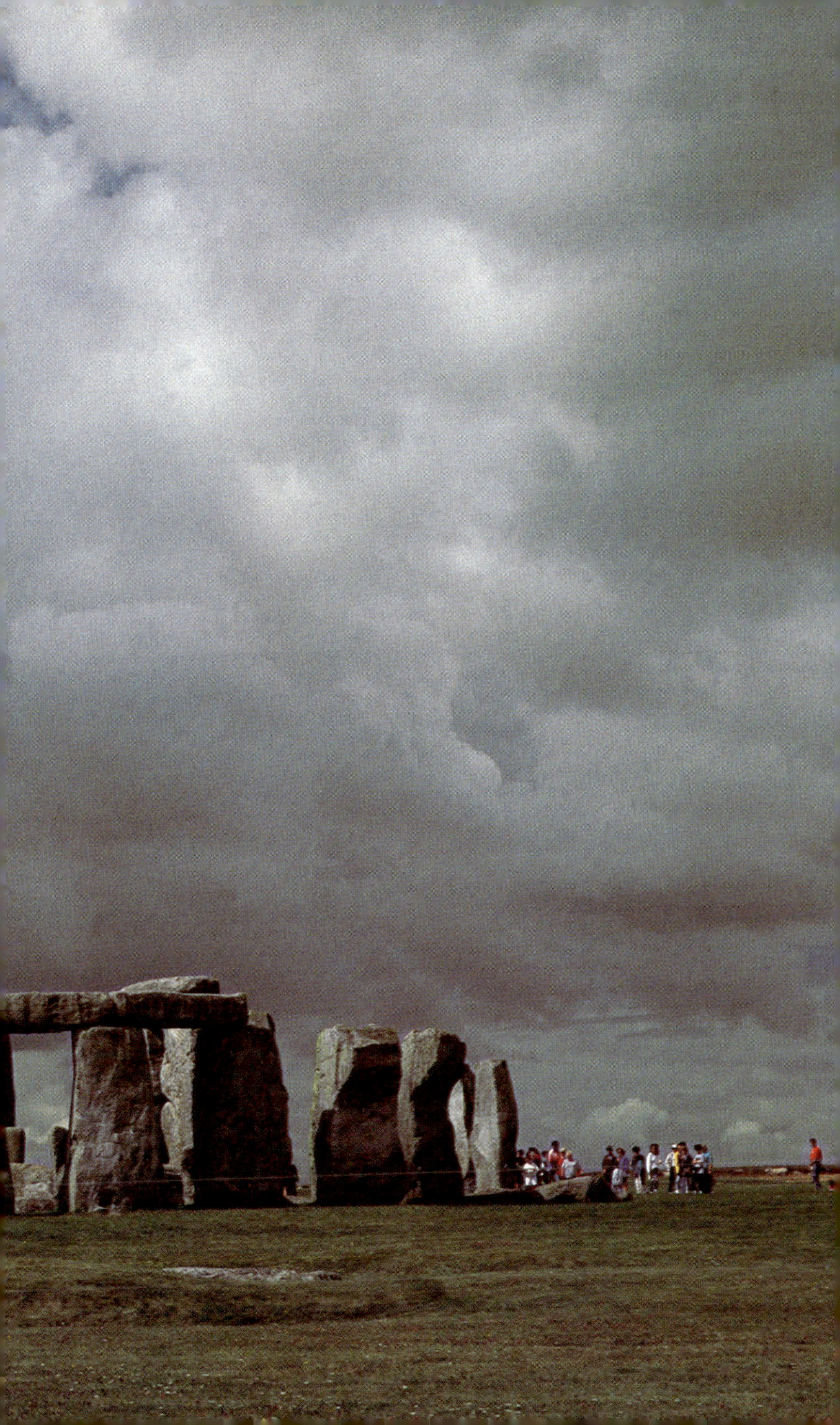

THE WEST COUNTRY

# THE WEST COUNTRY

AROUND STONEHENGE
SALISBURY
SOMERSET
BRISTOL / BATH
DEVON / CORNWALL
NORTH DEVON COAST

---

Southwest England has the mildest climate in the British Isles, and an exceptionally beautiful coastline. This idyllic countryside epitomizes the ideal of rural England as every traveler imagines it, with thatched cottages, hedge-lined roads and gently rolling moorland.

The region, also known as the West Country, is associated with many romantic tales and legends – not least with King Arthur – and has provided a setting for countless novels, from Daphne du Maurier's *Jamaica Inn* to Sir Arthur Conan Doyle's *The Hound of the Baskervilles*.

## AROUND STONEHENGE

In the county of Wiltshire near Amesbury is the most famous prehistoric site in England: the circular megalithic temple of Stonehenge, built between 3000 and 1500 BC. The site consists of a ring wall some 370 feet (114 m) in diameter. On the inner side of this ring, 56 hollows have been discovered; these doubtless served as graves.

During the second phase of building, around 2100 BC, a circle of 82 dolorite bluestones were transported in from

*Preceding pages: Stonehenge. Left: The picturesque coast at the Bedruthan Steps attracts tourists and seagulls alike.*

Wales; but this no longer exists. Around 2000 BC, heavy sandstone blocks known as sarsens, weighing up to 50 tons, were brought down from the Marlborough Downs and set up at the center of the site in the form of a horseshoe. Around this was a ring of rough arches consisting of 30 blocks of sandstone supporting flat lintel stones a yard thick. 500 years later, more bluestones were set up in another horseshoe form at the center, arranged around an altar stone. More than 300 barrows in the neighborhood suggest that Stonehenge probably had an important position in a cult of the dead. It also seems probable that it had some astronomical function, in view of the fact that the stones are exactly aligned with the winter and summer solstices; this may also indicate that the site served as a center for a sun-worshippers' cult.

Wiltshire has no fewer than 4,500 prehistoric sites, some from as early as 4,000 BC. West of Marlborough are Avebury and Silbury Hill. The mysterious stone circles of **Avebury**, the largest neolithic cult site in Europe, 980 feet (300 m) in diameter, were laid out between 2500 and 2000 BC using monoliths weighing up to 20 tons. Although the complex is bigger and older than Stonehenge, it is not nearly as well known. Replicas, information boards and various items discovered

## SALISBURY

at the site are exhibited in the **Alexander Keiller Museum**.

**Silbury Hill** (about 2800 BC) is the largest prehistoric artificial hill in Europe, rising to a height of 130 feet (40 m). No one knows exactly what its purpose was. The burial complex of **West Kennett Long Barrow**, 370 feet (113 m) long and 4,500 years old, has five graves made up of rows of dolmens. They contained the remains of 40 individuals.

In 1804, near **Marlborough**, the boys at the public school there carved a white horse in the turf of the downs. Marlborough boasts one of the widest High Streets in England, lined with pretty Tudor and Georgian houses.

### SALISBURY

South of Stonehenge and just before Salisbury is the Iron-Age hill fort of **Old Sarum**, which was later converted into a Roman settlement, from which the modern city of **Salisbury** emerged. The city, which is the county capital, has a magnificent **cathedral**, started in 1220 and completed by 1270. Because of this relatively short construction time, this cathedral provides a unified impression of the Early English style. The main portal consists of a three-part baldachin with peaked gables extending out in front of the façade and decorated sparingly with sculptural ornament. The interior arcades of the long house rest on unusually thin pillars of pale limestone and dark Purbeck marble. The spire was not added until the High Gothic period, finished in 1380. At 404 feet (123 m), it is the highest in England. In the octagonal Early English chapter-house, where the vaulting is supported by a single central pillar, you can see one of the four surviving copies of the *Magna Carta*. Within the grassy cathedral close, the largest in the country, stand the church servants' houses dating from the 14th to the 18th

*Above: The lions of Longleat. Right: Steps leading up to the chapter-room of Wells Cathedral.*

centuries. The **Salisbury and South Wiltshire Museum**, located within the 13th-century King's House, displays items found at Stonehenge and Old Sarum as well as paintings by Turner. A stroll through the enchanting old town will bring you to the parish church of **St. Thomas** and the impressive **market cross** (15th century). Across Crane Bridge on the corner of High Street by the meads of the Avon is the **Old Mill**, now accommodating a pleasant pub.

### Southern Wiltshire

West on the A36 is **Wilton**, once the capital of the Saxon kingdom of Wessex. **Wilton House**, home of the Earls of Pembroke, was started in 1647 by Inigo Jones and continued in 1656 by John Webb. Worth seeing here are the double-cube room, based on a 33-foot (10 m) module, with mythological paintings on the ceiling; paintings by Titian, Rembrandt, Van Dyck, Rubens, Breughel and Tintoretto; and the Tudor kitchen.

Continue on the A36 to **Warminster**, an elegant Georgian town. In the southwest is the Elizabethan **Longleat House** with a fine collection of porcelain, books and paintings. The wonderful gardens with a serpentine lake were laid out by Capability Brown. In 1966, Longleat Safari Park opened; today, giraffes, cheetahs, monkeys and hippos, as well as the famous lions, roam about the grounds.

To the north is **Westbury**, where in the 18th century a vast **white horse** was carved into the chalk hill below some enormous prehistoric earthworks. At **Uffington**, north of Marlborough, you can see a real prehistoric white horse 2,500 years old carved into the chalk.

On the B3092 at **Stourton** are some of the most beautiful 18th-century landscape gardens in England. An artificial lake is surrounded by rhododendrons and magnolias. A walk along its banks will take you to temples, grottoes and ornate bridges. On the edge of the park is an elegant Palladian house dating from 1722 and containing precious period furniture and paintings by Canaletto, Raphael and Poussin. For three days every July, the park hosts a "Fête Champêtre" with marvellous costumes and orchestra concerts on the shores of the lake, where fireworks are reflected in the water.

### SOMERSET
### Wells and Glastonbury

**Wells**, the little city at the foot of the **Mendip Hills**, boasts one of the most beautiful cathedrals in England. Built in 1150-1421, it has a magnificent Early Gothic façade, with a lower row of gables which zigzags across the entire width of the façade. Gables also top the niches formed by the buttresses, in each of which stands a sculpted figure; there were originally 176 of these, 127 of which have been preserved. Countless reliefs depict scenes from the Old and New Testaments.

## WELLS / GLASTONBURY

In the interior of this light, airy church, a unique piece of architecture in the crossing catches your eye: on three sides two pointed arches, one atop the other, were built to support the crossing-tower. Note also the staircase and the octagonal chapter-room in the Decorated style of the 14th century.

In **Vicar's Close**, north of the cathedral, forty 14th-century houses owned by the church constitute the oldest terraced houses in Europe; they are linked to the cathedral by a bridge. Wells is an intriguing city with many medieval buildings including the **Bishops' Palace** (13th century) and the church of **St. Cuthbert** in Perpendicular style.

The hill of **Glastonbury** was already settled in prehistoric times. The construction of what is today **Glastonbury Abbey** lasted from around 1200 until into the 16th century. The abbey was dissolved under Henry VIII and the church destroyed. Some of the most famous ruins in the country still convey a sense of their former size and beauty.

Glastonbury, set amidst the peat moors, is a place of legend and myths. Joseph of Arimathea is said to have come here in 60 AD with the Holy Grail, the cup used during the Last Supper, in order to convert the Celts. He planted his staff in the ground near the abbey, and it became a hawthorn bush which allegedly still flowers today. He is supposed to have buried the Grail in the conical hill of **Glastonbury Tor**, at the point whence now emerges the spring that fills the **Chalice Well**. King Arthur and Queen Guinevere are supposedly buried here too, as Glastonbury is claimed to be the Isle of Avalon, last refuge of the mortally wounded Arthur. His gravestone is located in the ruined abbey (probably faked by the monks in the 16th century). The only building to have survived reasonably whole is the abbey kitchen. Every year a gigantic pop festival is held here, swamping the town, much of whose old charm has in any case disappeared due to its colonization by so-called New-Agers.

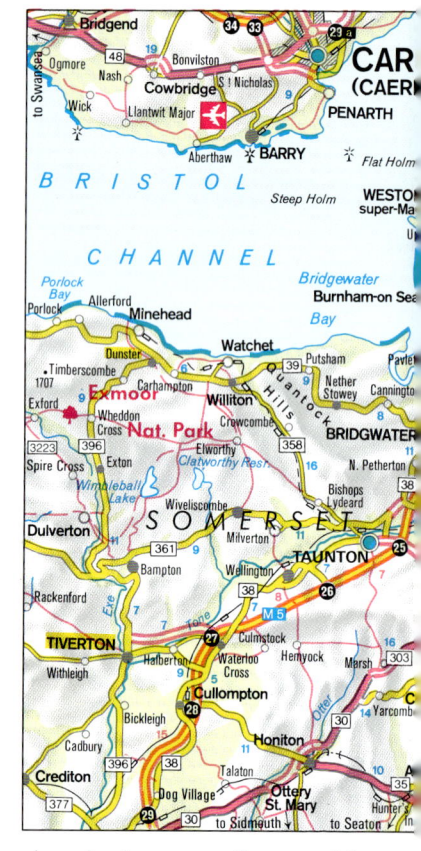

Another sight for footsore travelers is Clark's Shoe Museum in **Street**.

From Wells, the A371 leads to the caverns of **Wookey Hole**. Sixty thousand years ago they were a refuge for wild animals; today, the tour takes in an excellent fairground museum, an old slot-machine arcade, a mirror maze and a traditional paper mill. Continue on the A371 to the famous cheese town of **Cheddar** at the foot of the Mendips. Nearby is the impressive **Cheddar Gorge.** The caves here were inhabited up to 10,000 years ago, and a palaeolithic skeleton has been found here. Outside, rock climbers scale the 500-foot (154 m) walls of the Gorge.

# WILTSHIRE / SOMERSET

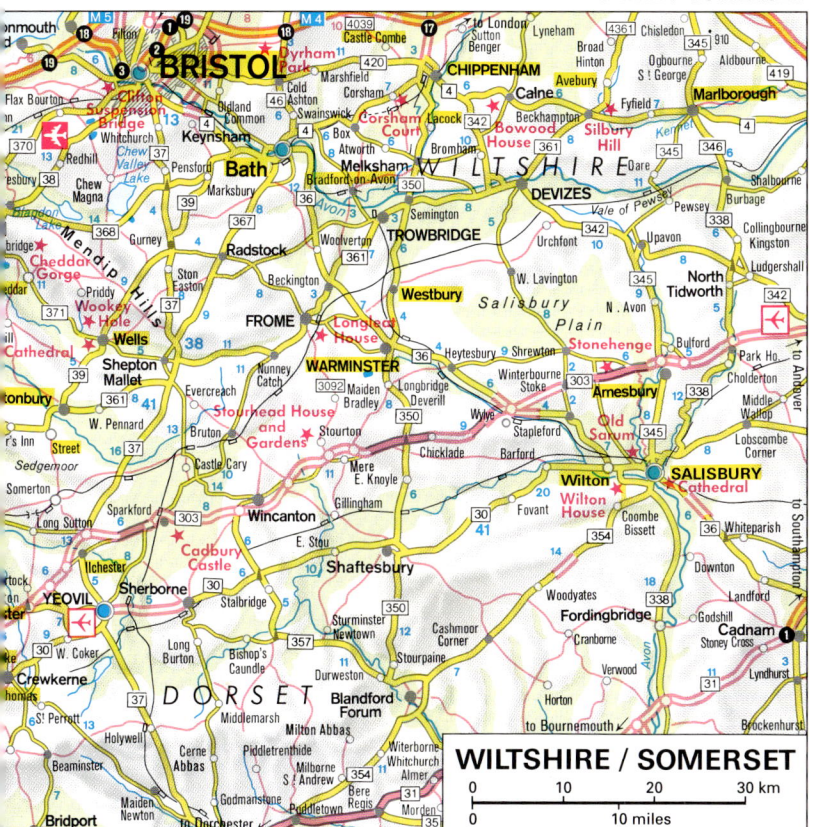

The A303 sweeps south towards the prehistoric hill fort of **Cadbury Castle**, one of several sites which claim to be King Arthur's fabled Camelot.

Near **Ilchester** is the Fleet Air Arm Museum with more than 40 historic aircraft, including the Concorde 002. The A303 continues on to Exeter; the longer coastal route leads south from Ilminster on the A358. Here, you can call in at the cider mill at **Dowlish Wake** (open all year) or at **Cricket St. Thomas**, east of Chard, to visit the wildlife park and manor house, before you come to the pebbly beaches at **Seaton** and **Sidmouth**.

The A396 continues north to **Tiverton**, where you can take a horse-drawn barge trip on the canal. Pretty little villages are scattered along the edge of Exmoor, once a royal forest and today a national park popular with hikers. At Ashway, deep in a remote valley, a medieval "clapper" bridge 150 feet (50 m) long, made of slabs of stone on stone pillars, crosses the rushing river. This type of bridge was once used by pack horses and is a typical feature of Devon and Somerset.

**Dunster** is a picturesque town, with a castle crowning the hill and a 17th-century yarn market; here, you can still see a hole made by cannon shot in the Civil War in one of the rafters. The castle was the last Royalist stronghold in Somerset. Other highlights of this medieval city include mills, an old dovecote, and a priory.

141

## BRISTOL

A safe harbor at the neck of the Bristol Channel, **Bristol** has long been an important port which grew rich on the trade in tobacco, wine and slaves. Today, the city specializes in the service sector and industry; one of its best-known products is the Rolls-Royce. Notable features are the cobbled streets and docks, where some ships have been turned into illuminated restaurants and nightclubs. Despite heavy bombing in World War II, some old half-timbered buildings survived, including the **Old Vic**, one of the oldest theaters in England (1766). In the legendary 17th-century half-timbered pub **Llandoger Trow**, Daniel Defoe and Robert Louis Stevenson are supposed to have created the stories of *Robinson Crusoe* and *Treasure Island*. The **cathedral** was founded in 1140 as an Augustinian monastery, and was, between the 14th and 16th centuries, extensively expanded and remodelled. The church of **St. Mary Redcliffe**, founded by wealthy merchants in the 13th century, was built in the Perpendicular Style; it has a particularly elegant interior, and is considered the most attractive parish church in England.

At the Great Western Dock, the highlight of the **Maritime Heritage Centre** is the *SS Great Britain*, Brunel's famous iron steamship, built and launched in Bristol in 1843. A hot-air balloon flight provides an unparalleled view of the city – including Brunel's superb suspension bridge at Clifton on the southwest edge of Bristol.

There are many fine museums and galleries to explore, including the **Exploratory Hands-on Science Center** in Brunel's 1840 railway engine-shed, or the **City Museum and Art Gallery**.

You can also take a guided tour of **Harvey's Wine Cellars**, complete with a gourmet meal afterwards at the adjoining restaurant.

*Above: When it's hot you don't have to wait long for customers. Right: The central basin of the Roman baths in Bath.*

## BATH AND ENVIRONS

Lying on a bend of the river Avon, the picturesque city of Bath, with its elegant 18th-century Georgian buildings of golden stone, is for some people the loveliest city on the whole island. Many of these old houses have been restored and are under landmark protection; while UNESCO has declared the whole city of Bath a world heritage site.

Three thousand years ago, the Celts discovered hot springs which they dedicated to the goddess Sulis; when the Romans arrived at the city of Aquae Sulis in 43 AD, they built a temple for their goddess Minerva above the springs. They also built the **Roman Baths**, and the large central basin, its green waters surrounded by statues, is still an impressive sight. Adjacent to this is the Georgian **Pump Room**, in whose elegant surroundings you can still take tea or a meal while listening to classical music. Behind the baths is the Late Gothic **Bath Abbey** (15th century) with richly-decorated fan vaulting. On the west façade, fallen angels try to climb back up Jacob's Ladder to heaven.

After Roman times, the spas at Bath were gradually forgotten. In the late Middle Ages, the city was a center of cloth production. But in 1702, with the visit of Queen Anne, the pendulum swung back. High society moved in, and the wealthy master of ceremonies Richard Nash (Beau Nash) made sure that etiquette and clothing were up to par. The **Assembly Rooms**, where people in that period took afternoon tea and attended the evening's events, today house the **Museum of Costumes** with a collection of costumes from the last four centuries.

Behind the Abbey, the Avon is crossed by the **Pulteney Bridge**, built in 1770 by Robert Adam and modeled on the Ponte Vecchio in Florence. In the northwest quarter of the old town are two more major sights: the classical terraces of the **Circus**, built in the 18th century by John Wood the Elder, and the semicircle of the **Royal Crescent** built by his son, John

## BATH AND SURROUNDINGS

Wood. Here, at No. 1, is a museum of Georgian life. To the west extend the botanic gardens of **Royal Victoria Park**.

Every year in June a famous international music festival is held in Bath. At other times, you can always take in a show at the recently restored and charming Georgian **Theatre Royal**.

To the south is lovely **Bradford-on-Avon** with its tiny Saxon church and steep tiers of stone buildings above the river. North of town is the 17th-century mansion **Dyrham Park** with fine interior decoration. Off the A4 is the Elizabethan manor house **Corsham Court** with a collection of Italian and Flemish paintings.

**Castle Combe**, northeast of Bath, is accounted one of the prettiest villages in England. This idyllic medieval spot is where *Dr. Doolittle* was filmed.

**Lacock**, south of Chippenham, is another village not to be missed. Besides its exquisite and beautifully preserved medieval stone houses, it boasts an abbey, founded in 1232, now a fine country house with traditional rose gardens. The **Fox-Talbot Museum of Photography** honors Henry Fox–Talbot (1800-1877), the inventor of photography, who lived here. His very first apparatus, from which modern cameras were developed, is displayed, together with old photographs and memorabilia, in a 16th-century barn.

North of Chippenham is **Malmesbury**. This beautiful Cotswold town has a magnificent Norman abbey (around 1150) with an elaborately carved doorway. Steep, winding streets; ladies in white hats meeting at the cricket match; a lovely old market cross; and the gently flowing river combine to create a quintessentially English flavor.

### DEVON

**Exeter**, the county town of Devon, is a cathedral and university town. Its cathedral was built in the Early English style

*Above: Music in stone – Exeter Cathedral.*
*Right: Still untamed and largely untouched – the landscape of Dartmoor.*

on Norman foundations; the two towers above the transepts date from the 11th century. The magnificent tripartite façade is ornamented with three rows of angels, kings and apostles depicting the heavenly Jerusalem. Inside, the cathedral boasts a wealth of pillars, mouldings, and vaulting. In the choir expressive misericords survive from the 13th century; there is also a carved wooden bishop's throne (14th century). A further attraction here is the Minstrel Gallery with its depictions of angels playing musical instruments. In St. Martin's Lane by the cathedral is the **Ship Inn** where once Sir Francis Drake and Sir Walter Raleigh raised their tankards. The picturesque and crooked half-timbered **Guildhall** in the High Street, one of England's oldest municipal buildings, dates from the 12th century. You can explore the underground passages (actually medieval aqueducts) below High Street. As you stroll through the cobbled streets, you will come across remnants of the old Roman walls, the ruins of the Norman **Rougemont Castle**, houses from Georgian, Regency and Victorian times, and the **Royal Albert Memorial Museum** (British paintings and Exeter silver). In the old harbor quarter is the **Maritime Museum**.

Northwest of Exeter, in a deer park on the Exe estuary, is **Powderham Castle**, home of the Earls of Devon, built between the 14th and 19th centuries. It has fine state rooms and a museum.

From here the A380 leads to the "English Riviera" and **Torquay**, an elegant resort with exotic plants, smart houses, a lively harbor and plenty of hotels and restaurants. This is the most popular part of Devon with busy resorts along the coast and a wide range of entertainment. Neighboring **Paignton** has an excellent zoo set in fine botanical gardens. In the dripstone **Kents Cavern**, north of Paignton, the remains of Britain's oldest inhabitants were found. A few miles west, tranquil **Brixham** is still as much a fishing port as a resort.

Down the coast the fjord-like estuary of the river Dart leads to **Dartmouth**,

## PLYMOUTH / DARTMOOR

whose houses tumble down to the quayside. It was from here that Crusaders set sail in the 12th century; today, you can take a steamer upriver to the medieval wool town (and modern shopping center) of **Totnes** with its narrow streets and the old castle.

The next estuary along the coast is that of **Salcombe** with its fishermen's houses and little white beaches fringing the wooded shores. It is a popular sailing center and has a sailing school.

Follow the coast round to the delightful thatched cottages at **Inner Hope** and eat crabmeat sandwiches at **Hope Cove** before driving on to **Plymouth**. The city lies on the river Tamar, on the border of Devon and Cornwall. The best view over Plymouth is from the breezy green sweep of **Plymouth Hoe**, where Sir Francis Drake once played bowls as he awaited the arrival of the Spanish Armada. The Hoe also has a lighthouse which accommodates the **Maritime Museum**. In 1620, the *Mayflower* set out from Plymouth for the New World. A memorial stone and the Stars and Stripes flag mark the actual departure point of the Pilgrim Fathers near the Old **Customs House** (1586) at Sutton Harbor. From these waters Captain Cook, Darwin and Captain Scott of the Antarctic also put to sea.

Just east of Plymouth is Devon's largest mansion, **Saltram House**. Within its palatial walls, paintings by Rubens and Reynolds, precious porcelain and period furniture are displayed. The A386 heads north to Yelverton, northeast of which stretches **Dartmoor**, a vast and untamed landscape which has been a National Park since 1949. It is a treacherous place. Snow can fall in midsummer, and walkers may suddenly be blinded by thick swirling mist. Even on sunny days, the moors should be treated with respect: always wear sturdy shoes and carry waterproof clothing, a map and a compass. Between the rolling moorland and gentle hills the tors stand high. These are granite formations deeply split and fissured by weathering and offering wide views of the landscape. You may catch a glimpse of the wild Dartmoor ponies which roam here.

Only a few roads traverse the moor. At its highest point (1,440 ft/440 m) is **Princetown** with its infamous prison, the English Alcatraz. Occasionally, prisoners have tried to take advantage of a sudden fog to run away from the working parties out on the moor, but few have gotten away.

A few miles further on, you come to the three-arched clapper bridge at **Postbridge**. In the Middle Ages, pack horses carried tin and copper along this route from the Dartmoor mines to the cities.

One of the most popular destinations for an excursion here is the picturesque village of **Widecombe-in-the-Moor** with its thatched granite cottages and a lofty church with a 16th-century rood screen.

At the attractive town of **Dartmeet** the East and West Dart rivers converge. To the south is **Buckfastleigh**, famous for its abbey, where the monks sell honey, cider and pottery. Here, too, is the terminus of the Dart Valley steam railway. To the north, at **Manaton**, there are remains of prehistoric settlements, such as Hound Tor. North of **Moretonhampstead** is a delightful valley and England's newest granite castle, **Castle Drogo**, built between 1910 and 1930 by Sir Edwin Lutyens, with an "armory" that actually contains fishing tackle. A little further on, the 400-year-old **Fingle Bridge** crosses the sparkling river Teign.

On the western fringes of Dartmoor is **Lydford**, fortified by King Alfred, where the later Norman castle boasts a noxious dungeon. South of the town is the dramatic **Lydford Gorge**, carved out by the river Lyd rushing between the sheer cliffs. The noise and rush of the water is terrifying, especially in the "Devil's Cauldron"; at the end of the ravine a waterfall plunges down 100 feet (30 m). Continue on the minor road south to the granite hill of **Brentor**; atop this, you have a magnificent view of the countryside from the tiny, ancient church.

*CORNWALL / POLPERRO*

**CORNWALL**

Thanks to finds of tin and copper, **Cornwall**, the region west of the Tamar, enjoyed an astonishing industrial revival and prosperity in the 18th and 19th centuries. At that time, many residents still spoke their Celtic language, Cornish; today, efforts are being made to give Cornish a second life. The region attracts countless tourists with its wild and rugged coastal landscapes, tranquil bays, mysterious moors and idyllic fishing villages. Tourism is a major source of revenue, together with vegetable farming, flower growing, slate quarrying and extraction of China clay.

The most important Tudor mansion in Cornwall is **Cotehele House** with its impressive dragon-beamed ceiling in the Great Hall. The house also has an exotic terraced garden with a working cider press. Not far away is the sombre **Bodmin Moor** with the historic Jamaica Inn, which inspired Daphne du Maurier's novel.

Near Minions, north of Liskeard, stand the **Hurlers**, a group of megaliths from the neolithic or bronze age. Legend has it that these circles were once men, turned to stone on the spot as punishment for playing the game of hurley on a Sunday. Nearby, set high above a deep quarry, is the **Cheesewring**, a natural rock formation weathered into a weird top-heavy pile, like a stack of wheels of cheese. South of Liskeard, just inland of the popular resort of **Looe**, a monkey sanctuary is tucked into a steep wooded valley near **Seaton**. This is the only place where Amazonian woolly monkeys have bred in captivity.

The old smugglers' den of **Polperro** lies a little further to the west. A jumble of pretty whitewashed cottages and narrow lanes above the harbor, it is swamped with visitors in the summer. Visit the **Museum of Smuggling** or

*Above: No longer for smugglers: the harbor of Polperro at low tide. Right: Reminiscences of the good old days.*

## LIZARD PENINSULA / ST. MICHAEL'S MOUNT

enjoy a stroll along the clifftop paths. From Polperro, drive westwards and take the car ferry from **Bodinnick** to the little port of **Fowey** (pronounced "Foy"). This is Daphne du Maurier country, and "Manderley" in *Rebecca* was based on the beautiful mansion of Menabilly, where the author lived, near **Polkerris**. There is a marvellous clifftop walk from Fowey to Polkerris, part of the long-distance **Cornish Coastal Path**.

A diversion inland, through Lostwithiel, leads to **Lanhydrock House** (built 1620-40), with splendid rooms, a huge kitchen, and the magnificent Long Gallery, 115 feet long (35 m), with an impressive stucco ceiling depicting Biblical scenes. South of **St. Austell**, center of Cornwall's kaolin industry, is coastal **Mevagissey**, a delight with its narrow streets and quaint shops above a very old and picturesque fishing port.

### The Lizard Peninsula

**Falmouth** is an excellent base from which to tour this area. Seven rivers feed its natural harbor, flanked by the castles **Pendennis** and **St. Mawes**, both built by Henry VIII. Palm trees line the streets and figureheads adorn the façades of some of the quaint old shops and pubs.

North of Falmouth are the subtropical gardens of **Trelissick**, while **St.-Just-in-Roseland** across the estuary has a pretty church among tropical trees beside the creek. At the water's edge is a workshop where figureheads are made.

In the wooded hills around **Gweek**, southwest of Falmouth, is a sea-lion sanctuary where injured seals are nursed back to health before being returned to the wild. Daphne du Maurier's *Frenchman's Creek* was set nearby, close to Helford itself. Today's visitors can take a trip underground into the 18th-century tin mines at **Wendron** near Helston.

Near **Coverack** and **Cadgwith**, the A3083 leads to the peninsula of the **Lizard**. From the wild, wave-tossed headland below the lighthouse, the ships of the Armada were first sighted four hundred years ago. To the northwest is **Kynance Cove**, one of the most beautiful coves in Britain, with dramatic rocks and a glorious deep turquoise sea below cliffs studded with wildflowers – definitely worth the steep climb down from the car park.

**Mullion Cove** is another glorious spot with its high stone harbor wall below steep grassy cliffs and a rock bearing a distinct resemblance to the head of a lion. There is splendid cliff walking all around here, such as, for example, the route to **Poldhu**, from where Marconi sent the first-ever wireless signals across the Atlantic.

### Around Penzance

The A394 towards Penzance passes a good beach at **Praa Sands** on its way to Marazion and the tidal island of **St. Michael's Mount**. At ebb tide the island is

## PENZANCE / ISLES OF SCILLY

connected by a causeway to the mainland. This may well have been the place from where Phoenicians shipped out tin two thousand years ago; it's certain, however, that there was a Celtic monastery here in the 6th century, and the Mount was a noted place of pilgrimage. Edward the Confessor gave the island to the Benedictine monks of Mont-St.-Michel in Britanny, and Henry VIII had it fortified. If the incoming tide prevents you walking back, you can avail yourself of the small ferry.

Back at **Marazion beach**, treasure-hunters scour the shingle for amethysts, while in the seaside resort of **Penzance** town, artists sketch the façade of the **Egyptian House** in Chapel Street, built in pseudo-Egyptian style in 1835. In front of **Penlee House** (1860), which houses an archaeological museum, stands an old market cross dating from the 9th century.

*Above: Summer sun and surf at the popular beach of St. Ives.*

### The Isles of Scilly

From Penzance, you can embark for the **Isles of Scilly**, a journey which takes 2 hours and 30 minutes by ferry or 20 minutes by helicopter.

Of the 140 or so islands and rocks, only five are inhabited. Two-thirds of the 2,000 islanders live on St. Mary's; the rest of the population is divided between Tresco, St. Martin's, St. Agnes and Bryher. Rocky outcrops fringed with silver white sands, surrounded by treacherous rocks, the islands cluster together in the sometimes stormy, but often warm Atlantic. A mild climate encourages rare flora and fauna as well as commercial horticulture. The wildlife is superb. There are seals, breeding and migrating birds, and countless butterflies in flowery fields. Ancient remains and burial sites, castles, shipwrecks, lighthouses and empty beaches add to the flavor.

**St. Mary's** is the main island and the largest (3 miles/5 km across). Its capital, **Hugh Town**, is home to the Scilly Museum, displaying prehistoric finds. This island is a good point of departure for boat trips to view the other islands' flora and bird life. On **Tresco**, you can see Tresco Abbey with its magnificent subtropical Abbey Gardens; King Charles' Castle (1651); and the Valhalla Maritime Museum, with the carved figureheads of 70 ships wrecked off the isles.

A visit to the Scillies offers a complete change of pace. Most visitors find themselves captivated by the clear turquoise water, lonely beaches and palms, fig trees and laurels. The 56 hotels and boarding houses in this mild climate are open the whole year round.

### From Land's End to Tintagel

Back on the mainland, head south from Penzance to the pretty fishing harbors of **Newlyn** and **Mousehole** (pronounced "Muzzle"). A narrow lane winds its way to the **Minack open-air theater,** which Rowena Cade built with her own hands into the natural rock of the cliffs in the 1930s. This Greek-style amphitheater hosts daily performances at 2 p.m. and 8 p.m. in summer, rain or shine, with the tumbling sea as a backdrop. Don't forget a thermos, a raincoat, and a cushion.

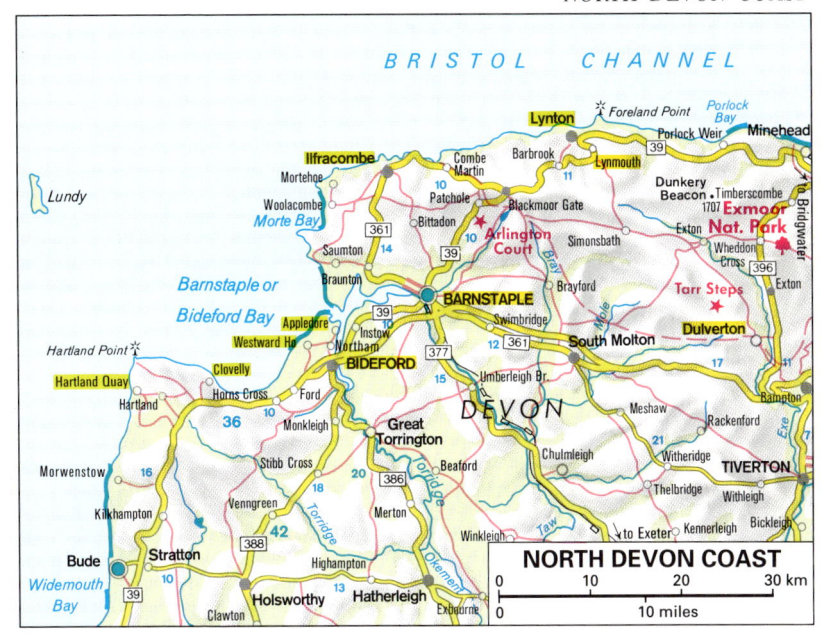

**Land's End** has belonged to an English millionaire since 1987. If the £5 entrance fee to the amusement park on the western tip of England seems unnecessary, you can take the path which leads behind the parking lot past a souvenir shop and café for two miles or so (3 km) along the cliffs to the harbor at **Sennan Cove.**

The B3306 now pursues its winding course to **St. Ives,** an artists' colony for over a century, whose main source of income is no longer tin and fish, but tourism. Worth visiting is the **museum** of the sculptor Barbara Hepworth.

The road winds north past relics of the tin-mining age before reaching the two resorts of **St. Agnes** and **Trevaunance Cove.**

A worthwhile detour leads to **Trerice,** a small but beautiful Elizabethan manor house (1570) set amongst luxuriant gardens and orchards. North of Newquay and the coast road, past small coves and rock arches, are the much-photographed **Bedruthan Steps.** The coastal scenery and steep steps to the beach are breathtaking. The B3276 continues along the coast to **Padstow,** a busy harbor since the Middle Ages. Boat trips from here allow you to explore the cliffs and caves and see seals, puffins, and sharks. Across the estuary is the sandy beach of **Rock,** good for sunbathing and relaxing while artists paint and yachts and windsurfers catch the breeze.

To the north is **Tintagel,** with a ruined castle (12th century) spectacularly placed atop a cliff high above the restless sea. Numerous legends say that this is the site of King Arthur's castle of Camelot. Accordingly, the entire village has fully dedicated itself to Arthurian tourism, except for the slate-roofed old post office (14th century).

## NORTH DEVON COAST

The A39 continues north to **Clovelly**, whose cobblestone streets are closed to all but pedestrians and donkeys. Every half hour, a jeep shuttle service ferries visitors up and down the steep path to the harbor, lined with pastel cottages and tea rooms. Apart from the flat concrete building at the entrance to the village, where you must pay an entrance fee, time seems to have stopped a century ago.

West of Clovelly is the raw lonely wilderness of **Hartland Quay** (shipwreck museum) and **Hartland Point**, while to the east is probably the most attractive town in Devon, **Bideford** (pronounced Bidford), which once traded in tobacco and wool. Further north is an idyllic little town with brightly-colored house doors and a rewarding pub on the seafront: **Appledore**. Westward Ho, which took its name from Charles Kingsley's novel, is today mainly a collection of mobile-home parks.

**Ilfracombe** is a quiet and well-kempt little fishing town on the north coast. To the east is the Victorian resort of **Lynton**, as well as the **Somerset and Devon Coast Path**. Also worth a visit is the little harbor at **Lynmouth** which was almost completely destroyed in 1952 by a torrential flood which followed a freak storm. Whole sections of the village beside the river were swept away and 34 people died.

Head inland now to visit **Arlington Court**, off the A39. Built in 1820, this elegant house contains fascinating collections of model ships, shells and costumes. **Barnstaple**, on the bay, is one of the oldest towns in England with a market which changes daily.

Inland lies **Exmoor National Park**, a paradise for nature lovers and ramblers. From Exmoor House in **Dulverton**, on the south edge of the moor, you can obtain information sheets on individual sights in the area.

*Above: A fire-eater entertains holidaymakers in Padstow.*

# GUIDEPOST WEST COUNTRY

## WEST COUNTRY
## AVON – BATH AND BRISTOL
### Accommodation
BATH: *LUXURY:* **Bath Spa**, Sydney Road, tel. 01225 444424. **Royal Crescent,** 16 Royal Crescent, tel. 01225 31090. **BRISTOL**: *LUXURY:* **Berkeley Square**, 5 Berkeley Square, tel. 0117 952970. *MODERATE:* **Courtlands**, 1 Redlands Court Road, tel. 01117 9424432. *BUDGET:* **Alandale,** 4, Tyndales Park Rd., Clifton, tel. 01117 9735407.

### Museums
BATH: **Roman Baths Museum**, tel. 01225 461111 ext 2785, March-Oct 9.00-18.00, Aug 9.00-18.00, Nov-Feb 9.00-17.00. **American Museum**, tel. 01225 460503, 26 March-6 Nov daily 14.00-17.00 except Mon. **Museum of Costume**, Bennett St., tel. 01225 46111, ext. 2785, March-Oct 9.30-18.00, Sun 10.00-18.00, Nov-Feb 10.00-17.00, Sun 11.00-17.00. **Victoria Art Gallery**, Bridge St., tel. 01225 46111 ext. 2772, Mon-Fri 10.00-17.30, Sat until 17.00. **Bath Postal Museum**, 8 Broad St., tel. 01225 460333, March-Dec Mon-Sat 11.00-17.00, Sun 14.00-17.00. **British Folk Art Collection**, Countess of Huntingdon Chapel, The Vineyards, The Paragon, tel. 01225 446020, April-Oct Tue-Sat and Bank Holidays 10.30-17.00, Sun 14.00-17.00. **Holbourne Museum and Crafts Study Centre**, Gt. Pulteney St., tel. 01225 466669, April-Dec Mon-Sat 11.00-17.00, Sun 14.30-18.00; Nov-Dec closed Mon. **BRISTOL**: **Bristol Industrial Museum**, tel. 0117 951470, Tue-Sun 10.00-17.00. **Harvey's Wine Museum and Cellars**, 12 Denmark St., tel. 0117 9637858, daily 10.00-17.00, Sat-Sun 14.00-17.00. **LACOCK**: **Fox Talbot Museum of Photography**, tel. 01249 73459, April-Oct daily 11.00-17.30.

### Tips and Trips
BATH: **No. 1 Royal Crescent**, tel. 01225 42126, open 1 March-30 Oct Tue-Sun 10.00-17.00, 1 Nov-11 Dec Tue-Sun 10.30-16.00. **BRISTOL**: **The Georgian House**, tel. 0117 9211362, all year Tue-Sat 10.00-17.00. **Maritime Heritage Centre**, SS Great Britain, tel. 0117 9260680, daily 10.00-18.00 in summer, 13.00-17.00 winter. **CHIPPENHAM**: **Sheldon Manor**, tel. 01249 653120, open 1 April-30 Oct Sun, Thur, Bank Holidays 12.30-18.00.

### Tourist Information
BATH: The Colonnades, 11-13 Bath Street, tel. 01225 462831. **BRISTOL**: St. Nicholas Church, St. Nicholas Street, tel. 0117 9260767.

## WILTSHIRE / SALISBURY
### Accommodation
SALISBURY: *LUXURY:* **Wilton Pembroke Arms Hotel**, Salisbury, tel. 01722 743328. *MODERATE:* **The Red Lion**, Milford Street, tel. 01722 323334. *BUDGET:* **The Kings Arms**, 9-11 St. John's Street, tel. 01722 327629.

### Museums
SALISBURY: **Salisbury and South Wiltshire Museum**, Cathedral Close, tel. 01772 332151, Mon-Sat 10.00-17.00, May 13-29, July and August Sun 14.00-17.00. **AVEBURY**: **Alexander Keiller Museum**, tel. 01672 539250.

### Tips and Trips
**STONEHENGE**: tel. 01980 624715, 1 April-31 Oct 10.00-18.00, 1 Nov-31 March 10.00-16.00. **STOURTON**: **Stourhead House and Gardens**, tel. 01747 841152, house April-Oct Sat-Wed 12.00-17.00, gardens all year daily 9.00-19.00. **WARMINSTER**: **Longleat House**, tel. 01985 844400, daily except Dec 25. Easter-Sept 10.00-18.00. Oct-Dec 10.00-16.00. **WILTON**: **Wilton House**, tel. 01722 743115, daily 11.00-18.00, 29 March-30 Oct.

### Tourist Information
SALISBURY: Fish Row, tel. 01722 334956.

## DEVON AND SOMERSET
## PLYMOUTH
### Accommodation
PLYMOUTH: *LUXURY:* **Copthorpe Hotel**, Armarda Way, tel. 01752 224161. *MODERATE:* **New Continental Hotel**, Mill Bay Road, tel. 01752 220782. *BUDGET:* **Invictor Hotel**, Lockyear Street, tel. 01752 664997.

### Tips and Trips
PLYMOUTH: **Plymouth Aquarium**, tel. 01752 222772, ext. 254, June-Sept daily 10.00-18.00, Oct-May 10.00-1700. **Saltram House**. Plymton, tel. 01752 336546, 1 April-30 Oct, 12.30-17.30, closed Fridays.

### Tourist Information
PLYMOUTH: Island House, 9 The Barbican, tel. 01752 264849.

## CORNWALL / ISLES OF SCILLY
### Accommodation
FALMOUTH: (Cornwall) *MODERATE:* **Falmouth**, Monglese Road, tel. 01326 211411. **Royal Duchy**, Cliff Road. tel. 01326 313042. *BUDGET:* **Broad Mede**, Kimberely Road, tel. 01326 315704. **ISLES OF SCILLY**: *LUXURY:* **Carnwethers**, Country House, Pelistry Bay, tel. 01720 22415. *MODERATE:* **The Beach Comber**, Thoroughfare, St. Mary's, tel. 01720 22680. *BUDGET:* **The Bylet Guest House**, Church Road, tel. 01720 22479.

### Tips and Trips
CORNWALL: **Tintagel Castle**, tel. 01840 770328, 1 April-31 Oct 10.00-18.00, 1 Nov-31 March 10.00-16.00. **Pendennis Castle**, tel. 01326 316594, 1 April-31 Oct 10.00-18.00. 1 Nov-31 March 10.00-16.00. **Trerice Manor**, 1 April-31 Oct 12.30-18.00.

### Tourist Information
FALMOUTH: 28, Killigrew Street, Cornwall, tel. 01326 312300. **ISLES OF SCILLY**: Porthcressa Bank, St. Mary's, tel. 01720 422536.

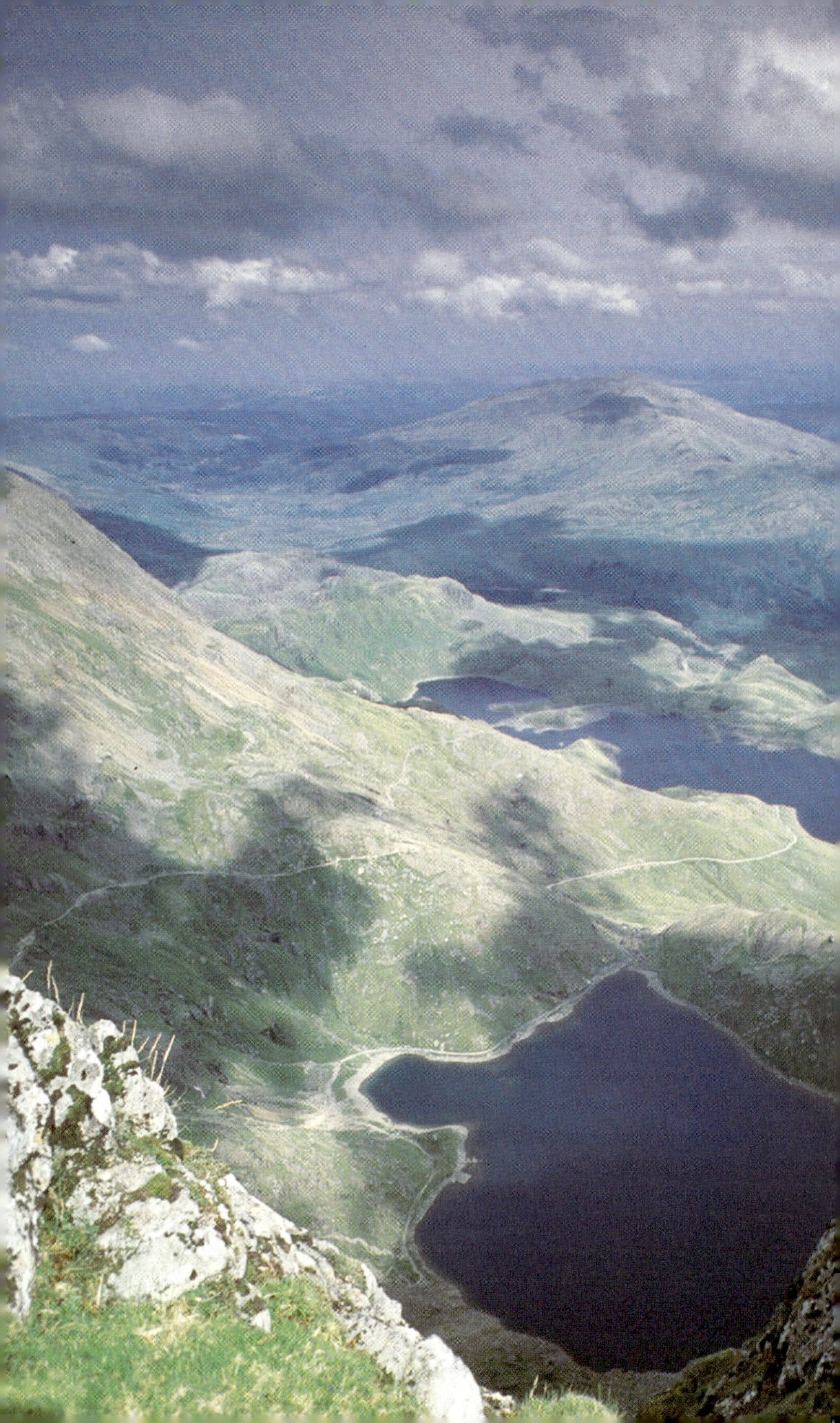

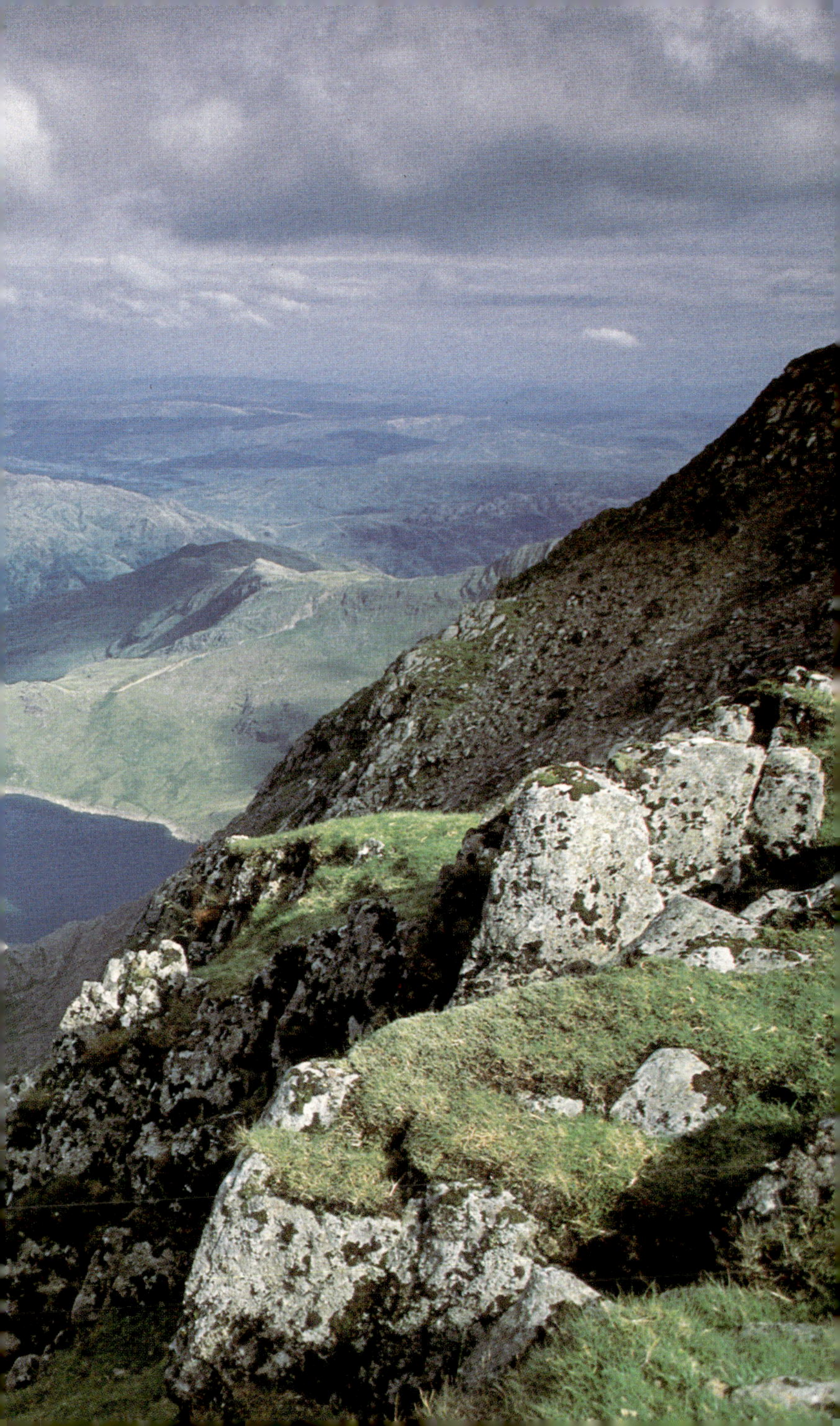

# WALES

# WALES

SOUTH WALES
MID WALES
NORTH WALES
ISLE OF ANGLESEY
NORTH WALES COAST

## SOUTH WALES

Wales is a land of hills and mountains, green valleys, defiant castles and a superb coastline. Long sandy beaches alternate with small, rocky bays. On the South Wales coast you can find deserted places to swim even at the height of the season. The mountainous hinterland is perfect walking country, and the Welsh landscape shows its most unspoilt side in the national parks. Washed by the Gulf Stream, South Wales has a very mild climate, and it rains the least between February and June.

The Welsh are proud of their independent culture and Celtic tongue. Since 1972 signposts have been in both English and Welsh, one of the first successes of the Welsh nationalist movement, the *Cymdeithas yr Iath Cymraeg*.

The M4 crosses the **Severn Bridge** just north of Bristol (a toll-bridge, but only for northbound traffic) with panoramic views of the Severn estuary. This route, like many others into Wales, begins with a castle. **Chepstow** lies on the banks of the Wye; its name derives

*Preceding pages: View from Snowdon over the austere landscape of Snowdonia National Park. Left: All aboard: the Llanberis Lake Railway.*

from the Saxon for "market town." The city began as a Roman stronghold, something reflected in the grid pattern of the streets in the old town. The Normans recognized the strategic importance of the site and built a fortress here in the 11th century. Opposite the castle is the **Chepstow Museum** which presents the turbulent history of the region.

From Chepstow, the A466 leads north into the **Wye Valley** and **Tintern**. Monks from Normandy founded **Tintern Abbey** here in 1137. Between 1270 and 1301, the Cistercians built the abbey church whose six-bayed nave includes elegant arches at the crossing and a beautiful rose window in the west façade. The magnificent Abbey ruins, open to the sky and set in thick woodland, inspired a famous poem by Wordsworth. Nearby is Tintern's old **Victorian Railway Station,** displaying a collection of old railway memorabilia.

North of Tintern is **Monmouth** (Welsh *Trefynny*), surrounded by three rivers and dominated by the ruins of the castle where Henry V was born in 1387. Shakespeare immortalized the monarch in a history play of the same name. Note the 13th-century **Monnow Bridge,** which still has a real bridge gatehouse.

Further southwest are the ruins of **Raglan Castle**, earlier seat of the Earls of

*SOUTH WALES*

Worcester. One of the last castles to be built in Britain, it's like a medieval palace, and its decorative towers contrast with the sturdy simplicity of Chepstow. During the Civil War it was the last castle to fall into the hands of Cromwell, after a siege of ten weeks.

**Crickhowell**, a small picturesque town at the foot of the eastern Black Mountains, makes an excellent center for exploring the exciting wild scenery of the **Brecon Beacons**, so called after hilltop beacons, or signal fires, in the Middle Ages. The **National Park** is very popular with walkers on account of its many marvellous views. From its highest point, **Pen y Fen** (2,900 ft/886 m), you can look out over the ranges of the parallel North-South ranges of the eastern and western Black Mountains.

At the foot of the Pen y Fen is the old market town of **Brecon** on the Usk. In the north of the town is a 12th-century **castle** which has been converted into a hotel. Nearby is the mighty **Cathedral of St. John**, built in the 12th century of red sandstone. The **Brecknock Museum** in Glamorgan Street shows pre-Christian finds as well as a collection of "lovespoons," wooden spoons which young men used to carve for their sweethearts. The museum also houses a reconstruction of an old courtroom.

Until a few decades ago, coal mining was still going on in the Beacons, and at the **Big Pit** mining museum at **Blaena-**

## SOUTH WALES

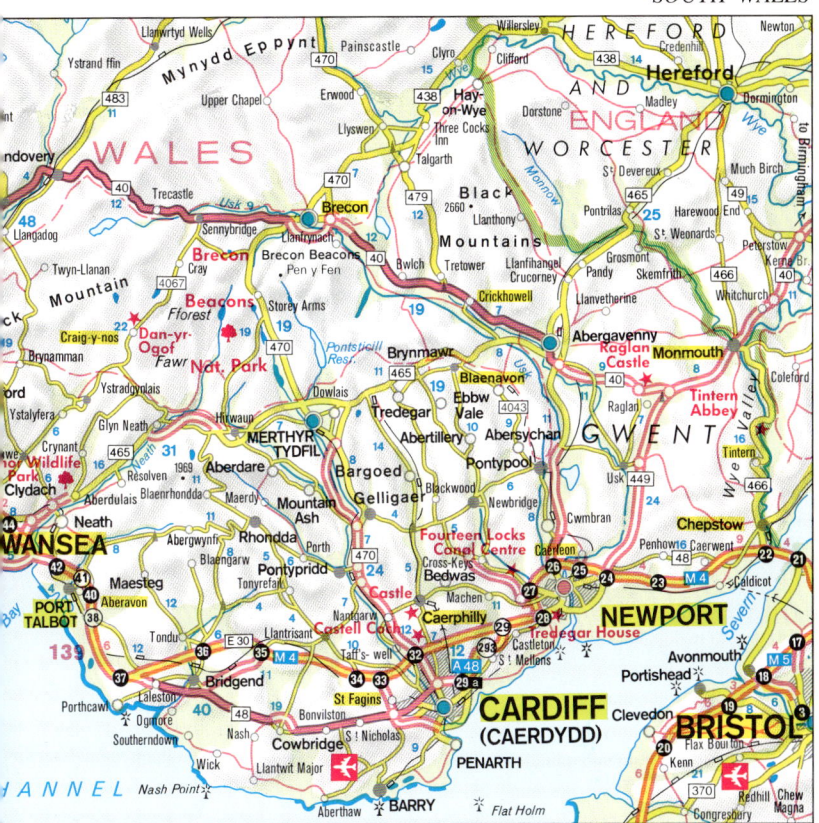

**von** you can don a helmet, descend into the depths in the pit cage, and tour the galleries and coal face.

Just before motorway exit 24 is the town of **Caerleon.** Here, over 50 acres (20 ha), the Romans laid out a military camp in 70 AD with a palace, a barracks, baths and a theater. Still visible are the green, grass-covered tiers of the oval amphitheater and parts of the buildings. The **Roman Legionary Museum** exhibits an outstanding collection of Roman finds.

**Tredegar House**, on the outskirts of **Newport**, is a magnificent 17th-century mansion, where the servants' quarters "below stairs" can be inspected as well as the splendors of life "upstairs." A little further north is the industrial city of **Caerphilly**. Built between 1268 and 1284 to keep the locals under control, **Caerphilly Castle** boasts an extremely complex defensive system with round towers and courtyards, one within another.

Worth seeing in **Cardiff**, capital city of Wales, is the **National Museum of Wales** with archaeological and early Christian exhibits, works of contemporary Welsh artists, and paintings by Gainsborough and Constable. **Cardiff Castle** was built in 1090 on 4th-century Roman foundations. The castle burned down in 1404 and was rebuilt 1865-1920; in the process, it was fitted out with a wealth of wall paintings and other pomp, according to the Victorian idea of a proper castle.

## SWANSEA / GOWER

On the western edge of Cardiff is another castle, built by the 3rd Marquess of Bute. **Castell Coch** (Red Castle) is a turreted fairytale fantasy not unlike King Ludwig's Neuschwanstein in Bavaria.

At the **Welsh Folk Museum** at St. Fagins, old cottages, farmhouses and other old buildings, including a toll house, school, blacksmith's forge and chapel, have been reconstructed.

The chimneys of **Port Talbot**'s steel works and oil refineries light up the sky at night; the swathes of smoke and the flickering flames paint a bizarre picture. Bordering directly on Port Talbot is the resort town of **Aberavon** with the Afan Lido leisure center. To the north is the **Neath Valley** with spectacular waterfalls and gorges. In the higher part of the Tawe valley at **Dan-yr-Ogof**, near Craig-y-nos, are huge caves where traces of Bronze Age settlement has been found.

*Above: Coastal cliffs near Trefin, Pembrokeshire. Right: Relaxing on the beach at Tenby.*

Where the Tawe flows into the sea lies **Swansea**, which in the 19th century was Wales' leading seaport and a center for copper processing and coal export. This university town was the birthplace of the poet Dylan Thomas (1914-1953). Works of Welsh artists are exhibited in the **Glyn Vivian Art Gallery**. The port area includes the marina, the **Maritime Quarter**, the **Maritime and Industrial Museum** and the **Little Theater**, where Dylan Thomas once rehearsed his plays. At the North Dock is a futuristic hothouse called **The Plantasia**, where desert and tropical climates are controlled by computer.

Southwest of Swansea, the **Gower** peninsula offers fine coastal scenery and beaches, particularly at Caswell Bay and Langland, which are prized not only by sunbathers and swimmers but also by windsurfers.

Even farther west are the old smugglers' haunts of Port-Eynon, Rhossili and Worms Head. All these towns are now popular resorts.

## Pembrokeshire

At the end of the M4 motorway, the A48 continues to **Carmarthen,** with its **Guildhall** (1766) and the **County Museum**. At St. Clears turn onto the A4066; near the mouth of the river estuary is the town of **Laugharne** and the boathouse (now a museum) where Dylan Thomas wrote *Under Milk Wood.*

The **Pembrokeshire National Park** takes in the coast of the Pembroke peninsula. Crossing it is the Coastal Footpath, leading 166 miles (267 km) from Amroth to St. Dogmaels near Cardigan. This is one of the most exciting and varied stretches of coastline in Britain, with turquoise seas, streams, bays, wide beaches and weird cliffs with a rich variety of wildflowers and birds.

The romantic castle of **Manorbier** (1275-1325) is surrounded by sand dunes, while vast lily ponds can be seen at **Bosherton**. At **St. Govan's Head** visit the old chapel (11th-13th centuries) tucked away in the cliffs, reachable only by a steep flight of steps. Its altar and pews are carved from the living rock. Inland is **Carew**, a pretty village with one of the loveliest High Crosses in Wales (c. 1033), a 14th-century church with a Perpendicular tower, and some magnificent castle ruins. By the river is the **Carew French Tidal Mill** (16th century).

At **Pembroke**, high on a wooded bluff above the river, looms the mighty Norman **Pembroke Castle**, (1090) with a watchtower 75 feet (23 m) high and a Norman hall. This was the birthplace of Henry Tudor, later to ascend the throne as King Henry VII.

Milford Haven is a major port with oil refineries. At the quays where fishing boats once tied up, tankers of up to 250,00 tons now moor. At nearby **Mill Bay** near **Dale**, Henry Tudor landed in 1485 before marching to Bosworth Field to defeat Richard III and claim the crown of England.

A nature reserve has been set up at the other end of St. Bridges Bay at **Skomer Island**; it's home to more than 30 species of birds. Boats ferry visitors to the island from **St. Martin's Haven**.

**St. David's**, the most sacred place in Wales, has a **cathedral** built at the end of the 12th century in a protected hollow and extended in the 14th century. It has an impressive interior: a three-aisled nave with Norman arcades and arches in Decorated style, and a filigree ceiling carved of Irish oak (15th century).

The small peninsula of **Strumble Head** is ideal for observing gray seals, which are seldom spotted in other areas; they return from their Atlantic fishing-grounds in September and stay here until October.

Follow the coast around St. Brides Bay. At little **St. Brides** the sea has encroached on to a graveyard and ancient stone coffins project from the cliffs behind the beach. After the wonderful sweep of **Newgale** beach comes **Solva**, a tiny harbor and deep inlet.

*MID-WALES*

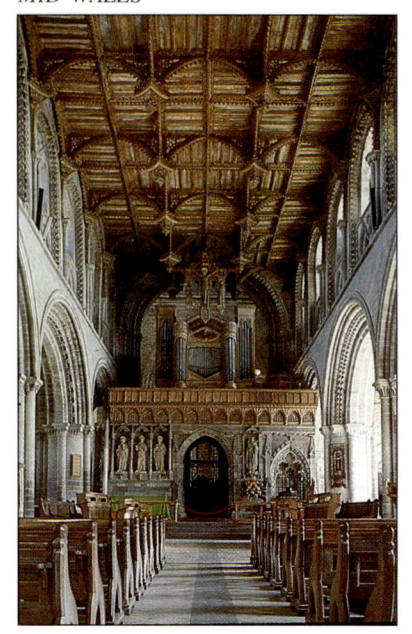

**Fishguard** is an important port for ferries to Ireland. East of Dinas Head on the Newport Bay is the popular resort of **Newport**. Southwest of Newport is the Neolithic cromlech of **Pentre Ifan**.

**Cardigan**, set on an elevation above the Teifi estuary, is a bustling market town with an old guildhall and coaching inns. Following the river inland will bring you to **Cenarth**, a romantic place with wide tumbling waterfalls, a watermill and the **National Coracle Centre**. Coracles are traditional round boats about a yard wide and about as long as a man, made of tarred canvas stretched over a wickerwork frame.

## MID WALES

The Welsh coast between Cardigan and Aberystwyth has some of the best sand beaches in Britain. At the cove of **Llangranog**, whitewashed houses and

*Above: St. David's, cathedral of the patron saint of the Welsh. Right: Harlech Castle.*

pubs high on the cliffs look down on the sand beach below. Picturesque **New Quay**, with its harbor and lobster pots, was supposedly the inspiration for the town of Llareggub in Dylan Thomas's *Under Milk Wood*. (If you think the name "Llareggub" reflects Thomas's knowledge of Welsh, read it backwards to discover its true etymology.)

At the mouth of the Ystwyth is **Aberystwyth**, capital of Mid-Wales. On the university campus is the **National Library College**, the cultural temple of the Welsh, which contains all major manuscripts in Welsh and other Celtic languages. Star exhibit is the *Book of Taliesin*, the oldest collection of Welsh legends and history. The Welsh are proud of their tradition of poets and bards. 1939 saw the founding here of the first elementary school in which the sole language of instruction was Welsh.

From Aberystwyth, the A4120 leads to **Devil's Bridge**, where the river Mynach plunges in a series of waterfalls 300 feet (91 m) into a wooded gorge. Below, in the mists and tumbling waters, you can see the **Devil's Punch Bowl** in the Rheidol valley, a hollow gouged out into weird shapes by the swirling river. You can also make the trip here by **steam train** on the narrow-gauge railway from Aberystwyth.

A picturesque old coach road leads from Devil's Bridge to the town of **Rhayader** and the **Elan Valley** reservoirs – an impressive chain of dammed lakes extending over 7 miles (11 km).

**Llandrindod Wells**, southeast of Rhayader, is a perfectly preserved Victorian spa town with tall gables, decorative ironwork, wide promenades and well-tended gardens. A Victorian Festival is held here every August. All year round visitors can take the waters at the Rock Park Spa and visit Lear's Magic Lantern Theater or the Victorian museum.

A diversion to **Kington** gives you a chance to see the remains of **Offa's Dyke** on the hills near the town. This earthen wall is about 15 feet (4.5 m) high, 60 feet (18 m) wide, and has a ditch nearly 12 feet (3.5 m) deep; the Saxon king Offa built it in the 8th century to divide Wales from England.

For 168 miles (270 km), **Offa's Dyke Path** follows the wall, a wonderful hiking trail from Chepstow in the south to Prestatyn in North Wales, which takes about 14 days to complete.

## NORTH WALES

At the mouth of the Mawddach river is the popular resort of **Barmouth**. The coastal road gives glorious views over the estuary, with broad sand beaches backed by dunes, while inland tower the Snowdonian mountains with Cader Idris (2,920 ft/893 m).

On the coast south of Tremadog Bay is the enchanting town of **Harlech**, which has a very well-preserved castle, towering in a strategic position on a rocky elevation. Built in 1283-89, with four round towers and a gatehouse, this fortress is protected today as a world heritage site.

In **Welshpool**, inland to the east, is **Powys Castle**. This grandiose mansion of red sandstone, with its two western towers (ca. 1300), was the residence of the Earls of Powys for more than 500 years. During renovations in the 16th century, the Long Gallery was added with its splendid stucco ceiling (1593). Besides the opulent apartments, you can also admire paintings (including Gainsborough), Gobelin tapestries and fine furniture. The terrace gardens were laid out in the 18th century in Italian style.

The little town of **Oswestry** has a well-preserved Iron-Age **hill-fort** and a **transport museum** full of vintage bicycles. Take the B4580 west to the highest waterfall, the largest natural lake and the highest road in Wales. In the hills near **Llanrhaeadr-ym-Mochnant**, the **Pistyll Rhaeadr** waterfall plunges 240 feet (74 m) over a sheer cliff. From **Pen-y-bont-fawr**, the B4391 curves around the shores of **Bala Lake**; you can also travel around it

# NORTH WALES

## NORTH WALES

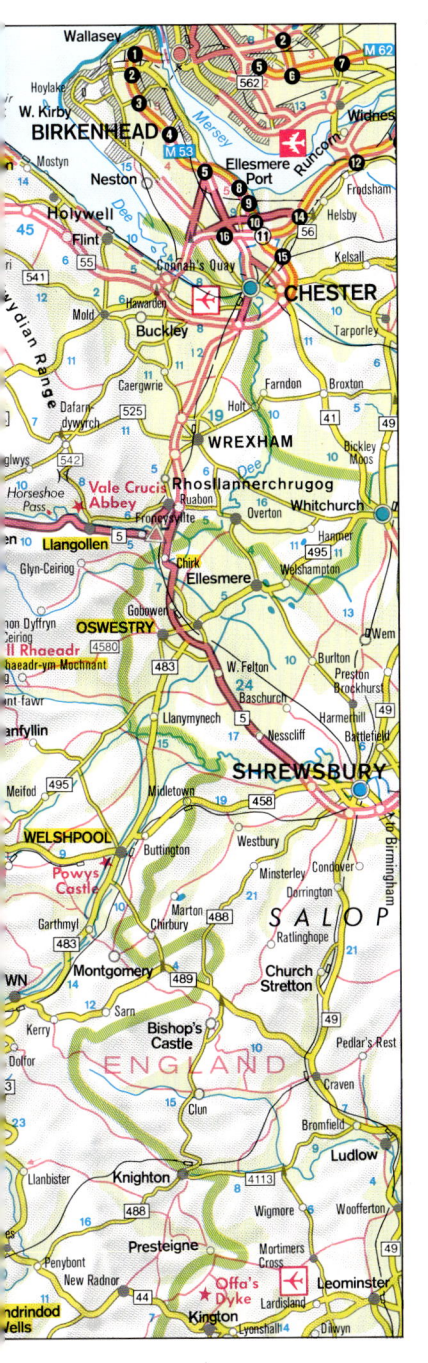

by narrow-gauge railway. From here, mountain roads snake north and south into high wild country. You can make a loop around Lake Vyrnwy via the highest road in Wales, Bwlch-y-Groes.

At **Chirk**, on the Welsh border, is one of the finest castles built by Edward I and the only one continuously occupied since the 14th century; it has magnificent entrance gates, gardens and dungeons. Inside, weapons and treasure are on display.

The A5 takes you on to **Llangollen**, a center for Welsh culture known for its colorful **Eisteddfod** festival every July, a contest for Welsh singers, poets and musicians. Worth seeing are the **Canal Museum**, the ruined fortress, and a fine half-timbered Tudor house, **Plas Newydd**. The valley of Llangollen is one of the most beautiful in the country; visitors can travel along the Llangollen canal in canal boats drawn by horses plodding along a towpath. East of the town at **Pontcysyllte**, canoes glide across Thomas Telford's magnificent 18-arched aqueduct, 121 feet (39 m) above the river Dee.

Spectacular views can be had from **The Horseshoe Pass** (1,130 ft/345 m) north of Llangollen on the A452. Set at the foot of the pass are the ruins of **Valle Crucis Abbey**, founded in 1202, with a High Cross from the 9th century.

The A525 leads north to **Ruthin**, an attractive town with medieval, Tudor and Georgian buildings and a crafts center. It is the only town in Britain where the curfew bell is rung every evening at 8 p.m.

The B5105, A5 and A470 will bring you back to the west coast and **Blaenau Ffestiniog**, which was a flourishing center of the slate industry until the 1970s. Slate is everywhere – on the roofs, covering walls, and around gardens; even the town fountain is a pillar of slate. An electric train carries passengers into the **Llechwedd Slate Caverns**. **Gloddfa Ganol**, once the world's biggest slate mine, is today a museum where you can

165

## CAERNARFON

explore on foot the half-lit tunnels and echoing caverns.

A narrow-gauge railway from 1836 connects Ffestiniog with Porthmadog, and steam trains regularly ply between the town and the sea. Near Porthmadog is **Portmeirion**. This is a real treasure, a surrealist Italianate village conceived in the 1920s by architect Sir Clough Williams Ellis and built on a wooded peninsula over nearly fifty years. Ellis also used parts of old buildings to build his fantasy village. A central piazza with a campanile; Burmese dancers on Ionic columns; Italian, Georgian and Victorian façades; a Jacobean town hall; domes and belfries combine to create an architectural fantasy. Also famous for its pottery, the town was the setting for the cult 1960s television series *The Prisoner*.

**Porthmadog**, on the Lleyn Peninsula, is a lively seaside resort with galleries,

*Above: Paddling across the aquaduct at Pontcysyllte. Right: Mount Snowdon (Yr Eryri) seen from Llyn Padarn.*

craft shops and a marina. To the west lies picturesque **Criccieth**. Its small castle, set on a promontory between two beaches, was a stronghold of the Welsh princes until seized by Edward I in 1283. Its twin-towered gatehouse is still in a good state of repair.

West is the little village of **Llanystumdwy**, where British prime minister David Lloyd George grew up and ended his days. Visit Highgate Cottage where he spent his youth, before following the coast around via **Pwllheli**, a busy resort with a large leisure and fairground complex, to reach **Abersoch**.

Next comes the wild windswept coast above Hell's Mouth and **Aberdaron** and the Land's End of North Wales with jagged cliffs and dangerous seas. Rounding the point, take time to walk barefoot across the Whistling Sands of **Porthoer**, just north of Aberdaron; the fine sand actually squeaks and whistles underfoot.

Inland, near **Llithfaen**, are the triple peaks of **The Rivals (Yr Eifl)**. At the top are the remains of hut circles, an ancient stone village – the **Town of the Giants** – and superb views of Caernarvon Bay. You can also walk through Vortigern's Valley (named for a Celtic chieftain said to have invited Saxons into Britain) to the ghost town of **Porth-y-Nant**.

At **Caernarfon**, located at the entrance to the **Menai Straits** which separate Anglesey Island from the mainland, stands the most famous castle in Wales. After King Edward I defeated the Welsh prince Llewellyn the Last in 1282, Caernarvon Castle, with its octagonal tower, was built as a symbol of English power. In 1284 Edward II was born here, as his father had promised an heir to the throne from Wales; the crown prince has been called the *Prince of Wales* ever since. The present Prince of Wales was invested here in 1969.

Close by the city walls is the church of St. Mary (1307). Many houses in the old town date from the 17th to 19th centuries.

*SNOWDONIA / ANGLESEY*

In **Bangor**, an interesting university town with a 16th-century cathedral and a charming old Victorian pier, the world's first iron suspension bridge was built in 1826. Thomas Telford's **Menai Bridge** spans the 1,300 yards (1.2 km) of the straits. East of Bangor is the 19th-century **Penrhyn Castle**, with a collection of paintings and some 2,000 dolls.

### Snowdonia

Snowdonia is a wild landscape of mountains and deep valleys, shaped by glaciers more than 100,000 years ago. In the past the region was densely populated, as is indicated by numerous relics such as stone circles, menhirs and old chapels.

**Snowdonia National Park** has gorgeous landscape to offer hikers, particularly those with waterproof clothing – the annual rainfall is 200 inches (5,000 mm). The National Park extends over 840 square miles (2,000 sq km), with **Snowdon**, at 3,560 feet (1,085 m), the highest of several majestic peaks.

At **Betwys-y-Coed** are the spectacular Swallow Falls; three rivers meet in this beautiful valley, and marked paths lead into the mountains and forests.

To the south is Beddgelert, a delightful village by the rushing river Glaslyn. Legend has it that the faithful hound Gelert of Prince Llewellyn has his grave (Bedd) here.

From Llanberis, the **Llanberis Pass** snakes its way between sheer rock faces and lakes past the keep of 13th-century **Dolbadarn Castle**. One easy means of ascent is the little rack-and-pinion mountain train which climbs up from Llanberis to the top of the mountain.

### ISLE OF ANGLESEY

Across the Menai Straits on the Isle of Anglesey is **Llanfair PG**. This is the short version of the longest place name in Europe: *Llanfairpwllgwyngyllgogerych-wyrndrobwllllantysiliogogogoch* – which means "St. Mary's by the white aspen over the whirlpool and St. Tysilio's by the red cave."

Many town names begin with *llan*, meaning a church; *aber* is a river mouth and *caer* a castle.

At **Bryn-Celli-Ddu**, you can see prehistoric burial chambers; there are also some with rock carvings near the sands of **Rhosneigr**.

Two bridges connect **Holyhead**, on **Holy Island**, to Anglesey; this is an important port for ferries to Ireland. As its name indicates, Holyhead (pronounced Hollyhead) was an important religious center of the Celts. In the 2nd century AD, this was a center for the druids' desperate resistance against the Romans. From Holyhead Mountain (720 ft/220 m) there is a wonderful view of the South Stack lighthouse.

East of Llanfair PG is **Beaumaris**. Its name is Norman French and means "beautiful marsh." Its moated castle, built

## NORTH WALES COAST

**LLANFAIRPWLLGWYNGYLLGOGERYCHWYRNDROBWLLLLANTYSILIOGOGOGOCH**
Llan-vire-pooll-guin-gill-go-ger-u-queern-drob-ooll-llandus-ilio-gogo-goch

in 1295, has rings within rings of defensive walls. It was the last, and perhaps the finest, of Edward I's many fortresses.

Also worth seeing is the **Tudor Rose**, one of the oldest 14th-century houses, which often hosts exhibitions. A museum has been set up in the **Old Gaol** which displays various methods of punishment, going all the way back to some outrageous tortures in the Middle Ages. There is also a delightful **Museum of Childhood** which exhibits old toys and dolls.

### NORTH WALES COAST

Back on the mainland, follow the A55 to **Conwy**, where another of Edward's castles, built in 1283-88, stands sentinel over the historic town beside the river estuary. Take a walk along the town walls and admire another elegant suspension bridge by Telford, which leads to the castle. Worth seeing too is **Aberconwy**, a medieval merchant's house, and **Plas Mawr** (1577-80) a wonderful mansion which is today home of the Royal Cambrian Academy of Arts. There is also **St. Mary's** church (13th century) and a building that claims to be the Smallest House in Wales.

**Llandudno** is Wales' most popular seaside resort, with a wonderful sandy beach at **North Shore**. North of the town center a limestone hump, the **Great Orme**, rises 679 ft (207 m) out of the sea; here, there are old copper mines to visit, while Lewis Carroll fans will enjoy the **Alice in Wonderland Center**.

Near **Conwy Bay** are the renowned **Bodnant Gardens** (laid out in 1875) with rare plants, a lily pond and the Welsh Mountain Zoo.

**Bodelwyddan**, near Rhyl, has a marble church and Bodelwyddan Castle, which contains many 19th-century paintings. The interiors, as well as the delightful walled garden and aviary, are all Victorian.

*Above: A nightmare for sign-painters – the longest place name in Europe.*

# GUIDEPOST WALES

## SOUTH WALES
### CARDIFF / CARMARTHEN
#### Accommodation
**CARDIFF**: *LUXURY:* **Angel**, Castle Street, tel. 01222 232633. *MODERATE:* **Glenmoor**, 150-152 Newport Road, tel. 01222 490230. *BUDGET:* **The Albany**, 14 Victoria Road, tel. 01222 701242.
**CARMARTHEN**: *LUXURY:* **Cuomtwrch Hotel**, Nantgaredig, tel. 01267 290238. *BUDGET:* **Spilman Hotel**, Spilman Street, tel. 01267 237037.
**LLYFYNDD**: *MODERATE:* **Trredyrhiw Country Guest House**, tel. 01558 668792.
**PEMBROKE**: *MODERATE:* **Court Hotel**, Lamphey, tel. 01646 672273.

#### Museums
**CAERLEON: Roman Legionary Museum**, High St., tel. 01633 423134, phone for opening times. **CARDIFF**: **National Museum of Wales**, Cathays Park, tel. 01222 397951, Tue-Sat and Bank Holiday Mon 10.00-17.00, Sun 14.30-17.00. **Welsh Folk Museum**, St. Fagins, tel. 01222 569441, April-Oct daily, Nov-March Mon-Sat 10.00-17.00. **CARMARTHEN: Country Museum**, Abergwili, 1,6 km east of Carmarthen, tel. 01267 231691, Mon-Sat 10.00-16.30. **SWANSEA: Swansea Arts Workshop**, Gloucester Place, tel. 01792 652016, all year Tue-Sat 11.00-16.00, Sun 12.00-16.30. **Glyn Vivian Art Gallery**, Alexandra Rd., tel. 01792 655006, Tue-Sun 10.30-17.30.

#### Tips and Trips
**BLAENAVON: Big Pit**, tel. 01495 790311, all year daily 9.30-17.00. **CAERPHILLY: Caerphilly Castle**, tel. 01222 883143, daily 9.30-18.00; Oct-March 9.30-16.00, closed Dec 25 and Jan 1. **CARDIFF: Cardiff Castle**, Castle Street, tel. 01222 822083, open daily March, April, Oct 10.00-17.00; May-Sept 10.00-18.00; Nov-Feb 10.00-16.30. **Castell Coch**, tel. 01222 810101, late March-late Oct daily 9.30-18.30; late Oct-March weekdays 9.30-18.30, Sun 14.00-16.00 **CHEPSTOW: Chepstow Castle**, Bridge Street, tel. 01291 624065, late March-late Oct daily 9.30-18.30. Late Oct-late March weekdays 9.30-16.00, Sun 14.00-16.00. **MONMOUTH: Raglan Castle**, tel. 01291 690228, 30 March-30 Oct daily 9.30-18.30; 31 Oct-29 March weekdays 9.30-16.00, Sun 14.00-16.00, closed Dec 25. **PEMBROKE: Pembroke Castle**, tel. 01646 681510, summer 9.30-18.00, winter 10.00-16.00, closed Dec 25. **TINTERN: Tintern Abbey**, tel. 01291 689251, late March-Oct daily 9.30-18.30; late Oct-March weekdays 9.30-16.00, Sun 14.00-16.00, closed Dec 25 and Easter.

#### Tourist Information
**CARDIFF**: Central Railway Station, tel. 01222 227281. **CARMARTHEN**: Lammas Street, tel. 01267 231557.

## MID WALES / ABERYSTWYTH
#### Accommodation
**ABERYSTWYTH**: *LUXURY:* **Bay Hotel**, The Promenade, Tel; 01970 617356.
*MODERATE:* **The Confah Country House Hotel**, Chancery, tel. 01970 617941. **Groves**, 44-46 North Parade, tel. 01970 617623.
*BUDGET:* **Marine Hotel**, The Promenade, tel. 01970 617356.

#### Museums
**LLANDRINDOD WELLS: Museum of Memorabilia**, Temple Street, tel. 01597 824513, all year Mon, Tue, Thur, Fri 10.00-16.30.

#### Tips and Trips
**ABERYSTWYTH: National Library of Wales**, tel. 01970 623816, Mon-Fri 9.30-18.00, Sat 9.30-17.00.
**LLYWERNOG: Silver Lead Mine**, on the A44, tel. 01970 85620, Easter-Oct daily 10.00-18.00.

#### Tourist Information
**ABERYSTWYTH**: Lisbon House, Terrace Road, Dyfed, tel. 01970 612125.

## NORTH WALES
#### Accommodation
**LLANDUDNO**: *LUXURY:* **Empire Hotel**, Church Walks, tel. 01492 860555.
*MODERATE:* **Bryn Derwen Hotel**, 34 Abbey Road, tel. 01492 876804.
*BUDGET:* **Glenvine Guest House**, 45 Church Walks, tel. 01492 875850.

#### Museums
**BEAUMARIS: Museum of Childhood**, 1 Castle Street, tel. 01248 712498, March-Jan daily 10.00-17.00, Sun 12.00-17.00.
**BETWS-Y-COED: Motor Museum**, (A5), tel. 01690 710632, March-Nov daily 10.00-18.00.
**CAERNARFON: Caernarfon Air World**, Air Caernarfon Ltd., Caernarfon Airport, Dinas Dinlle, tel. 01286 830800, Easter until end of October 9.00-17.00 daily.

#### Tips and Trips
**BODELWYDDAN: Bodelwyddan Castle**, tel. 01745 584060, April-June, Sept-Oct Sat-Thur; July-August daily. Nov-Feb Tue-Thur, Sat and Sun. Summer 10.30-17.00, winter 11.00-16.00. **HARLECH: Harlech Castle**, Castle Square, tel. 01766 780552, 30 March-30 Oct daily 9.30-18.30; 31 Oct-29 March weekdays 9.30-16.00, Sun 14.00-16.00, closed Dec 25. **PORTHMADOG: Criccieth Castle**, Castle Street, tel. 01766 522227. 30 March-30 Oct daily 9.30-18.30; 31 Oct-29 March weekdays 9.30-16.00, closed Dec 25. **WELSHPOOL: Powys Castle**, tel. 01938 554338, open 1 April-end of June; end of Sept-Oct daily except Mon and Tue; July-August daily except Mon (open Bank Holiday Monday).

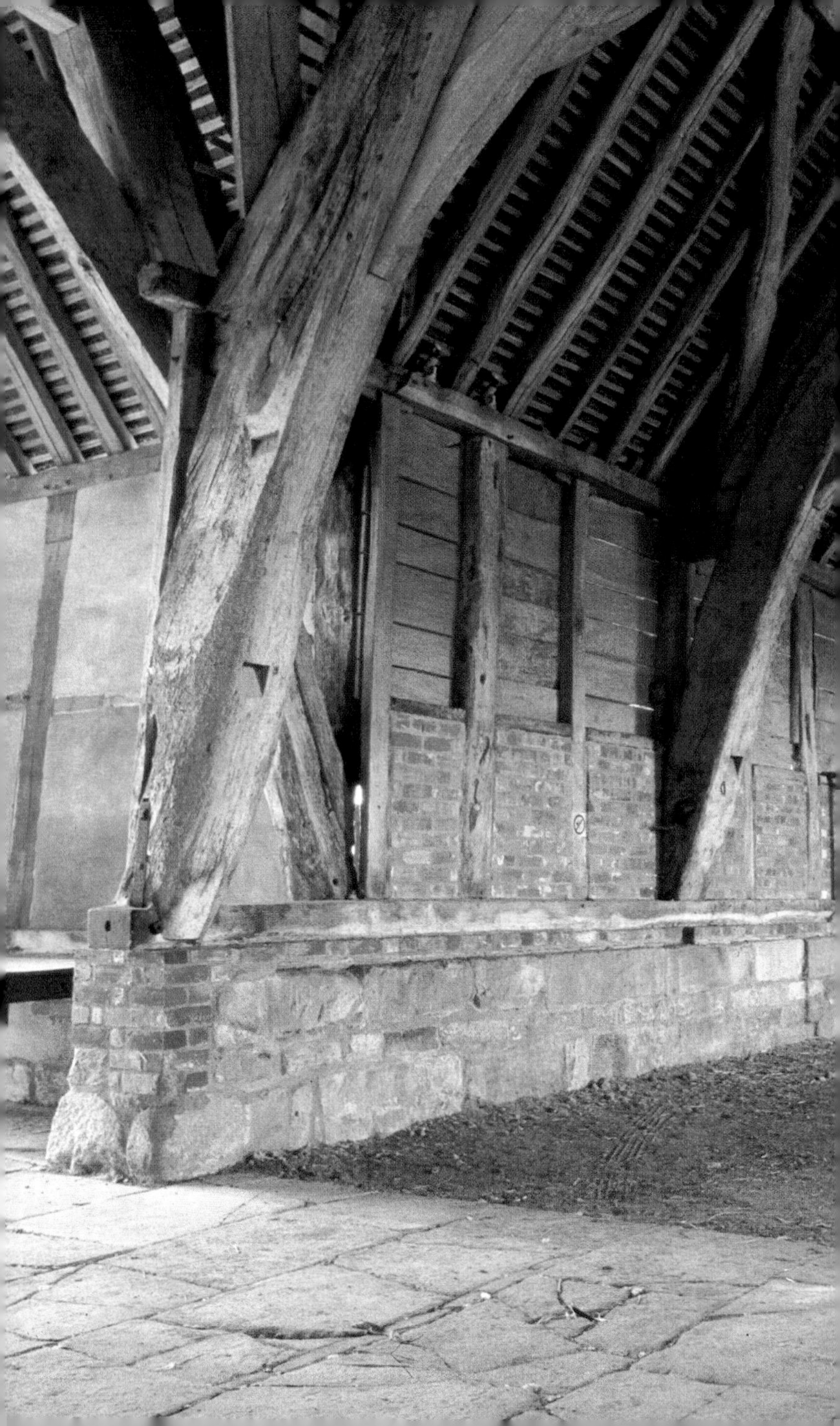

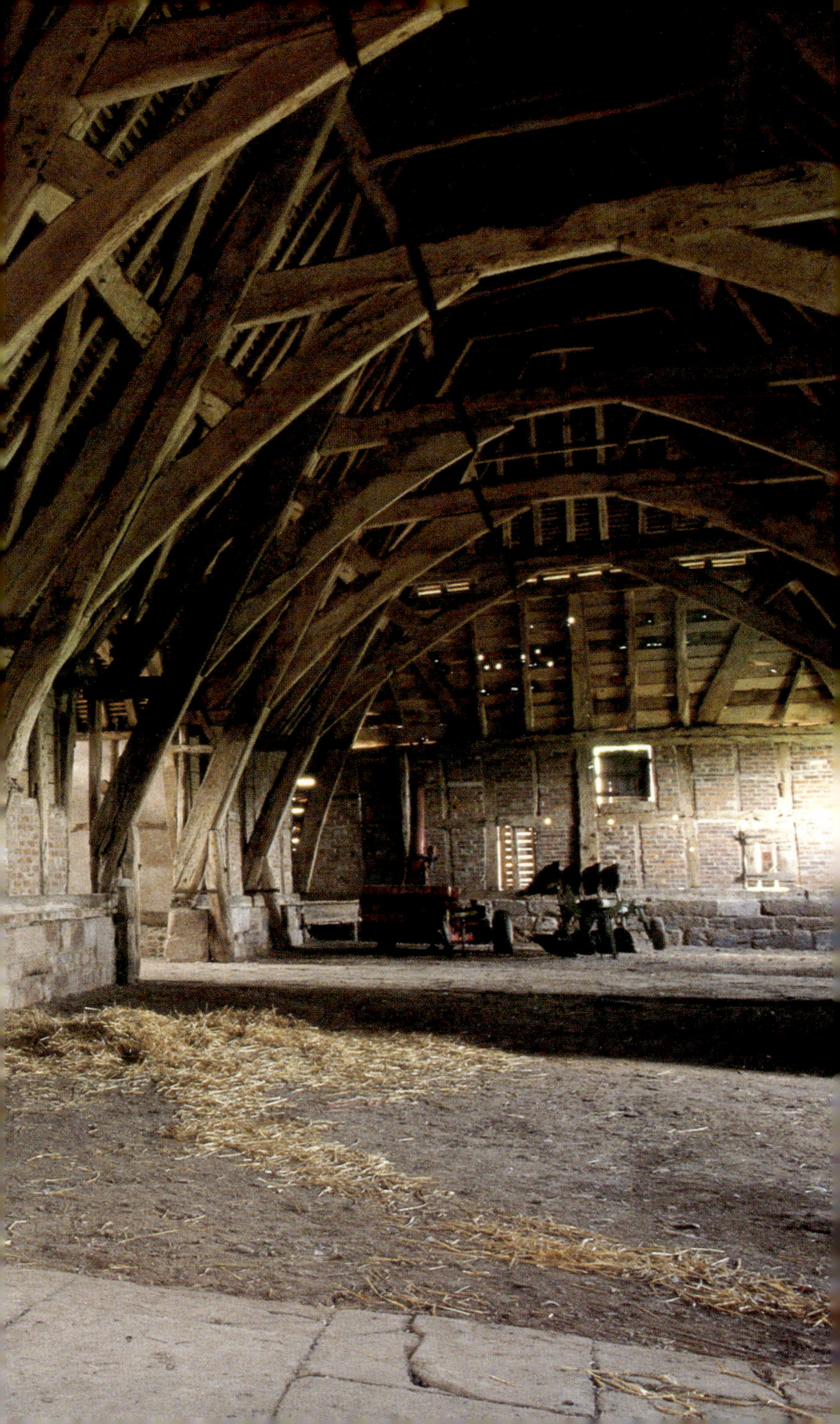

THE HEART OF ENGLAND

# THE HEART OF ENGLAND

**COTSWOLDS / BIRMINGHAM
WARWICKSHIRE
NORTHAMPTONSHIRE
LEICESTERSHIRE
LINCOLNSHIRE
NOTTINGHAMSHIRE
PEAK DISTRICT**

The name the Midlands – an area also known as "the heart of England" – actually is something of a misnomer. A glance at a map of the U.K. will show that the Midlands is not really in the middle at all. Although it encloses the middle part of the country, it lies mostly to the south of Birmingham, encompassing the counties of Herefordshire, Gloucestershire, Warwickshire, Shropshire and Worcestershire. The river Severn carves a broad valley through the region from south to north, with the Welsh hills to the west and the Cotswolds in the southeast.

## THE COTSWOLDS

There can be no better introduction to the heart of England than the Cotswolds. Cheerful streams purl between gentle hills; old stone buildings with slate roofs, lintels over the windows, and gable ends, seem to have grown out of the valleys and hillside. The color of the stone mutates from soft silvery gray in the south Cotswolds to butter-yellow and gold further north and east.

The limestone plateau of the Cotswold Hills is considered a region of great beauty, and is extremely popular with hikers. In the Middle Ages, trade in wool from the local sheep, the *Cotswold lions*, brought great wealth to the area, something reflected in the fine houses, churches, and mellow stone villages we see today. In small cities and towns, the rich wool merchants often financed the construction of oversized churches, which came to be known locally as *wool churches*. Even now, the region is mostly dependent on sheep-farming and cereals.

**Cirencester**, an ancient transportation hub of the Romans, is an ideal starting-point for touring the Cotswolds. The town's Roman origins can be explored in the excellent **Corinium Museum**. The parish church of **St. John the Baptist** with an impressive tower (1400) and the fan vaulting in St. Catherine's Chapel counts as one of the most beautiful wool churches in the country. Cirencester Park, home to the Earl of Bathurst, is set behind the highest hedge in England and has a chestnut avenue 5 miles (8 km) long.

In **Tetbury**, a pleasant old market town with many antique shops, the mansion of a rich wool merchant has been carefully restored and today houses a first-class hotel. Nearby are Highgrove and Gatcombe, the country homes of Prince Charles and Princess Anne.

*Preceding pages: Medieval barn in the Malvern Hills. Left: Barge enthusiasts in traditional clothing meet every year at Braunston.*

173

## THE COTSWOLDS

South of Tetbury, at **Westonbirt**, there is an extensive park with an arboretum, one of the best collections of rare trees and shrubs in the world. Northwest of Tetbury is the Elizabethan manor of **Chavenage House**, which is supposed to be haunted.

Northeast of Cirencester are the **Barnsley House Gardens** and pretty little **Bibury**, which William Morris once described as the most beautiful village in the Cotswolds. An old mill, the trout farm and Arlington Row – an idyllic higgledy-piggledy row of weavers' cottages – contribute to its distinctive charm.

East of Bibury and not far from the little market town of Burford is the Cotswolds Wildlife Park, one of whose special attractions is a herd of rhinoceros.

West of Burford on the A429, at **Yamworth**, lies the **Chedworth Roman Villa** with a bath house and mosaics. In the

*Above: A chat against the backdrop of typical Cotswold houses. Right: The picturesque Tewkesbury Abbey.*

little market town of **Northleach** in a former "House of Correction" – an 18th-century prison and court house – is an excellent museum of rural life, the **Cotswold Countryside Collection**. A 17th-century wool merchant's house contains a Magical Music Shop and Keith Harding's collection of every conceivable mechanical musical instrument.

Nearby **Bourton-on-the-Water** is a pretty and much-visited spot, with a model village, museums, a perfumery, bird park, and one of the best model railways in the country – but it can get very busy.

Wander off the main roads and there are lovely villages everywhere with mills and bridges and rushing streams, such as **Upper** and **Lower Slaughter**. You can take a pleasant stroll between the two villages along the River Eye.

Further north is **Stow-on-the-Wold** with its interesting old stocks, a reminder of how felons were once punished. There are other notable old stocks, shaped like eyeglasses, over at **Painswick**, south of

174

*THE COTSWOLDS*

Gloucester; the town is also famous for the 99 yew trees in the churchyard and its 18th-century Rococo Garden. The local butcher here sells what must be the world's most powerful cheese, called "Stinking Bishop."

Continuing north from Stow-on-the-Wold, you reach **Chipping Campden**, once a center of the wool trade, as still evidenced today by the wool merchants' houses from the 14th and 15th centuries, the town hall and other buildings.

**Hidcote Manor Garden**, northeast of Chipping Campden, is one of the most delightful gardens in England. It consists of a series of small gardens, each with its own distinct character or color scheme.

Turn west from **Moreton-in-Marsh** on to the A44 towards **Broadway**, aptly named after its wide main street. This is a classic Cotswold town which boasts beautiful Elizabethan houses – such as Tudor House and Abbots Grange – antique shops and cozy pubs. The **Teddy Bear Museum** is home to one of the best teddy bear collections in the world.

To the south are three particularly pretty Cotswold villages which justify abandoning the main roads. **Stanway** has a beautiful orange-gold stone Jacobean house; its vast gatehouse is adorned with magnificent stonecarving. Nearby **Stanton** has beautifully-restored 16th- and 17th-century houses in typical Cotswolds architecture. In **Snowshill**, a Tudor manor blends harmoniously with its village setting; inside, it's filled to the brim with collections of everything from Samurai armor to bicycles.

South of Stanton on the B4632 is **Winchcombe**, a lovely Cotswold town with weird gargoyles on the façade of the Perpendicular Style church (1490); a railway museum; and (an odd mix this) a folklore and police museum. Nearby are the picturesque ruins of the Cistercian **Hailes Abbey**, as well as **Sudeley Castle** which was once the home of Catherine Parr. The only wife to outlive King Henry VIII, she is buried in the chapel there. The castle park is ideal for extended walks.

175

## CHELTENHAM / GLOUCESTER

**The Severn Estuary**

In contrast to the rural country atmosphere of many of the small Cotswold towns and villages, **Cheltenham** is an elegant, sophisiticated place with a number of attractions for visitors. Medicinal springs were discovered here in 1718, and Cheltenham saw its heyday as a spa in the 18th and 19th centuries, when entire streets of elegant houses sprang up. In keeping with the spa ambience are the chic boutiques; the town is known for its shopping. Another nostalgic element are the horse-drawn carriage rides offered Sundays in Pittville Park. Sights include the **Art Gallery and City Museum** (containing archaeological finds, Chinese porcelain, English ceramics and Dutch paintings) Room and Museum. At the beginning of the 19th century, the great writer Jane Austen (1755-1817) occasionally worked on her novels in Cheltenham (including *Pride and Prejudice*).

In the city of **Tewkesbury**, many of the black-and-white half-timbered houses now accommodate little shops and cafés. The **Abbey Church** is one of the most attractive Norman churches in the country. Visitors with a taste for the Gothic should ask the prior to let them see the crypt with the bones of the Duke of Clarence. He was murdered by being drowned in a butt of malmsey on the orders of Richard III.

Head west of Cheltenham on the A40 to **Gloucester**, a major industrial center on the river Severn. The old docks and Victorian warehouses have been converted into a blend of specialty cafés, shops, countless antiques stalls, and museums – including the Opie Collection of Advertising and Packaging, the Waterways Museum and the Gloucestershire Regimental Museum.

The **Beatrix Potter Museum** in Gloucester Court will entertain young and old alike. Nearby is the **cathedral**, where William the Conqueror commissioned the *Domesday Book*. The southern transept and choir of this partially Anglo-Norman building were rebuilt in the Perpendicular style. Some of the stained-glass in the east windows is still the original article from the 14th century. There are superb cloisters with fan vaulting, as well as the tomb of King Edward II, who was, after systematic maltreatment, murdered with a red-hot poker at **Berkeley Castle**, southwest of Gloucester.

Not far from here is the world's largest wildfowl park at **Slimbridge**. These wetlands inspired many paintings by the Wildfowl Trust's inaugurator and naturalist, Sir Peter Scott.

**The Forest of Dean**

West of Gloucester, across the river Severn, lies the **Forest of Dean** with caves, Roman iron mines, and wonderful

*Above: A stained-glass window in the middle of the forest – one attraction of the sculpture trail in the Forest of Dean. Right: The Council House in Birmingham.*

*THE FOREST OF DEAN / HEREFORD*

hiking trails, including a "sculpture trail" with exhibits ranging from a composition made of railway ties to a huge stained-glass window that hangs in a broad green clearing. South of **Cinderford**, the Dean Heritage Centre at **Soudley** on the B4227 explains the changing pattern of life in the forest. **Symonds Yat**, on the B4432, is a mecca for rock climbers and offers a spectacular view down into the gorge of the Wye Valley. Travel north on the A40 to **Goodrich Castle**. Hewn directly from the sandstone above the river Wye, it has provided a spectacular vantage point ever since it was first built in the 13th and 14th centuries.

### Hereford and Worcester

The graceful town of **Ross-on-Wye** claims the only museum in England devoted entirely to buttons! It also houses the **Lost Street Museum** (which reconstructs a street from the time of Edward VII) as well as a candlemakers' workshop.

**Hereford** is a comfortably-sized city with a host of medieval buildings and a series of fascinating museums, including a cider museum and another devoted to steam engines. **Hereford Cathedral**, mainly Norman, houses the *Mappa Mundi*, one of the oldest maps in the world; in its Chained Library, many manuscripts and books from the 8th-15th centuries (more than 1,400 volumes) are chained to the shelves.

**Ledbury** is a pretty town with rows of half-timbered buildings, including the Market House and the Old Grammar School in a picturesque cobblestone lane.

Nearby, on the A438, is **Eastnor Castle**, which looks like a medieval fortress but was actually built around 1812. Its vast hall, splendid state rooms and beautiful grounds have served as a setting for many television and film productions, including *The Canterville Ghost* and *Sherlock Holmes*.

The **Malvern Hills** lie like a sleeping giant across the Midland plain. Footpaths criss-cross some of the most ancient hills in England; an Iron Age fort crowns their highest point. In the genteel Victorian spa of **Great Malvern**, you'll find, somewhat unexpectedly, the best kite shop in England. More in keeping with the mood is Little Malvern Court, set in acres of former monastic gardens. A few miles north is **Worcester** beside the river Severn, famous for its sauce and porcelain. The city boasts attractive Tudor houses, art galleries, museums and a **cathedral** that is a glorious mix of building styles from the 11th to the 16th centuries. John Lackland, the king who signed the *Magna Carta* and fought Robin Hood, is buried here.

The A44 leads westward to **Lower Broadheath**, where music-lovers can visit Edward Elgar's birthplace and the museum commemorating England's great composer. Porcelain enthusiasts can take a fascinating tour of the Royal Worcester factory.

The M5 motorway is a fast route into the center of Birmingham. Stop at **Bromsgrove** to see the **Avoncroft Museum of Buildings** with its working windmill, Georgian ice-house and earth closet – everything, in fact, from a 16th-century half-timbered house to a 1946 prefab.

## BIRMINGHAM

**Birmingham** is a much-maligned city. It is busy, sprawling and never beautiful, but it *is* vibrant with excellent museums and art galleries and is within easy reach of lovely countryside. Visit the **Botanical Gardens**, the Victorian streets of the jewelry quarter, or the **Museum of Science and Industry** with its excellent transport and aircraft sections, housed in an old factory. In this museum you can see the oldest functioning steam engine in the world, manufactured in 1779 by Boulton and Watt. In addition to a collection of Pre-Raphaelite paintings, the **Birmingham Museum and Art Gallery** shows an exhibition of handicrafts throughout the centuries. Birmingham has been the center of the jewelry industry for 200 years, but its rapid industrial growth began with the advent of the railway. Not surprisingly there is a **Railway Museum** near the city, at **Tyseley** on the A41. Canals also played their part in the city's growth, and it can be fun to take a "Brummage Boat" through the old network of waterways and out into tranquil countryside.

Culturally, Birmingham has also seen significant growth in recent years. The City of Birmingham Symphony Orchestra has become one of the world's leading ensembles since young conductor Simon Rattle – now a "Sir" – took it over in 1980. Birmingham is also home to the Royal Ballet, which moved from London as part of the ongoing effort to break that city's cultural monopoly in England.

Cadbury World at **Bournville** is an exhibition about chocolate – from a taste of the original unsugared drink at the court of Montezuma, the Aztec emperor, to a 1930s sweet shop and a demonstration of putting the yolk into a creme egg.

### The Upper Severn Valley

Other places within reach of Birmingham include **Aston Hall**, a splendid Jacobean house with a grand balustraded staircase and a *very long* Long Gallery. **Dudley** has a zoo in the grounds of its ruined castle (14th-16th centuries), and the 26-acre (10 ha) Black Country Museum with a chainmaker's house and an underground coal-mining display. On the canal nearby, visitors can have a go at "legging" a coal barge in the traditional way through the Dudley tunnel.

Heading southwest will bring you to **Kidderminster**, known for its carpets.

A little outside the town to the south on the A448 is **Harvington Hall** (16th-18th centuries). This moated manor house is positively riddled with secret passages

WEST MIDLANDS
0 10 20 30 km
0 10 miles
TELFORD
SHREWSBURY
Haughmond Abbey
Wrekin
Attingham Park
Wroxeter
Cound
Condover
Ironbridge
Shifnal
Boscobel House
Tong
Ivetsey Bank
Gailey
to Stafford
CANNOCK
to Derby
Lichfield
Tamworth
Twycross
Albrighton
Aerospace Museum
Moseley Old Hall
Bloxwich
Bassett's Pole
Fazeley
Atherstone
Kingsbury
Over Whitacre
Walsall
WOLVERHAMPTON
Much Wenlock
Norton
SHROPSHIRE
Morville
Shipley
Sedgley
Bridgnorth
Wenlock Edge
Shipton
Himley
Quatt
Cleobury North
DUDLEY
W BROMWICH
Aston Hall
Coleshill
BIRMINGHAM
Stone Br.
Corley
Allesley
Pedlar's Rest
Billingsley
STOURBRIDGE
TYSELEY
Bickenhill
SOLIHULL
COVENTRY
Bromfield
Cleobury Mortimer
Kidderminster
Bewdley
Harvington Hall
Shirley
Hockley Heath
Kenilworth
Ludlow
Cleehill
Clows Top
Alvechurch
BROMSGROVE
Royal Leamington Spa
STOURPORT
Hartlebury
Woofferton
Tenbury Wells
Teme
Little Hereford
REDDITCH
Henley in Arden
Warwick
Gt. Witley
Ombersley
Upper Sapey
Stockton
Vernon Arms
Studley
Holt Heath
DROITWICH
WARWICKSHIRE
Leominster
Lower Broadheath
Coughton Court
Cook Hill
Ragley Hall
Alcester
Charlecote Park
Hastings
Docklow
Broadwas
Bromyard
WORCESTER
Bidford
A. Hathaway's Cottage
STRATFORD-upon-Avon
Hope under Dinmore
Powick
Norton
Avon
Kineton
Ettington
Vale of Evesham
Alderminster
HEREFORD AND WORCESTER
Newton
GREAT MALVERN
Malvern Hills
Severn Stoke
Pershore
Evesham
Mickleton
Hidcote Manor Garden
Hidcote
Tredington
Compton Wynyates
Wynds Point
Eckington
Chipping Campden
Shipston on Stour
Dormington
Hereford
Mordiford
Preston
Ledbury
Longdon
Sedgeberrow
Broadway
Moreton-in-Marsh
Eastnor Castle
Snowshill
Stanton
Much Birch
Dymock
Abbey
Tewkesbury
Aston Cross
Stanway
Hailes Abbey
Long Compton
Staunton
Coombe Hill
Winchcomb
Wye
Harewood End
Bishop's Cleeve
Stow-on-the-Wold
Chipping Norton
St. Weonards
Newent
Sudeley Castle and Gardens
Peterstow
Ross-on-Wye
Lea
GLOUCESTER
CHELTENHAM
Slaughter
Evenlode
Goodrich Castle
Andoversford
Bourton-on-the-Water
Northleach
Windrush
to Oxford
Whitchurch
Huntley
Mitcheldean
Symonds Yat
GLOUCESTERSHIRE
Seven Springs
Colesborne
Burford
Cinderford
Hardwicke
Birdlip
Monmouth
Soudley
Yanworth
Forest of Dean
Arlingham
Painswick
Elkstone
Bibury
Aldsworth
Witney
Coleford
Blakeney
Barnsley House Gardens
OXFORDSHIRE
Bream
STROUD
Chalford
Barnsley
Slimbridge
Stonehouse
Poulton
Fairford
Bampton
Clanfield
to Newport
Lydney
Sharpness
Tintern
WALES
ENGLAND
Castle
Berkeley
Chavenage House
Nailsworth
Cirencester
Lechlade
Thames
Dursley
Gatcombe
Faringdon
Severn
Stone
Wotton under Edge
Crudwell
Cricklade
Highworth
Chepstow
Tetbury
Highgrove
Swindon
Thornbury
Alveston
Didmarton
Malmesbury
Purton
Shrivenham
Caldicot
Wickwar
Westonbirt
Sherston
Brinkworth
Wootton Bassett
Ashbury
River
Chipping Sodbury
Corston
Acton Turville
Sutton Benger
Filton
Avonmouth
BRISTOL
Castle Combe
Marshfield
M 54
M 42
M 6
M 50
M 5
M 4
E 05

and priestholes. Hounded Catholics could even lift up the stair treads and disappear inside.

From Kidderminster, the **Severn Valley Railway** runs frequent steam trains to Bewdley and along the beautiful river valley to **Bridgnorth**, a picturesque market town. Nearby is the **Midland Motor Museum**, full of sleek shiny racing cars.

If you leave Kidderminster on the A456 west and turn off onto the A4117, you'll pass through Shropshire. First comes **Ludlow** with its well-cared-for half-timbered buildings, among them the **Feathers Hotel** of 1603. Overlooking the Welsh marches and the Teme and Corve rivers, the impressive ruined castle in summer often provides a magical setting for Shakespeare performances. The castle was the last Shropshire fortress to surrender to the Parliamentarians in the Civil War.

*Above: The great banqueting hall of Warwick Castle. Right: Anne Hathaway's Cottage in Stratford-upon-Avon.*

The A48 leads to **Shrewsbury**. Possibly the best-preserved Tudor town in England, it is perched on a rocky hill in a loop of the river Severn. At the center of the town is the Square with the **Old Market Hall** (around 1596) and a statue of Lord Clive of India.

Abbeys, museums, stately homes and castles abound in the vicinity, and the avid historian or garden-lover might do well to spend a few days here. For example, an elegant, classical 18th-century house is set in beautiful **Attingham Park**, while at **Hawkstone Park** the landscape has been carved out into dramatic cliffs, stone steps, precipitous paths, tunnels, and grottoes. **Haughmond Abbey**, founded in 1135, has walls hewn directly from the living rock of the hillside; and there are magnificent landscaped gardens at **Hodnet Hall**.

The remains of a 2nd-century Roman city, with baths and forum colonnades, can be explored at **Viriconium**, near Wroxeter; while medieval **Much Wenlock**, southeast of Shrewsbury, has Nor-

# IRONBRIDGE / COVENTRY

man, half-timbered and Georgian buildings in immaculate condition. Geologists will appreciate a drive along the B4371 on the 400-million-year-old fossilized coral reef of **Wenlock Edge**.

### Cradle of the Industrial Revolution

An absolute must is the **Ironbridge Gorge Museum**, actually a complex of several extremely interesting industrial museums. It was in Ironbridge that Abraham Darby first smelted iron using coke in 1709, a technical breakthrough which led to the Industrial Revolution.

**Ironbridge** thereupon developed into the center of the cast-iron industry; here, for instance, were manufactured the ceremonial gates for Prince Albert's Crystal Palace. The secluded valley is now a vast living museum where you can watch molten iron being poured into Victorian molds, see the decorative **Iron Bridge**, the world's first cast-iron bridge (1778), or tour the **Coalport porcelain works** and see a unique collection of tiles at the Jackford Tile Museum. An appropriate conclusion to the visit is a meal in a Victorian gaslit pub.

From Telford, take the M54 east. Near exit 3 is **Boscobel House,** where Charles II hid when Cromwell's troops came searching for him. He also sought refuge in nearby 12th-century **White Ladies Priory** and in a priesthole at **Moseley Old Hall** (south of exit 2).

The history of military aviation is presented through the veteran aircraft at the Royal Air Force's **Aerospace Museum** in Cosford, a northern suburb of Birmingham. Or detour to **Bickenhill** to visit the **National Motorcycle Museum**.

### Coventry

East of Birmingham is the textiles and industrial city of **Coventry**. The historic old town was mostly destroyed by German bombs during the war. While there are guided tours of medieval Coventry and the history of its last 1,000 years is explained in the **Herbert Art Gallery and Museum**, most people come to see the **Cathedral**, one of the country's most notable post-war buildings. It stands next to the ruined Late Gothic cathedral, where the charred cross remains as a reminder of the bombing; the glass façade of the new building forms a visual link with the old. Inside are such outstanding works of modern art as the John Piper baptistry window and Jacob Epstein's statue of St. Michael and the Devil.

The **Museum of British Road Transport** displays street scenes from various epochs.

### WARWICKSHIRE

East of Coventry is **Rugby**, where you can tour Rugby School, birthplace of the sport rugby and made famous through *Tom Brown's Schooldays*. Rupert Brooke and Lewis Carroll (Charles Dodgson) were educated here.

## STRATFORD-UPON-AVON

To the south are two castles. At **Kenilworth**, Robert Dudley once entertained Elizabeth I with a 17-day feast and pageant. The second, **Warwick Castle**, is situated on the banks of the river Avon. It seems to epitomize the ideal image of an English castle, surrounded by parkland with greenhouses. Inside, in addition to pictures, porcelain, weapons and a grisly dungeon, there are splendid state rooms such as the *Great Hall* with a Venetian marble floor and oak eaves, or the *Drawing Room*, panelled with cedarwood and adorned with a baroque stucco ceiling and crystal chandeliers.

The old town of **Warwick** is full of half-timbered, top-heavy old buildings, with archways, alleys and attractive 17th- and 18th-century streets that invite exploration. The east and west gates of the town (the latter dating from the 12th century) include interesting chapels; note, too, the half-timbered **Leychester Hospital** (16th century).

*Above: William Shakespeare was born in Stratford-upon-Avon.*

### Birthplace of the Bard

**Stratford-upon-Avon**, birthplace of William Shakespeare, is still dominated by attractive half-timbered houses from the 16th and 17th centuries. Idyllically situated on the river Avon, once a cloth and farming town, Stratford today lives mainly through the marketing of its best-known native son.

**Shakespeare's birthplace** was an Elizabethan half-timbered house in Henley Street. The interior has never been remodeled, and here you can view a recreation of the living conditions of a well-to-do family of the 16th century with many Shakespearian memorabilia.

On the corner of Chapel Street and Chapel Lane is the site of **New Place**, where Shakespeare, after his return from London in 1611, spent the last five years of his life. A formal **knot garden** in the style typical of the Elizabethan period has been recreated here.

The poet's daughter, Susanna, married a doctor, John Hall, and **Hall's Croft** in the old town displays not only fine furniture of the time, but also the apparatus of a doctor's practice in the 17th century. A walk along an avenue lined with linden trees brings you to the parish church of the **Holy Trinity**, where Shakespeare was baptized and buried.

Stroll along the banks of the Avon towards the town center and you will see two of the great Shakespearian theaters here: the **Royal Shakespeare Theatre** and the **Swan Theatre**. Book ahead if possible, or see if there are any last-minute returned seats, for a performance by the Royal Shakespeare Company. Theatre at Stratford has a special magic of its own; the plays burst into life as if reanimated by their setting. North of the Royal Shakespeare Theatre are the elegant **Bancroft Gardens**.

West of Stratford on the A46, at **Shottery**, is the birthplace of Shakespeare's wife, **Anne Hathaway's Cottage**.

*EASTERN MIDLANDS*

# EAST MIDLANDS

0  10  20  30 km
0     10 miles

183

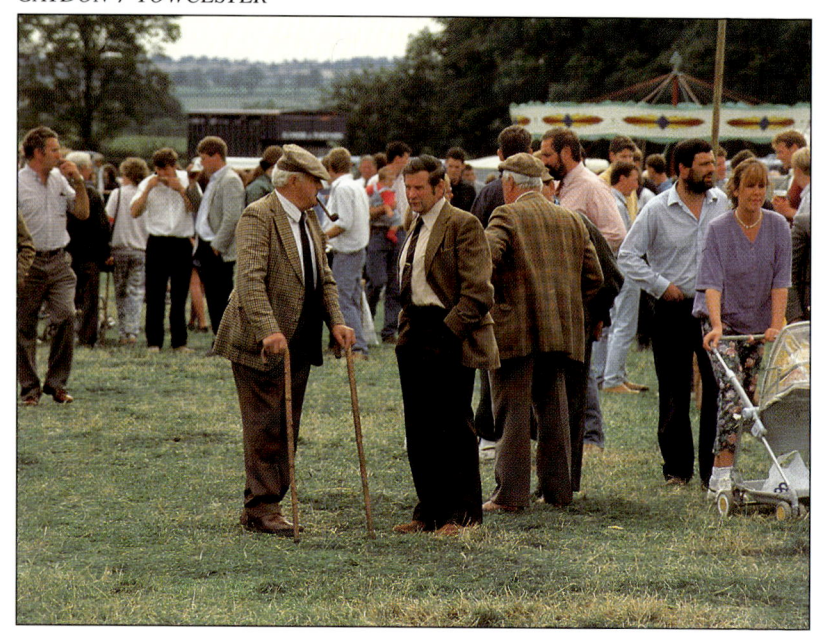

At Wilmcote, north of Shottery, the childhood home of the Bard's mother, **Mary Arden's House**, can also be visited. Here, county life and customs of the last three centuries are displayed and illuminated. **Charlecote Park**, where the young Shakespeare was alleged to have poached deer, is near **Wellesbourne**. Back in town, from the center of a darkened auditorium, the **World of Shakespeare** exhibition takes you back with sights and sounds through time to Elizabethan England, the horrors of the plague and the royal fireworks.

The Warwickshire countryside is rich in thatched cottages and stately homes. There are two fine houses on the A435 near Alcester: **Coughton Court**, where the anxious wives of Gunpowder Plotters awaited news as to whether their husbands' plans to blow up Parliament had succeeded; and **Ragley Hall**, a Palladian house with fine baroque plasterwork in the Great Hall, wonderful porcelain and paintings at every turn, and peacocks strutting outside. To the south, a gray stone country inn at **Ardens Grafton** near Bidford-on-Avon has a collection of 300 antique dolls.

Head to the M40 east of Stratford for a direct route to London. If time allows, come off at exit 12 for **Gaydon** and take the shuttle bus to the world's largest collection of historic British cars at the **Heritage Motor Centre**.

## NORTHAMPTONSHIRE

An old Roman road, known as Watling Street and today's A5, enters Northamptonshire just north of **Stony Stratford**, after which it leads through the center of the originally Roman town of **Towcester** (pronounced Toaster), known as *Lactodorum* to its founders.

Today a small market town typical of the area, Towcester is best known for its privately-owned horse racecourse, where

*Above: Agricultural shows are favorite social events in the country. Right: Locks at Stoke Bruerne Waterways Museum.*

steeplechase races take place regularly throughout the winter season, and two Arab horse race meetings (on the "flat") are held every summer.

Southwest of Towcester is the village of **Sulgrave** with **Sulgrave Manor**, the Tudor home of the family of George Washington, first President of the United States. The door of the house (1539) is decorated with the arms of the family, which supposedly served as a model for the Stars and Stripes.

Further north along narrow winding country lanes, but well signposted, is **Canon's Ashby**, the remarkably well preserved 16th-century family home of the poet John Dryden. The drawing room has a particularly fine Jacobean stucco ceiling.

Back in Towcester, anyone interested in canals and waterways can detour east to **Stoke Bruerne**, which lies on the **Grand Union Canal** as it passes on its way between London and Birmingham. The **Stoke Bruerne Waterways Museum** presents a comprehensive overview of the history of this and other great 18th-century canals of Britain. The village lies at the south end of the longest navigable canal tunnel in the country, some 3 miles (5 km) long, which comes out at the other end by the village of Blisworth; canal boat trips through the tunnel depart from the restored wharf alongside the museum.

If you take the A43 north, the next town is **Northampton**, the county town. This has been a center of human activity since prehistoric times; archaeological finds in the area date back as far as 6,000 years. To the Romans it was an important trading center, to the Saxons a vital hill fortress, and to the Normans an administrative center for the whole central part of the kingdom.

All of this history is well recorded and displayed in the **Northampton Central Museum**. Much of the old town was destroyed by German bombs in World War II, but the large market square, several old churches, and a number of other individual buildings of historic interest were

*LEICESTERSHIRE / ROCKINGHAM*

fortunately spared. For many centuries, Northampton has been a center for the shoe trade; a number of manufacturers in the town still operate factory shops where you can often find real bargains. The **Leathercraft Museum** documents this tradition. The **Derngate Theatre**, on the site of one of the medieval gates, occasionally mounts the first runs of plays which later go on to the West End, there to become hits.

## LEICESTERSHIRE

Northwest of Northampton on the A428, near the village of West Haddon, are the **Coton Manor Gardens**, and, just to the north of that, the **Guilsborough Grange Wildlife Park**.

Directly north from Northampton along the A508, is Market Harborough. On the way, the road passes through the little village of **Brixworth**, which is worth a stop for its magnificent Saxon church, described by one authority as "probably the most imposing 7th-century architectural monument north of the Alps."

**Market Harborough** is an attractive small market town with many fine Georgian houses and a large market square where both general and cattle markets have been held since as long ago as 1203. Its most remarkable building is the former Grammar School, built in 1614 on wooden stilts, so as to provide the vendors, whose stalls were set up beneath the building, some measure of protection from the elements. The **Harborough Museum** vividly records the town's long history.

From Market Harborough, take the A427 towards Corby. A left turn onto the A6003 at the outskirts of Corby leads to the village of **Rockingham**. To the east lies **Rockingham Forest**, part of a vast wooded area, once the favorite hunting-ground of William the Conqueror.

*Above: Fertile plains in Lincolnshire. Right: Spalding celebrates a flower festival every year in spring.*

*LINCOLNSHIRE*

From the lip of a steep hillside to the north of the village, that king's massive and imposing fortress, **Rockingham Castle**, broods over the valley of the River Welland, marking the border between Northamptonshire and Leicestershire. Having fallen into disrepair in the late Middle Ages, the castle was given by Queen Elizabeth I to Edward Watson, son-in-law of Lord Chief Justice Montagu; his family has owned it ever since. It was the model for "Chesney Wold" in Charles Dickens' novel *Bleak House*.

Returning south from Rockingham along the A6003, take a left onto the A6116 just before Corby. A minor road turning off to the left leads to **Kirby Hall**, a lovely 16th-century house built for Sir Thomas Stafford, and abandoned in the 18th century. Although its 17th-century gardens are currently being restored, the whole site is open for visitors. Nearby is **Deene Park**, another 16th-century Tudor mansion of great architectural and historical interest, with extensive formal and parkland gardens.

A worthwhile, if rather complicated, route leads along the A47 west of Peterborough to **Stamford**, a pleasant old coaching town with a good museum and several attractive coaching inns. South of the town is **Burghley House**, one of England's greatest Elizabethan houses, owned by the Exeter and Cecil families for over four centuries and crammed with great works of art, rare furniture, wall and ceiling paintings, and many other treasures.

## LINCOLNSHIRE

As you drive northwards, the land changes, gradually flattening out into a panorama of low, even plains and marshes extending as far as the coast of the North Sea.

This low-lying fenland countryside, most of it originally marshland, has been laboriously reclaimed by extensive drainage ever since Roman times. Because of its fertile, peaty soil, the entire area is covered with flower fields, bulb plantations, market gardens and seed nurseries, making it a gardener's paradise. To the west of the A15, the ground gradually rises to the more rolling countryside of the Lincolnshire Wolds.

From Market Deeping the A15 carries on northwards along the western edge of the fens. It passes through Bourne, where you can turn off onto the A151 to visit the impressive **Grimsthorpe Castle**, containing fine tapestries, furniture and works of art. The castle stands in spectacular parkland, where red deer roam; note, too, its unusual ornamental vegetable garden.

Gardeners and landscape architects should also note that the same turnoff leads to **Spalding**, a peaceful Georgian town showing strong Dutch influence in its architecture, which is the main center of Lincolnshire's flower industry. A world-famous flower festival is held here every spring.

North of Spalding, on the A16, is he old town of **Boston**, which was a thriving seaport in the 13th century. As the river Welland silted up, however, the coast was pushed farther and farther away from the town, sparking an economic decline, which was temporarily reversed by the building of a new channel and docks in the 1880s. Back in the 17th century, people were tried in the Guildhall for attempting to emigrate to America; those who did make the crossing gave the town's name to Boston, Massachusetts. The 18th-century **Fydell House**, containing the **Pilgrim College** (part of the University of Nottingham), still reserves a special room exclusively for visitors from the town's American namesake.

Walking around the city, you will see the town's emblem from a long way off: the **Boston Stump**, as St. Botolph's Church is referred to on account of its unfinished-looking, dumpy tower.

*Right: Testimony to the earlier power of the Church: Lincoln Cathedral.*

**Lincoln**

Further north on the A15, the city of **Lincoln** towers above the surrounding fens on a high narrow limestone ridge called the Lincoln Edge. The city itself is dominated by its superb cathedral, which can be seen from many miles away. Founded as *Lindum* by the Romans in 48 AD, Lincoln has remained an important strategic, cultural and commercial center for the whole region ever since.

The triple-towered **Cathedral of St. Mary** is a masterpiece of medieval church architecture. In 1185, the original church was badly damaged in an earthquake; it was rebuilt in the Early Gothic style, integrating such original Romanesque components as were left. As a result, Romanesque ornamentation and Gothic sculpture are juxtaposed on the building's imposing west façade with its twin towers. The three-aisled nave of this pillared basilica, 477 feet (146 m) long, ends in the so-called "Angels' Choir" (which is also tripartite), named for its 28 sculptures of angels. In this choir, you can easily spot the linear division of the walls, one typical characteristic of the Decorated Style.

The cathedral is surrounded by a maze of steep cobblestone streets, with many historic houses dating from the Middle Ages and subsequent eras, all well preserved and cared for. The 12th-century **Jew's House**, said to be the oldest inhabited town house in England, has been converted into a restaurant. Even Roman structures can be seen here and there.

Parts of the old Norman fortress, built by William the Conqueror still survive; among its treasures is one of the original Magna Carta documents. There is a good view from the Observatory Tower.

Antique shops abound in the old city. Other attractions here include the **Museum of Lincolnshire Life**, the **Usher Art Gallery**, **Ellis' Mill**, and specialist museums exhibiting everything from bicycles to antique toys.

## NOTTINGHAMSHIRE

From Lincoln the A46, an old Roman road known as the Fosse Way, heads back in a southwesterly direction into Nottinghamshire and leads to **Newark-on-Trent**.

Newark is noted for its large market square lined with elegant Georgian buildings, as well as its grandiose spired **Church of St. Mary Magdalen** and the nearby ruins of massive **Newark Castle**, which suffered three prolonged sieges during the English Civil War.

At one time the Great North Road (the A1) passed straight through the center of Newark, and the town became an important staging post for the coaches. There are therefore several attractive old coaching inns, ideal stopping point for a leisurely meal in traditional surroundings.

From Newark, you have a choice of two routes towards the southwest and Nottingham. The longer route follows the A617 west out of Newark, then branches left onto the A612 to Nottingham.

One of the highlights of this route is the small town of **Southwell**. Here stands the magnificent 12th-14th century **Southwell Minster**. Carved on the columns of the Chapter House are the unique **Leaves of Southwell**, immaculately executed stone carvings by an unknown 13th-century sculptor, depicting a variety of foliage, including oak, maple, hawthorn, grape leaves, and even buttercups, all in perfect detail.

Those interested in more recent history can visit the **Saracen's Head Inn**, where Charles I surrendered to the Scots in 1646.

The faster route to Nottingham is along the A46, the Fosse Way, which roughly follows the course of the River Trent and runs along the edge of the **Vale of Belvoir**, with rich agricultural countryside offering scenery not unlike that of the wolds. Once a year, there is a famous meet of the local hunt which departs from

## NOTTINGHAM / SHERWOOD FOREST

Belvoir Castle in search of the fox. The castle is worth visiting. It contains an excellent collection of paintings and some beautiful furniture and tapestries.

### Nottingham

Nottingham is a large, bustling university city in which a wealth of architectural, historical and cultural features exist cheek by jowl with all the elements of a modern, thriving industrial and commercial center. It is therefore an excellent place to break your journey; and it's well worth taking time to spend more than just a few hours exploring the city as well as its environs.

Dominating the scene is **Nottingham Castle**, first built by William the Conqueror in 1068, and destroyed, rebuilt and restored many times since. It now houses the **Nottingham Museum and**

*Above: Robin Hood of Sherwood Forest.*
*Right: Typical drystone walling and cottages in the Peak District.*

**Art Gallery**. You can also visit the labyrinth of caves and tunnels in the rock beneath it.

Among the many interesting old inns in the city are the old **Trip to Jerusalem**, said to stand on the site of an old alehouse where Crusaders gathered before journeying to the Holy Land, and the **Salutation Inn,** built in 1240 as a priory guest house.

Through the centuries, Nottingham has been an important centre for a number of industries and crafts, including lace-making, textile spinning, hosiery, tobacco, and bicycles, all of which are well represented in a wide variety of museums and exhibitions.

On the cultural front, the city has two fine theatres, the modern **Nottingham Playhouse** and the older **Theatre Royal** which specializes in opera, ballet and concerts. Southwest of the city is the university and nearby **Wollaton Hall**, built in the 1580s by Sir Francis Willoughby, and today housing the city's **Natural History Museum**.

### Sherwood Forest

No description of Nottingham would be complete without mention of the legendary Robin Hood, the outlaw and master archer who "robbed from the rich to give to the poor." Statues and images of him are found everywhere, some ancient, some modern: and whether or not he himself actually existed, very real parts of **Sherwood Forest**, where he is said to have roamed, still survive.

The forest extends well to the north of the city and west of the A614, which runs north to a multiple junction near Ollerton. Just to the west is **Edwinstowe**, where are the best-preserved sections of the original forest.

From Edwinstowe, you can make a brief diversion north to **Thoresby Hall**. Standing in nearly 12,500 acres (5,000 ha) of parkland, it is one of the many stately

## THE PEAK DISTRICT

The Peak District, a large area of open country in north Derbyshire, is a landscape dominated by wild moorlands interspersed with dramatic rocky crags and mountainous outcrops, known locally as "edges," and rising to heights of more than 2,000 feet (680 m) above sea level. The region is peppered with ancient stone circles, barrows and other relics from prehistoric times. Many of its tiny stone villages have remained virtually unaltered for hundreds of years.

Large tracts of the district are designated as a National Park and are thus protected from modern development. Thus the remoter parts of the area are best explored on foot, since road-building has been kept to a minimum.

From Sheffield, the A57 leads west, passing the **Ladybower Reservoir**, **Derwent Water** and the **Vale of Derwent**, homes which gave the area the nickname of "The Dukeries."

thence to wind its way up a small river valley, through **Hope Forest** to **Snake Pass** (1,680 ft/510 m). Even higher are **Kinder Scout** to the left (south) and **Bleaklow Hill** to the right (north), both good challenges for hill walkers and climbers.

After a pause at the top of Snake Pass, the A57 goes downhill into the small industrial town of **Glossop**. Turn south here onto the A624, which leads past Hayfield to Chapel-en-le-Frith; here, turn right onto the main A6 and continue west until you reach the left-hand turnoff of the smaller A5004, signposted to **Whaley Bridge**. Passing through that small town, this road proceeds on its tortuous way beside the very pretty river Goyt up the **Dale of Goyt**, well-wooded and rich in wildflowers; it continues on up the valley side and into **Buxton**.

More intrepid motorists can turn to the right after Whaley Bridge and follow a minor road to **Goyt's Bridge**, just upstream of the **Fernilee Reservoir**; turning left there, they can continue to follow

## BUXTON / BAKEWELL / CHATSWORTH

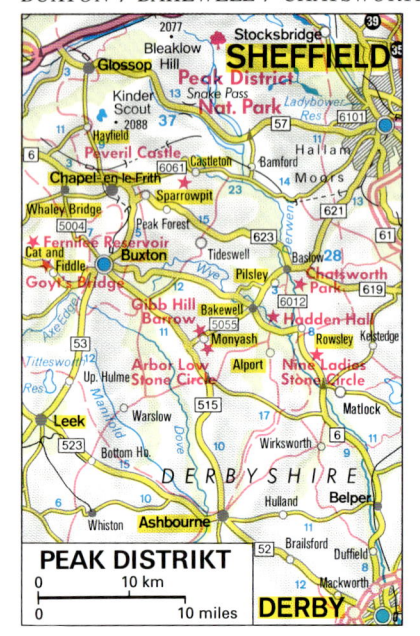

the road beside the river up to **The Cat and Fiddle**. This is not only, as its name implies, an inn, but a bleak pass at an elevation of 1,795 feet (547 m) above sea level.

To the southeast is **Axe Edge**, a popular spot for rock climbers, while the superb moorland below it attracts walkers. At this point the minor road joins the A537 and, after turning left, it in turn merges with the A54 which leads directly into Buxton. Here the route rejoins the A5004 from Whaley Bridge.

From a visitor's point of view, the old spa town of **Buxton** is the only major town in the whole Peak District. At an altitude of 1,007 feet (310 m), it is one of the highest towns in England, but because it is surrounded by even higher wooded hills, it is well sheltered.

The Romans were the first to appreciate its exceptional waters, and it has been a popular resort town ever since. Architecturally, its greatest benefactor was the 5th Duke of Devonshire, who, by financing the building of the magnificent **Crescent** in the 18th century, helped the town to become a serious and elegant rival to Bath. A huge dome, dating from 1859 and measuring 156 feet (47.5 m) in diameter, crowns the **Devonshire Royal Hospital**. Music-lovers will enjoy Buxton's small opera house, beautifully restored in 1979, which even hosts a popular annual opera festival.

One rewarding excursion from Buxton leads southeast down the A6 to **Bakewell**, a small spa town located on the banks of the river Wye with some fine 17th-century buildings. The town is famous for Bakewell tarts, traditional pastries which you can buy in many local shops; the delicious Bakewell pudding is equally worth investigating. Don't miss a visit to the **Old House Museum**. Bakewell is also patronized by climbers coming to ascend White Peak.

From here, the A6 continues eastwards toward **Haddon Hall** on the left. Originally a Norman castle, this building boasts an imposing banquet hall with wooden vaulting. Precious Flemish tapestries with hunting and allegorical motifs decorate the walls of the 14th-century Great Hall.

At **Rowsley**, a left turn onto the B6012 and over a bridge across the river Derwent takes you past the **Peacock Hotel** (a converted 17th-century stone manor house). Now cross a very narrow bridge into **Chatsworth Park**.

At its center is **Chatsworth House**, one of the country's finest and most impressive stately homes, which has been the seat of the Dukes of Devonshire since its construction in 1707. Fabulous collections of paintings, furniture, sculpture and old manuscripts, as well as magnificent gardens with an orangery, hothouse and rose garden, have made this great house world-famous.

*Right: In spring, pictures made of flowers are often displayed in Derbyshire villages, as here in Hope.*

From the northern edge of Chatsworth Park, close to the village of **Pilsley**, you can take the A619 to the left back to Bakewell.

However, if you continue on the A623 – which passes further to the north and rejoins the A6 just north of Buxton – you'll come, before the A6 junction and just outside the village of Sparrowpit, to a right turn onto the narrow B6061, which leads to **Winnats Pass** (1,312 feet/ 400 m), and then on into the large village of **Castleton**.

Situated at the head of **Hope Valley**, the town is dominated by the partly-restored ruins of the massive Norman **Peveril Castle**. Beneath the castle is a network of underground caverns and chambers, which can be explored.

Most spectacular of these caves is the **Peak Cavern**, just over half a mile long (1 km). The **Speedwell Mine**, rich in stalagmites and stalactites, can be visited by boat on an underground canal. Half an hour of foot will bring you to the **Blue John Mine**, distinctive for its blue feldspar.

Another excursion from Buxton follows the A53 toward Leek. This passes alongside **Axe Edge** and the slopes of **Axe Edge Moor**, where there are numerous fine walks and the sources of Derbyshire's four main rivers, the Wye, the Goyt, the Manifold, and the Dove. **Traveller's Rest**, on the main road nearby, is reputed to be the highest inn in England at 1535 feet (468 m) above sea level.

Another excursion leads you along the A515, heading southeast from Buxton to Ashbourne and then, after joining the A52, to Derby and the southerly parts of the county. On the way from Buxton, a small lane to the left, just after the B5055 turning, passes close to the mysterious **Arbor Low Stone Circle** and **Gibb Hill Barrow**, near **Monyash** village. In the east along a small road, near **Alport** village, is the **Nine Ladies Stone Circle**, near which Bronze Age relics have been unearthed. From here the B5056 drops into the Wye Valley, rejoining the A6 close to Haddon Hall. A left turn leads to Bakewell and back to Buxton.

## CIRENCESTER / THE COTSWOLDS
## STRATFORD-UPON-AVON
## COVENTRY

### Accommodation

**CIRENCESTER**: *LUXURY:* **Kings Head Hotel**, Market Place, tel. 01285 653322. *MODERATE:* **Clonsilla Guest House**, 7, Victoria Road, tel. 01285 652621. *BUDGET:* **The Leauseus**, 101 Victoria Road, tel. 01285 65364. **BIRMINGHAM**: *LUXURY:* **Swallow Hotel**, 12, Hagley Road, Five Ways, tel. 0121 4521144. *MODERATE:* **Forte Crest**, Smallbrooke Queensway, tel. 0121 6438171. *BUDGET:* **Hotel Ibis**, Lady Walk, tel. 0121 6226010. **The Pound**, Sheep Street, tel. 01451 830229.

### Museums

**BICKENHILL**: **National Motorcycle Museum**, tel. 01675 443311, daily 10.00-18.00. **BIRMINGHAM**: **Birmingham Museum and Art Gallery**, Chamberlain Square, tel. 0121 235 2834, all year Mon-Sat 11.00-17.00, Sun 11.00-17.30. **BRIDGNORTH**: **Midland Motor Museum**, Stourbridge Rd., tel. 01746 762992, July-Sept daily 11.00-17.00. Oct-June Sat, Sun and Bank Holidays 11.00-17.00. **BROADWAY**: **Teddy Bear Museum**, High Street, tel. 01386 858323, daily from 1 April-30 Sept 10.00-17.30. **BROMSGROVE**: **Avoncraft Museum of Buildings**, tel. 01572 831886, March-Nov 11.00-17.00. **CHELTENHAM**: **Art Gallery and Museum**, Clarence Street, tel. 01242 237431, Mon-Sat 10.00-17.20, closed on Bank Holidays. **CIRENCESTER**: **Corinium Museum**, Park Street, tel. 01285 655611, open 1 April-31 Oct daily 10.00-17.00, Sun 14.00-17.00; 1 Nov-31 March Tue-Sat 10.00-17.00. **COSFORD**: **Aerospace Museum**, tel. 01902 374872, daily 10.00-16.00, closed Dec 25 and Jan 1. **COVENTRY**: **Coventry Museum of British Transport**, Hales Street, tel. 01203 832425, daily 10.00-17.00. **DUDLEY**: **Black Country Museum**, tel. 0121 5579643, daily 1 March-31 Oct 10.00-17.00; 1 Nov-28 Feb Wed-Sun 10.00-16.00. **IRONBRIDGE GORGE**: **Ironbridge Gorge Museum** and **Coalport Porcelain Museum**, tel. 01952 433522, April-Oct daily 10.00-17.00; July-Aug until 18.00, in winter until 16.00. **ROSS-ON-WYE**: **Button Museum** Kyrle St., tel. 01989 566089, April-Oct daily 10.00-17.00. **Lost Street Museum**, Palma Court, 27 Brookend St., tel. 01989 562752, April-Oct daily 10.00-17.00, Sun 11.00-17.00. Phone for winter opening times. **SOUDLEY**: **Symonds Yat Museum**, tel. 01600 890360, Good Friday-30 Sept 11.00-17.30, closed during bad weather. **WINCHCOMBE**: **Folk Museum**, High Street, tel. 01242 602925, open 1 April-31 Oct Mon-Sat 10.00-17.00. **WORCESTER**: **Tudor House Museum**, Friar Street, tel. 01905 20904, Mon-Wed 10.00-17.00, Fri-Sat 10.00-17.00, Sun 13.30-17.30.

### Tips and Trips

**ALCESTER**: **Coughton Court**, near Alcester, tel. 01789 762435, April and Oct Sat and Sun 12.00-17.00, Mai-Sept Sat-Wed 12.00-17.00. **Ragley Hall**, near Alcester, tel. 01789 762090, April-Sept Tue-Thur, Sat, Sun and Bank Holiday Mon 12.00-17.00. **BIRMINGHAM**: **Altringham Park**, near Birmingham, tel. 01743 709203, house open 26 March-28 Sept Sat-Wed 13.30-17.00; in October Sat and Sun 13.30-17.00. Deer Park and Gardens open daily 10.00-18.00. **BOURNVILLE**: **Cadbury World**, Linden Road, near Birmingham, tel. 01214 334334, phone for opening times. **CIRENCESTER**: **Barnsley House Gardens**, near Cirencester. tel. 01285 740281, open Mon, Wed, Thur and Sat 10.00-18.00. **CHIPPING CAMPDEN**: **Hidcote Manor Garden**, tel. 01386 438333, April-Oct daily 11.00-19.00, closed Tue and Fri.
**GAYDON**: **Heritage Motor Centre**, Banbury Road, tel. 01926 641188, April-Oct 10.00-18.00; Nov-March 10.00-16.30. **HIDCOTE**: **Snowshill Tudor Manor**, near Hidcote, tel. 01386 852410, open April-Oct Sat and Sun 13.00-17.00; May-end Sept daily except Tue 13.00-18.00. **GLOUCESTER**: **Berkeley Castle**, near Gloucester, tel. 01453 810332, open April Tue-Sun 14.00-17.00; May, June, Aug and Sept Tue-Sat 11.00-17.00, Sun 14.00-17.00; in October Sunday only 14.00-16.30. **Goodrich Castle**, near Gloucester, tel. 01600 890538, open 1 April-30 Oct daily 10.00-18.00;1 Nov-31 March 10.00-16.00. **LEDBURY**: **Eastnor Castle**, tel. 01531 633160, open in August Sun-Fri 12.00-17.00, April-Sept open Sun and Bank Holiday Mon. **SOUDLEY**: **Dean Heritage Centre**, tel. 01600 822170, open 1 Feb-31 Oct daily 10.00-18.00. In February and March until 17.00; 1 Nov-31 Jan open Sat and Sun 10.00-17.00, closed Christmas. **STRATFORD-UPON-AVON**: **Shakespeare's Birthplace**, tel. 01789 204016, open 1 March-31 Oct Mon-Sat 9.00-17.00, Sun 10.00-17.30; 1 Nov-28 Feb Mon-Sat 9.30-16.00, Sun 10.00-16.00. **Charlecote Park**, Stratford-Upon-Avon, near Wellesbourne, tel. 01789 470277, open April-end Oct Fri-Tue 11.00-18.00. **World of Shakespeare Exhibition**, tel. 01789 269190, open daily 9.30-17.30, Sun 9.30-21.30. **TELFORD**: **Boscobel House**, near Telford, tel.01962 850244, April-Oct daily 10.00-18.00, Nov-March Wed-Sun 10.00-16.00, closed Jan. **TETBURY**: **Cavenage House**, near Tetbury, tel. 01666 502329, open March-Sept 14.00-17.00. **RUGBY**: **Kenilworth Castle**, near Rugby, tel. 01926 52078, April-Oct 10.00-18.00, Nov-March 10.00-16.00 daily. **WARWICK**: **Warwick Castle**, tel. 01926 495421, open daily all

year except Dec 25, 10.00-17.30, Nov-Feb 10.00-16.30. **WINCHCOMBE: Sudeley Castle**, tel. 01242 602308, daily 1 April-31 Oct 10.30-17.00.

### Tourist Information / Airport

**BIRMINGHAM**: 2, City Arcade, tel. 0121 6432514. **Birmingham International Airport**, information: tel. 0121 7675511
**CIRENCESTER**: Corn Hall, Market Place, tel. 01285 654180.
**WORCESTER**: Heart of England Tourist Board, Woodside, Larkhill Rd., tel. 01905 763436.

## NORTHAMPTONSHIRE LEICESTERSHIRE
### Accommodation

**NORTHAMPTON**: *LUXURY:* **The Moat House**, Ashley Way, Weston Favell, tel. 01604 406262. *MODERATE:* **Lime Trees Hotel**, 8 Langham Place, Barrack Road, tel. 01604 233012. *BUDGET:* **Hollington Guest House,** 22 Abington Grove, tel. 01604 32584.

### Museums.

**NORTHAMPTON**: **Abington Museum**, tel. 01604 39415, Tue-Sat 13.00-17.00. **Northampton Central Museum** and **Leathercraft Museum**, Guildhall Rd., tel. 01604 39415, Mon-Sat 10.00-17.00, Sun 14.00-17.00. **LOUGHBOROUGH**: **Bell Foundry Museum**, tel. 01509 233414, all year Tue-Sat 9.30-16.30. **STOKE BRUERNE**: **Canal Museum**, tel. 01604 862229, April-Oct 10.00-17.30 daily, Nov-March 10.00-15.30, closed Mondays.

### Tips and Trips

**BANBURY**: **Sulgrave Manor**, near Banbury, tel. 01295 760205, all year except Jan. 1st April-31 Oct daily except Wed 10.30-17.30, Nov-Jan 10.30.-16.30; March and Nov weekends only 10.30-16.30. **CORBY**: **Kirby Hall**, Deene, tel.01536 203230, daily 10.00-13.00, 14.00-18.00. **Deene Park**, tel. 0178 450278, Bank Holiday Sun and Mon, Easter to August; and Sun in June, July and Aug 14.00-17.00. **COTTESBROOKE**: **Cottesbrooke Hall**, tel. 01604 505808, open 23 April-24 March 14.00-17.30. **GRANTHAM**: **Belvoir Castle**, near Grantham, tel. 01476 870262, open April-1 Oct; 1 Oct-Maundy Thursday 10.00-18.00. **GREAT BRINGTON**: **Althorp House**, near Great Brington, tel. 01604 770042, open Sept-April 13.00.-17.30. **ROCKINGHAM**: **Rockingham Castle**, tel. 01536 770240, open Easter Sunday-30 Sept Sun, Thur and Bank Holiday Mondays. Tuesdays during August 13.00-17.30. **STAMFORD**: **Burghley House**, tel. 01780 450278, open April-Sept daily 11.00-17.00.

### Tourist Information

**NORTHAMPTON**: **Visitors Centre**, 10 St. Giles's Square, tel. 01604 22677.

## LINCOLNSHIRE / LINCOLN
### Accommodation

**LINCOLN**: *LUXURY:* **Washington Hall Country House**, tel. 0522 790340. *MODERATE:* **Hill Crest Hotel**, 15 Lindum Terrace, tel. 0522 510182. *BUDGET:* **Tennyson Hotel**, 7 Smith Street, South Park Avenue, tel. 0522 521624.

### Museums

**LINCOLN**: **Museum of Lincolnshire Life**, tel. 01522 228448, May-Sept 10.00-17.30, Oct-April Mon-Sat 10.00-17.30, Sun 14.00-17.30. **STAMFORD**: **Stamford Museum**, tel. 01780 66317, April-Sept Mon-Sat 10.00-17.00, Oct-March Tue-Sat 10.00-17.00.

### Tips and Trips

**LINCOLN**: **Lincoln Castle**, tel. 01522 511068, March-Oct Mon-Sat 9.30-17.30, Sun 11.00-17.30; Oct-March Mon-Sat 9.30-16.00, Sun 11.00-16.00. **The Incredible Fantastic Toy Shop**, tel. 01522 520534, 2 April-Oct Tue-Sat 11.00-17.00, Sun and Bank Holiday 12.00-16.00. **GRIMSTHORPE**:: **Grimsthorpe Castle**, tel. 01778 32205, June-mid September Sun and Bank Holidays 14.00-17.00.

### Tourist Information

**LINCOLN**: 9 Castle Hill, tel. 01522 529828.

## DERBY / NOTTINGHAMSHIRE
### Accommodation

**NOTTINGHAM**: *LUXURY:* **Forte Crest,** St. James's Street, tel. 0115 9470131. *MODERATE:* **Nuthall Lodge Hotel**, 432 Nuthall Road, tel. 0115 9784080. *BUDGET:* **Waverley Hotel**, 107 Portland Street, tel. 0115 986705.

### Museums

**DERBY**: **Industrial Museum**, tel. 01332 255308, open all year Mon 11.00 -17.00, Tue 10.00-17.00, Sun 14.00-17.00. **NOTTINGHAM**: **Nottingham Museum and Art Gallery**, tel. 0115 9483504, daily April-Sept 10.00-17.45, Oct-March 10.00-16.45. **D. H. Lawrence Birthplace Museum**, tel. 0115 9763312, all year daily April-Oct 10.00-17.00, Nov-March 10.00-16.00. **Wollaton Hall** and **Natural History Museum**, tel. 0115 9281333, April-Sept Mon-Sat 10.00-19.00, Sun 14.00-17.00, Oct-March Mon-Sat 10.00-16.00, Sun 13.30-16.30. **Nottingham Castle Museum**, tel. 0115 9483504, April-Sept daily 10.00-17.45, Oct-March until 16.45.

### Tips and Trips

**BAKEWELL**: **Haddon Hall**, tel. 01629 812855, April-Sept Tue-Sun 11.00-17.15, closed Sun in July and August. **CHATSWORTH**: **Chatsworth House and Gardens**, tel. 01246 582204, open 23 March-30 Oct 11.00-16.30.

### Tourist Information

**NOTTINGHAM**: 1-4 Smithy Row, tel. 0115 9470661.

195

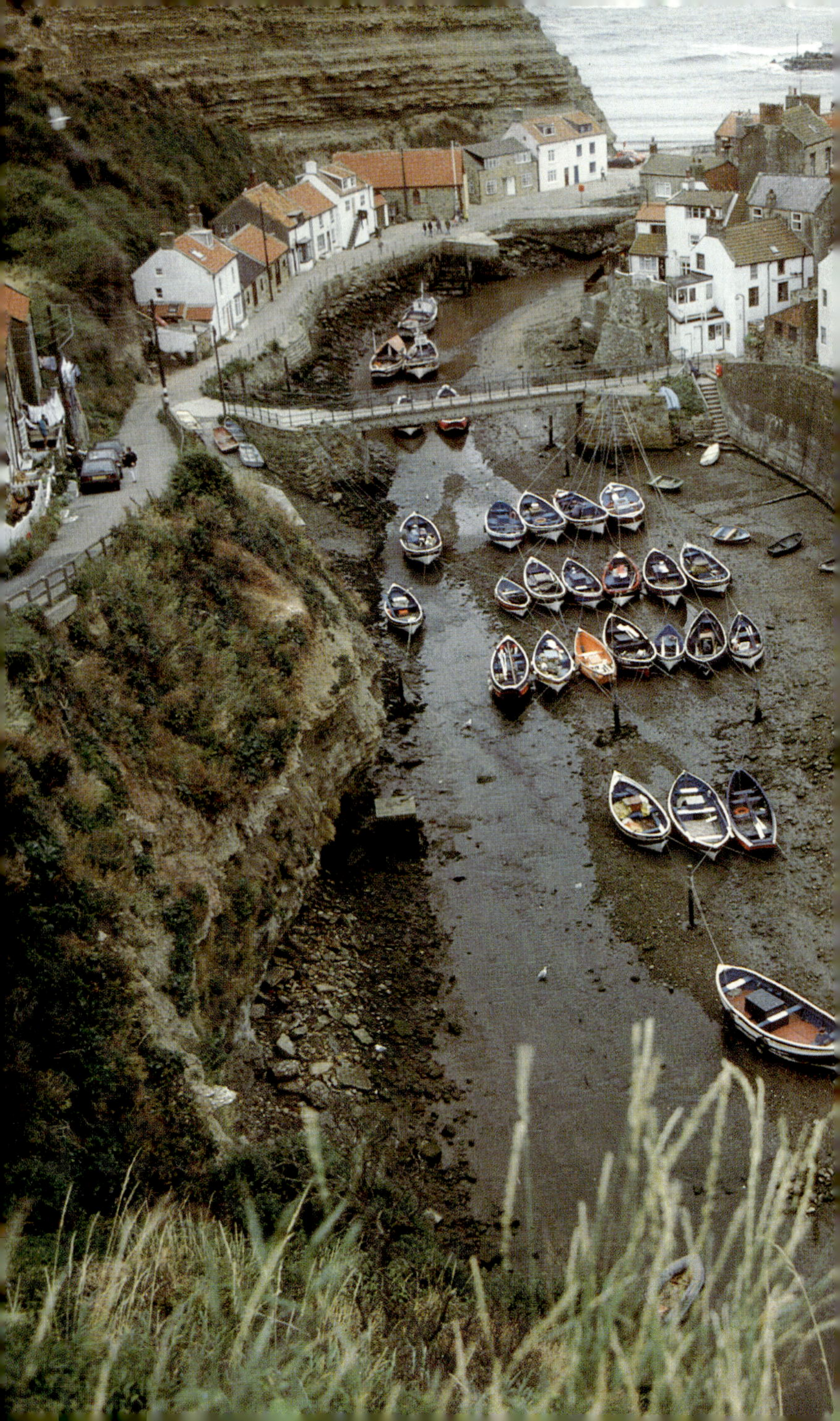

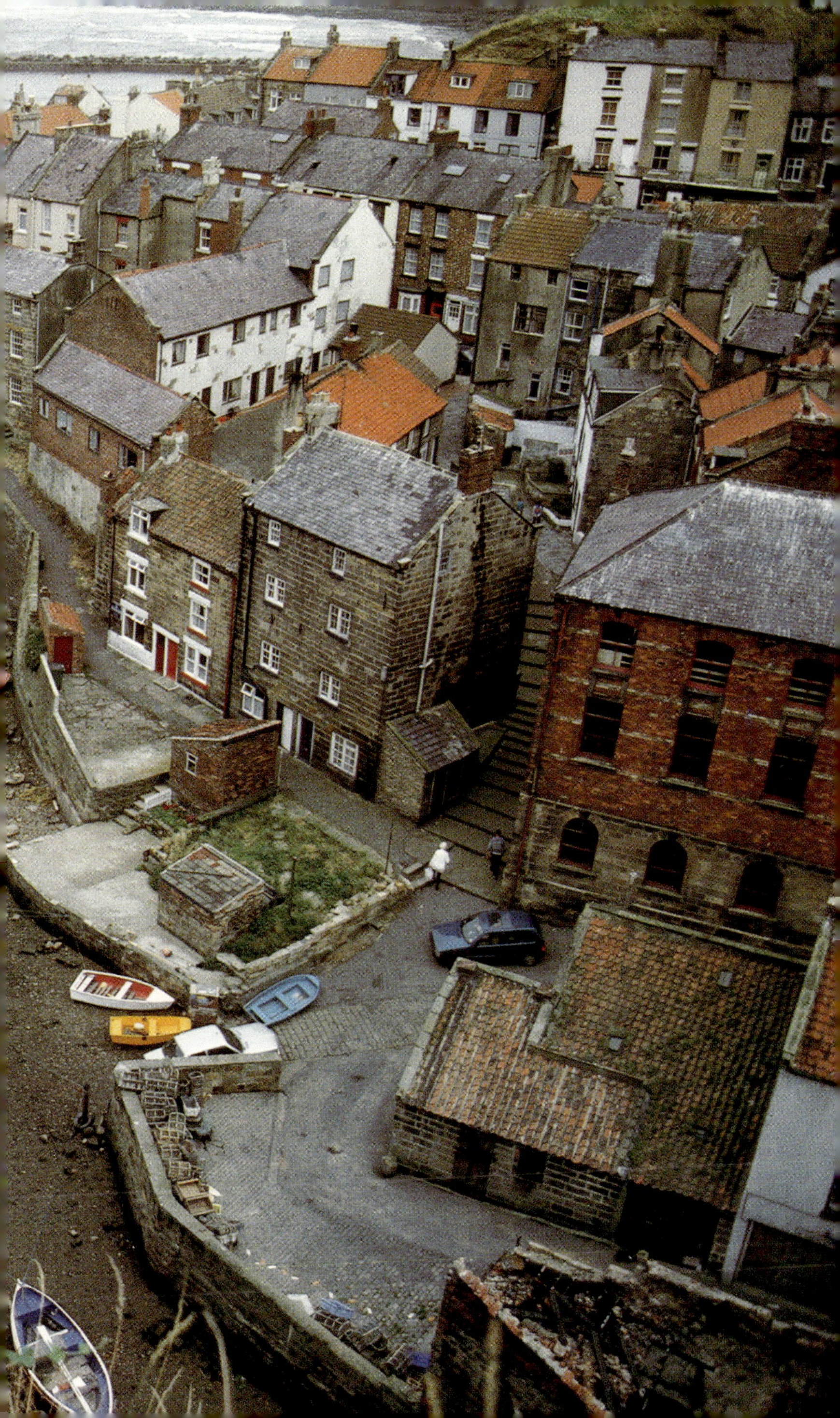

NORTHERN ENGLAND

# NORTHERN ENGLAND

**CHESHIRE**
**MANCHESTER**
**LIVERPOOL**
**HUMBERSIDE**
**YORKSHIRE**
**NORTH YORKSHIRE**

## CHESHIRE

The fastest route from Birmingham to the Scottish border is the M6 motorway which runs to the west of the Pennines. Exit 15 gives access to the complex of six towns that form **Stoke-on-Trent**, center of the ceramic industry since the 18th century and thus known as "The Potteries." Stoke's **City Museum** houses the largest display of Staffordshire ceramics in the world. In Etruria, at the junction of the Trent and Mersey Canal and the Caldon Arm, is the **Etruria Bone and Flint Mill**, opened in 1769, now an industrial museum.

Some of the traditional bottle kilns in which the pottery was fired are displayed in the **Gladstone Pottery Museum** in **Longton**, southeast of Stoke. South of the city in Barlaston, near the A34, is the world-famous **Wedgwood Pottery** with a visitors' center and museum. Ceramics enthusiasts can tour the porcelain factories where the vases and plates with their blue-and-white decorations have been manufactured since 1769.

If you leave Stoke by the A52 and turn off at Longsdon to **Horse Bridge**, you'll

*Preceding pages: Ebb tide in Staithes, North Yorkshire. Left: Shopping in the Chester Rows.*

come across a transport curiosity: one waterway is crossed by another. Further on is **Cheddleton**, where a lovely old flint mill stands beside the water and canal boats lie moored at the quay. Beyond, to the southeast off the A52, is the amusement park of **Alton Towers**.

From Stoke, the A34 leads north past Kidsgrove to one of England's most beautiful half-timbered houses, **Little Moreton Hall**, surrounded by a moat and gardens. To the east, the land rises towards the **Peak District National Park**; from the nearby eminence of **Mow Cop**, you can look out west over all of Cheshire spread below you. The A34 strikes north for Manchester through **Congleton**, a picturesque market town, and **Alderley Edge**, popular for its fine views. A mummified corpse from the Middle Ages was once discovered here, perfectly preserved in the peat.

An alternative route to Manchester is the A536 to **Macclesfield**, a mix of old half-timbered houses and 18th-century mills, once a center of the silk industry, as the Silk Museum and the Paradise Working Silk Mill demonstrate. To the east the A537 traverses a wild stretch of moorland on its way towards **Buxton**, while the B5470 ascends to **Whaley Bridge**. Close by, at **Buxworth**, the abandoned terminus of the Peak Forest

199

canal indicates what raw materials were once demanded during the Industrial Revolution.

Take the A6 towards **New Mills** and then the B6101 to **Marple**. Here, the Peak Forest canal flows into the Macclesfield canal, passing through a long series of locks and over a fine Roman aqueduct on the way to Manchester.

## Chester

In 79 AD, the Romans established the important camp of *Deva* to secure the land against the Welsh. In the early Middle Ages, Chester's city ramparts were erected atop the Roman ring wall. The Roman legacy is further evident not only in the amphitheater and garden, but also in the **Deva Roman Experience Museum**, close by the Heritage Centre. The 14th-century **cathedral** was part of a earlier Benedictine abbey.

*Above: The Victorian clock on the East Gate of the city walls of Chester.*

Most impressive of all are the city streets with their black-and-white half-timbered houses, and the Rows, arcaded walkways or galleries one story above the street. All manner of shops are to be found in this medieval setting, and the keen-eyed will notice ornate carvings on the ancient timbers.

A walk around the city walls is mandatory, including **King Charles' Tower** from which the ill-fated monarch witnessed the defeat of his troops at Rowton Moor in 1645.

### Merseyside

The M53 takes you north to **Ellesmere Port** on the Mersey, where the Waterways Museum is another reminder of the days when water transport supported the commerce of the nation.

If you take the M56 towards Manchester, get off at exit 8 for **Dunham Massey** near Bowdon. This large Georgian mansion is set in a deer-park with magnificent gardens, contains a vast collection of silver, and boasts a rare water-powered sawmill.

South of the motorway, towards Knutsford, is the former home of the Egerton family at **Tatton Hall**. This 19th-century house stands in the midst of formal gardens and woodlands laid out by Humphrey Repton. Besides the treasures of the house itself, there's a farm here still worked as it was in the 1920s.

Astronomers should head south again some 6 miles (10 km) to visit the observatory and radio telescope at **Jodrell Bank**, northeast of Holmes Chapel.

## MANCHESTER

If you're driving to **Manchester** from the south on the M6, leave the motorway at exit 19. Manchester itself is not a place to explore by car; vastly preferable ways to get around the city are public transportation or simply your own two feet.

# LANCASHIRE / CHESHIRE

## MANCHESTER

Although it was an important Roman center, the city is generally thought of as a manufacturing center that grew up during the Industrial Revolution. Enormous wealth was generated here in this period, and the revenues partly went to finance the building of temples of the arts and seats of learning. The down side of industrial progress was terrible environmental pollution and the shocking poverty of the working class. Manchester has long suffered under the stereotype of being a dirty, crime-ridden city, but in the last few years a city rejuvenation program has started to bring about a new and improved quality of life.

Not far from Piccadilly Station, in Dale Street, a stairway leads down to the banks of the **Rochdale Canal** which, to your left, passes through locks two centuries old beneath the 20th-century bustle of traffic on Piccadilly. This quiet towpath

*Above: Manchester's Piccadilly. Right: A new outfit: this bus ad reflects the city's economic progress.*

emerges next to the law courts. From here, go right on Chorlton Street to get to the busy shops on Portland Street. If you take Charlotte Street on the other side, you will find the **Chinese Arts Centre** at No. 36, with George Street, part of Manchester's **Chinatown**, on the left. The craftsmen who built the Chinese gateway here were brought in from Peking, as were the materials they used.

Turn right on Princess Street and walk to Mosley Street for the **City Art Gallery**. The gallery is renowned for its collection of French Impressionists and major British painters.

Further along Princess Street are **Albert Square** and the Town Hall, a beacon of mercantile Victorian confidence. A statue of Albert, consort to Queen Victoria, stands in the square, perhaps somewhat uncomfortable to find itself close to that of Abel Heywood, a former mayor so radical by the standards of the time that the Queen refused to visit Manchester while he held office.

Across the road, in the pedestrian precinct of Queen Street, there's a surprise for American visitors – the familiar figure of Abraham Lincoln. At the end of the street, on the other side of Deansgate, stands the **John Rylands Library**, another striking building from the 1890s. It has the finest collection of rare books in the North of England.

A left turn on Deansgate leads to Peter Street and the home of the world-famous Hallé Orchestra, the **Free Trade Hall**. Charles Hallé left Germany after the revolution of 1848 and came to Manchester where there was already a large German community. Appalled by the state of music in the city, he and his wife toured the world to raise money for an orchestra of international standard. The Hallé was founded in 1858. But the Free Trade Hall hosts a wide range of other events, as well, from classical concerts to pop to comedy evenings with local star Mike Harding.

# MANCHESTER

To the right of the GMex Centre, once a railway station and now a complex for trade fairs and congresses, is historic **Castlefield**; an elevator gives access to the site. Here the Romans built their fort, now partially restored, and here the first commercial canal, the Bridgewater, delivered passengers on its packet boats. Today the arena is a venue for concerts.

Nearby, the **Museum of Science and Industry** occupies the building that was once the world's first passenger train station. Exhibited in the Power Hall are machines built in Manchester, ranging from locomotives and steam engines to vintage Rolls-Royces from 1904. In the "Xperiment" in the Lower Byrom Street Warehouse, visitors can get hands-on experience in areas such as electricity and light. The Air and Space Gallery is more concerned with the history of flight: pride of place goes to Britain's first motorized aeroplane, the Triplane 1, manufactured in 1909 by engineer A. V. Roe.

At the end of Liverpool Street, in Water Street, television fans can join the **Granada Studios Tour**. Manchester is the location of Britain's longest-running and perhaps best soap, *Coronation Street*.

If you want another taste of the "real" Manchester, take in a game of the local football (soccer, that is) team Manchester United at **Old Trafford**. The **Manchester Museum** on Oxford Road, part of the university, is particularly known for its Egyptian, archaeological and ethnological collections. There is also a Jewish museum, a police museum, a transport museum, a museum of labor history and a museum of the women's movement housed in the home of the Pankhursts, leaders of the suffragette movement in England.

Elegant shops line St. Anne's Square. At night, theaters and concert halls, pubs and clubs (including the **Hacienda**) offer a wide range of entertainment.

### The Pennines

The **Pennine Hills**, east of Manchester separate Lancashire and Yorkshire. Walkers in good condition can hike the long-distance trail the Pennine Way the full length of the "Backbone of England," savoring to the full its natural beauty. But even from a car, you can get a sense of this wonderful landscape with its green hills criss-crossed with drystone walls.

From the M62, exit 21 puts you on the A640, which runs in a south-easterly direction to Newhey and on to Huddersfield. At Denshaw, a minor road leads to **Delph**, deep in a valley below the moors. The place name derives from the Old English "delfan," a cognate of "delve," meaning "to dig," reflecting ancient mining activities in the area. A walk up the river a mile or so (2 km) will bring you to an excavated **Roman fort** (beside **Castleshaw Reservoir**). The A6052 crosses the A62 to reach **Uppermill**, where a left turn onto the A670 leads to a car park by the canal. Before the waterway to Huddersfield was completed, goods were transferred, in the warehouse opposite, from canal-boat to pack-horses for the journey east over the hills – 600 horses were needed for every boatload! If you walk northeast along the canal, you'll come to the mouth of the Standedge tunnel, England's highest canal tunnel, at **Diggle**.

In the 19th century, the development of steam power and water transport led to the building of enormous mills (factories) in the valleys; but older, smaller mills powered by the rushing streams cascading down the hillsides, can still be found east of Uppermill, in the area around **St. Chad's Church** (also known as Saddleworth Church) and the Cross Keys pub. In the little valley, or "clough" (pronounced "cluff") to use the Yorkshire word, just north of the church, are the remains of two little woollen mills, typical of the hundreds that were scattered over the landscape in the 18th century.

If you follow the A640 northwards from exit 21, you'll come to **Smithy Bridge** and **Hollingworth Lake**. Set in lovely country,

*Above: A cricket match in Delph in the Pennines. Right: The "Fab Four" have become Liverpool's trademark.*

this is actually a reservoir used for supplying the canals. Here Matthew Webb, the first man to swim the Channel from England to France, trained – he later died attempting to swim the rapids at Niagara. The visitors' center tells the history of the area, and a walk through Smithy Bridge leads to another scenic canal, the Rochdale.

## LIVERPOOL

The commercial strength of Manchester grew with the development of transport links; but it was from the seaport of Liverpool that her goods reached the markets of the world. The M62 is the shortest route into the center of Liverpool, leading past the university and the great crown-shaped **Roman Catholic cathedral**, consecrated in 1967, a modernistic round building of glass and steel with a cylindrical lantern tower which John Lennon allegedly referred to as "Liverpool's largest public conveniences." The other cathedral, and in complete contrast, is the more traditional Neo-Gothic Anglican cathedral, begun in 1904.

The docks were the heart of Liverpool in its commercial heyday; today, however, they're dominated by a sad series of derelict buildings and vacant lots. Close to the Pierhead, however, is the **Albert Dock** complex (underground: St. James Street), which has been completely renovated and restored as a center of interest for the visitor.

In recent years, attempts to break London's monopoly on England's cultural life have benefited many cities, and Liverpool in particular. This applies less to the **Liverpool Museum** close to Lime Street station, where there's a planetarium on the top floor, but more to the nearby **Walker Art Gallery** with its collection of European and Pre-Raphaelite paintings. And definitely recommended is the extraordinary collection of modern art in Liverpool's **Tate Gallery**, a branch of the London museum of the same name. Like the **Maritime Museum**, it is located at Albert Dock. However, most visitors to the dock who were born after 1950 come not for art but for the Beatles: the exhibition **The Beatles Story** here is dedicated to them and their music.

As a climax to your visit a cruise on the great river Mersey is hard to beat. Upstream, off the A561 near the airport, is one of England's finest half-timbered houses, **Speke Hall**, a Tudor masterpiece with Victorian-era furnishings.

On Liverpool's eastern outskirts, the M57 leads off northwest from the M62 past **Knowsley Safari Park**; the A565 continues on towards the nature reserve at **Formby**. This large area of sand dunes and pine forest between the town and the sea is home to birds, butterflies and the rare (in England) red squirrels. The beach is one of the finest in the area.

Further north, **Southport** is the "classiest" of the Lancashire coastal resorts, with its internationally famous Royal Birkdale golf course and elegant shop-

*BLACKPOOL*

ping mile of Lord Street. Inland, just north of **Burscough**, is the **Martin Mere Wildfowl & Wetlands Centre** where duck and geese abound and, in winter, wild swans from the Arctic come to breed.

Also north of Burscough is **Rufford Old Hall**, a late 15th-century half-timbered house with an ornate hammerbeam roof and arms, tapestries and furniture from the 16th and 17th centuries.

East from exit 27 on the M6, via Standish and the A49 to Charnock Richard**,** is **Camelot Theme Park**, which offers entertainment in a medieval key.

### Blackpool

North of Southport, the coast is split by the estuary of the river Ribble, which penetrates 11 miles (18 km) inland to Preston. From here the road leads to

*Above: Liverpool's Pierhead and the Liver Building. Right: Blackpool Tower in the North's most popular seaside resort.*

**Blackpool**, the popular seaside playground of the industrial north.

Trams run along the oceanfront, past the honest vulgarity of **Pleasure Beach** with its rollercoasters (one the highest in the world) and other amusements, the piers, and the famous **Tower**, built in 1894 in emulation of Gustave Eiffel's celebrated construction in Paris. In autumn, the whole coast is illuminated with thousands of lights. On the estuary shore are two more of Britain's great golf courses, the Royal Lytham and the St. Anne's.

### Central Lancashire

East of Preston, the B6245 leads to a Roman fort at **Ribchester**. At **Whalley** the ruins of a Cistercian abbey stand above the river Calder; indeed, the remains of the medieval privies still overhang the water. Founded in 1172, the house was moved to the present site in 1296 where it endured until Henry VIII's dissolution of the monasteries.

North of Whalley, at **Clitheroe**, the old castle is still standing, and to the southeast at Padiham is **Gawthorpe Hall**. Built in the early 17th century and restored 150 years ago, it is known for its textile collection. North of here, the Forest of Pendle was once said to be the haunt of witches.

From **Newchurch in Pendle** off the A6068, anyone with sufficient energy can climb Pendle Hill. Numerous women were found guilty of witchcraft here in the 17th century, and executed at Lancaster castle.

## HUMBERSIDE

North of the junction of the M1 and the M18 is **Doncaster**, a busy industrial town with little left to recall its Roman and medieval history. It is famous, though, for the St. Leger Race, the oldest classic horse-race on the racing calendar. To the northwest is **Brodsworth Hall**, a perfect time capsule of a Victorian country house.

Further east, near Scunthorpe, is the Regency mansion **Normanby Hall**, built in 1820 by Sir Robert Smirk, architect of the British Museum. It is furnished in period style and has a costume display.

In **Grimsby** on the coast, visit the National Fishing Heritage Center for a look at the history of Britain's fisheries. A video display recreates life at sea on a trawler of 40 years ago. Back on the A15(T) a short drive brings you to **Humber Bridge**, which has the longest single span in the world, stretching 1,650 yards (1,510 m) across the Humber estuary.

**Kingston-upon-Hull**, or simply Hull, is the largest British port after London; freighters and North Sea ferries operate from the docks. Hull is the birthplace of William Wilberforce, the anti-slavery campaigner; his house is now a museum. In the city, the collection of the **Ferens Art Gallery** ranges from Old Masters to 18th-century portraiture and Victorian narrative works.

Northeast of Hull and north of Sproatley on the B1238, lies **Burton Constable**

*YORKSHIRE*

**Hall**, a 16th-century house with 18th-century additions by interior decorator Robert Adam and gardens landscaped by Capability Brown. North of Hull stands the unspoiled historic town of **Beverley** with its magnificent 13th-century cathedral. It contains the tomb of the Percy family of Northumberland, and wonderful wood carvings. The **Museum of Army Transport**, a short walk away, contains a fascinating history of military transport.

## YORKSHIRE

With its mountains, windswept moorlands, and a glorious coastline, Yorkshire is indubitably one of the finest of English counties. Green valleys shelter the crumbling ruins of abbeys; old cities boast stout castles and sublime cathedrals; and the region's turbulent and often bloody

*Above: The Yorkshire coast at Flamborough Head. Right: Today, more modern methods are used in the steel center of Sheffield.*

history has left a wealth of monuments in its wake. As you travel further north, the countryside changes from the large industrial towns in the south to the cultivated plains around York, thence up to the high moorlands and wild unspoiled countryside in the most northerly parts of the country. The heart of the northeastern part of the region is the broad lowland corridor which carries the main rail and road routes from London to the Scottish border.

York is the great city of this lowland country. First came the Romans, who noted the value of the Pennines to the west as a natural defensive rampart, and used them accordingly; the Normans later made York the capital of the north. The Pennines, incidentally, together with the North Yorkshire Moors, form one of the largest tracts of unspoiled countryside in England.

The huge expanses of the North Yorkshire Moors, stretches with little but grass, heather and peat, look much as they did thousands of years ago. Grouse

## SHEFFIELD / LEEDS / HALIFAX

and curlew are the main inhabitants, and you can walk for a whole day without meeting another human being. But in the northeast of the county, there's a whole series of castles and great houses, which demonstrate increasing fortification the nearer they are to the Scottish border. In contrast, the southern part of Yorkshire and Humberside reflects the more recent history of the Industrial Revolution in the 19th century.

**Cities of Steel and Wool**

**Sheffield** has developed in the shape of a natural amphitheatre on the southern Pennine slopes. The Industrial Revolution transformed Sheffield into the capital of the steel industry, but its famous cutlery trade dates back to Norman times. The fine **City Museum** contains a large collection of Sheffield plate, while the **Cutlers' Hall** is an impressive home for the cutlers' collection of silver. The **Ruskin Gallery** houses a collection formed in 1875 by artist and critic John Ruskin. It includes paintings, watercolors and illuminated manuscripts.

The M1 from London finishes at **Leeds**. The city is first mentioned by Bede in the 7th century; the cloth industry was established in the 14th century, and was the city's main industry until the 19th century, when it was joined by heavy industry. Notable are the classical revival **Town Hall** and, next door, the **City Art Gallery**, one wing of which is devoted entirely to sculptures by Henry Moore.

East of Leeds is **Temple Newsam**, a fine Jacobean house, birthplace of Lord Darnley, husband of Mary Queen of Scots. **Harewood House**, north of Leeds, has been the seat of the Earls of Harewood for more than 200 years. It has a fine collection of furnished rooms decorated by Robert Adam, with furniture by Thomas Chippendale; while the grounds, which include a famous bird garden, were designed by the ubiquitous "Capability" Brown.

West of Leeds lies **Bradford**, once the hub of the wool worsted trade. In the mainly 14th-century **cathedral** there is a stained-glass window by William Morris. The **National Museum of Photography, Film and Television** houses everything from a *camera obscura* to satellites as well as an ever-popular giant IMAX cinema screen.

From Bradford it is easy to reach the virtually unspoiled town of **Halifax** to the southwest. "From Hull, Hell and Halifax, good Lord deliver us": this old catch-phrase is a gruesome reminder of public executions which took place on market days until 1650 on Gibbet Street (the gibbet was a form of guillotine). Halifax is one of the more interesting industrial towns of West Yorkshire, thanks in part to **Eureka**, a deservedly popular museum for children, and the restored 18th-century **Piece Hall**, with its markets, colonnaded galleries and industrial museum.

*HAWORTH*

**Moors and Dales**

The A646 climbs up the Calder Valley, beside the river and the superb Rochdale Canal, towards **Hebden Bridge**. This stone-built mill town is well-known for its corduroy. You can find bargains in the clothing factory outlets.

The A6033 north to Keighley leads past the village of **Haworth**, famous for its literary associations with the Brontë family. The three sisters Anne, Charlotte and Emily wrote some great novels; *Jane Eyre* was one of Charlotte's masterpieces. The **Brontë Parsonage Museum**, with displays of family memorabilia, occupies the family's former home. Emily Brontë's beloved moors lie all around, and in wild weather her story of *Wuthering Heights* comes vividly to life.

Near Keighley is a delightful 17th-century merchant's house, **East Riddlesden Hall**. It houses a fine collection of Yorkshire oak furniture, early embroidery and ghosts. Heading back to Leeds, the A650, running down the valley of Airedale, is parallel to the Leeds and Liverpool Canal. This waterway boasts a dramatic staircase lock, the Bingley Five-Rise, at **Bingley**.

For those with time to spare, the route to York by way of Leeds can be exchanged for a more interesting tour. The A629 heads up Airedale to **Skipton**, known as "The Gateway to the Dales." The great **castle** of the **Cliffords** stands behind the church. Parts of the original Norman castle remain, including a banqueting hall 50 feet (15 m) long and a huge kitchen complete with roasting and baking hearths.

Scenery buffs should follow the B6265 as it winds up past the dale village of Hetton into Grassington, with its steep cobblestone streets, and thence up into the northern dales.

East of Skipton, the A59 leads to the 12th-century priory ruins of **Bolton Abbey**, standing amid meadows, woods

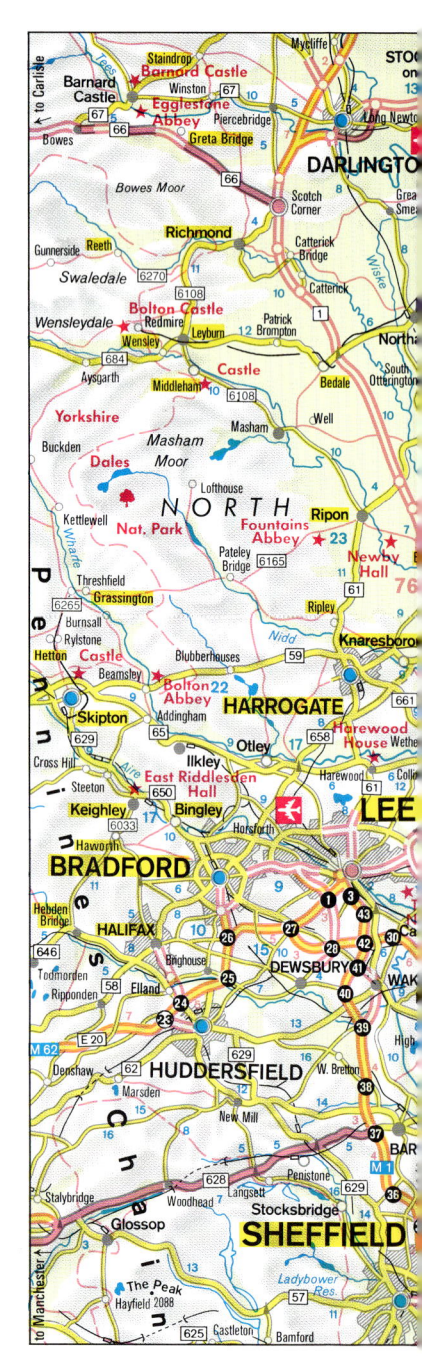

*YORKSHIRE*

and waterfalls. The nave, repaired and lengthened, is now the parish church. Stepping stones lead across the river Wharfe, and it is pleasant to stretch your legs beside its beautiful waters.

The A59 leads on through the spa town of **Harrogate**, known for its floral parks, dignified Victorian buildings and fine shops, and then on to **Knaresborough**. Here the Georgian houses line narrow streets and alleys which lead down to the river Nidd. **Mother Shipton's Cave**, where a famous soothsayer and prophetess was reputedly born in the 15th century, is open to the public.

If you don't want to go on to York, detour on the B 6165 to **Ripley**. The castle there has been the home of the Ingilby family since 1345. It is set in a 19th-century village and is a delightful stop on a summer's day. A few miles north are the truly magnificent ruins of **Fountains**

*Above: A spring walk to Fountains Abbey.*
*Right: Armorial bearings on one of the city gates of York.*

**Abbey**, situated in the impressive grounds of Studely Royal Park. Benedictine monks came to this remote spot in 1132 and founded the abbey. South of Ripon is one of Yorkshire's renowned Adam houses, the 18th-century **Newby Hall**, set in gardens that are full of rare and beautiful plants. Like most houses decorated by Robert Adam, the hall's interior and contents are superb.

The town of **Ripon** received its charter from Alfred the Great in 886. The cathedral's Saxon crypt holds many treasures. The building is also notable for its juxtaposition of Early English, Decorated and Perpendicular styles.

East of the A1, near the town of Boroughbridge, are the remains of the extensive Roman settlement *Isurium*.

The old Roman road of Dere Street, now the B6265, runs south to join the A59 eastward to York. A short diversion to the north brings you to **Benningborough Hall**. A showpiece of National Trust restoration, it is an early Georgian red-brick house built beside the river

Ouse. It houses more than 100 paintings on loan from the National Portrait Gallery in London.

## York

Historic capital of the north and the second of the two archbishoprics of the Church of England is the city of **York**. The street plan here has not greatly altered since the Middle Ages, and the principal places of interest are all within easy walking distance. The Romans chose this site beside the river Ouse for their fortress of *Eburacum*.

Later, the Danes founded a colony here, and the Normans built fortifications before, in the Middle Ages, the wool trade ushered in a period of prosperity. The city's history is written in its streets. Four great *bars*, or gates, still command the main roads and are a reminder of grimmer days when the strength of the city lay in its walls.

You can walk around the city along the ramparts of these largely-intact city walls. These enclose a maze of narrow winding streets lined with ancient half-timbered houses and exquisite churches. The pride of York is the breathtaking **Minster**. Built between 1220 and 1470, it is the largest English cathedral built in the Middle Ages; it is renowned for its traceried window (1338) which depicts scenes from the New Testament and for the other medieval stained-glass in the transept and choir. The Norman crypt adjoins the **Undercroft Museum**, which houses the cathedral's treasures.

The Romans were not the only early settlers in the area; in fact, it was the Vikings who gave York its name. Opened in 1984, the **Jorvik Viking Center** is built on the site of a Viking excavation in Coppergate: it tries to reconstruct the flavor of daily life in the Viking city of Jorvik down to the last detail, complete with sounds and smells.

**York Castle Museum** contains Kirkgate, an entire street of Victorian shops stocked with merchandise of the time. Other exhibits include period rooms, arms and armor. Another part of the castle is **Clifford's Tower**, built by Henry III and named after Roger de Clifford, one of the Lancastrian rebels, who was executed here on March 23rd, 1322, after which his body was hung in chains from the tower.

The **Merchant Adventurers' Hall** is a stunning guild hall built in the 1350s. The medieval guild of merchant adventurers was particularly concerned with foreign trade; now as then, merchants still use the facility to transact business or hold festive events. Described as a masterpiece of neo-classical architecture, **Fairfax Hall** is certainly one of the finest town houses in York. It holds a collection of 18th-century furniture and clocks.

The **York City Art Gallery** has a permanent collection of European painting from about 1350 to the present, including

*Above: York's Guildhall on the river Ouse. Right: St. William's College behind the cathedral. Far right: The beautiful grounds of Castle Howard.*

works by the well-known York artist William Etty.

200 years of railway history are documented at the **National Railway Museum**. Exhibits include a replica of Stephenson's Rocket; luxurious royal carriages; a model of the Trans Manche Super Train for the Channel tunnel; and the magnificent *Mallard*, the world's fastest steam locomotive ever.

Anyone with a disposition for adventure or horror may prefer to descend into the **York Dungeon**, which presents grisly tableaux of Dark Age deaths and medieval tortures and punishments set in dark, musty and atmospheric cellars.

After this, a visit to **Thomas Gent's Coffee House**, situated in a little alley called Coffee Yard, may be necessary to restore your spirits. This establishment takes you back to the year 1770, an age when coffee houses were the focus of social life.

In the narrow, winding alleyway known as the **Shambles**, the upper stories of the top-heavy medieval buildings jut out over the street and almost touch in the middle.

## NORTH YORKSHIRE

Rising from the great Plain of York, the **Howardian Hills** are a fine place to explore. Characteristic of their peaceful, quiet landscapes are villages nestling on hillsides, extensive lowland farms, and sheltered woodlands. If you take the A64 northwards out of York, you'll come to **Kirkham Priory** with ruins of an Augustinian foundation, including a gatehouse with magnificent stone-carving, set in a peaceful valley.

**Castle Howard** lies just off the A64 to Malton. John Vanbrugh started construction of this building in 1702, and it has been the home of the Howard family ever since. Its magnificent rooms contain a wealth of art and objects d'art, and the grounds are equally beautiful. Within 10,000 acres (4,000 ha) there are two large lakes, the Temple of the Four Winds, and a mausoleum.

Further along the A64, just north of Malton, is the modern theme museum of **Eden Camp**, constructed in the huts of a genuine prisoner-of-war camp from 1942. Here, scenes from World War II are recreated with the help of sound, lighting, and even smoke bombs.

The B1257 west from Malton winds through the Howardian Hills and picturesque villages such as Hovingham. Nearby is **Nunnington Hall**, a large 17th-century manor house on the banks of the river Rye. It houses the Carlisle Collection of miniature rooms.

The delightful small market town of **Helmsley** is a restful base from which to explore the surrounding countryside. The town has a 12th-century castle (now in ruins) once owned by the first duke of Buckingham.

Northwest of Helmsley, romantically situated in the secluded Rye valley, is **Rievaulx Abbey**. In the substantial remains of the 12th-century monastery and living quarters, you can clearly see the architectural transition from the rounded

## THE WOLDS

arches of the Romanesque style to the pointed Gothic arches of the Perpendicular style.

An interesting side trip from Rievaulx Abbey leads along the narrow road through the Hambleton Hills to the Cleveland Hills and the **Mount Grace Priory**. Under Henry VIII it suffered the same hard fate as all religious houses in England, but was converted into a private house in 1654 and is owned today by the National Trust.

South of the A170 and west of Helmsley is the noble ruined abbey at **Byland**; call in at the nearby village of **Kilburn**, where the famous "Mouseman" furniture is made. Robert Thompson began his career as the village wheelwright and moved on to make ecclesiastical furniture; his family continues the tradition today. In the local church, you can recognize examples of Thompson's own work from the mouse carved into the wood.

*Above: Fishing off Scarborough. Right: A view of the little village of Whitby.*

Close by is the village of **Coxwold** and **Newburgh Priory**, an Elizabethan mansion with 12th-century priory rooms. Laurence Sterne, author of *Tristram Shandy*, lived in Coxwold at **Shandy Hall**. It has been recently restored and is open to visitors. To the south is **Crayke**, a hilltop village straggling steeply up to its church and 15th-century castle. There are superb views from the top of this hill across the vale to York Minster. To the west, the A19 back to York takes you through the cobblestones and mellow red brick of **Easingwold.**

### The Wolds and the Coast

The A166 thrusts east of York towards the coast, passing through **Stamford Bridge**, the scene of Harold's successful battle against the Norwegian king Hardrada before Hastings in 1066. The B1251 leads northeast at Fridaythorpe to **Sledmere House**, the Georgian home of Sir Tatton Sykes; the exquisite long, vaulted library is the *pièce de résistance*.

*BRIDLINGTON / SCARBOROUGH / WHITBY*

In one of the prettiest villages in the wolds, outside Bridlington, is a magnificent example of Elizabethan architecture, **Burton Agnes Hall**. Still tenanted by descendants of the original family, it is filled with treasures accumulated over four centuries – and the ghost of the first owner's daughter.

The popular seaside town of **Bridlington** combines new and old. A fine Priory church, founded by Henry I, and the great Bayle Gate exemplify the old. In 1643, Queen Henrietta Maria, wife of Charles I, landed with arms purchased from the proceeds raised by selling the Crown Jewels. The harbor, however, was attacked, and she had to retreat to Boynton Hall nearby.

North on the A165, up a great sweep of bay, is a spectacular headland known as **Filey Brigg**. Further north, near the B1229 on a massive headland northeast of town, commanding magnificent views, is **Scarborough Castle**, dominating the seaside resort of **Scarborough**. Cockle stalls, amusement arcades and the like confer a kind of fun-fair atmosphere upon the old streets running down to the sea. Traditional fishing vessels, called cobles and mules, nose in and out of the harbor. A place of tranquility, on the other hand, is St. Mary's churchyard, where the writer Anne Brontë was buried in 1849.

Travelling further north along the coast on the A171 to Whitby, you can see vast open moors to the west and, to the east, the charming and quaint village of **Robin Hood's Bay**. The main street plunges giddily down to the sea, the little shops and houses crowding close. Once the inhabitants lived by fishing and smuggling; now it is a magnet for artists.

Further north is **Whitby**, with its maze of narrow streets and steps between the houses. In 1768 Captain Cook sailed in the Whitby-built *Endeavour* for Tahiti. His story is told in the **Captain Cook Memorial Museum**. On a high headland over the River Esk stands Whitby Abbey, founded in 657 but later destroyed by the Danes.

## NORTH YORKSHIRE MOORS

### The North Yorkshire Moors

The North Yorkshire Moors stand between the North Yorkshire coastline and the Yorkshire Dales. In the west, they drop to the vale from the steep scarp of the Hambleton Hills; to the northwest they extend to take in the Cleveland Hills, from which the River Esk runs down to the sea at Whitby. The region is at its loveliest between mid-summer and autumn, when the heather is in bloom and paints the slopes with great swatches of rusty reds and purples. Typical here, as in much of the north, are villages of gray stone clustered in beautiful secluded valleys, or sheep grazing contentedly by the roadside.

The whole area is fine walking country; but the steam trains of the **North Yorkshire Moors Railway** are another wonderful way of seeing the moors. Built

*Above: Sheep are part of the Yorkshire way of life. Right: Stone-walled fields are typical of the Yorkshire Dales.*

by George Stephenson, the line runs between Pickering and Grosmont, near **Egton**. The end of the line is at **Pickering**, a market town and tourist center for Pickering Vale. Parts of Pickering Castle still survive, and lovely 15th-century wall murals were discovered in the nave of the church under a layer of whitewash.

If you leave Pickering on the A170 and turn right at **Wrelton**, you'll drive up the Rosedale Valley to the remains of a 12th-century Cistercian nunnery, **Rosedale Abbey**.

To the southwest is **Hutton-Le-Hole**, a picturesque village built around a green and a stream crossed by numerous footbridges. With historical buildings such as a 16th-century mansion and an 18th-century cottage, the **Ryedale Folk Museum** illuminates rural history.

Further west, the A170 brings you to **Thirsk** and so-called "Herriot Country." The popular autobiographical books of the late James Herriot (a *nom de plume*), such as *All Things Bright and Beautiful*, recount the life of a country veterinarian in the fictional village of Darrowby, actually a combination of Thirsk, Middleham and Richmond. The period set of Herriot's own veterinary surgery has been preserved in Richmond Museum.

## The Dales

Since the recent reorganization of the English counties, the **Yorkshire Dales National Park** reaches deep into Cumbria. Thanks to restrictions on building imposed by the Park authorities, one of the most magnificent landscapes in England has survived: the dales between the Lake District and the North Yorkshire Moors. The park encompasses a contrasting array of dales, the Norse word for "valley," each of which has its own distinct character and customs.

Wensleydale, for example, one of the widest valleys in the region, is famed for its excellent cheese, which the monks of Jervaulx Abbey (today in ruins) were the first to produce.

**Bedale** marks the gateway to the region. From this market town, the A684 leads through Wensleydale and ultimately arrives at Kendal, the historic centre of the southern Lake District.

South of **Leyburn** on the A6108, **Middleham Castle** dominates the small town. This was the childhood home of Richard III and the massive keep still remains.

West of Leyburn, turn right at **Wensley** for the 16th-century **Castle Bolton**. Visitors can explore it from the subterranean dungeon to the top of its 100-foot (30 m) battlements, which command breathtaking views over the wide valley of Wensleydale.

From here the narrow road goes due north up over Redmire Moor to **Reeth**, situated on the crest between Swaledale and Arkengarthdale, and thus a good base for walkers and other visitors. The **Swaledale Folk Museum** here provides an intriguing glimpse into the rural life of local inhabitants in days gone by.

Moving east, the B6270 and the A6108 lead to the ancient town of **Richmond** with its marketplace and alleys known as "wynds." The 11th-century **castle keep** has been restored to what it must have been like in medieval times. In Friar's Wynd, the Georgian **Theatre Royal** of 1788 has been restored to its original state and is again in use.

To the north, the A66, another old Roman road, leads to Greta Bridge, where a right turn brings you to Egglestone Abbey and then to **Barnard Castle**. It perches precipitously on the steep banks of the river Tees.

To the east, just outside the town on the A67, lies the unusual **Bowes Museum**, which echoes the museum buildings in the Tuileries in Paris. It contains an eclectic collection of porcelain, furniture, and paintings.

Northeast on the A688 are **Staindrop** and **Raby Castle**, a magnificent 14th-century fortress complete with nine towers, medieval kitchens, and period furnishings.

# GUIDEPOST NORTHERN ENGLAND

## CHESHIRE PLAIN
## MANCHESTER / LIVERPOOL
### Accommodation
MANCHESTER: *LUXURY:* **The Gardens**, 55, Piccadilly, tel. 0161 2365155. *MODERATE:* **Castlefield Hotel**, Liverpool Road, Castlefield, tel. 0161 8327073. *BUDGET:* **Lindhurst**, 22, Whiterow, Cholton, tel. 0161 8629001.

### Restaurants
MANCHESTER: *LUXURY:* **Moss Nook**, Ringway Road, tel. 0161 4374778. **Victoria & Albert**, Water Street, tel. 0161 8321188. *MODERATE:* **Yang Sing**, 34 Princes Street, tel. 0161 2362200, Chinese. *BUDGET:* **Market**, corner Edge/High Street, tel. 0161 8343743.

### Museums
BARLASTON: **Wedgwood Pottery Visitor Centre and Museum**, tel. 01782 204218, Easter-Oct Mon-Fri 9.00-17.00, Sun 10.00-17.00, Oct-Easter Sat 10.00-16.00, closed Sun. **City Museum**, Hanley, Bethesda St., tel. 01782 202173, Mon-Sat 10.00-17.00, Sun 14.00-17.00. **Etruria Industrial Museum**, Lower Bedford St., tel. 01782 287557, Wed-Sun 10.00-16.00. CHESTER: **Deva Roman Experience Museum**, tel. 01244 343407, open all year daily 9.00-17.30. ELLESMERE PORT: **Waterways Museum**, tel. 0151 3555017, in summer daily 10.00-17.00.
MANCHESTER: **City Art Gallery**, Mosley St., tel. 0161 2365244, Mon-Sat 10.00-17.45, Sun 14.00-17.45. **Museum of Science and Industry**, Castlefield, tel. 0161 8321830, daily 10.00-17.00. **Manchester Museum**, The University, Oxford Rd., tel. 0161 2752634, Mon-Sat 10.00-17.00. LIVERPOOL: **City Art Gallery**, tel. 0161 2365244, Mon-Sat 10.00-18.00, Sun 14.00-18.00. **Liverpool Museum**, tel. 0151 6387144, all year weekdays and Sat 10.00-17.00, Sun 12.00-17.00. **Walker Art Gallery**, tel. 0151 4784199, weekdays and Sat 10.00-17.00. **Maritime Museum**, tel. 0151 2070001, all year daily 10.30-17.30, closed Good Friday, Christmas and New Year. **Beatles Exhibition**, tel. 0151 7091963, weekdays daily 10.30-17.30, Sat and Sun 10.00-17.00. **Tate Gallery**, tel. 0151 7093223, daily except Mon 10.00-18.00. **Atkinson Art Gallery**, tel. 0151 9342110, daily except Sun 10.00-17.00, Thur and Sat 10.00-13.00. MACCLESFIELD: **Macclesfield Silk Museum and Paradise Mill**, tel. 01625 613210. Museum open all year Tue-Sat 11.00-17.00, Sun 13.00-17.00. The Mill is open Tue-Sun 13.00-17.00.

### Tips and Trips
BURSCOUGH: **Martin Mere Wildfowl Centre**, tel. 01704 895181, daily 9.30-17.30, in winter until 16.00. CHARNOCK RICHARD: **Camelot Theme Park**, tel. 01257 453044, June-Aug daily 10.00-17.00, April-May, Sept-Oct Sat and Sun. KNOWSLEY: **Knowsley Safari Park**, Prescot. tel. 0151 4309009, March-Oct daily 10.00-16.00. MANCHESTER: **Granada Studio Tours**, tel. 0161 8329090, all year 10.00-15.00 daily, closed Mon and Tue. MERSEYSIDE: **Dunham Massey**, near Bowdon, tel. 0161 9411025, 2 April-30 Oct Sat-Wed 12.00-17.00. **Tatton Park**, Knutsford, tel. 01565 632611, 1 April-30 Sept daily 12.00-17.30. **Heaton Hall**, near Manchester, tel. 0161 236244, open summer by appointment only. **Wythenshawe Hall**, near Manchester, tel. 0161 2365244, open summer by appointment only. **Gullivers World Theme Park**, Jodrell Bank, tel. 01925 444888, 1 April-30 Oct Sat and Sun 10.30-17.00. **Observatory and Radio Telescope** Jodrell Bank, tel. 01477 571339, daily 26 March-30 Oct 10.30-17.30. November-Easter weekend only 11.00-16.30. HOLLINGWORTH: **Hollingworth Visitor Centre**, tel. 0161 706 373421, all year 11.00-16.00 weekdays, 10.30-17.00 Sat and Sun. LIVERPOOL: **Speke Hall**, tel. 0151 4277231, April-end Oct daily 12.00-17.30, closed Mon. SOUTHPORT: **Southport Zoo**, tel. 01704 538102, all year daily; Summer 10.00-17.00, Winter 10.00-16.00. BURSCOUGH: **Rufford Old Hall**, tel. 01704 821254, open 2 April-31 Oct daily Sat-Wed 13.00-17.00, Sun 13.00-17.30.

### Tourist Information / Airport
LIVERPOOL: **Merseyside Welcome Centre**, Clayton Square, Shopping Centre, tel. 0151 7093631. **Atlantic Pavilion**, Albert Dock, tel. 0151 7088854. MANCHESTER: Lloyd Street, tel. 0161 234315/8. **Manchester Airport**, flight information tel. 0161 4893000.

## STOKE-ON-TRENT / BLACKPOOL
## HUMBERSIDE
### Accommodation
STOKE-ON-TRENT: *LUXURY:* **The Grand**, Stakis, Trinity Square, tel. 01782 202361. *MODERATE:* **The George Hotel**, Swan Square, Burslem, tel. 01782 577544. *BUDGET:* **North Stafford Hotel**, Station Road, tel. 01782 744477.

### Tips and Trips
ALTON: **Alton Towers**, Stoke, tel. 01538 7072200, open Easter-5 November daily 9.00-dusk. BEVERLEY: **Museum of Army Transport**, tel. 01482 860445, all year daily except Mon 10.00-18.00. BLACKPOOL: **Blackpool Pleasure Beach**, Blackpool Pier, tel. 01253 341033, open 26 March-6 Nov daily. **Louis Tussaud's Waxworks**, tel. 01253 25953, all year daily 10.00-17.00 except Dec 25 and Jan 1. **Clitheroe Castle**, outside Blackpool, tel. 01200 24635, open Oct 11.00-16.00, April 10.00-17.00, May-Sept 11.00-17.00. GRIMSBY: **National Fishing Heritage Centre**, Alexandra

Dock, tel. 01472 344868, daily 10.00-18.00. **PADIHAM: Gawthorpe Hall**, tel. 01282 778511, April-Oct daily except Mon and Fri 13.00-17.00, open Good Friday and Bank Holiday Monday.

### Tourist Information
STOKE-ON-TRENT: Quadrant Road, Henley, tel. 01782 284600.

## YORKSHIRE / YORK
### Accommodation
YORK: *LUXURY:* **Middlethorpe Hall**, Bishopthorpe Rd., tel. 01904 641241. **Mount Royale**, The Mount, tel. 01904 628856.
*MODERATE:* **Ambassador**, 125 The Mount, tel. 01904 641316. **Clifton Bridge**, Water End, tel. 01904 640208.
*BUDGET:* **The Bedford**, 108-110 Boothham, tel. 01904 624412.

### Museums
**BRADFORD**: National Museum of Photography, tel. 01274 727488, Tue-Sun 10.30-18.00. **LEEDS: City Art Gallery**, Calverly Street, tel. 0113 2478275, open Tue-Fri all year 9.30-17.30, Sat 9.30-16.00. **HALIFAX: Eureka Children's Museum**, Discovery Rd., tel. 01426 983191, daily 10.00-17.00. **HAWORTH: Brontë Parsonage Museum**, tel. 0113 2642323, open April-Sept 10.00-17.00, Oct-March 11.00-16.30. **MALTON: Eden Camp Theme Museum**, tel. 01653 697777, daily 10.00-17.00. **SHEFFIELD: City Museum**, tel. 0114 2768588, open Mon-Sat all year 10.00-17.00 except Dec 25 and Jan 1. **YORK: York Castle Museum**, tel. 01904 653611, open April-Oct Mon-Sat 9.30-17.30, Sun from 10.30. **York City Art Gallery**, tel. 01904 623839, open all year Mon-Sat 10.00-17.00, Sun 14.30-17.00, closed Dec 25. **National Railway Museum**, Leeman Rd., tel. 01904 621261, open Mon-Sat 10.00-18.00, Sun 11.00-18.00.

### Tips and Trips
**BRIDLINGTON: Burton Agnes Hall**, tel. 01262 490324, 1 April-31 Oct 11.00-17.00.
**COXWOLD: Shandy Hall**, tel. 01347 868465, June-Sept Sun and Wed 13.30-17.00. **FRIDAYTHORPE: Sledmere House**, tel. 01377 236208, daily April-Oct 12.30-16.30, closed Mon and Fri. **GRASSINGTON: Bolton Abbey**, tel. 01756 710238, daily all year 8.00-19.00, Friday 8.00-16.00. **HOWARTH: North Valley Railway**, tel. 0113 2645214. Time table details tel. 01833 236477, runs April-October daily. **LEEDS: Temple Newsam**, tel. 0113 2647321, Tue-Sun 10.30-17.30. **Harewood House**, near Leeds, tel. 0113 2886331, mid-March-Oct daily11.00-17.00. **RIPLEY: Ripley Castle**, tel. 01423 770152, April, May, October weekends only 11.30-16.30. June, August daily 11.30-16.00. **RIPON: Newby Hall**, tel. 01423 322583, April-Sept 11.00-17.00, closed Mon. **SPROATLEY: Burton Constable Hall**, tel. 01964 562400, open 3 April-30 Sept daily 12.30-17.30. **YORK: Jorvik Viking Centre**, tel. 01904 643211, all year daily 9.30-18.30 except Dec 25 and Jan 1. **Fairfax Hall**, Castlegate, tel. 01904 655543, March-Dec Mon-Sat 11.00-17.00, Sun 13.30-17.00, closed Fri. **Castle Howard**, near York, Malton, April-Oct daily 11.00-16.30. **Benningborough Hall**, near York, tel. 01904 470666, April-Oct Fri-Wed 11.00-17.00.

### Tourist Information
**LEEDS**: The Arcade, City Station, tel. 0113 2478301/2. **SHEFFIELD**: Peace Gardens, tel. 0114 2734671/72.
**YORK**: De Grey Rooms, Exhibition Square, tel. 01904 621756.

## SCARBOROUGH / WHITBY
### Accommodation
SCARBOROUGH: *LUXURY:* **Royal Hotel**, St. Nicholas Street, tel. 01723 3643333.
*MODERATE:* **Palm Court**, St. Nicholas Street, tel. 01723 368161. *BUDGET:* **Peace Home Park Hotel**, 21-23 Victoria Park, tel. 01723 500954.

### Museums
**HUTTON LE HOLE: Ryedale Folk Museum**, tel. 01751 417367, 19 March-29 Oct daily 10.00-16.30. **MIDDLEHAM: Richmond Museum**, tel. 01748 825611, Easter-30 October 11.00-17.00 daily. **REETH: Swaledale Folk Museum**, tel. 01748 884373, Easter-Oct daily 10.30-17.00. **WHITBY: Captain Cook Memorial Museum**, tel. 01947 601900, open 31 March-31 Oct daily. 10.00-16.30, Sat and Sun 11.00-15.00.

### Tips and Trips
**HOVINGHAM: Nunnington Hall**, tel. 01439 748283, 26 March-30 Oct Tue, Wed, Thur, Good Friday, Sat and Sun 14.00-18.00. Bank Holiday Monday 12.00-18.00. July and Aug on Friday also. **MALTON: Castle Howard**, tel. 01653 648333, open 1 April-31 Oct daily. House open 11.00-16.30, grounds open 10.00-16.30. **Kirkham Priory**, tel. 01653 81713, open 1 April-30 Sept. **MIDDLEHAM: Jervaulx Abbey**, tel. 01677 460391, open daily all year. **Middleham Castle**, tel. 01969 23899, April-Oct daily 10.00-18.00, Nov-March Wed-Sun 10.00-16.00. **REETH: Barnard Castle**, tel. 01833 38212, 1 April-31 Oct 10.00-18.00. 1 November-31 March 10.00-16.00, closed Mon and Tue. **SCARBOROUGH: Scarborough Castle**, tel. 01723 372451, April-Oct 10.00-18.00 daily; 1 Nov-31 March 10.00-16.00. **WENSLEY: Bolton Castle**, tel. 01969 23981, March-Nov 10.00-17.00.

### Tourist Information
**SCARBOROUGH**: St. Nicholas Cliff, tel. 01723 373333.

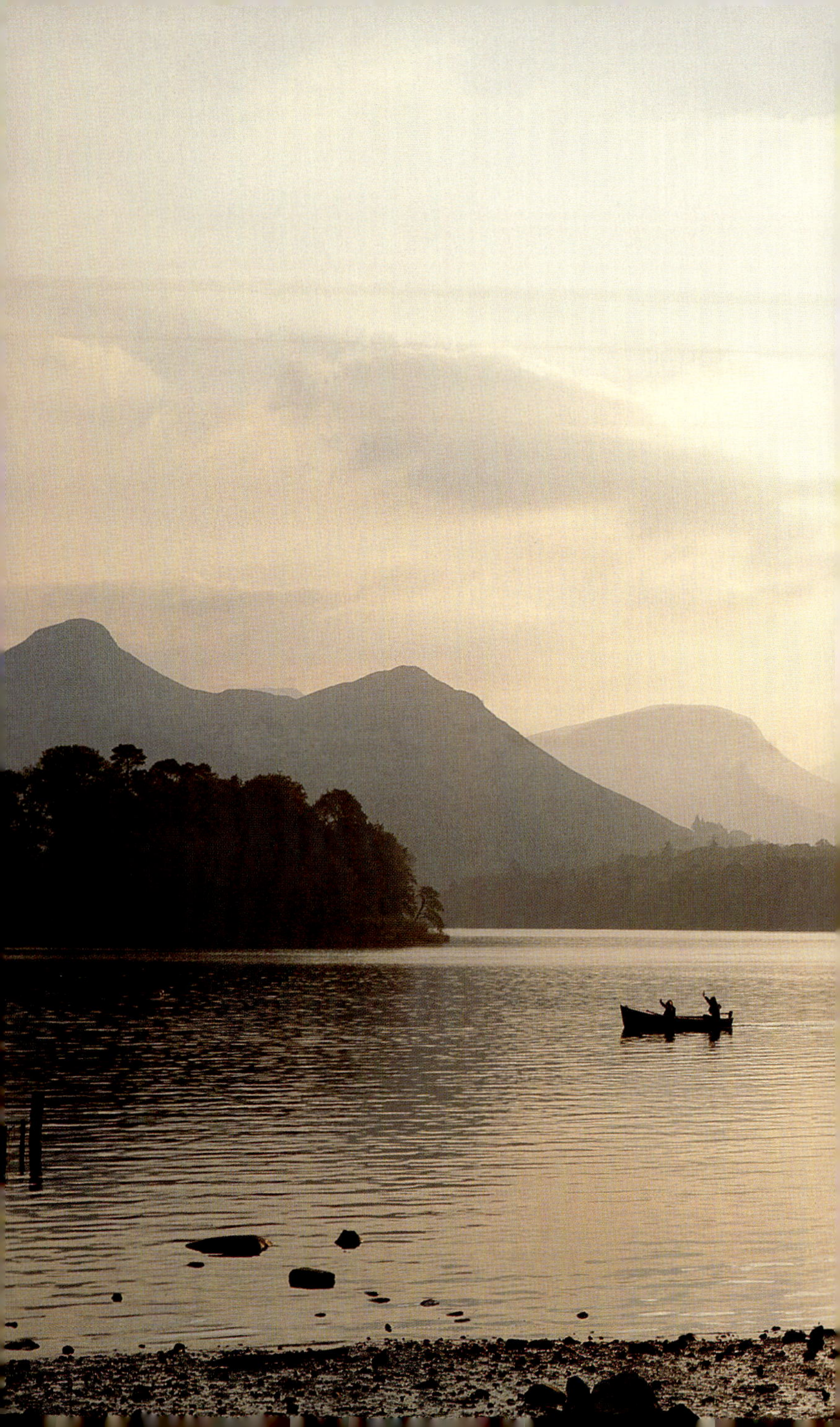

LAKES AND BORDERS

# THE LAKES AND BORDERS

CUMBRIA / LAKE DISTRICT
CARLISLE / BORDERS
DURHAM
NORTHUMBERLAND

## CUMBRIA / LAKE DISTRICT

**Cumbria**, in the northwest of England, contains some of the most beautiful country in the land. The greater part (900 sq mi/2,300 sq km) of the region is taken up by the **Lake District**, a national park which attracts floods of visitors every year. In the south, the landscape is hilly and green; it grows increasingly dramatic and wild, however, the further north and west you go. England's highest peak, Scafell (3,200 ft/979 m), and many other notable elevations surround the 16 fair-sized lakes, and the district boasts a wide variety of flora and fauna. There is something for everyone, and Kendal makes a good base from which to conduct explorations.

### Kendal

**Kendal** is the gateway to the Lake District. It first attained some measure of prosperity in the 14th century as a center of the wool weaving industry; its trademark product was the heavy cloth known as "Kendal green." The medieval layout of the town endures in the narrow alleys

*Preceding pages: Dusk on Derwent Water. Left: Climbers on Shepherd's Crag in the Lake District.*

that branch off the main street. The old stables in the 12th-century castle ruins now house the **Museum of Lakeland Life and Industry**. Catherine Parr, later to marry Henry VIII, was born in this castle in 1512. Also worth a visit is the art collection at **Abbot Hall**, an 18th-century Georgian building, which includes watercolors by Turner and drawings by Ruskin, another Lake District regular.

From Kendal, take the A590 to **Levens** and **Levens Hall**, the largest Elizabethan house in the region, based on an earlier pele tower, a defensive tower typical of the border country. The house itself is interesting but even more fascinating are the gardens (especially the famous **Topiary Gardens**), which have not changed since the 17th century, much like those at Hampton Court, which happened to have been laid out by the same man, a certain Beaumont. From here, you can detour to see the 17th- and 18th-century houses in **Cartmel**, or the town's **Priory**, the finest medieval building in the Lake District.

The picturesque little market town of **Ulverston** is the birthplace of Stan Laurel (1890-1965), commemorated in the **Laurel and Hardy Museum**.

The A590 ends at **Furness Abbey**. In the 12th century, this was one of the most important Cistercian abbeys in England. The monks were known for settling in

*CUMBRIA AND DURHAM*

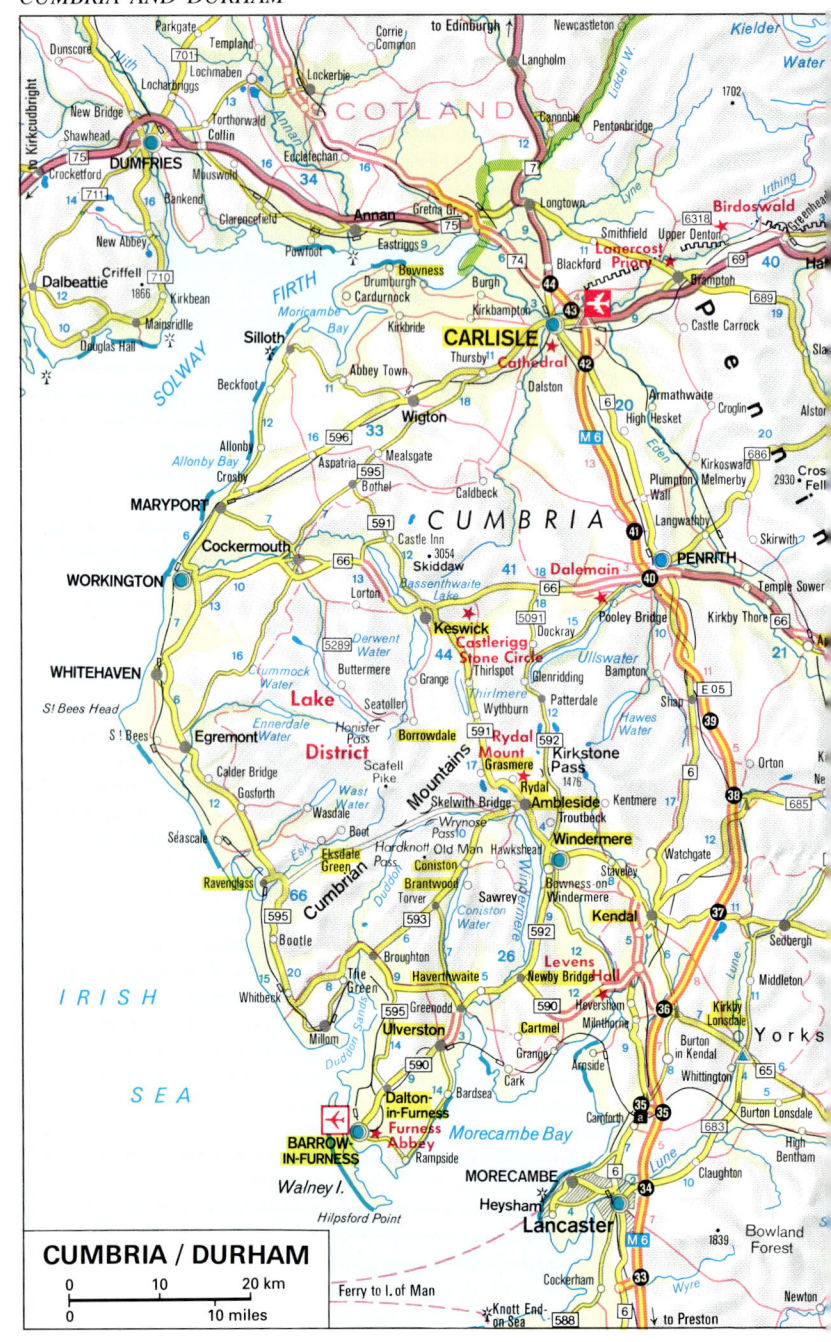

*CUMBRIA AND DURHAM*

227

idyllic surroundings, so it is hardly surprising that even as a ruin the abbey in the *Vale of the Deadly Nightshade* is still an impressive sight today. At **Dalton-in-Furness** there is a watchtower which the Cistercian monks erected to protect the abbey against Scottish attacks.

**Barrow-in-Furness** dates from as recently as the last century; it's one of those towns stamped out of the ground during the Industrial Revolution. Iron and steelworks sprang up here to supply the shipyards nearby. Today the docks are operated by the firms British Nuclear Fuels and British Gas, but the town's glory days are past.

### Lake Windermere

At **Haverthwaite**, the road crosses into the national park. Since 1847, the Lakeside and Haverthwaite Railway has been carrying passengers to Windermere, by steam or diesel, helping the region to become the most popular holiday destination in England. Crossing Newby Bridge, you come to **Bowness-on-Windermere**, an attractive village with a well-known lakeside promenade. In the high season Bowness gets quite crowded; not only is it a terminus of the ferry across the lake, but many boat and coach trips also start from here.

Above Bowness is the village of **Windermere** which owes its birth to the coming of tourism in the 19th century. Not surprisingly, it consists almost entirely of shops, hotels and boarding houses.

**Lake Windermere** itself is the longest (10 miles/16 km) and largest in England. Its name derives from the Scandinavian, *Vinandr's Mere*. It's surrounded by charming countryside, with woods and green hills divided up by dry-stone walls: a more pastoral setting than the landscapes of most of the district's other lakes, where the dark volcanic stone creates a more sober, stark scenery, espe-

*Above: Driving sheep in Cumbria. Right: High Sweden Bridge in the fells near Ambleside.*

cially in the rain. Boating enthusiasts should peruse the **Windermere Steamboat Museum** and take a trip on the lake in the 1902 steam launch.

Above the western shore of Windermere is the village of **Sawrey** where, at Hill Top, Beatrix Potter lived and raised sheep after retiring as a writer of children's books. Her house is now open to lovers of Peter Rabbit, Jemima Puddleduck and their friends; her original watercolors show her talent as an amateur naturalist. True fans should also take in the **World of Beatrix Potter Exhibition** in Bowness.

**Ambleside** stretches along the north shore of the lake and dates back to long before the tourists discovered the Lakes. The site of a Roman fort is nearby, one of a ring of military structures established around the central mass of high hills which the Romans did not bother to conquer. The one sight here is the **Bridgehouse**, built actually over the river to free its owner of the obligation to pay land tax. Ambleside is on the fringe of true hill country, the fells. In order to appreciate this landscape, you have to don a pair of sturdy shoes and hike. For routes, consult the works of Wainwright, who documented, in detail, every trail in the Lake District, easy and hard; his books are available in every local bookshop.

One must in this region is **Grasmere**. As well as being a village of great beauty it was home to the poet William Wordsworth (1770-1850) and his family. He is buried in **St. Oswald's Church** in Grasmere. Just outside Grasmere is tiny **Dove Cottage** where he lived with his sister; next to it, the **Wordsworth Museum** houses manuscripts, paintings by Constable and Gainsborough and memorabilia of the Romantic movement. Nearby is **Rydal**, where the poet lived until his death. The house, Rydal Mount, still belongs to descendants of the family and contains many of the poet's personal possessions. A more prosaic Grasmere highlight is Sarah Nelson's Grasmere Gingerbread, a truly delicious confection unlike anything else known as "gingerbread."

*FURNESS FELLS / NORTHERN LAKES*

**The Furness Fells**

From Grasmere, the A593 leads to **Coniston** on Coniston Water. In nearby **Brantwood** lived another notable Lakelander: the writer, artist and critic John Ruskin (*The Stones of Venice*). His house commands a view of the highest mountain in the area, the **Old Man** (2,600 ft/ 800 m), which in turn offers the best panorama of Windermere, Coniston Water and also Scafell Pike and the sea.

From Coniston, the A593 leads to **Duddon Sands** by the sea and then turns right to **Eskdale Green**. The roads here are very narrow and in the high season very busy, so caution is advised, especially as sheep graze beside the road. Due to its proximity to the sea, the landscape here seems harsher, with barren slopes of gray scree contrasting markedly with the softer shapes of the eastern Lake District.

*Above: The Lilliput Lane workshops in Penrith. Right: Older than Stonehenge: the stone circle at Castlerigg.*

From Eskdale Green the route leads back to Grasmere and Ambleside via **Hard Knott** and **Wrynose Pass**. This round trip gives a good introduction to the most attractive places around Furness Fells.

**The Northern Lakes**

Going north from Grasmere, you come to **Thirlmere**, a lake surrounded by mountains and forests. Despite human intervention – the lake is dammed and the trees planted by man – it is still an attractive sight. On the hillsides, you can see traces of ancient industry, slate and lead mines; while the minute figures of rock climbers scale the cliffs. Before the road reaches Keswick, a track leads off to the right to **Castlerigg stone circle**, which is older than Stonehenge. From here there is a good view back to Thirlmere and north to Keswick.

Dating back to the Middle Ages, **Keswick** became an important mining town in the 16th century. Graphite was mined in nearby **Borrowdale**, and in 1832 the world's first lead pencil factory opened in Keswick. The industry survives today and a survey of its history, as well as the methods of pencil manufacture, is presented at the **Cumberland Pencil Museum**.

South of the town is **Derwent Water**, which, in its unspoiled setting, is one of the most beautiful lakes in England. In the north is **Ullswater**, by whose shores Wordsworth wandered lonely as a cloud and saw the daffodils that inspired the poem.

**CARLISLE AND THE BORDERS**

For centuries, **Carlisle** was the center of border conflicts between England and Scotland. Even in Antiquity, it marked the border of the Roman empire and the Celtic realms. In the 2nd century, attacks and encroachments by the Celtic tribes increased so much that a fortified frontier wall was built from sea to sea within ten years. Named after the emperor of the time, **Hadrian's Wall** begins at Bowness on the Solway Firth and stretches 73 miles (117 km) across to Newcastle-upon-Tyne, from the Irish Sea to the North Sea. It consisted of two walls of stone with a fill of earth and mortar, making it wide enough for a legionary to use as a rampart. Ditches on either side made it more difficult for barbarians to attack. Nineteen castles were located along the wall, each garrisoned by a thousand soldiers. A total of 10,000 men were stationed at the wall, and a military road was built parallel to it to allow them to move quickly to the scene of the action. But despite all these efforts the constant pressure of the northern tribes could not be withstood forever. In the 4th century the Romans were forced to abandon the wall, and the locals soon started using it as a quarry for building materials for houses and churches.

**Carlisle**, originally known as *Luguvalium*, retained its strategic importance here even after Roman times. Its position at the mouth of the river Eden in the Solway Firth favored trade and brought the city prosperity. In the Dark Ages the Scots tried again and again to take the city; in reaction, the Norman king William II had the locality so strongly fortified that Carlisle was not taken until the 17th century. During the Civil War the city was captured and plundered by a Scottish army under General Leslie after a bitter nine-month siege. Precisely one hundred years later the Scots were at the gates once more, this time lead by Bonnie Prince Charlie, who took the castle without firing a shot. At the market cross he declared his father king of Great Britain. After the defeat and massacre of the Scots during the Jacobite Rebellion of 1745, the Duke of Cumberland recaptured the city. Culloden was the last attempt of the Scots to achieve their independence from England.

The **Market Cross** is a good point to start your tour of Carlisle; it stands on the erstwhile site of the Roman forum.

231

Around the **market square** are some of the most attractive historical buildings in the city, such as the **Guildhall** or the **Tullie House,** which houses a museum and art gallery. Exhibits include prehistoric and Roman finds as well as around two thousand works of art from the last 300 years, including paintings by Peter Blake.

The city **cathedral** is one of the most attractive churches in the North of England. The eventful history of the city is reflected in the cathedral as well. Building started at the beginning of the 12th century. Originally a small abbey, the building grew as the city grew in importance, becoming Carlisle's principal church, continually added to and modified as architectural styles changed through the ages and as the population increased. The cathedral stands on Norman foundations, and both the exterior and interior are predominantly Gothic in style. Its most impressive features include the great east window in Decorated Style, depicting the Last Judgment; the sculptured decorations of the columns; and the painted ceiling vaulting.

In the northwest of Carlisle is the city's **castle**, built in the 11th century by William Rufus and continually extended and strengthened to withstand the Scots. In 1568 Mary Stuart, Scots rival of Elizabeth I, was imprisoned for two months in its tower, called Queen Mary's Tower.

## COUNTY DURHAM

**County Durham** may be divided into two very different parts: there is the densely-populated, typically industrial region along the coast where the rivers **Tyne**, **Wear** and **Tees** join the sea, and then there is the rural, western part, with the city of **Durham** at its center.

Historically, Durham was one of the most important political centers in England. Under the Normans it was the residence of the Prince Bishops, who were at once spiritual and secular rulers.

*Above: Durham Cathedral, the earliest example of English Gothic.*

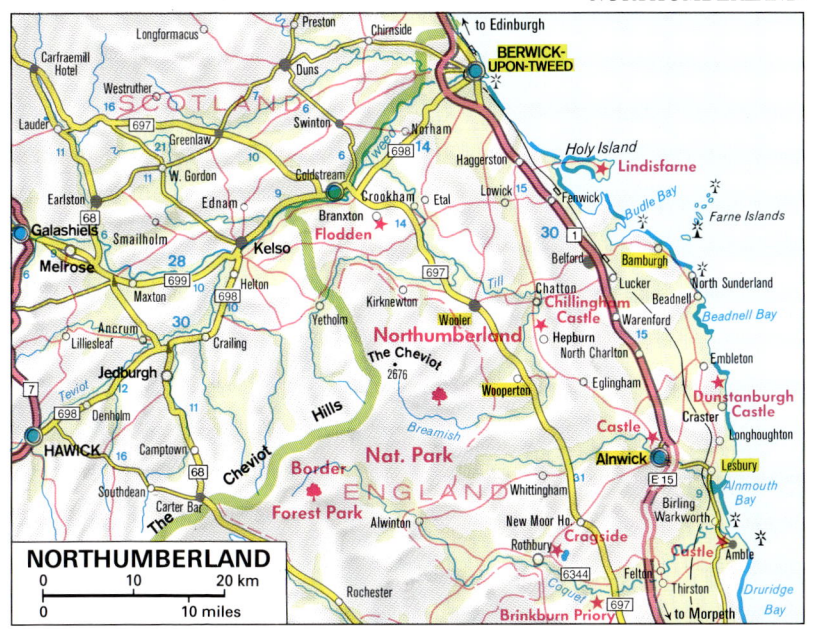

The city is among the most beautiful in England. It is dominated by the castle and the massive bulk of the Norman **cathedral**; the design of the latter, started in 1093 by the Norman bishop William of Calais, was revolutionary in its day. The choir was given cross-ribbed vaulting, the galleries were supported externally by flying buttresses, and the transverse arches dividing up the nave were Gothic (pointed), not rounded. The robust, incised pillars of the nave rise to perfect rounded arches, with yet more arches above, all patterned with typical Norman geometric carving. This cathedral was the foundation of Gothic architecture in England. In addition to the chronicler of early English history, the Venerable Bede, it is also the final resting place of the revered, but misogynistic, St. Cuthbert.

Opposite the cathedral stands **Durham Castle**, once in the front line of conflicts with the Scots and later, in the 12th century, residence of the bishops who ruled the region. Like the cathedral, it stands within the ancient town on a bluff overlooking a curve of the river Wear, which once acted as a natural moat.

South of Durham is the busy market town of **Darlington**, a byword among railroad buffs the world over. This is where George Stephenson built his Locomotive No. 1, displayed in a **museum** in the old Northwest Railway Station. Darlington was the terminus of the world's first commercial passenger railway, and the museum celebrates the dawn of the age of the steam train. In the Victorian age there were major textile mills here, another reason for the railway's advent.

## NORTHUMBERLAND

**Northumberland** is the northernmost region of England. At the mouths of the rivers Tweed, Tyne and Tees there arose over the centuries major centers of trade and commerce such as Berwick, Newcastle and Stockton. The Romans landed on the Northumberland coast, followed by the Vikings, while a thousand years later, in the 19th century, great steam-

*NEWCASTLE-UPON-TYNE*

ships departed from here, delivering the industrial products of Great Britain to the entire world. The interior, on the other hand, is dominated by untouched landscapes, such as the **Cheviots**, where the *Border Forest Park* and the *Northumberland National Park* have been set up. South of the Tyne, the **Pennines** also offer impressive landscapes.

### Newcastle-upon-Tyne

The county town of **Newcastle-upon-Tyne** is the largest of a complex of industrial and commercial towns along the river, but was in fact founded as the easternmost end of Hadrian's Wall; the wall itself ran down what is now Westgate. The south bank of the Tyne is dominated by industrial and modern residential districts; it's on the north bank that you find the old town and all of the sights.

*Above: The Norman castle of Bamburgh.*
*Right: Cormorant breeding-grounds on the Farne Island bird reserve.*

The best place to start a tour is at the **Quayside** with a view of three of the six bridges that cross the river: the Tyne Bridge (1928), the Swing Bridge (1878) and the **High Level Bridge**. This last is the best-known, designed in the 19th century by Robert Stephenson, son of the railway pioneer George Stephenson, as a double-decker railway and road bridge, and opened by Queen Victoria in 1849. The neighboring rehabilitated **quay district** is enchanting with its historical houses, small shops and restaurants. On Sunday there is a colorful **flea market**. At Sandhill are the **Guildhall** (17th century, rebuilt in the 19th century), the **Custom House**, and the restored half-timbered **Bessie Surtees House**, dating back to the 16th/17th centuries and with rotating exhibitions recalling the days of the merchant adventurers. A favorite place to meet is the 137-foot (42 m) **Earl Grey Monument** at the center of town; its viewing platform offers a fantastic panorama of the city. Grainger Street, one of Newcastle's busiest shopping streets, starts at the monument. Only a few steps away from the popular shopping mall at Eldon Square begins Newcastle's **Chinatown**. Newcastle also boasts a number of museums, such as the **Museum of Antiquities**, which also has a model of Hadrian's Wall, or the **Museum of Science and Engineering**, which presents a look at the city's industrial heyday.

### Along the Coast

**Alnwick Castle** has been in the possession of the Percy family, the Dukes of Northumberland, since the 12th century. It contains French period furniture, Meissen porcelain, and works by Turner, Titian, Tintoretto and van Dyck.

Not far from Alnwick, an extremely beautiful section of coast with some beaches begins at **Lesbury**. Via the stark ruins of **Dunstanburgh Castle**, destroyed in the Wars of the Roses, past the huge Norman fortress of **Bamburgh Castle,** the road leads on across a causeway to **Holy Island** and the priory and castle of **Lindisfarne**. Here was the first great stronghold of Christianity in the north, and the magic survives despite the crowds. The island is cut off twice a day by the tides; be sure to pick up a listing of safe times to cross before heading out over the 3-mile (5 km) sand bar.

Irish monks arrived here in the 7th century from the island of Iona in the Irish Sea in order to convert the pagan Saxons. The monastery which they built developed quickly into a spiritual center, and the monks' skill with their hands was soon renowned: costly gospels, filigree work and reliquaries issued from their workshops.

These treasures attracted the Vikings, too, and in 955 the monks fled with the bones of St. Cuthbert to Durham. Only ruins remain of the Benedictine abbey on Lindisfarne which was founded 100 years later.

All along the border with Scotland stand the castles and fortified towers, or pele towers, that speak of the long years of conflict between English and Scot. The A1 crosses the border river Tweed to the last outpost of England, **Berwick-upon-Tweed**. Once, Berwick was an important Scottish port; it changed hands 13 times before finally being incorporated into England in 1482. You can stroll along Berwick's city walls, which date back to Elizabethan times.

The A697 leads to **Wooler**, a fine center for exploring the hills, after passing close to **Flodden**, a name that invokes memory of Henry VIII's defeat of the Scots in 1513, though the battlefield is further north, close to the village of Branxton. Further south take the B6348 to **Chillingham Castle** (14th century), an absolute must. In the castle park roam a herd of extremely rare white cattle of an archaic type which *may* well be the direct descendants of a herd kept by the ancient Celts for sacrificial purposes, white cattle being sacred to the sun.

*GUIDEPOST LAKES AND BORDERS*

## LAKE DISTRICT
### Accommodation
**KENDAL**: *LUXURY:* **Garden House Hotel**, Fowl-Ing Lane, tel. 01539 731131.
*MODERATE:* **Higher House Farm**, Oxenholme Lane, Natland, tel. 015395 61177.
**KESWICK**: *MODERATE:* **Chaucer House Hotel**, Derwentwater Place, tel. 017687 72318. **Applethwaite Country House Hotel**, Applethwaite, Underskiddaw, tel. 017687 72413.
**WINDERMERE**: *LUXURY:* **Hillbeckghyll Country House Hotel**, Hillbeckghyll Lane, Trout Beck, tel. 015394 32375. **Miller Howe**, Rayrigg Rd., tel. 015394 42536, with good restaurant. **Sharrow Bay**, Howtown (east side of Ullswater), tel. 017684 86301, with good restaurant.
*MODERATE:* **Cedar Manor Hotel**, Ambleside Road, tel. 015394 43192. **Gilpin Lodge**, Crook Rd., tel. 015394 88818, with good restaurant. **Linthwaite House**, Crook Rd., tel. 015394 88600, with good restaurant.
*BUDGET:* **Burn How Garden House**, Back Belsfield Rd., Bowness, tel. 015394 46226, with good restaurant. **Hideaway Hotel**, Phoenix Way, tel. 015394 43070.
### Restaurants
**WINDERMERE**: *MODERATE:* **Porthole Eating House**, 3 Ash St., Bowness, tel. 015394 42793, Italian cuisine.
*INEXPENSIVE:* **Rogers Restaurant**, 4 High St., tel. 015394 44954.
### Museums
**CARTMEL**: **Cartmel Motor Museum**, tel. 01539 58509, open 1 April-31 Oct 10.30 a.m-17.00 p.m, open on Saturdays.
**GRASMERE**: **Wordsworth Museum** and **Dove Cottage** (home of William Wordsworth) tel. 015394 355444, open daily 9.30-17.30, closed in January.
**KENDAL**: **Museum of Lakeland Life and Industry**, Kirkland, tel. 01539 722464, April-Oct 10.30-17.00, phone for opening times in winter.
**KESWICK**: **Cumberland Pencil Museum**, tel. 017687 73626, open all year daily 9.30-17.00. **Cars of the Stars Museum**, tel. 01768 773757, open daily 10.00-17.00, closed in January.
**WINDERMERE**: **Windermere Steam Boat Museum**, tel. 015394 45565, open daily 10.00-17.00.
### Tips and Trips
**BOWNESS-ON-WINDERMERE**: **World of Beatrix Potter**, The Old Laundry, Crag Bow, tel. 015394 88444, open all year 10.00-16.00.
**KENDAL**: **Sizergh Castle**, 5 km south of Kendal, tel. 01539 560070, April-Oct Sun-Thur 13.30-17.30, gardens open from 12.30.
**KESWICK**: **Beatrix Potter's Lake District**, Packhorse Court, tel. 017687 75173, open all year.
**LEVENS**: **Levens Hall**, tel. 015395 60321, open 3 April-30 September daily 11.00-17.00.
**RAVENGLASS**: **Muncaster Castle**, tel. 01229 717614, open 20 March-30 October Tue-Sun 13.00-16.00. **ULVERSTON**: **Cumbria Crystal Glass Factory**, tel. 01229 584400, open all year 9.00-17.00, Mon-Fri 10.00-16.00, Sat 10.00-16.00, Sun 12.00-16.00.
**WINDERMERE**: **Lakeside and Hatherwaite Railway**, tel. 015395 31594, runs all year daily 10.00-17.00.
### Tourist Information
**KENDAL**: Town Hall, Highgate, tel. 01539 725758. **KESWICK**: Moot Hall, Market Sqare, tel. 017687 72645. **WINDERMERE**: Victoria Street, tel. 015394 46499.

## CARLISLE
### Accommodation
**CARLISLE**: *LUXURY:* **Crown and Mitre Hotel**, Highgate, tel. 01539 725758.
*MODERATE:* **Pinegrove Hotel**, 262, London Road, tel. 01288 24828.
*BUDGET:* **The Woodlands Hotel**, 262-266 London Road, tel. 01228 45643.
### Tips and Trips
**BIRDOSWALD**: **Roman Fort** and **Hadrians Wall**, tel. 01697 747602, open daily 26 March-31 October 10.00-17.00.
**CARLISLE**: **Carlisle Castle**, tel. 01228 591922, open 1 April-30 Sept 10.00-18.00; 1 Oct-30 Sept 10.00-16.00. **Tullie House**, tel. 01228 34781, open all year Mon-Sat 10.00-17.00, Sun 12.00-17.00. **Brougham Castle**, tel. 01768 62488, open daily 1 April-31 Oct 10.00-18.00.
**GREENHEAD**: **Roman Army Museum**, tel. 016977 47485, open daily 10.00-17.00.
**LANERCOST**: **Lanercost Priory**, tel. 01697 73030, open daily 1 April-30 Sept 10.00-17.00.
### Tourist Information
**CARLISLE**: Old Town Hall, Green Market, tel. 01228 512444

## NEWCASTLE / DURHAM
### Accommodation
**NEWCASTLE**: *LUXURY:* **Imperial Swallow Hotel**, Jesmond Road, tel. 0191 2815511.
*MODERATE:* **Cairn Hotel**, 93-107 Osborne Road, tel. 0191 281135
*BUDGET:* **Whitemare Pool Forte Motel**, A1 / A194 Little Chef, tel. 0191 438333.
### Restaurants
**NEWCASTLE**: *MODERATE:* **Fisherman's Lodge**, Jesmond Dene, Jesmond, tel. 0191 281321.

# GUIDEPOST LAKES AND BORDERS

**Fisherman's Wharf**, 15 The Side, tel. 0191 2321057. **21 Queen Street**, 21 Queen St., Quayside, tel. 0191 2220755. **Vermont**, Castle Garth, tel. 0191 2331010.

### Museums
**CORBRIDGE**: **Corbridge Museum**, tel. 01434 632349, open 1 April-31 Oct daily 10.00-18.00. 1 Nov-31 March Wed-Sun 10.00-16.00.

**DARLINGTON**: **Railway Centre and Museum**, North Road Station, tel. 01325 460532, daily 9.30-17.00.

**DURHAM**: **Museum of Archaeology**, tel. 0191 3743623, open Nov-March 12.30-15.00, April-Oct 11.00-16.00.

**HEXHAM**: **Border History Museum**, tel. 01434 652349, Nov, Feb-Easter Sat-Tue 10.00-16.30. Open daily Easter-October.

**MIDDLESBOROUGH**: **Captain Cooks Museum**, tel. 01642 311211, open daily March-Oct 10.00-17.30; Oct-March 9.00- 16.00.

**NEWCASTLE**: **Greek Museum**. The University, Classics Department, tel. 0191 2227966, Mon-Fri 9.30-13.00 and 14.00-16.30. **Hancock Museum**, tel. 0191 227418, open all year Mon-Sat 10.00-17.00, Sun 14.00-17.00. **Beamish Museum**, tel. 01207 2301811, open 14 March-31 Oct daily 10.00-17.00. 1 Nov-31 March Tue, Thur, Sat and Sun. **John George Joicey Museum**, tel. 0191 2324562, open all year Mon-Sat 10.00-17.00.

### Tips and Trips
**DURHAM**: **Durham Heritage Centre**, tel. 0191 3843720, open 2 April-10 April daily, then Sat and Sun only from 16 April-22 May, then 28 May-25 Sept. **Durham Castle**, tel. 0191 3743800, Easter and Spring Bank Holiday 14.00-16.30, July-Sept Mon-Sat 10.00-12.00 and 14.00-16.30, Sun 14.00-16.30. Oct-June Mon, Wed and Sat 14.00-16.30. **Belsay Hall**, tel. 01661 881636, open 1 April-31 Oct 10.00-18.00. **Durham River Trips**, tel. 0191 3869525. Daily boat trips start at 12.30 and 14.00.

**GUISBOROUGH**: **Guisborough Priory**, tel. 01287 638301, open 1 April-30 Sept daily from 10.00-18.00. 1 Nov-31 March Wed-Sun 10.00- 6.00.

**HEXHAM**: **Howsteads Fort** and **Hadrians Wall**, tel. 01433 44363, open daily from 1 April-30 Sept 10.00-18.00.

**JARROW**: **Jarrow Monastery**, open April-Oct, Tue-Sat 10.00-17.30, Sun 14.30-17.30. Nov-March Tue-Sat 11.00-14.30.

**STAINDROP**: **Raby Castle**, tel. 01833 660202, open from Easter Sunday until Easter Wed only in April. May and June: Wed-Sun. July, Aug and Sept: daily except Saturday. Hours of opening: 13.00-17.00. **Barnard Castle**, tel. 01833 38212, open 30 April-10 October daily from 9.00-18.00. 10 October-31 March from 10.00-18.00.

**STOCKTON-ON-TEES**: **Butterfly World**, tel. 01642 791414, open daily 10.00-16.00 November-February.

### Tourist Information / Airport
**DURHAM**: Market Place, tel. 0191 3843720. **NEWCASTLE**: The Central Library, Princess Square, tel. 0191 2610610.

**Newcastle International Airport** is situated approximately 22 minutes from the city centre, tel. 0191 2860966.

## BERWICK-UPON-TWEED
### Accommodation
**BERWICK-UPON-TWEED**: *LUXURY:* **Kings Arms Hotel**, Hide Hill, tel. 01289 308867. *MODERATE:* **Berwick Walls Hotel**, 31-36 Ravensdowne, tel. 01289 330770. *BUDGET:* **The Castle**, 103 Castle Gate, tel. 01289 3079000.

### Restaurant
**BERWICK-UPON-TWEED**: *MODERATE:* **Funnywayt' Mekalivin**, 41 Bridge Street, tel. 01289 308827.

### Museums
**BERWICK-UPON-TWEED**: **Museum and Art Gallery**, tel. 01289 330933, open Easter-30 Sept 10.00-18.00. 1 Oct-Easter Tue-Sun 10.00-16.00. **Berwick Barracks Museum**, tel. 01289 304493, open daily 1 April-31 Oct 10.00-18.00. From Nov-31 March closed Mon and Tue.

**LINDISFARNE**: **Lindisfarne Museum**, tel. 01289 89200, open 1 April-30 Sept 10.00-18.00. 1 Oct-31 March 10.00-16.00.

### Tips and Trips
**Bamburgh Castle**, tel. 01228 591922, open Easter-End of Oct Mon-Sat 9.30-18.00. 1 Nov Mon-Thur 10.00-16.00. **Cragside House and Gardens**, tel. 01669 203333, open daily 1 April-30 Oct 13.00-17.30. **Floors Castle**, tel. 01573 223333, open daily 10.30-17.30. October: open Sun and Wed only 10.30-16.30. **Paxton House**, tel. 01289 386291, open daily from Good Friday-31 Oct 9.00-17.00. **Thirlestane Castle**, tel. 01578 722430, open daily 9.00-17.00 Easter-Sept, except Sat.

**ALNWICK**: **Alnwick Castle**, tel. 01665 603942, open daily Easter-Mid Oct 11.00-17.00.

**LINDISFARNE**: **St. Coombes Open Farm**, tel. 01850 635585, open daily 1st April-31 Oct 10.00-18.00. **Lindisfarne Castle**, tel. 01289 89244. 1 April-30 Oct daily 1300-17.30 except Fri. **WOOPERTON**: **Chillingham Castle,** tel. 01668 5359, open 1 May-30 Sept daily except Tue 13.30-17.00.

### Tourist Information
**BERWICK-UPON-TWEED**: Castle Gate Car Park, tel. 01289 330733.

*GUIDELINES*

## PREPARATIONS

### Climate

The British weather is well-known for its moods and caprices. The areas of low pressure constantly arriving from the Atlantic pass over and onwards to the east as quickly as they came. Days of continuous rain are seldom, with the Gulf Stream keeping temperatures on the mild side. However, for your trip to England you should take an umbrella, a raincoat, sturdy shoes and a warm pullover. In the summer there may be extended periods of fine weather and even a heat wave is conceivable. In London and the larger cities in the south it can be very humid at these times, with poor air quality. A good time to travel is during the months of March to July and from the second half of September and October. Travellers to northern England or Wales need not avoid August.

Average temperatures and rainfall:

|  | Temperature in C | Rainfall in mm |
|---|---|---|
| January | 4 | 87 |
| February | 4 | 66 |
| March | 6 | 65 |
| April | 8 | 56 |
| May | 11 | 64 |
| June | 14 | 64 |
| July | 16 | 69 |
| August | 16 | 84 |
| September | 14 | 82 |
| October | 11 | 80 |
| November | 7 | 85 |
| December | 5 | 93 |

### Arrival

**By air**: Every major city in the United Kingdom has an international airport. London alone is served by five airports: Heathrow, Gatwick, Stanstead, Luton and London City Airport, the last being a small airport for shuttle services.

Since the more important and larger airports lie at some distance outside the metropolis, you will need a transfer upon arrival. If you land at the world's busiest passenger airport, **Heathrow** (13 miles or 20 km west of London; tel. 0171 594321), you can take the underground into central London (**Piccadilly Line**, about 45 minutes). The way to the underground is signposted in the terminals (North American visitors should note that a subway in this part of the world is simply a tunnel across a street for pedestrians). Heathrow has two underground stations: one for Terminals 1, 2 and 3, and one for Terminal 4. The red double-decker "Airbus" connects the airport with the main hotel districts in London and with Victoria Station. The most expensive way is by taxi: insist that the meter be switched on and that you are not charged excessively for extras.

**Gatwick Airport** (tel. 01293 535353) is used particularly for charter flights and lies about 25 miles (40 km) south of London. There is a rapid train service into London, the **Gatwick Express**, which departs every 20 minutes between 5:30 am and 11:00 pm; outside these times, there is an hourly service. The journey takes 45 minutes and ends at Victoria Station. For the same route the **Green Line bus** requires one hour and 45 minutes.

**London City Airport** (tel. 0171 4745555) is situated 6 miles (10 km) to the east in the Docklands. Connections to central London: British Rail and the Thames River Bus.

**Luton Airport** (tel. 01582 405100) is 30 miles (50 km) north. Connections: British Rail and airport bus.

**Stanstead Airport** (tel. 01279 680500), connections: British Rail and Green Line bus.

**Birmingham Airport** (tel. 0121 7677145), there is a rail connection into Birmingham City.

**Liverpool Airport** (tel. 0151 4868877), there is a bus connection into Liverpool City.

## GUIDELINES

**Manchester Airport** (tel. 0161 4893000), there is a bus connection into Manchester City.

**Newcastle Airport** (tel. 0191 2860966), underground and buses run into the city.

**Ferries**: In the main season you should book ahead on car ferries in particular, although the opening of the Channel tunnel has eased the situation. Ferries link major ports on the Continent (Calais, Cherbourg, Le Havre, Ostende, Zeebrugge, Rotterdam, Vlissingen, Hamburg and others) with numerous towns on the south and east coasts (Dover, Ramsgate, Newhaven, Harwich, Portsmouth, Plymouth, Hull, Newcastle). Details may be obtained from any travel agent, where you can also book.

**Channel Tunnel**: Around the clock on every day of the year, the car trains speed back and forth between Calais and Folkestone. With a journey time of 35 minutes this is the fastest connection with the Continent. Tickets can be purchased in advance, but as a rule it is enough simply to turn up and book onto the next train. You can pay in pounds or in French francs. The cost of a return ticket for one car and passengers varies between £200 and £310 (1995) depending on the time of year. For foot passengers the high-speed train, the *Eurostar*, is recommended; it connects Paris or Brussels with London in 3 hours.

If you take the **train** through to London, your journey will end either at Victoria Station (built in 1860) or in the renovated Waterloo Station (built 1848). Both stations are also linked with the underground system.

### Arrival Formalities
### Import and Export Restrictions

Medicines requiring a prescription, certain plants, meat, meat products and products of animal origin (such as hides, furs, eggs, poultry, milk and milk products) are subject to import and export restrictions. However, per person 1 kg of completely cooked meat or meat products in tins or in hermetically sealed containers is permitted.

There are no exchange controls affecting banknotes, traveller's checks and so on in any currency.

Precise details may be obtained from: HM Customs & Excise, New Kings Beam House, 22 Upper Ground, London SE1 9PJ, tel. 0171 6201313.

**Pets** may not be brought into the United Kingdom unless the intention to do so has been reported in advance and the pet spends 6 months in a recognized quarantine facility. Animals imported illegally may be destroyed and the importer subjected to a heavy fine. Information from the Ministry of Agriculture, Fisheries and Food, Government Buildings (Toby Jug Site), Hook Rise South, Tolworth, Surbiton, Surrey KT6 7NF, tel. 0181 330441.

**Customs**: If you are arriving directly from a member state of the European Union, no customs regulations apply. At airports you may proceed straight through the blue channel for arrivals from EU countries. A customs declaration is therefore not required, although there are random checks for narcotics, weapons and products injurious to the health or the environment.

**Travel Documents**: If your country of origin is not a member of the European Union, you will require a valid passport to enter the United Kingdom. Nationals of the EU may present their identity card instead. Please contact the British Embassy in your own country for advice.

### GETTING AROUND

### By Car

The roads and motorways network in Britain is eminently suitable for touring by car. Even the minor roads, which are the best ways of getting to know the country, are of good quality. Brown signposts point to nearby sights. You do not require an international driving permit, your own driver's license will suffice.

**Highway Code**: This is is the body of regulations which prescribes how anyone using the highway should proceed. It can be obtained at all ports of arrival at the offices of the AA (Automobile Association) or RAC (Royal Automobile Club). Most traffic regulations and signs correspond to the international standard (including the priority to the right rule at intersections of equal status, although road markings usually indicate which is the major road).

It should be noted that the United Kingdom is one of the countries where driving is on the left, which means overtaking on the right. Speed restrictions on traffic signs are given in miles per hour and distances in miles. Unless specified otherwise, there is a speed limit in built-up areas of 30 mph (48 km/h), on roads with one lane in each direction 60 mph (97 km/h) and on motorways and roads with more than one lane in each direction 70 mph (113 km/h). Use of seatbelts is obligatory for drivers and all passengers.

**Petrol (gas)**: Unleaded fuel is available at virtually all filling stations.

**Breakdown**: Automobile driver's associations (similar to AAA in the USA) are the **AA** (Automobile Association) and **RAC** (Royal Automobile Club), which both have numerous branches in all parts of the country and a large staff of patrolmen-mechanics who provide on-the-spot assistance in the event of breakdowns. This service is free for members or if your home automobile association has an arrangement with the AA or RAC.

**Car rental**: Car rental companies have offices at all airports and major railway stations. The larger companies will even allow you to return the car to another office, thus obviating the necessity for a round trip. Many airlines offer a fly-drive service: when you buy your air ticket you also rent the car, which is waiting when you land in Britain. For details see the brochure "Britain: Vehicle Hire" which can be obtained from the British Tourist Authority (see Addresses section).

## By Bus

Remoter areas are sometimes badly served by the railways network. In these cases we recommend the use of public bus services. Purchasing the **Discount Coach Card** (obtainable at 2000 National Express agencies in Britain) gives you a 30% discount on National Express bus tickets in England and Wales. Young people between 16 and 25, students and senior citizens over 60 can buy the card for about £7. Also available from National Express agencies is the **Tourist Trail Pass** which permits unlimited travel on National Express buses. You can choose between 3 and 15 days of travel within a particular time period. Prices start at £49 for 3 days of travel.

## By Train

Britain has a very well developed railways network. The main cities are connected by frequent, fast and punctual InterCity trains. The new InterCity 225, for example, will take you from London to Edinburgh in just 4 hours. In addition to modern trains, some local sections of the network are supplemented with steam trains for railway enthusiasts. On some long-distance services, sleeping cars are available and in this way you can save a day's travelling and the price of a hotel room. Supplements for a standard-class berth start at £25 ; for a first-class berth at £30. The fare structure has been made highly complex by the ongoing process of privatization of the railways; it is best to check with your travel agent first.

**The BritRail Pass**: This pass is a highly recommended way for foreign visitors to the United Kingdom to save on travelling costs. It permits unlimited travel in England, Scotland and Wales, with an unlimited number of stops. Available for

1st and standard class. Children between 5 and 15 pay half, while the **Youth Path** is available for young people between 16 and 25 (2nd class only). Senior citizens (60 and above) are also entitled to reductions. The pass is valid for 4, 8, 15 or 22 consecutive days or for a full month.

If you wish to take a break from train travel, the **BritRail Flexipass** is available for 4, 8 or 15 travelling days per month. Important: BritRail passes can **only** be purchased in your home country before you start your trip.

### Combining Means of Transport
### Fare Reductions

The **Visitor Travelcard** means unlimited travel on almost all London buses and underground lines. In addition it gives you a selection of discount vouchers for London's main sights and some restaurants. The card cannot be purchased in Britain, but **only** in travel agents abroad.

### PRACTICAL TIPS

### Accommodations

There is a wide variety of accommodations available, ranging from the luxurious 5-crowns hotel (British classification) to the typical bed-and-breakfast.

Hotels generally accept traveller's checks and credit cards. B&B and boarding houses will usually expect to be paid in cash.

**Bed and breakfasts** (or B&B) will be found in just about every town and village and are the least expensive form of accommodation. They can be recommended not only for their cheapness but also for the contact they afford with the people who run them. Many families offer B&B in their own homes to earn a little extra money. Usually you will not need to book, unless it is the main season, or you are planning to stay in a major city. Listings of B&B establishments in England and Wales with prices and location maps are available by mail order from AA Publishing, Fanum House, Basingstoke, Hampshire RG21 2EA, tel. 01256 20123. Outside London, prices vary between £12.50 and £30 per night, per person. Some working farms also offer B&B. Note also that accommodation prices in the UK are always quoted per person, and not per room as in the USA and elsewhere.

**Boarding houses** can be found particularly in seaside towns and tourist areas and are somewhat more expensive as a rule than B&B; on the other hand, there is often a wider choice of rooms with or without bathrooms. There is a list of these establishments included in "AA Bed & Breakfast" for England. Prices start at £20 per person per night.

**Self-catering**: This type of accommodation ranges from simple cottages in the country to city apartments. A security deposit is paid in advance; all equipment and utensils in the unit are then at your disposal. Typical prices for a cottage for 4 people vary between £95 and £1100 per week. There is a list of self-catering facilities in "Britain: Self-Catering Holiday Homes", available from the British Tourist Authority.

**Hotels**: Britain offers a great range of hotels of the most varied type and character. The British Tourist Authority classifies the hotels and awards them crowns (the highest accolade is five crowns). In addition to this there are the evaluations of "approved", "commended", "highly commended" and "de luxe". Outside the towns there are plenty of hotels of country house style, even old castles and mansions have been converted into hotels. Occasionally one could wish perhaps for a little more comfort, but on the whole this is amply compensated for by atmosphere. Information may be obtained from: **Country Homes and Castles**, 118 Cromwell Road, Kensington, London SW7 4ET, tel. 0171 3704445; **Small Luxury Hotels of the World**, 21 Blades

Court, Deodar Road, London SW15 2NU, tel. 0181 87795000; **Wolsey Lodges,** 17 Chapel Street, Bildeston, Ipswich, Suffolk IP7 7EP, tel. 01449 74129).

**Youth hostels**: The Youth Hostels Association (YHA) maintains over 240 hostels in England, Wales and Scotland. Do not let the name mislead, not only young people but all ages are welcome, including families. For further information: Youth Hostels Association, Trevelyan House, 8 St Stephen's Hill, St Albans, Herts AL1 2DY, tel. 01727 55215.

**Camping sites**: These are marked on most road maps and are up to international standards. They are set up for tents, caravans and mobile homes, provide mains power outlets and a series of facilities such as showers and washrooms, laundries, shops, restaurants and bars. Camping off authorized sites without permission is prohibited. If you do find a picturesque well-located meadow which simply begs you to spend the night there in your tent or caravan, obtain the permission of the landowner first. And of course you should leave the place in the state you found it in; take your rubbish with you.

### Banks

Banks are open from at least 9 am to 3:30 pm, although many offer counter services until 4:30 pm. Some large banks are also open on Saturday. Most of the banks' own cash machines take EC cards and credit cards, although not all banks appear to accept American Express cards. These machines are the simplest and quickest ways of obtaining cash.

Money exchange offices are open in addition to the banks and operate outside banking hours too; however, they offer bad exchange rates and charge high commission. If you do use them make sure you check the exchange rates first. The law states that they must clearly display details of exchange rates and commission charges at the entrance.

### Electricity

The mains power supply in the UK is 240 V, 50 Hz. Appliances working on 220 V volts can be used, but US appliances (120 V) must **not** be used (this includes hairdryers, shavers) unless you can switch them to 220/240 V or have a transformer. British plugs are three-pin with flat pins; adapters can be bought in electrical stores or at the airport.

### Emergency Calls

Dial 999 on any phone free of charge to be connected with the police, ambulance or fire service.

### Food and Drink

English cooking generally suffers from a bad reputation. It is easy to eat appalling food in Britain, but not too difficult to find places offering a standard as high as anywhere in the world. The original British cuisine was virtually extinguished in the 19th century by a combination of pseudo-French faddery and the dreary cooking of the impoverished working classes in the cities. Country cooking managed to survive and its high quality ingredients and unfussy preparation are the strengths of English cooking today.

Eating habits are changing and the traditional English breakfast of bacon and eggs, toast and marmalade and much more besides (often enough to cover your requirements through to the evening) is giving way to the so-called Continental Breakfast. Home-baked cakes and pastries can also be excellent but it is not easy to find a bakery which really does bake its own bread and cakes. Finding a restaurant which cooks to the traditional English or Welsh recipes is not easy either, as many are seduced by French styles.

Restaurant guides can be obtained from book stores to help avoid nasty shocks. The AA issues the guide **Best Restaurants in Britain**, which can be ordered from AA Publishing, Fanum House, Basingstoke, Hamps. RG21 2EA, tel. 01256 20123.

The wide variety of Indian, Chinese, Thai and Japanese restaurants in all larger cities should not be forgotten: London, Manchester and Cardiff even have their own Chinatowns. For many people an Indian or Chinese meal is part of a night out on the town.

**Main meals**: For breakfast you have the choice between the rather insipid Continental Breakfast so beloved by hotels or the hearty English speciality, the **full breakfast**. In its more traditional and most comprehensive form it includes: orange, tomato or grapefruit juice; porridge or cornflakes with milk; stewed fruit; kippers, scrambled eggs or fried eggs with bacon and sausages and fried tomatoes; toast, various kinds of bread, with marmalade and jam, honey; tea or coffee. Sometimes you may be offered grilled kidneys or kedgeree (cooked, flaked fish, sometimes smoked, with rice). It should be stressed that this impressive list is more a tourist experience than an everyday event.

At this point it may be a good idea to clear up some potential confusion. The main meal of the day is called dinner, and for the middle classes this is in the evening. The working man still tends to refer to his midday meal as "dinner" and his evening meal (which may well be a hot meal) as "tea". The usual term for the midday meal is **lunch** and it tends to be kept short and simple. Many office workers buy sandwiches and something to drink, and take their lunch to the park in fine weather. Others go to the pub, which more and more frequently serves hot meals over the bar (especially in the big cities). Avoid pubs which can only offer sad steak-and-kidney pies kept hot in glass cases, but go to those which have a good lunchtime menu: shepherd's pie (minced meat topped with mashed potatoes and glazed, sometimes with onions and vegetables in the filling), ploughman's lunch (fresh bread, cheese and pickles) are typical pub meals.

England is famed for its **afternoon tea**, which is celebrated at 4 o'clock in the afternoon. Like the full English breakfast this is a meal which is a regular feature of the day for very few people indeed. I venture most afternoon teas are served in restaurants and tea-shops to people in town for the day. In some families it still survives as a regular Sunday afternoon feature, after the heavy Sunday lunch of roast beef. Afternoon tea in its classic form is Earl Grey tea, cucumber sandwiches with the bread crust removed, and scones (pronounced *sconns*) with butter and jam or homemade cakes. In Bath, the "Bath buns" (sweet rolls) are eaten, "stotty cake" in Northumberland and "bara brith" (fruitcake) in Wales.

**Dinner** tends to be eaten somewhat late, between 7 and 8 pm, although in the cities eating out later is quite normal. Some of the more important British specialities are listed below, with a number of regional delicacies too.

Hors d'oeuvres, now generally termed "starters", are not always served, but are frequently found in more traditional establishments: **anchovies** (often on lettuce leaves); **angels on horseback** (oysters rolled in strips of bacon, grilled and served on toast); **devils on horseback** (pitted prunes stuffed with calf's liver or chicken sautéed in butter with herbs and pepper, and then rolled in bacon and grilled); **fresh crayfish**; **gammon** (cured ham). In Yorkshire, the famous **Yorkshire pudding** (dough baked in the juice of a joint of meat) is served with onion sauce as an hors d'oeuvre although most people only know it as an accompaniment to roast beef.

**Fish**: The national dish of the English could be said to be **fish and chips**, now that the traditional Sunday roast is on the wane. The first fish and chips shop was opened in Mossley near Manchester by John Lee in 1863 and his idea conquered the kingdom. This dish was until recently

*GUIDELINES*

always packed in newspaper (now plain white paper, supposedly more hygienic, must be used) and often simply opened up and eaten in the street. Various types of fish are available (cod, haddock, sole, hake, plaice) and all are deep-fried in batter, and then served with chips and often, especially in the north of England, with mushy peas. Most people sprinkle salt and vinegar on their fish and chips. You will need to go to a restaurant to try **Scottish salmon**, and you should check whether it is wild or farmed salmon. The Scottish **Finnan haddie** is haddock which has been smoked over a fire of oak wood. On the Yorkshire coast, try the **shrimps**, while the fishing towns along the Channel coast are famed for their **oysters**. **Dover sole**, the queen of the flatfish, is not restricted to the Dover coast but has been given this name by the fishermen to distinguish it from the less noble flounder. It is at its best grilled on the bone. Countless fish dishes can be tried throughout Britain, including **pike, fish pie, poached haddock** with parsley sauce, and **trout** (smoked, boiled or baked).

**Meat**: The British have long had the reputation of being a nation of meateaters, and until meat prices skyrocketed in the 1970s roast beef reigned supreme as the national dish, appearing on virtually every table for Sunday lunch, traditionally served with roast potatoes, Yorkshire pudding and horseradish sauce. The Aberdeen Angus cattle from Scotland supply the best meat. **Beef stew** is another solid British dish which manifests itself in different ways in different parts of the country: Welsh stew with leeks, Exeter stew with carrots, turnips, onions and parsley dumplings. The tenderest lamb comes from Kent and Wales: try Welsh roast lamb (the meat is first marinated in honey, garlic and rosemary). In the north-west of England, the speciality is Lancashire hotpot (a lamb and potato stew with kidneys and oysters, with one simpler version being layers of lamb, scalloped potatoes and onions topped by a piecrust). Throughout Britain, roast lamb is eaten with mint sauce, a remnant, like roast pork with apple sauce and turkey with cranberries, of the mediaeval penchant for mixing sweet and sour. Yorkshire is famed for its York ham.

**Game**: In the autumn the shooting season starts and on the high moors of northern England and Scotland grouse, pheasant and partridge fall to the sportsman's gun. Grouse-shooting in particular has settled into a strict ritual since the 19th century and for many people it is more of a social event. Today shooting must frequently be suspended to allow the populations to recover. The birds are speeded to the shops and soon appear on restaurant tables, metamorphosed into tasty dishes. One speciality is game pie, made of grouse, woodcock or partridge. In Sussex there is a variant of the famous **steak and kidney pie** where the beef is replaced by pheasant meat. Of course, during the season there is plenty of roast pheasant, which is served with potato crisps (US: potato chips). Rabbit stew (although rabbit is not strictly game) is a favourite country dish, especially as hunting rabbits is not a rich man's sport. **Cumberland sauce** is particularly good with game.

**Cheese**: Since cheese is produced almost exclusively by large cheesemaking companies, there are still maybe a dozen different cheeses produced in Britain, some of which are of impressive quality. Even the French relish **Cheshire** cheese which originates in the north-west of England. It releases its special taste particularly when toasted and slightly runny. Connoisseurs speak with respect of the **Blue Cheshire**, with its sharp taste and soft consistency. For many **Cheddar** is virtually synonymous with chees, and it is famous throughout the world. Try the farmer's lunch of cheddar, home-made bread and slices of onion, washed down with a mug of beer. The best blue cheese in Britain is **Stilton**. It probably originated in the area of Stilton, south of Peterborough in Huntingdonshire. The writer Daniel Defoe is supposed to have tried some there back in 1720. A cheese originally produced in Wales is **Caerphilly**, white, mild and with a delicate taste of buttermilk. From Derbyshire (pronounced Darbyshire) comes **Derby** cheese, firm in consistency and mild of taste. **Sage Derby** is the same cheese when greenly suffused with sage. **Lancashire** cheese is a white, crumbly creamy cheese which locally is often eaten on bread with blackcurrant jam.

**Vegetarian dishes**: Savorsome indigenous herbs and plants have helped Britain produce a good vegetarian cuisine, in line with international trends. Wales even has two traditional vegetarian dishes: the **herbal cheese sausage** from Glamorgan and **laver bread**, a dish prepared from seaweed. Laver bread can be eaten raw or added to soup.

**Drinks**: The number of different **beers** is vast since there are countless local breweries, and over the last twenty years the real ale movement has resulted in many old breweries reopening and brewing the old beers again. Good pubs often have a whole battery of beer pumps at the bar: the usual mass-produced draught beers, some imports and, if you are lucky, some real ales which tend to be stronger and tastier (the latter are often the landlord's pride). **Mild** is a slightly old-fashioned beer with an alcohol content of around 4%, and is often drunk mixed (**brown and mild**) with **brown ale**, which is dark and sweet. One of the strongest beers is **Yorkshire Stingo**, while the Midlands are the home of the best **pale ales** (this kind of beer is brewed with water containing gypsum). The most typical English beer is **bitter**, which is consumed cool, but not cold. Bitter has lost ground over the last twenty or thirty years to **lagers**, which are served chilled. Guinness is a beer familiar to nearly everyone, but there are also many English-brewed **stouts** (a stout is a very dark and creamy malt beer that is actually darker and sweeter than a **porter**).

**Cider** of course is made from apples and is a particular speciality of the West Country and also Herefordshire. In its roughest form it is called **scrumpy** and is very potent. Local opinion in Somerset has it that too much scrumpy leads to mental derangement. Of late, cider has undergone a renaissance, with numerous strong, dry ciders being launched onto the market, the older brands being too sweet (or weak?) for the modern palate. **Perry** is cider made from pears.

English **wine** made from grapes grown in English vineyards was famous in the milder early Middle Ages and with the apparent warming-up of the climate vineyards are even being established in Wales (Pembroke, Aberavon). Otherwise vines are to be found almost exclusively in the south of England. The wine is predominantly white wine, of the Müller-Thurgau and Seyval Blanc grapes.

**Port**, favourite after-dinner drink of elderly gentlemen, is not produced in Britain but in Portugal, having been "discovered" in 1700 and imported into England in order to drive French wines off the market. It consists of 75% semi-fermented red wine and 25% brandy.

**Gin** is a favorite drink of the middle classes and the Royal Navy, and consists of a mixture of distilled grain and a bouquet of botanical additives such as juniper, orange peel, coriander seeds, cassia bark, angelica, liquorice and violet root. The Navy's drink is **pink gin** – Plymouth gin with a hint of angostura bitters. The Scots are regular drinkers of **single malt whisky**, and the English and Welsh like to include one in their bars. The whisky is manufactured from malt (barley allowed to germinate three days), yeast and the distillery's own spring water. Its brown coloring it obtains from the sherry vats in which it must be stored for at least three years. Its alcohol content

*GUIDELINES*

lies at around 40%. *Single malt* means that the constituents of the whisky come from just one distillery, while *blended* clearly denotes a mix from several distilleries. Blends also can be of an excellent quality. It is a solecism to drink malt whisky any way but straight up at room temperature: in other words, no ice!

And finally, **tea**: On average, each adult in Britain drinks about six cups of tea a day. As Dr. Johnson once said, the teapot hardly has time to cool. Tea first came into fashion around 1662 when Charles II married a princess from Portugal, Catharina, who introduced her homeland's custom of tea-drinking to the English court. The English custom of adding milk to tea is not another example of British culinary barbarity but actually a practice learnt from the southern Chinese.

### Health Insurance

Tourists in the UK are granted emergency treatment at no cost in hospitals maintained by the National Health Service (NHS). In the case of treatment as an in-patient, you will have to pay some of the costs unless you were born in or reside in an EU country. It may be advantageous to take out an additional holiday insurance policy. Details may be obtained from your insurance company.

### Hours of Business

For banks and post offices, see the corresponding sections. Shop opening times vary greatly but generally are from 9 am to at least 5:30 pm in the week, until 5 pm on Saturdays. Newsagents selling newspapers, magazines, sweets and cigarettes have longer hours, including Sundays. In the last few years trading laws have been extensively liberalized and most supermarkets and many larger stores are open on Sundays and some are open until late on weekdays.

**Pubs** in England and Wales may serve alcohol from 11 am to 11 pm. In many pubs a bell is sounded for last orders. Many pubs, particularly in rural areas, close in the afternoons from 3 to 5:30 pm. The landlord has more discretion these days in when he opens; the safest thing to say is that you will not get a drink in a pub between 11 pm and 9 am.

### Language

English is the official language and is spoken in all parts of the country. The Celtic tongues still survive in some remote mountainous districts of Wales and Scotland. In Wales the language is called Welsh or *cymraeg,* and is still spoken in western parts. Place-names is where the visitor most often encounters Welsh: it is almost an impossibility that he will be greeted by someone saying *bore da* (good morning), unless by another tourist.

### Cymraeg:

*Aber* (ah-bear) . . . river mouth, estuary
*Blaen* (bline) . . . . . . source of a river
*Bach, fach* (bakh, vakh) . . . . . . little
*Bryn* (brin) . . . . . . . . . . . . . . hill
*Bwlch* (bulkh) . . . . . . . pass, gorge
*Capel* (cap-ell) . . . . . . . . . . chapel
*Castell* (cass-tell) . . . . castle, fortress
*Coch, goch* (cokh, gokh) . . . . . . red
*Caer,* gaer (kyre) . . . . . . . . . . fort
*Coed* (co-ed) . . . . . . . . . . wood
*Ddu* (dhee) . . . . . . . . . . . . . black
*Ffynnon* (finnon) . . . fountain, spring
*Glan* . . . . . . bank of river or stream
*Hafod* (have-odd) . . summer pastures
*Llan* (hlan) . . . . . . . . church, parish
*Llyn* (hlinn) . . . . . . . . . . . . lake
*Mawr* (mao-er) . . . . . . large, great
*Mynydd* (minn-idh) . . . . . mountain
*Nant* . . . . . . . . . . . . . . . . stream
*Pen* . . . . . . . . . . . . peak, end, top
*Tre* (tray) . . . . . . homestead, town
*Hwyl* (hweel) . . . . . . . . . . cheers
*Diolch* (dee-olkh) . . . . . . . . thanks
*Diolch yn fawr iawn* (dee-olkh en vow-er yown) . . . . . . . many thanks
*Croeso i Gymru* (croisaw ee gumry) . . . . . . . . . . . welcome to Wales
*Sut mae?* (sit my) . . . How's it going?

*Lechyd da!* (yacky da) . . . . . . cheers
*Dymuniadau gorau* (dim-inny-ah-die gorr-eye) . . . . . . . . . . All the best

## Money

One pound sterling is made up of 100 pence (singular penny, and often simply "p" is heard). You will often hear a pound referred to as a "quid" (note: there is no plural form; so, "five quid" and so on). The tourist exchange rate is currently (September 1995) around DM 2.25 to the pound, US dollar 1.51, Australian dollar 1.97. For information on changing money, see the Banks section above. Coins in circulation: 1, 2, 5, 10, 20 and 50p and £1. Banknotes: £5, 10, 20 and 50. Credit cards are widely accepted in Britain, including American Express, Visa, Diners Club and Mastercard. Eurocheques can also be used, although subject to a limit.

## Post Offices

Post offices are usually open Monday to Friday between 9 am and 5:30 pm, and Saturdays until 12:30 pm.

In small towns and villages the post office often combines with the local general store, which means lunch-time closing may often be the rule.

## Public Holidays

January 1: New Year's Day. Good Friday and Easter Monday (variable). May 1: May Day-Labour Day. Spring Bank Holiday: Last Monday in May or first Monday in June. Summer Bank Holiday: Last Monday in August or first Monday in September. December 25 and 26: Christmas Day and Boxing Day.

## Telephone

There are two telephone companies in Britain, British Telecom and Mercury Communications. Both install and maintain public telephones. More and more often the classic red telephone boxes once so typical of the English street are being replaced by modern, grey functionalist telephone cabins. There are coin-operated and card telephones (CardPhone). British Telecom telephone cards are available at face values of between £2 and £20 in all post offices and in shops displaying the green telephone card emblem. It is often possible to use your credit card when phoning from Mercury phone boxes; Mercury telephone cards are also available from many kiosks and shops. To make a call from a coin-operated box you will need 10, 20 or 50 p coins, or £1 coins. Hotels often add a high surcharge to every unit for calls from your room. To prevent unpleasant surprises, check at reception.

To make international calls from the UK you will need to dial 00 followed by the country code (see the phone directory). Then dial the area code, omitting the 0 if there is one. In the UK the area codes now all begin with 01. The changeover was in April 1995 so you will still see the old style printed. For example, Luton numbers were 0582 and are now 01582. Mobile phone numbers and the like do not necessarily start with 01.

## Time

Usually you will need to put your clock back one hour when travelling to Britain from Europe. Summer time in Britain is from the end of March to the end of October.

## Tipping

A service charge is usually contained in hotel and restaurant bills, and amounts to 10-15% All the same it is quite customary to give a personal tip (up to 10%) to indicate your satisfaction, particularly in restaurants. In a pub the barman or barmaid will always give back the exact change; it is unusual to tip cash. The way to do it is to offer the barman a drink while paying: he may refuse with thanks, actually take a drink or put the equivalent into his tips glass. Porters at hotels and

*GUIDELINES*

railways stations should be given 50-75p per suitcase, and taxi-drivers will be pleased with a tip of 10% of the fare.

### Weights and Measures
1 inch (in.) = 2.54 cm
1 foot (ft.) = 12 in. = 30.48 cm
1 yard (yd.) = 3 ft. = 91.44 cm
1 mile (mi.) = 1.61 km
1 pint (pt.) = 0.57 l
1 quart (qt.) = 2 pt. = 1.14 l
1 gallon = 4 qt. = 4.56 l
1 ounce (oz.) = 28.35 g
1 pound (lb.) = 16 oz. = 453.6 g.

These are Imperial measure, which differs from the system in the USA.

## ADDRESSES

### Airlines
**British Airways**, 156 Regent St., W1R 5TA, tel. 0171-8974000. **Canadian Airlines International**, ticket office: 15 Berkeley Street, London W1X 6AE, open daily 5-10 pm; reservations London: tel. 0181 5777722, outside London: tel. 0345 61767. **Continental Airlines**, Beulah Court, Albert Road, Harley, Surrey RH6 7HP, tel. 01293 827411. **Lufthansa**, 23-26 Piccadilly, W1R 0EJ, tel. 0171 4080442. **Quantas**: 359 King Street, Hammersmith, London W6 9NJ; Travel Centre: tel. 0181 8460466; reservations: tel. 0345 747767.

### Automobile Associations
**Automobile Association** (AA), Fanum House, Basingstoke, Hampshire RG21 2EA, tel. 01256 20123; **Royal Automobile Club (RAC),** 89-91 Pall Mall, London SW1Y 5HS, tel. 0171 9302345.

### British Embassies and Consulates Abroad
**AUSTRALIA: British High Commission**, Commonwealth Avenue, Yarralumla, Canbera ACT 2500, tel. (61) 6 270666, fax. (61) 6 2575857. **CANADA: British High Commission**, 80 Elgin St., Ottawa K1P 5K7, tel. (613) 237 1530, fax. (613) 237 2980. **NEW ZEALAND: British High Commission**, 44 Hill St., Wellington 1, tel. (64) 4 472 6049, fax. (64) 4 473 4982. **USA: British Embassy**, 3100 Massachusets Ave. N.W., 20008 Washington DC, tel. (0202) 462 1340, fax. (0202) 216 6760. **British Consulate General**, 845 Third Avenue, New York 10022 N.Y., tel. (212) 745 0495, fax. (212) 745 0456.

### Embassies and Consulates in the UK
**American Embassy**, 24-31 Grosvenor Sq., London W1A 1AE, tel. 0171 4999000. **Australian High Commission**, Australia House, Strand, London WC2B 4LA, tel. 0171 3794334. **Canadian High Commission**, McDonald House, 1 Grosvenor Square, London W1X 0AB, tel. 0171 2586600. **New Zealand High Commission**, New Zealand House, Haymarket, London SW1Y 4TQ, tel. 0171 9308422.

### British Tourist Authority Abroad
**AUSTRALIA**: 210 Clarence St., Sydney NSW 2000, tel. 261 603-7. **CANADA**: Suite 450, 111 Avenue Rd., Toronto M5R 3J8, Ontario, tel. 961 8124, 925 6326. **NEW ZEALAND**: Suite 305, 3rd Floor, Dilworth Bldg., Corner Customs/Queen Sts., Auckland 1, tel. 303 1446. **USA**: 551 Fifth Avenue, Suite 701, New York NY 10176-0799, tel. 986 2266.

### Tourist Information
**British Tourist Authority**, Thames Tower, Black's Rd., London W6 9EL, tel. 0181 8469000. **British Travel Centre** and **Wales Tourist Board**, 12 Regent St., Piccadilly Circus, London SW1Y 4PQ, tel. 0171 7303400. **London Tourist Board**, 26 Grosvenor Gardens, London SW1W 0DU, tel. 0171 7303450. **Tourist Information Centre**, Victoria Station Forecourt, London SW1, tel. 0171 8248844. **Wales Tourist Board**, Brunel House, 2 Fitzalan Rd., Cardiff CF2 1UY, tel. 01222 499909.

## AUTHORS

**David Arscott** worked for the BBC and various radio stations before becoming a freelance writer. He is the co-author of the chapter "Southern England".

**Heather Barraclough** lives in Yorkshire. Together with Michael Z. Brooke she wrote the chapter "Northern England".

**Michael Z. Brooke** has lived for many years in Manchester and has explored the modern city with its historical roots and the surrounding countryside. He is co-author of the chapter "Northern England".

**Joe da Casa** is an Englishman of Spanish descent. After a career in public relations he has dedicated himself to writing. He contributed the chapter "The Home Counties" and was co-author of "The Heart of England".

**Gill Davies** lives in Wales and is the author of a successful series of children's books and textbooks for adults. She wrote the chapters "The West Country", "Wales" and "The Heart of England".

**Martin Marix Evans** is a writer, photographer and publisher. He is particularly interested in the influence past generations have had on the European landscape. He contributed the chapters "History and Culture" and "The Lakes and Borders".

**Angus McGeoch** is a historian, author and editor. He has written articles for numerous travel guides. Together with David Arscott he wrote the chapter "Southern England".

**Andrea Russ** is an ethnologist and journalist; on journeys of explorations to the Tuareg she crossed the Sahara many times. Since London for her is the most fascinating city in the West, she leads study trips not only to North Africa but also to southern England. She is the author of the chapter "London".

**Alexander Sabo** has led tours worldwide for many years. Great Britain, especially East Anglia, is of particular interest to him as an economic historian. He wrote the chapter "East Anglia".

**Philipp Zitzlsperger** studied history of art in London and Rome and leads tours to Britain and Italy. Much of the travel information in this book is from his pen.

## PHOTOGRAPHERS

| | |
|---|---|
| **Archiv für Kunst und Geschichte**, Berlin: | 12, 14, 17, 18, 20 21, 23, 25, 27, 28, 29, 30, 31, 32, 182 |
| **Beck, Josef** | 36, 54, 60, 68 |
| **Bondizio, Bodo** | 76, 202, 203 |
| **Chambers, W. M.** | 166, 176, 196/197, 212 |
| **Elliot, Dough** | 49 |
| **Haafke, Udo** | 100, 130, 149, 181, 186, 198, 228 |
| **Heathcote, Terry** | 102 |
| **Hühn, Holger** | 33, 62, 71 L., 71 R., 82, 94, 95 |
| **Jonkmanns, Bernd** | 81, 142, 205 |
| **Kaempf, Bernhard** | 8/9, 69, 103, 128, 129, 132, 143, 144, 170/171, 175, 189, 200, 208, 213, 215 L., 216, 217 |
| **Liese, Knut** | 47, 53, 59, 74, 86, 88, 131, 161 |
| **Lyons, David** | 15, 89, 92, 93, 96, 105, 118, 138, 139, 148, 152, 191, 193, 204, 209, 214, 215 R., 222/223, 224, 229, 234 |
| **Marix Evans, Martin** | cover, 112, 113, 172, 184, 185 |
| **Müller, Kai Ulrich** | 10/11, 19, 34/35, 39, 50, 61, 64, 67, 79, 97, 108, 114, 116, 117, 120/121, 124, 125, 134/135, 136, 150, 154/155, 156, 162, 163, 167, 168, 174, 177, 180, 190, 207, 219, 230, 231, 232 |
| **Nesbit, Mike** | 206 |
| **Phillips, Diana** | 122 |
| **Pitkin Pictorials, Ltd.** | 55 |
| **Playne, David** | 160, 187 |
| **Radkai, Marton** | 38, 41, 42, 45, 48, 51, 52, 63, 65, 73 |
| **Russ, Ivan** | 43, 46 |
| **Scheibner, Johann** | 145 |
| **Schwarz, Berthold** | 78 |
| **Stadler, Hubert** | 218 |
| **Stankiewicz, Thomas** | 40, 57 |
| **Tlusty, Ivana** | 66, 235 |

# INDEX

## A

Abbotsbury 104
Aberavon 160
Aberdaron 166
Aberystwyth 162
**Adam**, Robert 78, 80, 110, 111, 143, 208, 209, 212
**Albert**, prince 68, 69, 100, 116, 202
Alcester 184
Aldeburgh 131
**Alfred the Great**, king 15, 40, 102, 147, 212
Alfriston 94
Alnwick Castle 235
Alport 193
Alton Towers 199
Amberley 96
Ambleside 229, 230
Appledore 152
Ardens Grafton 184
Arlington Court 152
**Arthur**, king 14, 103, 137, 140, 141, 151
Arundel 96
Ascott House 114
Aston Hall 178
Attingham Park 180
Avebury 13, 137
Aylesbury 113, 114
Aylesford Friary 87

## B

Bakewell 192, 193
Baldock 110
Bamburgh Castle 235
Bangor 167
Barlaston 199
Barmouth 163
Barnard Castle 219
Barnsley House Gardens 174
Barnstaple 152
Barrow-in-Furness 228
Bath 13, **143-144**
Battle 93
Bayham Abbey 91
Beaulieu Abbey 101
Beaumaris 19, 167
**Becket**, Thomas à 18, 88, 126
Bedale 219
Bedford 110
Belvoir Castle 190
Benningborough Hall 212
Berkeley Castle 176
Berwick-upon-Tweed 235
Beverley 208
Bexhill 93
Bibury 174
Bideford 152
Biggleswade 110

Birmingham 31, 178
Blackpool 206
Blaenavon 158
Blaenau Ffestiniog 165
Blandford Forum 105
Blenheim Palace 26, 118
Bodelwyddan, castle 168
Bodinnick 149
Bodnant Gardens 168
**Boleyn**, Anne 22, 23, 52, 92, 114
Bolton Abbey 210
Boroughbridge 212
Borrowdale 230
Bosherton 161
Boston 188
Bournemouth 103
Bourton-on-the-Water 174
Bowness-on-Windermere 228
Box Hill 97
Bradford 209
Bradford-on-Avon 144
Brantwood 230
Brecklands 123, 131
Brecon Beacons Nat. Park 158
Bridgnorth 180
Bridlington 217
Brighton 94, **95-96**
Bristol 142
Brixham 145
Brixworth 186
Broadlands Mansion 101
Broadstairs 89
Broadway 175
Brodsworth Hall 207
Bromsgrove 178
Brookland 90
**Brown**, Lancelot "Capability" 28, 80, 95, 96, 111, 113, 139, 208, 209
Bryn-Celli-Ddu 167
Buckfastleigh 147
Buckler's Hard 101
Burghley House 187
Burnham Thorpe 129
Burscough 206
Burton Agnes Hall 217
Burton Constable Hall 207
Bury St. Edmunds 131
Buxton 192, 193, 199
Buxworth 199

## C

Cadbury Castle 141
Cadgwith 149
Caerleon 159
Caernarfon 166
Caerphilly Castle 159
Cambridge **123-125**
Canon's Ashby 185
Canterbury 14, 18, **88-89**
Cardiff 159, 160

Cardigan 161, 162
Carew 161
Carlisle 230, 231, 232
Carmarthen 161
Cartmel 225
Castle Bolton 219
Castle Combe 144
Castle Drogo 147
Castle Howard 215
Castleton 193
Celts 13, 14, 40, 104, 118, 140, 143, 150, 157, 167, 230
Cenarth 162
Cerne Abbas 105
Chalfont St. Giles 115
Charing 88
Charlecote Park 184
**Charles I.** 25, 55, 61, 80, 189
**Charles II.** 25, 59, 181
Charnock Richard 206
Chartwell 92
Chatham 87
Chatsworth House 192
Chatsworth Park 192
Chavenage House 174
Chawton 97
Cheddar 140
Chedworth Roman Villa 174
Cheesewring 148
Cheltenham 176
Chepstow 157, 163
Cheriton 89
Chester 13, 15, 200
Chichester **96-97**
Chillingham Castle 235
Chiltern Hills **114-115**
Chippenham 15
Chipping Campden 175
Chirk 165
Chiswick 79
Christchurch 103
**Churchill**, Sir Winston 33, 56, 62, 92, 118
Cinderford 177
Cirencester 173
Clandon Park 97
Claydon House 113
Clitheroe 207
Clovelly 152
Colchester 13, 123, 132
Congleton 199
Coniston 230
**Constable**, John 29, 48, 77, 123, 132
Conwy 168
**Cook**, James 28, 56, 76, 80, 146, 217
Corby 186
Corfe Castle 104
Corsham Court 144
Cosford 181
Cotehele House 148

250

# INDEX

**Coton Manor Gardens** 186
**Cotswolds** 173-175
**Coughton Court** 184
**Coventry** 181
**Coverack** 149
**Cowes** 100
**Coxwold** 216
**Criccieth**, castle 166
**Cricket St. Thomas** 141
**Crickhowell** 158
**Cromwell**, Oliver 25, 41, 44, 52, 104, 114, 125, 158, 181

**D**

**Dalton-in-Furness** 228
**Darlington** 233
**Dartmeet** 147
**Dartmoor** 147
**Deene Park** 187
**Defoe**, Daniel 44, 48, 142
**Delph** 204
**Denmead** 97
**Derwent Water** 191
**Dickens**, Charles 31, 50, 73, 187
**Diggle** 204
**Dolbadarn Castle** 167
**Dorchester** 104-105
**Dorchester-on-Thames** 116
**Dover** 87, 89
**Dowlish Wake** 141
**Drake**, Sir Francis 24, 56, 145
**Dudley** 178
**Dulverton** 152
**Dunham Massey** 200
**Dunstable** 112
**Dunstanburgh Castle** 235
**Dunster** 141
**Dunwich** 131
**Durham** 232, 233
**Durham Castle** 233
**Dyrham Park** 144

**E**

**Easingwold** 216
**East Bergholt** 132
**Eastbourne** 93
**East Horsley** 97
**East Lulworth** 104
**Eastnor Castle** 177
**East Riddlesden Hall** 210
**Edward I** 18, 51, 60, 90, 165, 166, 168
**Edward II** 19, 166, 176
**Edward III** 20, 115
**Edward IV** 21, 22
**Edward the Confessor** 16, 41, 55, 56, 150
**Edward V** 22
**Edward VI** 23
**Edward VII** 32

**Edward VIII** 32
**Edwinstowe** 190
**Egglestone Abbey** 219
**Elizabeth I** 24, 52, 56, 57, 105, 110, 115, 182, 187, 232
**Elizabeth II** 33, 81, 115
**Ellesmere Port** 200
**Ely** 126-128
**Eskdale Green** 230
**Eton** 116
**Etruria Bone and Flint Mill** 199
**Exbury Gardens** 101
**Exeter** 144-145
**Exmoor** 141
**Exmoor National Park** 152

**F**

**Falmouth** 149
**Felixstowe** 132
**Fens** 123, **125-128**
**Firle Place** 94
**Fishguard** 162
**Folkestone** 89
**Formby** 205
**Fountains Abbey** 212
**Fring** 128
**Furness Abbey** 225

**G**

**Gainsborough**, Thomas 27, 123, 132
**Gawthorpe Hall** 207
**Gaydon** 184
**George II** 28, 80, 115
**George IV** 28, 57, 95, 115
**George V** 32
**George VI** 33
**Glastonbury** 140
**Gloddfa Ganol** 165
**Glossop** 191
**Gloucester** 176
**Glyndebourne** 94
**Godmanstone** 105
**Goodrich Castle** 177
**Goodwood House** 96
**Grasmere** 229, 230
**Grassington** 210
**Great Malvern** 178
**Great Orme** 168
**Great Yarmouth** 129
**Grimes Graves** 13, 131
**Grimsby** 207
**Grimsthorpe Castle** 188
**Guildford** 97

**H**

**Haddon Hall** 192, 193
**Hadrian's Wall** 13, 231

**Hailes Abbey** 175
**Halifax** 209
**Hambledon** 97
**Hampton Court** 22, 79, **80-81**
**Hardy**, Thomas 103, 104, 105
**Harewood House** 209
**Harlech** 19, 163
**Harrogate** 212
**Harvington Hall** 178
**Harwich** 132
**Hastings** 92-93, 216
**Hastings Country Park** 93
**Hatfield** 110
**Haughmond Abbey** 180
**Hawkhurst** 90
**Haworth** 210
**Helmsley** 215
**Helston** 149
**Henley-on-Thames** 116
**Henry I** 17, 80, 87
**Henry II** 17, 18, 88, 89
**Henry III** 18, 19, 51, 56, 103
**Henry IV** 21
**Henry V** 21, 157
**Henry VI.** 21, 24, 116, 124
**Henry VII** 22, 56, 81, 161
**Henry VIII** 22, 23, 52, 59, 60, 63, 76, 79, 80, 87, 93, 95, 98, 101, 104, 112, 114, 125, 128, 140, 149, 150, 175, 206
**Hereford** 177
**Hever Castle** 92
**Hidcote Manor Garden** 175
**High Wycombe** 114
**Hitchin** 110
**Hodnet Hall** 180
**Hogarth**, William 27, 49, 79
**Holyhead** 167
**Hood**, Robin 18, 178, 190
**Hove** 95
**Huddersfield** 204
**Hughendon Manor** 115
**Hunstanton** 128
**Huntingdon** 125
**Hutton-Le-Hole** 218
**Hythe** 89

**I**

**Ightham Mote** 91
**Ilchester** 141
**Ilfracombe** 152
**Ipswich** 132
**Ironbridge** 181
**Isle of Wight** 98, **99-101**

**J**

**James I** 24, 61, 76, 97, 114
**James II** 26, 27
**John**, king 115
**John Lackland**, king 18, 128, 131, 178

251

## INDEX

**Johnson,** Samuel 27, 50, 117
**Jones,** Inigo 61, 62, 76, 139
**Jordans** 115

**K**

**Kenilworth,** castle 182
**Keswick** 230
**Kew Gardens** 79, 80
**Kidderminster** 178
**Kilburn** 216
**Kimbolton** 125
**King's Lynn** 128
**Kingston** 104
**Kirby Hall** 187
**Kirkham Priory** 215
**Knaresborough** 212
**Knebworth House** 110
**Knole** 91
**Knowsley Safari Park** 205

**L**

**Lacock** 144
**Land's End** 151
**Lanhydrock House** 149
**Laugharne** 161
**Ledbury** 177
**Leeds** 209
**Leeds Castle** 87
**Letchworth** 110
**Levens** 225
**Lewes** 94, 95
**Lincoln** 18, **188-189**
**Lindisfarne** 15, 235
**Liskeard** 148
**Little Moreton Hall** 199
**Liverpool** 205
**Lizard,** peninsula 149
**Llanberis** 167
**Llandrindod Wells** 162
**Llandudno** 168
**Llanfair PG** 167
**Llangollen** 165
**Llangranog** 162
**Llechwedd Slate Caverns** 165
**London** 13, 16, 17, 19, 21, 26, 30, **37-82**, 131, 132, 207
  Albert Memorial 68
  Bank of England 39, 45, 46
  Banqueting House 61
  Barbican Centre 37, 43, 44
  Big Ben 53, 55
  Bond Street 39, 65
  British Museum 67, 131, 207
  Brompton Oratory 69
  Buckingham Palace 38, 57, 59
  Cabinet War Rooms 61
  Carlton House Terrace 59
  Carnaby Street 64
  Chelsea 39, 54, 72
  Cheshire Cheese 50

  Chinatown 64
  City 37, 40-54
  Clarence House 59
  Commonwealth Centre 59
  Commonwealth Institute 70
  Courtauld Institute Galleries 63
  Covent Garden 38, 39, 62, 81
  Crown Jewels 52
  Customs House 54
  Dickens House 68
  Docklands 38, 53, 75
  Downing Street 61
  Dr. Johnson's House 50
  Dulwich Picture Gallery 77
  Fenton House 77
  Fleet Street 49-51
  Florence Nightingale Museum 72
  Fortnum & Mason 64
  Freud Museum 77
  Geological Museum 69
  George Inn 74
  Gray's Inn 50
  Green Park 38, 59
  Greenwich 75-76
  Guildhall 46
  Hampstead 39, 77
  Harrods 39, 70
  Hayward Gallery 73
  Holland House 71
  Holland Park 70, 82
  Horse Guards 61
  Houses of Parliament 39, 55, 61
  Hyde Park 67, 68, 69
  Imperial College 30, 69
  Imperial War Museum 72
  Institute of Contemporary Arts 59
  Iveagh Bequest Museum 78
  Keats Memorial House 78
  Kensington Gardens 68
  Kensington Palace 68
  Kenwood House 78
  King's Road 72
  Lambeth Palace 72
  Lancaster House 59
  Leicester Square 64
  Leighton House 70
  Lincoln's Inn 50
  London Bridge 40, 54
  London by Night 81-82
  London Dungeon Museum 75
  London Transport Museum 62
  London Zoo 66
  Madame Tussaud's 65
  Mansion House 46
  Marble Arch 67
  Marlborough House 59
  Mithraic Temple 54
  Monument 54
  Museum of London 43, 44, 54
  Museum of Mankind 65

  Museum of the Moving Image 73
  National Army Museum 72
  National Film Theatre 73
  National Gallery 60
  National Maritime Museum 76
  National Portrait Gallery 60
  Natural History Museum 69
  Nelson's Column 60
  New Globe Theatre 74
  Old Admiralty 61
  Old Bailey 48
  Oxford Street 67
  Piccadilly Circus 64
  Planetarium 66
  Portobello Road 71
  Regent's Park 66, 82
  Regent Street 64
  Royal Academy of Arts 65
  Royal Albert Hall 37, 69
  Royal Exchange 45
  Royal Festival Hall 37, 73
  Royal National Theatre 73, 82
  Royal Opera House 63, 82
  Sadler's Wells 82
  Science Museum 69
  Sherlock Holmes Museum 66
  Sir John Soane's Museum 67
  Soho 38, 39, 63-64, 81, 82
  Somerset House 63
  South Bank Arts Centre 72, 82
  South Kensington 39, 68-70
  Southwark Cathedral 73
  St. Bartholomew the Great 49
  St. Bride's Church 50
  St. Giles Cripplegate 44
  St. James's Palace 59
  St. James's Park 38, 59
  St. Katharine's Docks 53
  St. Margaret's Church 55
  St.-Martin-in-the-Fields 60
  St. Paul's Cathedral 26, 39, 42, 46-49
  St. Paul's Church 62
  St. Stephen Walbrook 46
  Tate Gallery 38, 56, 132
  Theatre Museum 62
  The Temple 50
  Tower 21
  Tower Bridge 53, 75
  Tower of London 41, 51-54
  Trafalgar Square 39, 59-61, 63, 82
  Victoria and Albert Museum 30, 69
  Victoria Memorial 59
  Wallace Collection 67
  Westminster Abbey 16, 19, 39, 41, 55-56
  Westminster Cathedral 56
  Westminster Hall 55
  White Tower 17
  Wigmore Hall 82

252

*INDEX*

Longleat House 139
Longton 199
Lower Slaughter 174
Ludlow 180
Luton 111
Luton Hoo 111
Lydfort 147
Lyme Regis 104
Lymington 101
Lyndhurst 101
Lynmouth 152
Lynton 152

**M**

Macclesfield 199
Magna Carta 18, 55, 67, 116, 131, 138, 178, 188
Maidstone 87
Malmesbury 144
Malton 215
Manaton 147
**Manchester 200-203**
Manorbier, castle 161
Margate 89
Market Deeping 188
Market Harborough 186
Marlborough 138
Middleham Castle 219
Midhurst 97
Mildenhall 131
Milford Haven 161
Milton, John 24, 44, 115
Milton Keynes 112
Minions 148
Monmouth 157
Moretonhampstead 147
Moreton-in-Marsh 175
Morris, William 30, 69, 70, 72, 90, 116, 174, 209
Moseley Old Hall 181
Mottisfont Abbey 101
Mount Grace Priory 216
Much Wenlock 180

**N**

Nash, John 57, 60, 66, 67, 95
Nelson, Lord Horatio 28, 48, 60, 61, 101, 129
Newark-on-Trent 189
Newburgh Priory 216
Newbury 118
Newby Hall 212
**Newcastle-upon-Tyne** 14, 231, **234-235**
Newchurch in Pendle 207
New Forest 101
Newhaven 94
Newhey 204
Newlyn 150
Newmarket 131

New Mills 200
Newport 100, 159, 162
Newquay 151
New Quay 162
New Romney 90
Norfolk Broads 123
Normanby Hall 207
Normans 15, 17, 19, 98, 100, 123, 157, 185, 209, 213, 233
Northampton 185
Northleach 174
**Northumberland National Park** 234
Norwich 123, **129-131**
Nottingham 189, 190
Nunnington Hall 215

**O**

Offa's Dyke Path 163
Old Sarum 138, 139
Old Warden 110
Oswestry 163
Oxborough Hall 131
Oxford 115, **116-118**
  Christ Church College 116
  Magdalen College 116
  Merton College 116
  Sheldonian Theatre 117
  Ashmolean Museum 118
  Divinity School 117
  Holywell Music Room 117
  New College 117
  Old Bodleian Library 117
  Radcliffe Camera 117

**P**

Paddock Wood 91
Padiham 207
Padstow 151
Paignton 145
Pangbourne 116
Parham House 96
**Peak District National Park** 199
Pembroke Castle 161
**Pembrokeshire National Park** 161
Pennine Hills 203
Pennines 199, 208
Penrhyn Castle 167
Penshurst Place 92
Pentre Ifan 162
Penzance 150
Peterborough 126
Petworth House 96
Peveril Castle 193
Plymouth 146
Poldhu 149
Polesden Lacey 97
Polkerris 149
Polperro 148, 149

Poole Harbour 103
Pontcysyllte, aqueduct 165
Portchester 98
Port-Eynon 160
Porthoer 166
Portland Castle 104
**Portsmouth 98-99**
Port Talbot 160
Powderham Castle 145
Powys Castle 163
Praa Sands 149
Prestatyn 163
Preston 206

**Q**

Quainton 114
Quebec House 92

**R**

Raglan Castle 157
Ragley Hall 184
Raleigh, Sir Walter 51, 52, 53, 105, 117, 145
Ramsgate 89
Raynham Hall 129
Reeth 219
Rhayader 162
Rhosneigr 167
Rhossili 160
Rhyl 168
Ribchester 206
**Richard I Lionheart** 18, 41, 51, 128
**Richard II** 18, 20, 53
**Richard III** 21, 22, 161, 176, 219
Richborough Castle 89
Richmond 80, 219
Rievaulx Abbey 215, 216
Ripley 212
Ripon 212
Robin Hood's Bay 217
Rochester 87
Rockingham 186
Romans 13, 14, 40, 43, 54, 89, 99, 104, 109, 123, 124, 131, 143, 157, 159, 167, 173, 180, 184, 187, 188, 192, 200, 203, 208, 212, 213, 229
**Romney Marsh 89-90**
Romsey Abbey 101
Rosedale Abbey 218
Ross-on-Wye 177
**Royal Shakespeare Company** 37, 43, 82
Rufford Old Hall 206
Rugby 181
Ruskin, John 209, 225, 230
Ruthin 165
Ryde 100
Rye 90

253

# INDEX

## S

Sackville-West, Vita 90, 91
Saffron Walden 132
Salcombe 146
Salisbury 18, **138-139**
Saltram House 146
Sandbanks, peninsula 103
Scarborough 217
Scilly, Isles of 150
Scotland 17, 19, 24, 25, 27, 56, 230
**Scotney Castle** 90
Seaford 93
Seaton 141, 148
Shaftesbury 105
Shakespeare, William 24, 37, 56, 64, 74, 157, 182, 184
**Shandy Hall** 216
Shaw, George Bernard 62, 67
Sheffield 209
**Sheffield Park** 95
Sherborne 105
**Sherborne Castle** 105
Sherwood Forest 190
Shrewsbury 180
Sibury Hill 137, 138
Sidmouth 141
Silbury Hill 13
**Sissinghurst Garden** 90
Skipton 210
**Sledmere House** 216
**Snowdonia National Park** 167
Snowdonian, mountains 163
Snowdon, mount 167
**Somerset and Devon Coast Path** 152
Soudley 177
Southampton 101, 102
Southport 206
Southsea 99
Southwell 189
Southwick 97
**Speke Hall** 205
St. Agnes 151
St. Albans 13, 21, 109
Stamford 187
**Stamford Bridge** 216
Stanton 175
Stanway 175
St. Austell 149
St. David's 161
St. Dogmaels 161
Stevenson, Robert Louis 31, 142
Stilton 125
St. Ives (Cambridgeshire) 125
St. Ives (Cornwall) 151
**St. Martin's Haven** 161
St. Mawes 149
**St. Michael's Mount** 149
Stockbridge 101
Stockton-on-Tees 233
Stoke Bruerne 185
Stoke-on-Trent 199
Stonehenge 13, 137, 139
Stourton 139
**Stowe Landscape Gardens** 113
Stow-on-the-Wold 174
Stratford-upon-Avon 182
Stretham 125
**Studely Royal Park** 212
Studland 104
Sudbury 132
**Sudeley Castle** 175
Suffolk 131
**Sulgrave Manor** 185
Swanage 104
Swansea 160
**Syon House** 79

## T

**Tatton Hall** 200
Tetbury 173, 174
Tewkesbury 176
Thatcher, Margaret 20, 37, 38, 75
Thaxted 132
Thetford 131
Thirlmere 230
Thomas, Dylan 160, 161, 162
**Thoresby Hall** 190
Tintagel 151
**Tintern Abbey** 157
Torquay 145
Totnes 146
Towcester 13, 184, 185
**Tredegar House** 159
Trelissick, gardens 149
Tunbridge Wells 91
Turner, William 29, 48, 56, 72, 80, 96, 123, 225

## U

Uffington 118, 139
Ulverston 225
Undercliff 104
Uppermill 204
Upper Slaughter 174

## V

**Valle Crucis Abbey** 165
Vanbrugh, John 26, 215, 118
Ventnor 100
**Victorian Age 30-32**
Victoria, queen 33, 57, 59, 68, 81, 100, 115, 202, 234

## W

**Waddesdon Manor** 114
**Wakehurst Place** 95
Wallingfort 116
Wareham 103
Warminster 139
**Wars of the Roses 21-22**, 42, 109, 235
**Warwick Castle** 182
**Wells 139-140**
Wells-next-the-Sea 129
Welshpool 163
Wendover 114
**West Kenett Long Barrow** 138
West Lulworth 104
Westonbirt 174
Weymouth 104
**Whipsnade Wild Animal Park** 112
Whitby 217, 218
**White Ladies Priory** 181
**Wicken Fen Nature Reserve** 128
William II 115, 231
William III 26
William IV 28, 30
William the Conqueror 16, 41, 51, 55, 93, 101, 176, 186, 188, 190
**Wilton House** 139
Winchcombe 175
Winchelsea 90
**Winchester 102-103**
Windermere 229, 230
**Windsor Castle** 57, 115
**Winslow Hall** 113
Wisbech 126
**Woburn Abbey** 112
**Woburn Safari Park** 112
Wolsey, Thomas 22, 80, 91
Woodstock 118
Woolf, Virginia 79, 90
Worcester 178
Wordsworth, William 29, 229
World War, First 31
World War, Second 33, 43, 88, 98, 101, 117, 142, 185, 215
**Worth Matravers** 104
Wrelton 218
Wren, Sir Christopher 26, 42, 46, 54, 56, 113, 115, 117
Wroxeter 180
Wroxham 129

## Y

Yarmouth 101
York 13, 14, 15, 208, **213-215**
Yorkshire 17, 208
**Yorkshire Dales National Park** 219

# Explore the World
## NELLES MAPS

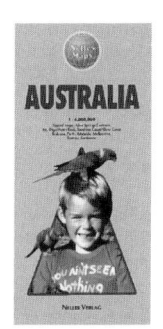

**AVAILABLE TITLES**

**Afghanistan** 1 : 1 500 000
**Australia** 1 : 4 000 000
**Bangkok** - *Greater Bangkok, Bangkok City* 1 : 75 000 / 1 : 15 000
**Burma** - *Myanmar* 1 : 1 500 000
**Caribbean Islands 1** *Bermuda, Bahamas, Greater Antilles* 1 : 2 500 000
**Caribbean Islands 2** *Lesser Antilles* 1 : 2 500 000
**Central America** 1 : 1 750 000
**Crete** - *Kreta* 1 : 200 000
**China 1** - *Northeastern* 1 : 1 500 000
**China 2** - *Northern* 1 : 1 500 000
**China 3** - *Central* 1 : 1 500 000
**China 4** - *Southern* 1 : 1 500 000
**Egypt** 1 : 2 500 000 / 1 : 750 000
**Hawaiian Islands** 1 : 330 000 / 1 : 125 000
**Hawaiian Islands 1** *Kauai* 1 : 125 000
**Hawaiian Islands 2** *Honolulu - Oahu* 1 : 125 000
**Hawaiian Islands 3** *Maui - Molokai - Lanai* 1 : 125 000
**Hawaiian Islands 4** *Hawaii, The Big Island* 1 : 330 000 / 1 : 125 000
**Himalaya** 1 : 1 500 000

**Hong Kong** 1 : 22 500
**Indian Subcontinent** 1 : 4 000 000
**India 1** - *Northern* 1 : 1 500 000
**India 2** - *Western* 1 : 1 500 000
**India 3** - *Eastern* 1 : 1 500 000
**India 4** - *Southern* 1 : 1 500 000
**India 5** - *Northeastern - Bangladesh* 1 : 1 500 000
**Indonesia** 1 : 4 000 000
**Indonesia 1** *Sumatra* 1 : 1 500 000
**Indonesia 2** *Java + Nusa Tenggara* 1 : 1 500 000
**Indonesia 3** *Bali* 1 : 180 000
**Indonesia 4** *Kalimantan* 1 : 1 500 000
**Indonesia 5** *Java + Bali* 1 : 650 000
**Indonesia 6** *Sulawesi* 1 : 1 500 000
**Indonesia 7** *Irian Jaya + Maluku* 1 : 1 500 000
**Jakarta** 1 : 22 500
**Japan** 1 : 1 500 000
**Kenya** 1 : 1 100 000
**Korea** 1 : 1 500 000
**Malaysia** 1 : 1 500 000
**West Malaysia** 1 : 650 000
**Manila** 1 : 17 500
**Mexico** 1 : 2 500 000
**Nepal** 1 : 500 000 / 1 : 1 500 000
**Trekking Map** *Khumbu Himal / Solu Khumbu* 1 : 75 000
**New Zealand** 1 : 1 250 000

**Pakistan** 1 : 1 500 000
**Philippines** 1 : 1 500 000
**Singapore** 1 : 22 500
**Southeast Asia** 1 : 4 000 000
**Sri Lanka** 1 : 450 000
**Tanzania** - *Rwanda, Burundi* 1 : 1 500 000
**Thailand** 1 : 1 500 000
**Taiwan** 1 : 400 000
**Vietnam, Laos, Cambodia** 1 : 1 500 000

**FORTHCOMING**

**Colombia - Ecuador** 1 : 2 500 000
**Trekking Map** *Kathmandu Valley / Helambu, Langtang* 1 : 75 000
**Venezuela** - *Guyana, Suriname, French Guiana* 1 : 2 500 000
**Uganda** 1: 700.000

*Nelles Maps in european top quality!*
*Relief mapping, kilometer charts and tourist attractions.*
*Always up-to-date!*

# Explore the World

# NELLES GUIDES

## AVAILABLE TITLES

**Australia**
**Bali / Lombok**
**Berlin and Potsdam**
**Brittany**
**California**
  *Las Vegas, Reno,*
  *Baja California*
**Cambodia / Laos**
**Canada**
  *Ontario, Québec,*
  *Atlantic Provinces*
**Caribbean**
  *The Greater Antilles,*
  *Bermuda, Bahamas*
**Caribbean**
  *The Lesser Antilles*
**China**
**Corsica**
**Crete**
**Cyprus**
**Egypt**
**Florida**
**Greece** - *The Mainland*
**Hawaii**
**Hungary**
**India**
  *Northern, Northeastern*
  *and Central India*

**India**
  *Southern India*
**Indonesia**
  *Sumatra, Java, Bali,*
  *Lombok, Sulawesi*
**Ireland**
**Israel** - with Excursions
  to Jordan
**Kenya**
**London, England and Wales**
**Malaysia**
**Mexico**
**Morocco**
**Moscow / St Petersburg**
**Munich**
  *Excursions to Castels,*
  *Lakes & Mountains*
**Nepal**
**New York** - *City and State*
**New Zealand**
**Paris**
**Philippines**
**Portugal**
**Prague / Czech Republic**
**Provence**
**Rome**
**South Africa**
**Spain** - *North*

**Spain**
  *Mediterranean Coast,*
  *Southern Spain,*
  *Balearic Islands*
**Sri Lanka**
**Thailand**
**Turkey**
**Tuscany**
**U.S.A.**
  *The East, Midwest and*
  *South*
**U.S.A.**
  *The West, Rockies and*
  *Texas*
**Vietnam**

*Nelles Guides – authorative, informed and informative.*
*Always up-to-date, extensivley illustrated, and with first-rate relief maps.*
*256 pages, appr. 150 color photos, appr. 25 maps*